Between a River & a Mountain

Between a River & a Mountain

The AFL-CIO and the Vietnam War

Edmund F. Wehrle

The University of Michigan Press
Ann Arbor

For Jacqueline, My Love

Published in the United States of America by
The University of Michigan Press
Manufactured in the United States of America
♾ Printed on acid-free paper

2008 2007 2006 2005 4 3 2 1

A CIP catalog record for this book is available from the British Library.

Library of Congress Cataloging-in-Publication Data

Wehrle, Edmund F., 1964–
Between a river and a mountain : the AFL-CIO and the Vietnam War / Edmund F. Wehrle.
p. cm.
Includes bibliographical references and index.
ISBN-13: 978-0-472-09900-9 (cloth : alk. paper)
ISBN-10: 0-472-09900-0 (cloth : alk. paper)
ISBN-13: 978-0-472-06900-2 (pbk. : alk. paper)
ISBN-10: 0-472-06900-4 (pbk. : alk. paper)
1. AFL-CIO—History. 2. Labor movement—United States—History—20th century. 3. Vietnamese Conflict, 1961–1975. 4. Labor movement—Vietnam—History—20th century. I. Title.

HD8055.A6W44 2005
331.8'0973'09047—dc22 2005014441

ISBN13 978-0-472-02579-4 (electronic)

Contents

	Acknowledgments	vii
	Introduction	1
1	Free Trade Unionism	9
2	"No More Pressing Task Than Organizing in Southeast Asia"	29
3	"It's a Vast Jungle and We're Working on the Periphery"	51
4	New Frontiers	75
5	Into the Quagmire	101
6	Free Fall, 1968–69	135
7	Entangling Alliances and Mounting Costs, 1970–71	153
8	"The Last of the Cold War Mohicans," 1972–75	173
	Notes	201
	Bibliography	279
	Index	297

Illustrations following page 152

Acknowledgments

I have incurred a great many debts in the preparation and writing of this book. The faculty and staff at the University of Maryland at College Park provided significant encouragement and support as I began my initial investigations. Stuart Kaufman, the sage editor of the *Samuel Gompers Papers*, provided invaluable early guidance. That this project survived his sudden death is a testament to his powers to inspire. I am indebted to a number of other individuals, who carefully read my manuscript for both style and substance, including David Sicilia, Gary Clifford, Frank Ninkovich, Peter Levy, Marc Jason Gilbert, and Allan E. Goodman. One individual's support and aid stands out, that of my father, Edmund S. Wehrle, who read and commented on countless drafts, offering crucial insights and encouragement. In the final stages of manuscript preparation, my wife Jacqueline carefully read drafts and attended to footnotes.

The staff at the George Meany Memorial Archives, especially Lee Sayres, put up with my almost constant presence for several years. My European research was greatly enhanced by the help of Marie-Paule Blasini at the French National Archives for Overseas Affairs and by Pascal Clerc at the French Confederation of Democratic Workers Archives. Likewise I am indebted to archivists at the Kheel Center for Labor Documentation; the Gerald Ford Library; the Hoover Institute on War, Revolution, and Peace; the National Security Archives; the National Archives; the British National Archives; the Wagner Archives; the Walter Reuther Library; the Lyndon Baines Johnson Presidential Library; the John F. Kennedy Presidential Library; and the Library of Congress Manuscript Reading Room. Numerous individuals provided me with invaluable firsthand impressions; particular thanks go to Nguyen Duc Dat, Robert Senser, and Vy Pham.

A Hearst Travel Grant from the University of Maryland History Department, as well as grants from the Lyndon Johnson Foundation and the Eastern Illinois University Office of Grants and Research, facilitated my extensive research for this project.

While the aid and support of these many individuals have enhanced this work, its flaws and shortcomings rest solely on my shoulders.

Introduction

Two dramatic incidents of violent working-class protest stand at either end of this study. The first occurred in April 1950, at the port of the French city of Nice. A mob—organized by communist trade unionists—gathered to protest the French war in Indochina. As the rabble grew unruly, it forcibly boarded a ship loaded with war supplies destined for Southeast Asia. Rampaging through the vessel, the mob destroyed everything in its wake, eventually catapulting an artillery-launching ramp into the Mediterranean Sea.[1] Twenty years later, in May 1970, New York City "hard hat" construction workers, resentful of the eruption of "unpatriotic" peace protests against the recent Cambodian invasion, spontaneously descended on an antiwar demonstration in Manhattan, savagely beating scores of protesters.

These episodes, separated by just over two decades, represent very different reactions to costly and painful wars in Vietnam, yet each suggests the deeply held passions of working people in response to complicated, frustrating, foreign engagements. In America's Vietnam War, a disproportionate number of combatants came from blue-collar backgrounds—to the extent that it is remembered today as a "working-class" war. But beyond the prominent presence of the sons of workers on the front lines, from the early 1950s to the fall of Saigon in 1975 the leadership of American organized labor also was deeply involved in unfolding events in Vietnam.[2] Indeed, the AFL (American Federation of Labor), and subsequently the AFL-CIO (American Federation of Labor-Congress of Industrial Organizations), played pivotal roles following both violent clashes. In response to the 1950 communist riots in France, the European representative of the AFL, Irving Brown, organized counterprotests to undermine the sabotage campaign. Two decades later, Jay Lovestone, the director of the AFL-CIO's International Affairs

Department, helped orchestrate a series of hard hat rallies in New York City following the clash between construction workers and protesters. Indeed, in several decades of bitter opposition to communism in Southeast Asia and support for the American war, the AFL-CIO helped shape the contours of U.S. involvement in Vietnam—and the war in turn reshaped the American labor movement.

To a generation of progressive-minded unionists and intellectuals, the federation's hawkish stance on Vietnam seemed an unforgivable error, the product of a mindless anticommunism that poisoned dreams of an activist labor movement working in coalition with a revitalized Left. The 1970 hard hat demonstrations, in particular, still stir painful memories. "The possibility of igniting trade union passion among America's young was lost as images of pro-war hardhats charging anti-war marchers filled television screens," reflected Richard Trumka, current secretary treasurer of the AFL-CIO.[3] Labor historians, a particularly politically engaged breed, have echoed Trumka's view. In his first book, historian Nelson Lichtenstein lamented the "sclerotic and increasingly unimportant" state of the labor movement and regrettably tied its decline to the AFL-CIO's support for "a vigorous prosecution of the Vietnam War."[4] Trumka and Lichtenstein are correct in identifying the Vietnam War as a crucial turning point for organized labor. But both the AFL-CIO's pro-war stance and the way that hard-line approach backfired so terribly are far more complex than has generally been understood. In its foreign policy, the federation could be chauvinistic, intolerant, obdurate, and even paranoid, but its position on the Vietnam War was much more than simply the product of a myopic, knee-jerk anticommunism.

First and foremost the federation's support for the war rested on its hopes that a substantial and politically savvy labor movement in South Vietnam, the Vietnamese Confederation of Labor (CVT), might be transformed into a vehicle for social, political, and economic reform.[5] Founded by nationalists formerly allied with the Viet Minh, in its two decades of existence the CVT represented an authentic force for democracy in a troubled country. In their enthusiasm for the CVT, representatives of American labor went so far as to tout the organization as a potential "paramilitary" force, capable of challenging the Viet Cong in the trenches.

Separated by deep cultural chasms, relations between U.S. labor and its South Vietnamese counterpart were not always placid. But the AFL-CIO offered a valuable lifeline to the CVT, and at heart the two organizations, operating in very different environments, had much in common and even suffered the same fundamental contradictions. In particular, both organizations idealized independence of action, both striving to be autonomous actors, free of the taint of compromising alliances with the state, employers, the church, or any sullying forces. Survival, however, especially in the case of the CVT, required that each organization compromise these ideals and enter into numerous questionable alliances. As U.S. labor grew increasingly involved in the Vietnam War and more determined to aid the CVT, it accepted generous subsidies not only from U.S. foreign aid agencies but also from the Central Intelligence Agency (CIA). The CVT likewise reluctantly accepted the patronage of a succession of mercurial, corrupt Saigon governments and the benefaction of interested American parties, especially the AFL-CIO. In both cases, the compromises—though necessary to advance trade union agendas—severely discredited the labor movements in the eyes of many. The intertwined ambitions of both organizations in effect spun a Gordian knot that was beyond disentanglement by the early 1970s.

Both the elevation and betrayal of trade union autonomy, so central to the story of labor's Vietnam War, cannot be understood without reference to "free trade unionism"—a governing ideology put forth by an ambitious group of internationalists at the AFL in the 1940s. Above all, free trade unionism stressed the paramount importance of maintaining labor's autonomy. The AFL-CIO's intense and activist anticommunism and its "guns and butter," full-employment approach to economics both derive from this mandate for autonomy. In the years after World War II, free trade unionism came to dominate the American organized labor movement, providing unifying themes and an efficacious rhetoric in consonance with cold war imperatives. Buttressed by the free trade unionism ideology, the AFL and CIO, separately and then together as the AFL-CIO, delved into international affairs, supporting noncommunist trade unions around the world—ambitions often pursued in close alliance with U.S. officials, businessmen, and other potentially tainted collaborators.

The American military intervention in Vietnam in 1965, which was supported enthusiastically by both the AFL-CIO and the CVT, exposed the contradictions at the core of each movement's efforts to realize its ideals. In America, the far-reaching internationalism of free trade unionism always ran against the grain of the populist, nationalistic orientation of most rank and file workers. As the war grew divisive, increasing numbers of American trade unionists—both leaders and members—joined the antiwar movement. Meanwhile the federation's questionable dealings with the CIA and close ties to other government agencies became public knowledge, bruising the organization's carefully constructed facade of independence. Political leftists, in fact, began mocking the AFL-CIO as the "AFL-CIA," an obeisant arm of a reactionary government and the antithesis of the autonomy and virtue that free trade unionists sought to convey.[6]

Clinging to its anticommunist global agenda, AFL-CIO leaders forged an intensely close relationship with President Lyndon Johnson and later an awkward but mutually beneficial alliance with President Richard Nixon.

These associations also cost U.S. labor dearly in terms of support from increasingly dovish liberal allies. By the mid-1970s, U.S. labor was a weak and divided force that faced enormous economic challenges. While other factors contributed, including race and an increasingly globalized economy, at the center of U.S. labor's decline lay the divisive and painful Vietnam War.

The U.S. intervention similarly strained the CVT, adding new tangles and twists to its struggle to preserve its autonomy while obtaining necessary outside support. As its dependence on U.S. benefactors, in particular the AFL-CIO, deepened, so did a sense of resentment, as its hopes of offering leadership to the rudderless masses abraded with every alliance it made with outsiders. South Vietnamese labor, full of promise and potentially a third force in a bitterly divided country, never overcame an insoluble paradox: its dependence on outsiders was necessary for its survival but it fatally weakened its claim to the mantle of Vietnamese leadership. These compromises, similar to the AFL-CIO's bending of free trade unionism—though rendered significantly more intense in an atmosphere of civil war—undermined the CVT's claim to legitimacy. Surveying his organization's limited choices, one CVT officer lamented that it was "pinched between a river and a mountain."[7]

The AFL-CIO, struggling with the same entangling issues, lived to fight another day. The CVT faced obliteration in 1975. Still, the paradoxes plaguing both organizations intimate much about the agendas and potential of mid-twentieth-century organized labor, as well as the awkward, and in many cases insurmountable, obstacles blocking such ambitions.

The story of labor's Vietnam War cannot be told solely from the perspective of either Washington or Saigon. This study interweaves several narratives to provide the context and content necessary to understand the larger story. A brief introductory chapter discusses the ideological rooting of the post–World War II U.S. labor movement in the philosophy of Samuel Gompers and a subsequent group of New York City trade unionists that included Jay Lovestone, David Dubinsky, and most importantly George Meany. In their rise to power in the AFL, these labor leaders promulgated an ideology they termed free trade unionism, stressing activist internationalism, a commitment to maintaining the essential autonomy of trade unions, and advocacy of aggressive full-employment economics. The second chapter treats the emergence and early struggles of the Vietnamese Confederation of Labor, as well as the AFL's protracted battle against communism in Western Europe and its growing interest in Southeast Asia. Driven by the burgeoning goals of both organizations, the first contacts between American and Vietnamese trade unionists came in 1950.

The frustrating Eisenhower years are the subject of chapter 3. Despite the

AFL's and subsequent AFL-CIO's ambitions to advance their anticommunist agenda in the third world, American labor found little support from either the Republican administration or its financially costly alliance with the International Confederation of Free Trade Unions. Vietnamese labor similarly struggled under the repressive regime of Ngo Dinh Diem. Increasingly the CVT sought international help, but the AFL-CIO, with limited resources of its own, had little success in pressing the Eisenhower administration to develop programs and policies for South Vietnamese labor.

With much relief, labor embraced the Kennedy and Johnson presidencies, as recounted in chapters 4 and 5. The new Democratic administrations offered exactly the activist foreign policy and aggressive spending programs at home for which labor had long called. In an atmosphere of great expectations, the AFL-CIO moved to strengthen its bonds with the CVT.

In chapters 6 and 7, the hopes invested by the AFL-CIO in the Kennedy and Johnson administrations suddenly shatter. Even while basking in what historian Kevin Boyle calls "the heyday of American liberalism," the Vietnam War became an increasingly divisive issue for labor.[8] Nevertheless, the AFL-CIO offered its support to President Johnson and devoted itself to cooperative programs to aid the CVT. Then, beginning in 1968, in rapid succession the Democrats lost the presidency (signaling perhaps the final blow to the liberal–New Deal coalition), full-employment economics came under fire, and antiwar activism grew within the labor movement. In Vietnam, the CVT came under increasing attack from both the South Vietnamese government and the Viet Cong. Chapter 8 covers the painful final years of the CVT, including the fall of Saigon.

Between 1965 and 1975, the social, economic, and political atmosphere in which the AFL-CIO operated was completely transformed. A powerful and politically influential organization at the beginning of the 1960s, by the early 1970s it was a divided and weakened force. At the center of this seismic shift was the war in Vietnam.

Historians have not been charitable when dealing with postwar American organized labor and its relations with the state. Most depict trade unions as entering, of their own volition, a junior partnership with the state, compromising the interests of its membership. Christopher Tomlins, for instance, has argued that by participating in mechanisms such as the National Labor Relations Board organized labor, once proud and independent, helped transform itself into a series of "quasi-public instrumentalities whose function was . . . defined by the state." Others take a harsher view, lamenting both labor's failure to broker a stronger corporate bargain for itself and a loss of the activist spirit supposedly so prevalent in the 1930s.[9]

While few studies have examined labor's foreign policy, those that have depict trade union leaders as slavishly following the official American foreign policy. Written at the height of New Left revisionism, Ronald Radosh's seminal 1969 study, *American Labor and United States Foreign Policy: The Cold War in Unions from Gompers to Lovestone,* argued that from "World War I to the present era of Cold War, the leaders of organized labor have willingly offered their support to incumbent administrations, and have aided the Department of State in its pursuit of foreign policy objectives."[10]

By contrast, my study disputes previous formulations as too simplistic. In its foreign affairs, the federation tried and often managed to pursue its own independent agenda. Yet, as political realities and the anticommunist imperative intruded it made convenient alliances with the state to further its endeavors. Organized labor sought to use such arrangements to its own advantage and insisted that its work with the CIA and other government agencies in no way impinged on its autonomy. Still, when revelations of CIA connections and other questionable activities found their way to the public, the AFL-CIO's reputation palpably suffered.

This study also speaks to a second body of scholarship—that dealing with American foreign policy and the Vietnam War. Obviously, the Vietnam War has received more than its fair share of attention from scholars. Yet most studies focus closely on elite decision makers centered in the State Department, White House, and military.[11] Likewise, as historian George Herring has pointed out, "the interaction between the Americans and the South Vietnamese is one of the least developed areas in the burgeoning literature of the Vietnam War."[12] This study directly addresses these gaps. It argues that trade unionists pressed their own series of initiatives for Vietnam, dating back to the early 1950s, centered on transforming the CVT into a shaping force in South Vietnam. Moreover, while not presenting a comprehensive history of the South Vietnamese labor movement under Tran Quoc Buu, this work makes the first effort to resurrect a genuine social movement that is absent from standard accounts of the war.

For some, my assertion that a war in Southeast Asia represented a major turning point for organized labor, a movement supposedly focused on domestic issues, may push credulity. Yet by the second half of the twentieth century American foreign and domestic affairs were so hopelessly intertwined that they must be treated as one entity—a reality well understood by the internationalist leaders of the AFL-CIO. The political, economic, and cultural ramifications of the Vietnam War sent shock waves across the country. For American organized labor, those waves brought lasting, perhaps permanent, repercussions, exposing deep internal contradictions and contributing mightily to its ongoing decline.

While an international history of labor's Vietnam War that fully details and balances the parallel experiences of both the CVT and the AFL-CIO would have been ideal, the available sources do not allow for such a study. In no way is this work to be construed as a dual history of the AFL-CIO and the CVT. Indeed, the official records of the CVT did not survive the fall of Saigon. Hence a complete history of South Vietnamese labor that balances leadership and the grass roots and details the organization in its multifaceted entirety appears to be a near impossibility. Instead, using available American, French, and British records, this study focuses on relations between the CVT and the AFL-CIO at the leadership level. For the unique perspective of South Vietnamese trade unionists, I relied on oral interviews with former CVT officers, a published official history of the organization, and the occasional surviving speech or copy of *Cong Nhan,* the CVT's newspaper. While acknowledging the limitations and biases inherent in my sources, what follows, I feel confident, is an accurate and balanced rendering of an important and little-known chapter in our recent history.

1 Free Trade Unionism

Why did a labor movement devoted to domestic, economic concerns become so intensely consumed by affairs overseas—so much so that its involvement in the Vietnam War wrought wounds still painful even today? Historians have approached this question from a variety of vantage points, alternatively constructing explanations around the obsessive anticommunism of organized labor's leadership, the prestige and status foreign affairs offered supposedly parochial trade union leaders, or the jobs provided by the cold war economy.[1] While each interpretation contains seeds of veracity, the real roots of American organized labor's all-consuming internationalism are deeper and more complex.

Asked about their remarkable engrossment with foreign affairs, labor leaders such as George Meany invariably referred to *free trade unionism*. No mere throwaway line, the term encapsulated the aspirations and ambitions of a generation of trade union leaders—ideals largely responsible for labor's tragic involvement in the Vietnam War. Principally, this ideology meant that independent trade unions were essential components of democracies—the sole defense of workers against a multitude of threatening interests and institutions. To be deprived of the opportunity to join an autonomous trade union, operating independent of business, government, church, or other potentially corrupting influences, was to be denied a basic human right. Countries restricting independent trade unions could not rightfully be called democracies. Such preoccupations with autonomy were not unique to U.S. labor. Indeed, Vietnamese organized labor struggled with surprisingly similar concerns.

The anticommunism driving mainstream post–World War II labor in the United States flowed directly from its fixation with trade union independence, and as such it should be viewed (alongside full-employment economics) as a principal component of free trade unionism. The proliferation of "unfree" labor unions, such as those in communist countries, represented menacing precedents mandating vigilant opposition.

Yet not all mandates of free trade unionism were as clear. The ideology emerged, in fact, as an imperfect resolution of an identity crisis—a crisis perhaps best understood in terms of two rival sets of ideals, each proposing to pilot organized labor through the turbulent early decades of the twentieth century. The first, championed most articulately by Samuel Gompers, prescribed the absolute separation of labor and the state, with independent, potent trade unions focusing solely on immediate job-related issues. The second ideology, the "new unionism," associated largely with Sidney Hillman, envisioned close labor-government cooperation in a corporate state structure.

Free trade unionism emerged as an amalgam of the two approaches. Led by George Meany, free trade unionists accepted many of the basic tenets of the new unionism, in particular industrial organization and the efficacy of political alliances. Yet Meany and his followers also preached the gospel of labor autonomy with an uncompromising rhetoric differing little from that of Gompers. Simultaneously, however, especially on issues of foreign policy, free trade unionists worked closely with the state in a manner absolutely consistent with Hillman's approach. The Meany and Hillman camps did sharply part company on the issue of international communism. Hillman and his followers advocated tolerance of world communism. Free trade unionism, conversely, divined a world starkly divided—West versus East, freedom versus slavery.

After World War II, free trade unionism eclipsed both Hillman's corporatism and the entrenched "voluntarism" still practiced in isolated corners of the AFL. Yet until its demise in the 1960s free trade unionism as practiced by the AFL-CIO remained an unsatisfying, self-contradictory settlement of labor's identity crisis, in which key principles, labor-state separation in particular, incessantly would be stretched, bent, and finally shattered by the Vietnam War. Because the history of organized labor and the Vietnam War is largely the story of trade union independence betrayed, the ideological edifices erected by labor leaders, in which autonomy and anticommunism competed as primary goals, require some elaboration.

"Tell the Politicians to Keep Their Hands Off": Gompers's Elastic Antistatism

In the strongly worded ideals of Samuel Gompers—the diminutive but supremely self-confident first president of the AFL—lies the genesis of the philosophical approach later known as free trade unionism. From his earliest days at the helm of the AFL in the 1880s, Gompers unceasingly championed a single vision: the exigency of a potent, independent labor movement operating solely in the interest of the laboring classes. Only strong, autonomous trade unions—certainly not the state—could defend the interests of working people. "Tell the politicians to keep their hands off," Gompers pronounced, "and thus . . . preserve voluntary institutions and opportunity for individual and group initiative."[2] Often labeled voluntarism, Gompers's approach flowed from a realistic assessment of late-nineteenth-century labor relations in an era of state-sponsored strikebreaking, one-sided court injunctions, and resistance to all forms of unionization. For Gompers, quixotic calls to radicalism and revolution endangered the meager gains of working people, and he brazenly dismissed revolutionary socialists as dangerous "impossiblists."[3] Only an independent labor movement focused on immediate economic issues could effect positive short- and long-term change.

Despite the clarity of his rhetoric, in practice Gompers balanced ideological rigidity with pragmatism. When the early twentieth century brought signs of new flexibility from some business and government leaders, Gompers saw an opportunity. He eagerly joined the National Civic Federation, an organization espousing business-labor-state dialogue as an antidote to the costly labor strife of the times. Increasingly, he involved the AFL in politics, supported social legislation, and forged a working alliance with the Democratic Party.[4]

The outbreak of war in Europe in 1914 abetted Gompers's ideological elasticity.[5] Jettisoning earlier predilections toward pacifism, Gompers embraced the war as an epochal confrontation, pitting democracy against tyranny.[6] Practical interests also motivated the AFL chief. Speaking to a Philadelphia audience in 1915, he admitted that "the war has opened up tremendous economic opportunities—some temporary, others permanent."[7] As American doughboys fought in Europe, workers prospered at home, inaugurating in earnest a lucrative, though often awkward, nexus between organized labor and what later became known as the military-industrial complex.[8]

Even those in labor who lacked Gompers's ideological commitment to the war appreciated its material benefits. Frank Rosenblum, an executive of the Amalgamated Clothing Workers of America (ACWA), advised union vice president Jacob Potofsky that, despite their mutual reservations about the war, as a "question of expediency" they should avoid doing "anything which will antagonize anyone."[9] Fifty years later, in the heat of the Vietnamese conflict, Rosenblum and Potofsky chose the opposite course—open opposition.

Amid the fervor of national emergency, Gompers, seeking to transcend the status of a parochial labor leader, repackaged himself as a national statesman. An immigrant heavily influenced by Marxism as a young man, Gompers always viewed labor affairs from an international perspective and rarely held his tongue on international issues. With the war, he became increasingly outspoken and preoccupied with international events.

It was primarily Gompers's abhorrence of radicalism, however, rather than his appetite for prestige, that drove his internationalism. Already a vehement critic of socialism, Gompers discovered a new enemy in 1917: Russian bolshevism. Quickly, he situated himself as one of the country's most vocal anticommunists. To the point of obsession, he assailed bolshevism as a threat to free labor.[10] Vehemently attacking the Russian revolution, Gompers reaffirmed his ideal of trade union autonomy; the subversion of labor's autonomy would lead inexorably to the horrors of bolshevism. Yet, as the first Red Scare flared, his fervent rhetoric left little room for nuance and no doubt fed the hysteria of the times.

Until his death in 1924, Gompers focused his tireless energy on his campaign against bolshevism. At the behest of President Woodrow Wilson, in the fall of 1918 he traveled to Europe to participate in an allied labor conference, which Gompers aimed to transform into an international labor organization to counter communism. In 1921, he published *Out of Their Mouths: A Revelation and Indictment of Sovietism*, an exposé of "slave labor" conditions in the future Soviet Union based on interviews with refugees.[11]

In the final years of his life, as a postwar counteroffensive by employers severely weakened trade unionism, Gompers strove to fashion a rhetorical defense of the American labor movement around his critique of communism. In a series of articles in *McClure's*, he posited the AFL as "Our Shield against Bolshevism." Absent a "labor movement in America devoted to the ideals of liberty . . . there would be Bolshevism in America," he charged.[12] The rhetorical juxtapositioning of American labor as the antithesis of communism remained a rallying cry for leading trade unionists through the Vietnam War period.

As early as 1919, then, key components of what later would become free trade unionism already had fused—in particular a relentless emphasis on trade union independence coupled with a vehement anticommunism. And already in evidence was the central paradox destined to plague U.S. trade unionists (and later South Vietnamese labor) for much of the century: the near impossibility of maintaining autonomy while profiting from the myriad opportunities proffered by labor-state cooperation.

Hillman's Corporate Model and the Communism Question

If Gompers remained, at least rhetorically, insistent on absolute trade union independence, by the 1920s new voices were championing an unapologetically corporate formulation—one infusing the state directly into labor relations. At the core of the movement, which was quickly dubbed the "new unionism," was a group of socialist trade unionists and liberal-minded employers in the New York City needle trades, in particular ACWA president Sidney Hillman.[13]

The bespectacled Hillman never lacked for ambition or vision. He dreamed, as historian Nelson Lichtenstein has suggested, of transforming "an immigrant, industrial peasantry into an organized body of social citizens."[14] But, in contrast to Gompers's rhetorical emphasis on self-reliance, Hillman and the new unionists, many of whom were dedicated socialists, eagerly sought the fellowship of intellectuals, political parties, and government officials. "Labor cannot act independently, in isolation from other progressive groups," argued Hillman.[15] He moved instead to forge close working alliances with progressives such as Jane Addams, Clarence Darrow, and Louis Brandeis—ties surpassing anything imagined by Gompers. Both the ACWA and the International Ladies Garment Workers Union (ILGWU) promoted social legislation and rabidly sought political alliances—especially with the Democratic Party.[16] With the advent of the New Deal, Hillman forged an intimate personal and working relationship with President Franklin Roosevelt. The ACWA president personally helped draft the labor provisions of the National Industrial Recovery Act (an overhaul of labor relations designed along the lines of Hillman's corporate model) and worked closely with the architects of the National Labor Relations Act, Senator Robert Wagner and New Deal economist Leon Keyserling. Finding the AFL less receptive to his ambitious agenda, Hillman joined in founding the Congress of Industrial Organizations. He remained a zealous apostle of the New Deal and became a fixture in Roosevelt's three reelection campaigns.[17]

The new unionism agenda hardly ended at the nation's borders. Born in Jewish Lithuania, Hillman, like Gompers, was an immigrant profoundly sensitive to world affairs. Unlike Gompers, however, Hillman and most of his followers saw little threat from communism, either in the Soviet Union or in the ranks of American labor. Building on corporatist ambitions, Hillman and other CIO leaders worked to incorporate communists, whom they saw as potential "shock troops" for the new unionism, into their planned coalition. Having visited Russia in 1921, Hillman admired the Bolshevik revolutionaries, who shared his intense interest in "democratic Taylorism" and his faith in the potential of industrial production and progress. Hillman later sought to facilitate East-West cooperation by organizing the World Federation of Trade Unions (WFTU), which, according to historian Victor Silverman, "envisioned a corporative world—one ruled by global institutions that would represent all elements of society."[18]

With the outbreak of World War II, Hillman's grand democratic vision gained considerable momentum. Philip Murray, president of the CIO, who (at least temporarily) shared Hillman's policy of tolerance for communists, talked openly of using the war to reorient labor's place in the nation's polity. Modeled on his study of Roman Catholic corporatist teachings (principles that would later shape the Vietnamese labor movement), Murray proposed the formation of tripartite "industrial councils" aimed at fostering harmony among government, labor, and capital.[19] Walter Reuther, a rising activist from the United Auto Workers, proposed his own version of corporatism—his alluring "5,000 planes a day" plan.[20] Such corporate initiatives appeared to be the wave of the future. Hillman and others enthusiastically tied their destinies to the New Deal, envisioning a fully integrated labor movement at the core of a corporate political economy—a synthesis the CIO eventually planned to export worldwide. With unbridled relish, new unionists cast aside the cautiousness of Samuel Gompers and moved swiftly toward socialist-inspired ideals of corporatism.[21] But not all followed without qualms.

The AFL Internationalists

By the early 1940s, Hillman's corporate model appeared to be ascendant. Even rising figures in the less progressive AFL, including George Meany, appropriated the general framework of Hillman's approach. Soon Meany and others of like mind would seize control of the AFL and institute something of a counterreformation, introducing to the federation many of the ideals central to new unionism. Yet amid the dizzying pace of change and opportunity, the AFL reformers concurrently grew apprehensive, fretting that labor had relinquished too much autonomy. Moreover, some—Meany and David Dubinsky in particular—watched with mounting apprehension the growing presence of communists in the American labor movement and the threat of international communism worldwide.

The leader of the emerging AFL internationalists was George Meany—the cigar-chomping, blunt-talking, plumber turned AFL-CIO president, easily caricatured as an Archie Bunker with a national pulpit. Despite his reputation as a narrow "bread and butter" business unionist, Meany was more complex than his popular image. As a young man, he became enamored with Hillman's new unionism and was drawn to the lively socialist-inspired debates over economics, labor, and politics swirling around New York City in the 1920s.[22]

Born in the Bronx in 1894 into a third-generation Irish-Catholic family, Meany received only limited formal education as a boy. Following in his father's footsteps, he joined the potent plumbers Local 463 and quickly ascended to the puissant office of union business agent by the early 1920s.

Unlike Hillman's Amalgamated Clothing Workers, which appealed to employers on the basis of mutual interest, construction industry unions operated from positions of brute strength and exclusivity, seeing no need for state interference and enjoying a monopoly on skilled workers and hence the luxury of closed shops and virtual control over work sites. Plumbers in particular evinced an aura of potency, solidarity, and toughness.[23] As a business agent all but equal in power to employers, Meany could shut down a work site instantly if building materials or labor conditions fell short of contract specifications.[24] Out of this background, Meany adopted a hard-edged, straight-talking idiom, frequently curt and dismissive but suggestive of strength and autonomy. Throughout his life, Meany carried himself—even in his dealings with U.S. congressmen, cabinet officers, and presidents—with the self-assurance (at times bordering on arrogance) of a business agent.

While a product of the conservative construction trades culture, from the start Meany was intrigued by politics and captivated by the world beyond his plumbers' local. "I was just a plumber from the Bronx. . . . But then I began to listen to people," he later reflected.[25] Through his wife, a member of the International Ladies Garment Workers Union, Meany remained closely apprised of the pitted ideological battles between communists and socialists in the garment industry. In 1922, Meany became secretary of the New York City Building Trades Council. Despite its parochial reputation, the council engaged many of the burning labor issues of the time. There Meany came into contact with pacifist activist A. J. Muste (later a leading early figure in the anti–Vietnam War movement), and an educator, John R. Commons, an influential labor economist from the University of Wisconsin.[26]

Meany's fellow council members, a diverse and politically active group, also broadened the young plumber's horizons. Philip Zausner, a Polish-born Jew who headed the New York City painters' union, quickly became his mentor. Zausner "introduced me to the socialists of New York City," Meany recalled. Inspired by the painter, Meany dove headfirst into the intellectual world eddying around the new unionism, attending, for instance, a debate between the socialist Morris Hillquit and lawyer Samuel Untermeyer on the proposition "Shall the unions be regulated by the Law?"[27] Representing the council, Meany journeyed to Albany for a meeting of the Conference for Progressive Political Action, an organization espousing industrial unionism and government planning.[28]

While he was drawn to the world of New York socialists (many of whom had personal experience fighting communism) and Hillman's new unionism, Meany also evolved into a vehement anticommunist. As was the case with others, firsthand experience contributed. During the 1920s, communist agents launched an initiative to infiltrate vulnerable trade unions, the so-called boring from within strategy. Zausner took the lead in fighting a determined drive to penetrate his painters' union and clearly fed his youthful friend's emerging distaste for communism.[29] Meany himself recalled that communists "made a lot of noise and we had some excitement" in his Bronx-based plumbers' union. He later proudly recounted his part in exposing and foiling the communists' designs.[30]

Despite the cosmopolitan draw of Zausner's world, Meany became equally intrigued by the outlook and ideas of Samuel Gompers, in particular the former cigar maker's emphasis on trade union independence and power—an outlook that meshed well with the Bronx plumber's business agent sensibilities and his developing anticommunism. Meany met Gompers at the 1922 New York State Federation of Labor convention. Two years later Meany traveled to his first AFL convention in El Paso, Texas, where he again met President Gompers.[31] Gompers clearly impressed the young man, who a half century later could quote at length from the AFL president's writings.[32]

As Meany weighed countervailing influences, another future leader of the AFL internationalists was on the ascent. During the 1920s, Meany encountered future ILGWU president David Dubinsky. Sharing an intense anticommunism and both intrigued by the new unionism, the two became fast friends.[33] Dubinsky's diminutive stature and easy smile masked an intensely combative nature. As a youth in tsarist Poland, he became an energetic member of the General League of Jewish Workers, popularly known as the Bund. His activism quickly drew the attention of local officials, who jailed and moved to deport the young troublemaker. Faced with exile to Siberia, Dubinsky managed to escape to New York City—all before his twentieth birthday. In America, he faced continuing challenges. A leading figure in ILGWU by the late 1920s, he led the union's battle to thwart communist infiltrators—a struggle that essentially pitted Jewish socialists against Jewish communists. Dubinsky emerged from the conflict victorious but with a deep, lifelong enmity for communists, who, he insisted, were "directed from the outside toward goals that served the interest of the party rather than the ILGWU." Intolerant of "any dissent from party doctrines or criticism of Russia," communism, to Dubinsky, fundamentally imperiled legitimate trade unionism.[34]

In his anticommunist crusade, Dubinsky found a tireless ally in Jay Lovestone, a former leader of the American Communist Party. A compulsively secretive, Lithuanian-born Jew who had become a fanatical communist while a student at the City College of New York, Lovestone rose to secretary treasurer of the American Communist Party by the late 1920s. At a 1929 Moscow conference, however, he made the near fatal error of openly criticizing Stalin's plans to abandon boring from within strategies in favor of creating a string of competing or dual communist unions, a move Lovestone saw as destined for failure in America. According to legend, Stalin's attendants subtly warned Lovestone that space remained open in Russia's Jewish cemeteries. Taking the hint, the American agent fled back to New York City, where he organized fellow defectors into an anti-Stalin circle known as the Lovestonites. The hard-driven Lovestone—never abandoning the stealth tactics he had adopted as Stalin's agent—soon became a valued adviser to the ILGWU and Meany on the domestic and international dangers of communism.[35] Lovestone devoted the rest of his life to anti-Soviet pursuits, eventually heading the AFL-CIO's International Affairs Department in the Vietnam War era.

Lovestone issued repeated warnings to Meany and Dubinsky of growing communist infiltration in progressive sectors of the labor movement and government. Yet Lovestone could not fully offset the allure of New Deal labor-state cooperation for those he advised. Assuming the presidency of the ILGWU in 1932, Dubinsky became a rabid supporter of Roosevelt. With Hillman, he helped form the breakaway CIO in 1935 and cofounded a political party, the American Labor Party (ALP), in 1936 to help reelect Roosevelt. Meany also embraced the New Deal. In 1932, he gained election to the New York State Federation of Labor (the state AFL body); two years later, at the age of thirty-nine, he became its president.[36] In many ways emulating Hillman's political model, Meany used his new offices aggressively to forge bonds between government and labor. He readily jettisoned AFL reservations about politics and became a tireless lobbyist in Albany for a host of new legislation, including unemployment insurance, social security, and minimum wage provisions. In the process, Meany formed an unusually intimate alliance with New York governor Herbert Lehman—analogous to Hillman's partnership with FDR.[37] Though dedicated to the AFL, Meany generally recognized the key CIO ideals of pluralism and industrial unionism.[38]

Yet Meany and Dubinsky's embrace of the new unionism and New Deal remained a wary one. Lovestone's warnings about communist influence did resonate. CIO leaders, including Hillman, eagerly recruited communists to aid in the massive undertaking of organizing industrial workers. As Meany later bitterly recalled, CIO president John L. Lewis "picked up commies—every commie he could—and they were good organizers."[39] But the communists in the CIO, according to labor's anticommunists, even when they were effective organizers, were hardly silent partners in a united front. Suspicions peaked in 1940, when left-leaning unionists, under the spell of the Hitler-Stalin pact, refused to endorse Roosevelt as the ALP candidate in response to the president's support for Great Britain.[40] As tensions smoldered, Dubinsky feared another communist drive to infiltrate the ILGWU. Anxiety over left-wing influence in the labor movement finally drove him to leave the CIO and reaffiliate the ILGWU with the AFL in 1940.[41]

Other aspects of the emerging New Deal order troubled Meany and Dubinsky as well. Both remained committed to maintaining an essential independence as the state grew ever more involved in labor relations. As a result, both occasionally clashed with New Deal officials. In 1935, Meany led a dramatic strike in New York City against the Works Progress Administration (WPA). For several months, Meany traded invective with General Hugh Johnson and other New Deal officials over issues related to wage rates for relief construction workers; finally the government capitulated.[42] On a lesser scale, Dubinsky quarreled bitterly with the Rural Resettlement Administration over its plans to build a combination farm and factory for garment workers in New Jersey, a plan Dubinsky suspected to be the invention of an industrialist hungry for government subsidies.[43]

As Meany and Dubinsky struggled to balance autonomy with opportunity, they also grew increasingly consumed with foreign affairs. Bucking the national trend toward isolationism, Dubinsky, Meany, Lovestone, and other internationally minded trade unionists gathered in 1933 at New York City's Aldine Club to organize a boycott of German goods and establish the German Labor Chest to aid unionists and socialists fleeing Nazi persecution.[44] In 1938, Meany and Dubinsky joined sympathetic unionists in the AFL to launch Labor's League for Human Rights, Freedom and Democracy, a body determined to challenge fascism and aid antifascist refugees.[45] Early and unforgiving critics of European and American appeasement of Hitler, labor's internationalists fashioned a potent analogy around Neville Chamberlain's 1938 capitulation at Munich, a favorite rhetorical device employed ceaselessly for forty years, whenever they were pleading for foreign policy activism—such as in Vietnam during the 1950s and 1960s.

While antifascism consumed their immediate energies, the communist menace always loomed in the shadows for both Meany and Dubinsky. Early subscribers to the concept of "Red Fascism," they consistently depicted their war against fascism as one side of a two-sided coin. The real enemy was all forms of totalitarianism—especially communism. An endlessly expressed article of faith for the AFL's human rights league remained a refusal, as Meany explained, "to recognize any important difference between a dictatorship of the Nazi-Fascist type and a dictatorship like that of Stalin."[46]

Meany brought his intense internationalism to the national AFL in late 1939. His election as AFL national secretary treasurer marked the beginning of something of a counterreformation within the AFL. The Bronx plumber clearly represented a more progressive brand of unionism unthreatened by the industrial unionism, cultural pluralism, and aggressive politics of the CIO. And, like many in the CIO—and in contrast to remaining isolationist elements within the AFL—Meany was closely attuned to world events.[47] In Washington, he and other like-minded internationalists, such as AFL vice president Matthew Woll, an old ally of Gompers, quickly made their presence felt in the federation.[48] David Dubinsky's return to the AFL in 1940 added another hard-line anticommunist with an internationalist perspective.[49] From his command post in New York City, Lovestone and his Lovestonites, a close-knit coterie of several hundred followers and agents, became a major influence on and constant source of intelligence for the assembling group of anticommunist internationalists.[50]

As the war heated up in Europe, Labor's League for Human Rights, under the direction of Lovestone, threw itself into the propaganda battle over American intervention, distributing millions of posters warning of Nazi infiltration and the day when "Heil Hitler replaces God Bless America."[51] Indefatigable, Lovestone also served as labor secretary to William Allen White's Committee to Defend America by Aiding the Allies. Through White's committee, the ex-communist "crusader" made important, lifelong contacts with State Department officials and figures from the intelligence world.[52]

With America's intervention in the war, the AFL's League for Human Rights intensified its operations, distributing roughly $25 million to assist in the relief and resettlement of refugees in Europe.[53] Lovestone coordinated his efforts closely with those of the Office of Strategic Services (OSS) and its labor bureau in London, which was under the direction of Arthur Goldberg, a future secretary of labor and Supreme Court justice.[54] Lovestone's European contacts, including the Dutchmen Omer Becu and J. H. Oldenbroek, who both became key figures in the postwar International Confederation of Free Trade Unions (ICFTU), proved invaluable in plotting reconnaissance operations in Europe.[55]

The decade leading up to World War II, then, witnessed the rise of a cadre of like-minded labor internationalists in the AFL. Melding aspects of the new unionism with the cautious approach of Samuel Gompers, the group quickly established an institutional base and an expanding network of contacts. The ramifications of appeasement confirmed for them the exigency of aggressive, early challenges to international threats. Initially focusing on the defeat of fascism, never far from the thoughts of AFL internationalists was the other great international evil—Soviet-driven communism.

An Early Cold War

Wartime alliances, however, temporarily straightjacketed the AFL internationalists.[56] In public pronouncements, free trade unionists discreetly avoided reference to the Soviets; Meany and others noted only an alliance with "the people of Russia." "We would do everything we could to help Russia as an ally in the fight against Hitler, but we would do nothing to advance communism," explained Dubinsky.[57] This policy produced awkward moments. In 1942, Walter Citrine, general secretary of the British Trade Union Congress (TUC), traveled to Washington to seek AFL participation in an Anglo-Soviet Union Committee, designed to symbolize cooperation between the Allies. To the chagrin of both the British and the Roosevelt administration, the federation flatly rebuffed its British counterpart.[58]

Increasingly, President Roosevelt's willingness to work with the Soviets stirred misgivings. Troubled by FDR's deteriorating health and apparent tolerance of the Soviets, Meany privately voted for fellow New Yorker Thomas Dewey in the 1944 presidential election. "I just felt that in dealing with the Russians after the war, we would be better off with Dewey," he later explained.[59]

As the war wound down, the AFL internationalists tired of muting their anticommunism and began mobilizing for the next great struggle—the battle against Soviet postwar designs. The stark absence of free trade unions in the Soviet Union, Meany announced, would soon spell an end to wartime cooperation. "[W]hile we can work together for victory in war," he editorialized in the *American Federationist,* "we cannot plan together for peace."[60] In 1944, the federation launched a semiautonomous organization, the Free Trade Union Committee (FTUC), to pursue its postwar foreign policy objectives. Lovestone, serving as FTUC secretary from his offices in New York City, essentially ran the organization, which AFL internationalists envisioned as a base for mounting an anticommunist counteroffensive in Western Europe.[61]

Such anticommunist activism contrasted sharply with Hillman's conciliatory postwar approach toward the Soviets. The clothing workers president needed little encouragement from his Roosevelt administration allies to pursue closer relations with Soviet trade unionists. Already intoxicated with visions of an organic, smoothly functioning corporate state, Hillman dedicated himself to the creation of the World Federation of Trade Unions, through which he intended to globalize his corporatist ideals. The AFL internationalists, however, saw things in a starker light. Conceiving of the world in strictly polarized terms, they viewed cooperation with the Soviet Union as a betrayal of the basic rights and liberties of labor—the first step toward a calamitous forfeiture of trade union autonomy and potency. The Soviet system, therefore, had to be aggressively resisted. Even as one war concluded, for labor's internationalists a new cold war had already begun.

Free Trade Unionism

As the AFL internationalists organized and plotted their early cold war, the political winds began to shift against Hillman's corporate model of labor relations. New unionism proponents had expected a large-scale military mobilization organized by New Dealers to further their cause, establishing alluring precedents for cooperative labor relations and a planned economy. But what emerged resembled chaos more often than harmony. As conservatives staged a political comeback, darkening clouds gathered over organized labor.[62] Congress passed the Smith-Connally Act, the first antilabor legislation enacted since before the New Deal. Representing labor in supposedly balanced wartime planning agencies, trade unionists often found their voices stifled.[63] From his perch on the War Labor Board, George Meany emerged as a leading voice of dissent, loudly protesting that rising prices were outpacing stagnant wages. In one network radio address, Meany assailed the "handful of unpatriotic men . . . whose desire it is to wreck the price control program so that food profiteers may enjoy a field day at the expense of the general public."[64] (Almost thirty years later, he employed similar language to denounce Richard Nixon's price and wage controls program during the Vietnam War.)

Increasingly, even many formerly enamored with corporatism shifted positions in favor of a reassertion of labor's autonomy. Having clashed repeatedly and bitterly with the federal government during the war, CIO founder John L. Lewis returned to the AFL and became an ardent supporter of trade union independence (although he remained cool toward the internationalism and anticommunism of free trade unionists such as Meany). By the fall of 1945, Lewis was bellowing, "What Murray and the CIO are asking for is a corporate state, wherein the activities of the people are regulated and constrained by a dictatorial government. We are opposed to the corporate state."[65] Soon even Philip Murray, despite an earlier infatuation with corporatism, began echoing Gompers's famous lament, "What the government gives, the government can take away."[66]

With the arrival of peace, Meany wasted no time in demanding a termination of wartime economic controls. At the AFL Bricklayers' annual convention in 1946, he issued a blunt directive: "[W]e have to say to the government, we want no control over working conditions and wages." For emphasis, Meany, a lifelong disciple of hyperbole, added that "government control leads to communism and fascism, if it is allowed to run its course."[67] Before San Francisco's Commonwealth Club that summer, he reiterated his Gompersesque theme: "[G]overnment interference in business leads to more and more bureaucratic control and eventually to state socialism, whether under the name of communism or fascism."[68]

To Meany and the AFL internationalists, the war against totalitarianism directly reflected an urgent need to restore balance to the domestic order. Without greater determination to maintain autonomy, labor risked being subsumed by the state—a tragic fate befalling impotent trade unions under communist and fascist regimes. Although Meany's message may have seemed harsh and inflexible to some, a conservative political resurgence, wartime frustrations, and outright hostility from business interests increasingly discredited reveries of corporate cooperation and planning.[69]

By the end of World War II, as their views gained traction, AFL internationalists openly began identifying themselves as free trade unionists and loudly trumpeted their ideals as the future of both national and international labor. Staking out their ground in uncompromising rhetoric, free trade unionists spoke and wrote incessantly of labor autonomy and *freedom*—a word they elevated to near sacramental status. Discussing trade union growth in 1946, George Meany pronounced that "we have been free to organize, free to appeal to public opinion, free to use our economic strength, [and] it has only been because of our freedom to act that the wage-earners of America are today so far ahead."[70]

First among freedoms for Meany was freedom from an encroaching state. Labor, he insisted, must remain an "independent force" and "at no time can we serve or act as an agency or dependent of our government."[71] He even went so far as to criticize "labor's Magna Carta," the Wagner Act. The original purpose of the act, he remonstrated, was "broadened and extended," hence "the fears of a great many labor men—that the Wagner Act would bring the government too deeply into the field of employer relations—was realized."[72] Matthew Woll, the AFL vice president, took Meany's admonitions further, warning in 1948 of the "shackles of statism, which were increasingly curtailing and negating the rights of all."[73] Soon some in the CIO were echoing this neo-Gompers line. As early as 1946, future CIO president Walter Reuther urged that "free labor" and "free management" establish a postwar accord lest a "superstate will arise to do it for us."[74] Far from clarifying and delineating the proper relationship between an autonomous labor movement and government, the rhetoric of free trade unionism seemed more often to slide toward angry antistatism.

For the AFL internationalists, maintaining trade union strength and autonomy was not only the best way to defend labor at home but was essential to defending democracy abroad as the world entered the tense postwar era. "A democratic way of life is essential to a free labor movement and free trade unions are equally essential to free institutions," pronounced AFL president William Green in 1944.[75] And no threat loomed larger than communism—a system ceaselessly disparaged by Meany and his followers as the antithesis of free trade unionism. In the parlance of present-day historians, communism represented the discursive "other," a menacing and debasing presence to be reviled and resisted at all turns and in contrast to that which free trade unionists positively defined themselves.[76]

In the early years of the cold war, Meany and his ilk competed energetically to denounce the Soviet system, forever reminding audiences that Soviet workers were "little better off than slaves."[77] The slavery analogy had historical moorings, of course. The present struggle with the Soviets, according to free trade unionists, echoed the central labor question of American history: the epic battle of "free labor versus slave labor." The cold war, pronounced one free trade unionist, was an "irrepressible conflict."[78] Consciously or unconsciously, such language recalled the "free labor, free soil" rhetoric of the Civil War and even the republican language of the American Revolutionary War.[79]

Far from a purely historical problem, however, free trade unionists imagined a dire, immediate threat. "[M]ake no mistake about it," Meany warned the New York State Federation of Labor, "the prime objective of the brutal rulers in the Kremlin is the control and enslavement of the people of the USA."[80] Subversion of free labor unions, free trade unionists tirelessly maintained, was step one of Lenin's revolutionary strategy. Potent, independent, anticommunist unions thus represented the front line in the modern battle between slavery and freedom. To Meany, no "partnership, united front or joint action of even the most limited sort" could be tolerated between free and communist trade unions. To the contrary, free labor must "be the spearhead of the democratic world in energetically exposing totalitarianism of all shades and stripes."[81] Well before most trade union leaders could place Indochina on a map, the ideological intensity and inflexibility propelling U.S. labor toward the Vietnam War was set.

Paradoxically, however, free trade unionism's grand vision of labor leading a historical battle precipitated a compromise involving the very value deemed most indispensable—labor's autonomy. Seeking to strengthen anticommunist unions worldwide, both the AFL and CIO worked increasingly in alliance with state agencies, including the CIA, all the while proclaiming the primacy of independence. Even in more mundane domestic affairs, labor-state cooperation expanded rather than contracted in the postwar years. Spurred by Meany, the postwar AFL dove further into the legislative process by forming a political action committee, Labor's League for Political Education. The federation also broadened its advocacy of social legislation. In the case of health care, the AFL, working at times almost interchangeably with the Truman administration, outdid its supposedly more socially conscious counterparts in the CIO with an aggressive campaign in support of national health insurance.[82] Yet such developments barely made a dent in free trade union discourse. The intense rhetorical celebration of trade union independence, in stark contrast to the reality of growing state-labor cooperation, was so pronounced that it suggests an unconscious quest to counterbalance or compensate for compromised autonomy.

Free trade unionism, in the end, emerged an entity caught awkwardly between Hillman's vision and Gompers's ideals. The exact boundaries guarding labor's autonomy remained obscure. Busy gearing up to wage a cold war and hardly given to introspection, free trade unionists rarely pondered the dilemma of a movement committed to preserving its autonomy yet forced to pursue compromising alliances to further far-reaching causes.[83] Still, such festering contradictions would dog them. Pondering many of the same difficulties, Vietnamese trade unionists later metaphorically spoke of being "pinched between a river and a mountain." Americans similarly refer to being caught between a rock and a hard place—essentially where the Meany internationalists found themselves during the painful Vietnam War.

Full-Employment Economics

Undergirding assumptions central to free trade unionism lay a "bastard" variant of Keynesian economics, popularly known as full-employment economics. An aggressive fiscal approach that prescribed massive government spending to stimulate production and consumption, full-employment economics propelled the labor movement toward greater involvement in foreign affairs, culminating in its support for the war in Southeast Asia.

"Proto-Keynesian" theories linking employment and consumer spending to economic growth first surfaced in the 1920s among progressive labor and business leaders—including Hillman and proponents of the new unionism.[84] During the New Deal, government officials such as labor-friendly Leon Keyserling, even before they were exposed to the theories of John Maynard Keynes, began actively promoting government spending as a vehicle to promote consumption, job creation, and growth.[85] Wartime prosperity, driven by immense government investment, bolstered the confidence and claims of full-employment enthusiasts.

To the AFL, beset by an awkward ambivalence toward state activism, full employment had a natural appeal; it prescribed a confined and defined role for government, one not threatening trade union autonomy. By the early 1940s, with the particular support of Meany and Dubinsky, the AFL became a spirited sponsor of full-employment economics. During the war, the federation's mouthpiece, *The American Federationist,* ran a high-profile series of articles extolling the approach.[86] With the arrival of peace, the federation enthusiastically endorsed the Keyserling-authored Employment Act of 1946, which encoded key elements of the full-employment agenda.[87] While some liberals and many in the CIO might have preferred fundamental economic reform and planning programs, as these options fizzled they, too, embraced full-employment economics.[88]

A harsh postwar political climate, however, yielded only barren ground for the new economic formulations. An increasingly conservative Congress essentially ignored the Employment Act and thwarted Truman's efforts to initiate Keynesian social-spending programs. Frustrated, the AFL and CIO turned increasingly to defense spending for full-employment fuel. Leon Keyserling, as a member of the Council of Economic Advisers, personally tutored National Security Council (NSC) members on his brand of aggressive Keynesian economics, teaching them that the U.S. economy could afford—and even prosper as a result of—a massive military buildup; it could have both guns and butter. In 1949, he helped draft NSC-68, which recommended generous increases in defense spending.[89] While often promoting creative applications of defense procurements, such as directing spending to regions with high unemployment, organized labor's vigorous support for defense spending, particularly its warm relations with companies and political figures associated with the defense industries, spurred critics, who by the 1960s were denouncing the AFL-CIO as yet another cog in the machinery of a garrison state.[90]

By the late 1940s, full employment, replete with a growing dependence on defense spending, became a central component of free trade unionism. The nation had, according to the full-employment champions, all the means at its disposal to fight communism abroad and enjoy healthy economic growth at home. For the next thirty years, such optimism buttressed not only labor's domestic initiatives but also its self-assured, expansionist outlook toward the world.

Yet it would be a mistake to overemphasize the role of economics in labor's growing internationalism. Rather it was ideology that overwhelmingly propelled the growing internationalism of key U.S. trade unionists. One examines the written and spoken record of American labor leaders almost in vain for evidence of anything other than diehard anticommunism motivating labor's international aspirations. Speaking publicly or privately, the trade union leaders who presided over the post–World War II era were consistent: they believed free and independent trade unions were essential to the preservation of human rights and that the spread of communism *anywhere* represented a grave threat to those rights. While some historians have depicted amorphous notions such as the allure of "new corporatist international structures" as intoxicating American labor, the historical record provides virtually no evidence that such notions shaped the thoughts of U.S. labor leaders.[91]

"In Those Early Years It Was Rather Lonely"

Only weeks after the end of the war, Meany traveled to Blackpool, the gritty British resort town on the Irish Sea. There he was to address the annual

Trade Union Congress Convention. He arrived as a fraternal delegate with a pointedly unfraternal message: his branch of the American labor movement would adamantly oppose any postwar international labor organization affiliated with Soviet trade unions. In a tense speech before a hostile TUC crowd, including a visiting Russian delegate, Meany threw down the gauntlet. "We do not recognize or concede that the Russian worker groups are trade unions," he pronounced. No common ground could exist between communist "fronts" and Western unions. "What could we talk about?" Meany mockingly demanded, "the latest innovations being used by the secret police?"[92] As the Russian delegate leaned forward and listened intently to a translation, the audience members shuffled their feet and coughed loudly. Heckles of "tommyrot" and "shame" met Meany's lambasting of "pseudo-trade unions" in Russia.[93] The oldest delegate present could not remember a speech so frequently interrupted by chants of "Withdraw! Withdraw!" (a British form of booing) and other jeers.[94] The episode, high-profile news in England and America, underscored not only free trade unionists' determination to preemptively launch a cold war but also the striking degree of national and international opposition facing those designs.

While Meany rejected any postwar labor confederation that would admit Soviet trade unions, Sidney Hillman, free of the consuming anticommunism driving the free trade unionists, worked hard to create just such an organization. He became a key architect of the World Federation of Trade Unions, an endeavor his biographer described as "a world labor organization committed to a global version of the New Deal."[95] Founded in October 1945, WFTU affiliates included the CIO, the British Trade Union Council, the French Confédération Générale du Travail, and other world labor organizations, both communist and noncommunist.[96] The new organization, for Hillman and others, represented a key step toward a new, grand international system based on accommodation between East and West—an agenda the free trade unionists aimed to thwart.[97]

Disturbed by the formation of the WFTU and communist gains in Western Europe, in late 1945 the AFL's Free Trade Union Committee dispatched special agent Irving Brown to Paris to coordinate the counteroffensive. Simultaneously, the AFL moved to establish its influence with trade union movements in Latin America and elsewhere in the third world.[98]

Thirty-three years old when he arrived in Paris, Brown already had experienced some of the most bitter labor conflicts of the 1930s. He had earned distinction as an AFL organizer in East Saint Louis, South Chicago, and Harlan County, Kentucky—all focal points of Depression era labor insurgency and violence. A secular Jew and native of the Bronx, Brown's father, a militant Teamster, had sparked his son's devotion to trade unionism. As a student at New York University in the early 1930s, the younger Brown fell under the spell of Jay Lovestone. Recognizing Brown's skills and potential, Lovestone immediately dispatched his disciple to help thwart CIO organizing campaigns in the Midwest. Through Lovestone, Brown began his international work during World War II, operating in London in league with "Wild Bill" Donovan and the OSS. Assigned to cultivate the European labor underground, Brown parachuted into France only days after the Allied invasion. A natural linguist, he quickly became fluent in French, German, and Italian. Tireless, talented, driven, and ruthless, Brown was the ideal agent to press the AFL's anticommunist agenda in Europe.[99]

But Brown was largely on his own. Most European trade unions had affiliated with the WFTU, and the continent remained in political and economic disarray. "In those early years it was rather lonely, because everybody was in the WFTU except us," Brown later recalled.[100] No U.S. government support existed, and within the AFL itself conservative elements resisted funding expensive overseas programs. In correspondence with Lovestone, Brown lamented the lack of material assistance from the federation. Lovestone assured his protégé that their sponsors were "growing and changing" but cautioned that "you must be careful not to step on old traditions and illusions."[101] As Brown's "lonely" efforts attest, during the immediate postwar years free trade unionists struggled both to maintain a requisite independence and to press an ambitious anticommunist agenda in Western Europe. The AFL's Paris-based agent accomplished little before 1948 save the cultivation of a network of European anticommunists.[102] New opportunities to advance the cause would arrive soon, however, as the U.S. government moved to expand its engagement in Europe and the world. For labor's internationalists, such sponsorship was welcome, even if it compromised the autonomy mandated by free trade unionism.

Conclusion

The forces that propelled American labor toward its costly involvement in Southeast Asia were virtually all in place by the end of World War II. Blending the competing philosophies of Sidney Hillman and Samuel Gompers, free trade unionists articulated a compelling vision of labor as an autonomous actor and an uncompromising and indispensable opponent of international communism. Driven by ideology, labor's internationalists moved to launch an early cold war well before the rest of their country joined the battle against Soviet communism.

Free trade unionists, however, would struggle to adhere to their strict rhetorical mandate for autonomy, especially after the AFL embarked on numerous labor-state cooperative ventures intended to advance its anticommunist foreign policy. Meanwhile, a world away in French Indochina a labor movement was also coalescing, one that would struggle with many of the same convictions and contradictions as its American free trade union counterpart.

2 "No More Pressing Task Than Organizing in Southeast Asia"

For two years following World War II, the AFL internationalists fought a lonely, largely solitary cold war against communist infiltration of Western European unions. In 1947, however, the fortunes of free trade unionism turned markedly for the better. With the Truman Doctrine and the Marshall Plan, the federal government emerged as a new, generous partner in the anticommunist cause. While a partnership between labor and the U.S. government risked compromising trade union autonomy, its fruits—greater resources with which to battle communism in Western Europe—were too alluring to resist. By 1950, anxious to expand its crusade, labor's internationalists prepared to take their cold war to the third world. High on the list of regions drawing U.S. labor's interest was Indochina.

In Vietnam, a nascent trade union movement was struggling to carve out an independent existence in the midst of violent revolution. Much like their American counterparts, Vietnamese trade unionists prized autonomy, ambitiously seeking to break cycles of national impotence. Caught in a nether land between French colonizers and revolutionary communists, the middle course chartered by the leaders of Vietnam's labor movement carried its own perils. With few available resources, early Indochinese trade unionists sought outside aid and leverage from any source available, including American labor.

The Origins of Vietnamese Organized Labor

While the history of mid-twentieth-century American organized labor can be told with reasonable certainty and the aid of abundant primary and secondary sources, the early history of Vietnamese trade unionism is considerably more shadowy. Indeed, what became the South Vietnamese labor movement took root in the late 1940s as an illegal underground assemblage of anticolonial nationalists, many of whom were veterans of the revolutionary Viet Minh. Despite stiff opposition from the French authorities, from its inception the nascent movement showed remarkable resilience, militancy, and pragmatism.

Geographically, religiously, and ethnically diverse, and taking the shape, as natives described it, of a pole supporting two rice baskets, Vietnam was unlikely terrain for the emergence of a labor movement. The population—roughly 80 percent of which toiled in subsistence agriculture, with few owning land and many working on large, French-owned plantations—struggled under the oppression of French colonialism.[1] Vietnamese not working the land might serve the French in supporting roles. By the 1940s, over one hundred thousand served the colonial army. Little in the way of industry existed. As historian Alexander Woodside noted, "Vietnam could barely match the labor force of preindustrial England."[2] In the north, some small industries, such as coal mining (eventually employing some fifty thousand miners), took root. By midcentury, small factories producing cigarettes or other items sprang up in cities throughout Vietnam. Companies such as the Société Indochinese pour Eaux et l'Électricité en Annam employed native workers in power plants supplying energy to central Vietnam. Still, Vietnam remained underdeveloped throughout the period considered in this study.[3] Despite the paucity of industry, an Indochinese version of the "labor question" did emerge and eventually took center stage in the battle against French colonialism. Directly from these developments the movement later calling itself the Vietnamese Confederation of Labor evolved.

"From the beginning," explained historian William Duiker, "there was little question that the primary objectives of French colonial policy in Indochina were economic."[4] And cheap labor was crucial to this equation. Driven largely by rapacity, colonizers, beginning in the late nineteenth century, devised brutal means by which to control labor, creating conditions in many ways analogous to slavery. French colonists, scrambling to forge a profitable commercial agricultural sector, forcibly uprooted hundreds of thousands of Vietnamese peasants, many of them former landowners. Cruel native recruiters, known as *cai,* preyed on this newly landless population, harnessing it for labor on large plantations.[5] Conditions on rubber plantations were particularly horrific, bordering on vassalage; workers suffered long hours, physical punishment, and rampant disease. In the interwar years, the mortality rate at one Michelin rubber plantation approached 50 percent. Overseers identified laborers solely by assigned numbers. In one infamous case, a foreman beat to death a worker known only as Brother 70, generating a story that painfully lingered in the collective memory of Vietnamese workers well after the end of French rule. Elsewhere, working conditions in Vietnam's light industries and the coal mines north of Haiphong were almost as miserable.[6]

The heavily bureaucratic French colonialists vigilantly guarded against dissent among natives. A central intelligence agency, the Sûreté Générale, maintained an extensive network of informants and kept close tabs on suspected nationalists.[7] "The French state's perennial anxiety to keep control of every activity and its jealous husbanding of power" permeated the colonial administration, observed Virginia Thompson, one of the few Americans to study Indochina before World War II. All signs of resistance brought immediate reprisals.[8] "The French hold us in hatred and contempt," reported the Vietnamese nationalist Phan Chau Trinh in 1906. "They consider us not merely as savages, but as dogs and swine. . . . More than a few people in the countryside have been beaten to death by Frenchmen."[9] To support the top-heavy, oppressive bureaucracy, peasants and workers paid crippling taxes. Poverty spread rapidly, especially in the countryside, where in the early twentieth century a French bureaucrat reported that most of the population "lives at the border of famine and misery."[10]

Such repression never dampened the nationalistic impulses brewing among the Vietnamese—sentiments often inflamed by anger and frustration surrounding exploitative colonial labor practices and conditions. During the 1920s, Ton Duc Thang, a radical nationalist, began organizing workers in Saigon's factories and docks into secret unions. French authorities quickly broke the campaign, but the rebels soon turned to more violent measures.[11] In 1929, Vietnamese nationalists murdered René Bazin, a French official in charge of a brutal labor-recruiting network.[12]

The emerging primacy of the labor issue spoke directly to an ongoing struggle to unify and direct the nationalist movement. As historian Alexander Woodside suggests, "one theme does seem to have united many Vietnamese of a great variety of political loyalties and ideological outlooks in the twentieth century," and that is "the search for better collective organization or more effective 'organized communities' and 'organized groups,'" known by the Vietnamese as *doan the*.[13] For many nationalists, the goal of organizing a new, equitable labor system to supplant the glaring cruelties of French rule emerged as the crucial component in forging this elusive *doan the*.

A sharp economic downturn in the early 1930s caused by a worldwide collapse in rubber and rice prices lent even greater urgency to the Indochinese "labor question." As conditions worsened, frustrations could not be contained. In 1930, unrest at rubber plantations in Bien Hoa in Cochinchina rapidly spread to both urban and rural areas, where workers in large numbers walked off their jobs. While the strikes focused on material issues, the scope of the rebellion and accompanying violence fundamentally threatened colonial control.[14] In response, authorities launched a mammoth counteroffensive, brutally breaking the strikes and even mounting aerial bombings of villages. As insurance against future troubles, the French colonial Criminal Commission ordered 699 executions without trial.[15]

By 1931, the French had quelled the uprisings, but small-scale work stoppages, often inspired by communist operatives, persisted throughout the decade. Communists launched the first sustained drive to organize Saigon's dockworkers in the early 1930s (a struggle later revived with limited success by the South Vietnamese labor movement).[16] Saigon's impoverished drivers of "tombstone carts," small horse-driven carriages, mounted strikes in 1935, and again the police reacted ruthlessly.[17]

As labor tensions smoldered, the Marxist-Leninist analysis of colonialism, rooted in blistering critiques of labor exploitation, gained a growing following. French success in weakening the Vietnamese Nationalist Party (VNQDD) essentially left the communists to dominate the nationalist movement and reorient it further toward questions of labor and revolution. In 1930, activists founded the Indochinese Communist Party. While earlier nationalist campaigns focused on the small, educated elite of Vietnam, communists targeted the country's proletariat (numbering roughly two hundred thousand, including small factory employees, shipyard workers, and coal miners) and the large peasant class.[18]

Nationalist pressure and international criticism of labor conditions in Vietnam did bring some relief for the toiling masses. In 1927, the colonial government issued a labor code, which limited work hours; established basic health, safety, and housing standards; and prescribed recruiting procedures. But labor inspectors had little power, and employers routinely disregarded the code. A more serious effort at reform came in 1936 with the election of the French "Popular Front" government under Léon Blum. The new socialist prime minister introduced a host of reform legislation that granted new rights to colonial workers. On January 1, 1937, Blum issued a new colonial labor code mandating an eight-hour day, pensions for victims of accidents, weekly rest periods, restrictions on night work for women, and prohibitions against the activities of the brutal *cai* labor recruiters. The reformed code, however, still strictly prohibited labor unions.[19]

Ignoring the prohibition, Vietnamese communists and nationalists continued their clandestine organizing, particularly in the coal and textile industries. In early 1937, Saigon-based American journalist William Henry Chamberlin watched nationalist agitators disrupt welcoming ceremonies for a visiting former French cabinet officer. As a military band broke into the *Marseillaise,* protestors unleashed a chorus of cries demanding labor unions and self-government. Police instantly descended on the group, arresting four. Chamberlin left Indochina shaken by the incident and convinced that any hope for the future of Southeast Asia "depends on the ability of the Indo-Chinese laborers to build up permanent labor organizations."[20]

The French, however, continued to resist reform, and native unrest only grew. In 1939, elements of the developing labor movement joined with other nationalist groups to mount a general strike (a familiar French labor tactic) in the port city of Haiphong.[21] As organizing efforts spread, some employers found it expedient to sidestep colonial prohibitions and bargain directly with "worker representatives," although labor organizers had much to lose through such contacts.[22]

Among those deeply affected by the momentous labor upheavals of the times was Tran Quoc Buu. The future leader of the South Vietnamese labor movement, Buu was born on May 13, 1912, in Tan Nghi, near Qui Nhon, the capital of Binh Dinh Province in central Vietnam. From an early age, he felt the pull of the anticolonial movement. His eagerness to partake in protests and agitation angered his stern father, a local mandarin. Exasperated, the patriarch finally banished his fourteen-year-old son from the family home for participating in anti-French rallies. School officials followed suit, expelling Buu and banning him from further education. Lost and alone, Buu wandered the country for a time. In 1932, he surfaced in Hanoi, where he completed his education and then spent several years teaching high school in Saigon and Qui Nhon. However, Buu could not shake his commitment to the anticolonial cause and remained an active agitator as nationalism engulfed French Indochina.[23]

Joining forces with socialists and communists, Buu was drawn increasingly into the armed struggle against the French. In 1940, with Japanese influence spreading and a new French Vichy government in place in Indochina, nationalists decided to test the new regime with a large-scale uprising. Buu eagerly joined in a massive insurrection by peasants and urban workers in southern Vietnam. The labor question—outrage over deteriorating working conditions—united the diverse demonstrators. Protesters brandished signs bearing communist-inspired slogans designed to appeal directly to the Vietnamese peasantry and proletariat: "The Cultivators Must Have Land" and "Liberation for the Industrial and Agricultural Workers." The Vichy government, however, was more resilient than revolutionaries expected, and the French authorities quickly counterattacked. They arrested Buu and other leaders of the protests.[24]

At a military tribunal, the judges sentenced Buu to ten years at Paulo Condore, the Devil's Island of Vietnam. Grim, subhuman conditions met the young nationalist at the island prison, where most of his fellow inmates were political prisoners. Convicts were packed together in squalid, five-by-nine cells roofed with iron bars. Meager daily rations of rice and water provided the only sustenance. Those who violated the rules suffered torture and confinement in tiger cages. But if the intent was to break the will of the prisoners the result was often the opposite. For many, incarceration proved both politically radicalizing and the source of lifelong friendships. Prisoners plastered the gritty walls with portraits of Mao, Lenin, and Marx and maps of the world. They published secret journals, and discussion groups on Marxist-Leninist ideology met clandestinely.[25] "Friendships forged behind bars," explained historian David Marr, "were often the closest of any in the revolutionary movement."[26] Buu's cellmates were two young militants, Vo Van Giao and Tran Huu Quyen, who shared his intense nationalism. In prison, this trio, later known as the "three musketeers," developed a lifelong bond that became the nucleus of the South Vietnamese organized labor movement.[27]

Besides Buu, Quyen, and Giao, in the early 1940s Poulo Condore was home to numerous influential members of the Viet Minh, including Le Duan, the intense founding member of the Indochinese Communist Party and the de facto leader of North Vietnam after Ho Chi Minh's death in 1969. Buu and Le Duan came to know each other while toiling in the prison dispensary, where one worked as a clerk and the other as an orderly's aide. Later Buu recalled of his onetime friend that "the most striking thing about him was his fanaticism about Marxism-Leninism" (a conclusion shared even by Le Duan's communist allies).[28] From his youth through his time in prison, Buu shared a common anticolonial militancy with the likes of Le Duan. But early on he manifested deep doubts as to whether the Viet Minh ideology represented *doan the,* the glue capable of holding the revolution together and rebuilding Vietnamese society.

On March 9, 1945, the Japanese, already a lurking presence behind the Vichy collaborationist government in Vietnam, seized control of the country, temporarily ending eighty years of French rule. Although the sequence of events remains murky, the Japanese appear to have arranged for Buu's release. They then trained him alongside members of an eccentric religious sect, Cao Dai, as part of the drive to maintain Japanese control.[29] Founded in 1919, the Cao Dai aimed to realize *doan the* through its synthetic religious practices. Cao Daists considered "all religions as one," positing Jesus, Buddha, Joan of Arc, and an eclectic mix of other religious figures as all equally worthy of veneration. Whatever the extent of Buu's adherence to the strange, new denomination, by 1945 he was serving as its political officer. Following the Japanese defeat, in August 1945 Buu and elements of the Cao Dai allied themselves with the Viet Minh, seeking to halt the reimposition of French colonial rule.[30]

For over a year, Buu made common cause with the Viet Minh as the first

Vietnamese war began. By 1947, however, he and other nationalists battling alongside communists began to question the alliance. At best, they seemed to be facing years of bitter fighting in the jungle—at worst, defeat seemed to be on the horizon. The Viet Minh cadres were "reduced to a struggle for sheer survival" after successful French attacks on their headquarters in northern Vietnam.[31] Concurrently, the French began a serious pacification campaign, granting new rights and "a semblance of autonomy" to the Vietnamese.[32] Many nationalists began to consider working within the system to bring about change and ultimately an end to colonialism.

Buu, who always viewed the Viet Minh as tainted by ties to outsiders, increasingly sought to distance himself from his former collaborators.[33] For a time, he and the Cao Dai fought both the French and the Viet Minh. In a sense, the Cao Dai–Viet Minh conflict represented a struggle for the soul of the revolutionary movement. The Cao Dai and the Viet Minh, as Alexander Woodside has argued, offered "two polar reactions or types of reactions in Vietnam to French colonialism and the decay of the old society," with both claiming to be "prophets of universal faith."[34] For Buu, however, neither the "spiritual response" nor that centered on the inexorable conflict between social classes represented a viable, transcendent *doan the*. Infighting within the nationalist camp increasingly sent Buu into a deep depression. Despondent, he moved to separate himself from the violence and acrimony; he swore on the graves of his ancestors he would never again have anything to do with politics.[35]

Buu was not the only member of the future South Vietnamese labor movement to experience an epiphany in 1947. Trinh Quang Quy, for instance, future research director for the South Vietnamese labor movement, hailed from a well-to-do landlord's family in North Vietnam. Nevertheless, the August Revolution of 1945, in which Ho Chi Minh and the Viet Minh briefly seized power before being ousted by the French, deeply captivated the young man. Quy leaped at the opportunity to join the revolutionaries. For several years, he fought as a loyal member of the Viet Minh.

In 1947, Quy found himself uncomfortably witnessing "a typical people's trial" of Mrs. Cat Hanh Long, a landlady at Dong-Bam plantation in Thai-Nguyen Province. As the interrogation proceeded, Quy grew increasingly uneasy. He shared the same background and many of the supposed "crimes" of the defendant. He imagined the inadequate responses he would offer if the interrogators turned on him. "Why did you learn French? Why did you become a wealthy man? Why were your grandparents and parents top leaders of your village?" In torment, Quy "realized the brutal truth that a group of international communists were doing everything they could to enslave my beloved country."[36] Ironically, though obscured from their followers, most of the early leaders of the Viet Minh, including Ho Chi Minh and Pham

Van Dong, shared Quy's "petit bourgeois" background, but by the late 1940s the revolutionary imperative endangered any who remotely resembled "class enemies."[37]

As Buu and other nationalists broke from the Viet Minh, trade unionism was making its first concrete advances in Vietnam. French officials, seeking to advance their pacification campaign and feeling the sting of international criticism of their colonial labor practices, moved to ease the tight restrictions on Vietnamese workers.[38] Between the end of World War II and the French return, the Viet Minh, briefly seizing control of Vietnam, had begun organizing workers into what it foresaw as "one big union," the Tong Lien Doan Lao Dong (TLD), modeled on the French Générale Confédération du Travail (CGT), France's largest labor federation. The TLD, however, made little headway in the south or in Vietnam's cities, which were still controlled by the French.[39] When the communist-leaning CGT organized a meeting of native workers in Saigon, Sûreté Générale agents showed up to intimidate the gathering, making note of those present and conspicuously taking down license plate numbers. The next day, complained the CGT general secretary for Vietnam, several of his "comrades were arrested."

While harassing the CGT, the secret police looked the other way as anticommunist socialist and Christian trade unions moved to organize Vietnam's workers.[40] With encouragement from the AFL, in June 1947 the Force Ouvrière, an anticommunist breakaway group from the left-leaning CGT, began organizing French civil servants working in Vietnam. While the Force Ouvrière signaled an interest in unionizing native workers, its representative in Indochina lacked the confidence of his superiors and proved unable or unwilling to launch a recruitment campaign.[41]

In contrast to the indolent Force Ouvrière organizer, a French customs officer named Gilbert Jouan, with twenty years experience in Indochina, took an interest in native workers. Jouan first worked with the left-leaning CGT, but quickly grew disillusioned with the inertia and ideological rigidity of the organization. He turned instead to the French Confederation of Christian Workers (CFTC), a Roman Catholic labor federation determined to organize native workers even in the volatile atmosphere of French Indochina.[42] Jouan and other Catholic trade unionists in 1947 formed a "delegation" representing CFTC interests in Vietnam. The group focused first on organizing French workers stationed there, founding the Syndicat Général des Fonctionnaires d'Indochine and a second organization for workers in private industry.[43]

But Jouan was not content to stop with French workers. In 1948, he notified the French authorities of his intention to begin "an authentic Christian trade union in Indochina . . . for the Indochinese themselves."[44] Already Jouan had sought out disaffected nationalists and organized them in "study circles," convening at the Palais Mutualité on 14 rue du Président Thinh (later renamed Le Van Duyet Street) in Saigon.[45] Among those he recruited was Tran Quoc Buu. The two immediately bonded, becoming almost inseparable. An American observer described Jouan as a "kind of evangelist" who lived "native style" with Buu's family. Influenced by Catholic social teaching, Jouan stressed the virtues of corporate labor relations, in particular *chambres mixtes de métiers,* or trade councils, in which employers, employees, and representatives of the state would meet and jointly make management decisions (along the lines of the corporatist model advanced by Philip Murray in America during World War II). Buu and other Vietnamese nationalists appeared to be motivated students, and Jouan was evidently a dedicated teacher.[46] In Western-style trade unionism and the concept of *chambres mixtes de métiers,* Buu seemed to find a viable *doan the*—his roadmap for unifying and reconstructing Vietnamese society.

Buu's conversion to trade unionism in many ways reflected a man teetering between two cultures—a condition that seemed to afflict his entire revolutionary generation. Educated under the French colonial system, Buu, to observers, seemed very much a French gentleman—reserved, with an air of sophistication, conducting business in French (never learning English), influenced deeply by western ideas and institutions. A gourmet, he indulged a lifelong love affair with good food, resulting in a lifelong struggle with his weight. But Buu was also a Vietnamese revolutionary, seeking fundamental change—*doan the*—for his country. He could surprise American visitors with fiery speeches, complete with revolutionary exhortations. Just as startling, Buu could revert quickly to his customary formal, detached demeanor. The Southeast Asian labor leader, mirroring a national search for identity, often seemed a maze of contradictions, a man neither fully of the East nor of the West, a riddle his American friends and supporters never completely solved.[47]

That Buu and Jouan's brazen move to organize native workers was permitted at all by colonial officials was attributable to the French pacification campaign, which included a quasi-independent government under Bao Dai. But Buu and Jouan still faced colonial prohibitions against trade unions. As one colonial official explained in 1948, nascent trade unions had "absolutely no legal standing; these such groups are only tolerated by public officials."[48] French colonial law, however, did allow the formation of "professional organizations." Sensing a loophole, Jouan and Buu concocted a scheme to launch their planned labor movement as a professional organization. In 1948, they christened their project the Association for Protection of Professional Interests of Workers in Craft, Industry, Commerce, Agriculture and in Liberal Professions.[49] In keeping with its "tolerance" policy and hoping the association would contribute to the pacification campaign,

French officials chose to allow its existence. Still, Jouan moved to safeguard his nascent movement with the leverage of international recognition. He arranged for the International Federation of Christian Trade Unions, with which the CFTC was federated, to recognize the Vietnamese organization. In 1950, the International Labor Organization (ILO) in Geneva also extended recognition. Eager to establish themselves on the world stage, Jouan and Buu dispatched delegates to that year's ILO conference.[50]

In fact, the budding trade unionists had little to fear from Saigon officials. Jouan, with many years of service in French Indochina, was a trusted and admired man. As one official report on Christian trade union organizing described him, "the mentality of an apostle, his faith in his work, [and] his dynamic personality, make him worthy of our esteem." The colonial government even arranged time off for Jouan at the customs office so he could focus on the organizing work that officials obviously hoped would counterbalance the appeal of the Viet Minh.[51] "The consolidation of the support of the working class in Vietnam is mainly to be achieved by close collaboration with the Christian Trade Union," the Vietnamese minister of social action told an American official. He considered trade unions to be "a strong point against Communist infiltration."[52] The result was an awkward modus vivendi between budding labor organization and state.

Nevertheless, while granting it a lease on life the colonial government's self-interested benevolence tainted Buu's organization. In the early 1950s, rumors swirled through Saigon (a city permanently in the throes of sensational gossip) that Pierre Perrier, head of the Sûreté Générale, had infiltrated the burgeoning labor movement. While acknowledging that there was "much truth" in the rumors, Donald Heath, the American ambassador in Saigon, concluded that Buu and Jouan's movement was not "an easily manipulated instrument in the hands of the government."[53]

Whatever relationship existed between Buu's movement and the French authorities, it represented only the first of many such awkward alliances reluctantly but willingly entered into by the organization to ensure its survival. Still, as the rumors attest, such pragmatism could be compromising. An outgrowth of a painful colonial past, Vietnamese culture—to the point of fixation—prized reputation, independence, and "moral purpose." These expectations, known as *uy tin,* placed tremendous pressure on those aspiring to forge *doan the* for their troubled country.[54] The exigencies of life in colonial Southeast Asia left the nascent Vietnamese labor movement facing bitter dilemmas for which there existed few attractive alternatives. Though in much magnified form, in their struggle with issues of dependence and independence Buu and his followers found themselves trapped in a paradox similar to that afflicting their American counterparts. Both movements valued sovereignty and independence of action, but for self-preservation they often depended on careful compromise and tenuous alliances.

The leaders of the Viet Minh, in the eyes of many, were better situated to present themselves as the genuine representatives of the people, less encumbered by ties to outsiders. Yet already they had a reputation for ruthlessness and, especially compared to the budding future CVTC, had little presence in southern Vietnamese cities. Nevertheless, especially in the countryside, the Viet Minh cadres had proven themselves proficient fighters and organizers. In many ways, the CVTC and communist guerrillas would remain rivals for the next two decades.[55]

These complex issues aside, Buu and Jouan were eager to advance their cause. Disregarding legal prohibitions, the two launched an aggressive campaign to organize workers, recruiting roughly eight thousand members by the end of 1950. That year they renamed their organization the Federation of Employees in the Private Sector and established an official headquarters at the Palais Mutualité, a large compound that remained their home until 1975. The organization quickly grew to include at least ten "illegal" unions, representing the employees of Citroën and Air Vietnam, as well as shoemakers, typesetters, tailors, and barbers.[56]

While tolerating the burgeoning labor movement, French authorities at times sought to circumscribe its activities. Colonial officials denied, for instance, Buu's petition to hold a public demonstration on May 1, 1950, in honor of May Day. Manifesting a determined militancy, Buu and his fellow incipient unionists instead announced a "requiem mass" at the Cathedral of Saigon. Following the services, union leaders directed members to the federation's headquarters, where they approved a series of resolutions to be presented to the government. Their demands included the closing of a gambling house in Cholon (the ethnic Chinese city adjacent to Saigon), an end to the subcontracting system at Saigon's port, and new labor codes that would decriminalize labor unions.[57]

In 1952, under pressure from the ILO and IFCTU and due to the increasing communist success in organizing peasants, Bao Dai finally issued a new series of labor regulations, which at last permitted Vietnamese workers to organize.[58] The decrees generated strong opposition from Vietnam's bourgeoisie—both French and native. Nonetheless, the Bao Dai government and French officials clung fatuously to the hope that the reforms would generate support among the working classes.[59]

Buu and Jouan, seizing on their new legal status, renamed their organization the Vietnamese Confederation of Christian Workers (known best by its French acronym, CVTC).[60] They focused considerable energy on recruiting rural workers, especially plantation workers and tenant farmers;

the organization's rural unions quickly became and would remain the confederation's largest. A little over a year later, the Sûreté Générale estimated that the CVTC's membership had grown to 38,990, including around 1,300 unionists in Hanoi.[61] Catholics, despite the organization's ties to the Christian International, remained in the minority. Officially, the CVTC "was open to all workers" and set out to attract a diverse membership, inclusive of all religious and minority groups.[62] Although Buu considered himself a Buddhist, he recognized diversity as a necessary ideal.[63] The CVTC downplayed religion when recruiting, focusing instead on immediate economic issues. Such a pragmatic, ecumenical approach fit well with Vietnamese society, in which religious affiliation and worship tend to be fluid. Multiple shrines to Christian, Buddhist, and other religious figures often adorn the homes of Vietnamese, who see little contradiction in venerating more than one religion.

While on one hand it was seeking to maintain peace with the French and Vietnamese authorities, on the other the CVTC strove to maintain an active militancy. In 1953, it initiated strikes by employees of Air France, five hundred shoemakers in Cholon, and workers in the five largest printing houses in Saigon. That same year, when government officials, seeking to facilitate labor organizing by the Dai Viet Nationalist Party, moved to disrupt CVTC operations in the north, Buu and Jouan loudly protested, notifying the ILO in Geneva and "unleashing a violent campaign in the press for trade union freedom."[64]

While focusing on its survival and bread and butter issues, the confederation also strove steadfastly to achieve a larger goal as well: to create new, durable workplace arrangements, in particular the formation of tripartite committees, consisting of representatives of government, employers, and labor, to settle future conflicts.[65] Through such reforms, Buu and the CVTC ambitiously hoped to mold *doan the* around Western-style trade unionism—nonviolently harnessing a near century's worth of labor-related anger and resentment to challenge the French and reinvigorate Vietnamese society. A Catholic priest with close ties to the CVTC explained that "another goal no less dear to the leaders of the CVTC is to propagate the doctrines of Christian trade unionism beyond the borders of Vietnam to all of East Asia."[66]

The early success of the CVTC could not be denied. Observers saw far-reaching social and political implications. Joseph Buttinger described the early movement as "a vehicle through which the 'socialist' tendencies of the masses and their hostility towards the Bao-Dai regime might be expressed more openly."[67] Yet despite enormous strides in a relatively short period, the CVTC remained fragile, caught between the surging Viet Minh and repressive French colonial overlords. Out of necessity the organization sought outside support. The AFL and CIO, already seeking to cultivate noncommunist third world labor movements, could not help but take an interest in Indochinese developments.

Partners in the Early Cold War

If 1947, the pivotal year when Buu and others broke with the Viet Minh, proved a turning point for the Vietnamese nationalists who later founded the Vietnamese Confederation of Labor, it marked a similar watershed for the AFL internationalists. Since 1945, free trade unionists had waged a lonely and frustrating struggle against a perceived international communist conspiracy to undermine free labor unions in Western Europe. By 1947, however, Meany and his circle gratifyingly watched the tide turn as their brand of virulent anticommunism and internationalism increasingly gained the upper hand. Tensions between the Soviets and Americans over the postwar future of Europe had mounted in the months following the defeat of Hitler. By 1947, U.S. officials more in tune with the impassioned anticommunism of the free trade unionists emerged triumphant over those advocating accommodation. Increasingly President Truman and others came to see the Soviets as essential threats to freedom in Western Europe and ultimately the United States—a view long held by free trade unionists. The Truman Doctrine embodied this new spirit and official resolve. Most importantly for the AFL internationalists, the U.S. government became a generous, deep-pocketed partner in the federation's once lonesome battle for the fate of Western European labor.

Ironically, in the years that preceded the consummation of this partnership, labor and state appeared to be moving farther apart. In 1946, Sidney Hillman died; soon thereafter his vision for labor relations and international coexistence expired as well. The corporatist cause, already wounded by volatile World War II labor-state relations, came increasingly under fire as Republicans seized control of Congress in 1946, gutting Truman's Fair Deal programs and relentlessly targeting organized labor. Passage of the "slave labor" Taft-Hartley Act served as a painful admonition of the state's capacity for malfeasance. Faced with an antagonistic federal government, even more radically inclined labor leaders suppressed impulses toward economic planning and corporatism in favor of a return to defensive, pure and simple unionism.

Taft-Hartley also signaled the growing potency of anticommunism. Alongside prohibitions against closed shops and boundaries on labor's right to strike, the act obliged trade union leaders to sign affidavits disclaiming affiliation with the Communist Party. Free trade unionists, while outspoken in denouncing Taft-Hartley, appreciated the new stipulation—if for nothing else than the trouble it promised to cause left-leaning trade unionists. "So far as that affidavit is concerned," advised Meany, "I don't see why we should pull the Communist chestnuts out of the fire."[68] Pivoting to accommodate shifting ground, CIO leaders scrambled to oust communists from their ranks rather than risk public repudiation. Quickly any connection to communism in organized labor became anathema. In San Francisco, at the 1947 AFL convention, Secretary Treasurer Meany bitterly denounced United Mine Workers president John L. Lewis for his tolerance of communism while president of the CIO. Unlike Lewis, Meany crowed, "I was never a comrade to the comrades."[69] An intensely anticommunist wind blew through the labor movement—and through the country. Free trade unionism's bellicose, unyielding anticommunism was no longer an anomaly; it was mainstream politics. Left-leaning or communist trade unions and unionists remained (as did conservative, isolationist elements in the AFL), but increasingly anticommunist internationalists, guided by the principles of free trade unionism, charted the course for organized labor.

The full-scale arrival of the cold war and the concurrent sudden shift in American priorities also brought dramatic changes to the AFL's foreign policy in Western Europe. The inauguration of a large-scale, American-funded recovery program for Europe, proposed by Secretary of State George C. Marshall in the summer of 1947, salvaged the AFL's struggling overseas programs, which earlier had been described by Irving Brown as "an international business [run] on a five-and-dime-store basis."[70] Seeking to siphon resources and funding from the Marshall Plan, Meany leaped to support the European economic relief program, linking it to free trade unionism's war against the "aggressive slave system" of the Soviet Union.[71]

Both the AFL and the CIO relished the Marshall Plan's New Deal orientation and its commitment to a substantial role for organized labor in the planning and execution of the relief program.[72] Together they generously lent personnel to the Office of Labor Advisers in the European Recovery Program (ERP). At the height of the program's operation, the Marshall Plan employed nearly eighty American trade unionists in Europe.[73] Corporatism, on the wane and under attack from the AFL at home, thrived in the ERP.

The American infusion of funds and expertise into Europe reenergized Irving Brown's stalled efforts to buttress anticommunist trade unions. Flush with Marshall Plan dollars, he successfully cultivated anticommunists within the French communist-leaning CGT labor federation. American money then established the anticommunists in a separate rival federation, known as the Force Ouvrière, which soon moved to organize French civil servants in Vietnam.[74] When French communist labor unions attempted to disrupt Marshall Plan shipments to the port of Marseilles, Brown organized a counteroffensive in league with local crime syndicates.[75] Throughout Western Europe, the Marshall Plan similarly rescued AFL operations with infusions of much needed cash.[76]

Alongside the Marshall Plan, the AFL found another willing benefactor for its activities in Western Europe—the CIA. Beginning in 1949, the AFL inaugurated an informal arrangement through which its semiprivate auxiliary, the Free Trade Union Committee, received yearly grants from the CIA. Between 1949 and 1958, the CIA transferred nearly half a million dollars to the FTUC. However, as historian Anthony Carew has concluded, the relationship between American labor (particularly the AFL) and the CIA "was not a smooth one."[77] American labor resented the supposed Ivy League elitism of CIA agents, while agency officials harbored misgivings about left-wing former communists such as Jay Lovestone. More seriously, even while accepting agency subsidies, U.S. labor strove to retain at least a semblance of the autonomy mandated by free trade unionism. Relations grew particularly sticky when the CIA demanded careful accountings for financial grants—stipulations particularly needling to free trade union sensitivities. Denouncing the "bookkeeping psychology" of the intelligence officers, the AFL consistently refused audits. Organized labor and the agency terminated the formal arrangement in 1958, by which time the frayed, tension-ridden relationship had become too much for both parties.[78]

Nevertheless, the agency provided American labor officials such as Brown and Lovestone with intelligence community contacts that later proved useful. Lovestone, for instance, cultivated Samuel Berger, a student of the labor theorist Selig Perlman at the University of Wisconsin and postwar U.S. labor attaché to the London embassy. Berger proved a remarkably useful liaison between the FTUC and the CIA. Later, during the Vietnam War, Berger, then serving as deputy ambassador to Saigon, again proved helpful as a vigorous supporter of South Vietnamese labor.[79] Despite the end of their formal relationship with the CIA, Lovestone and Brown maintained personal connections to the agency, ties that remained advantageous until they became public at the height of the Vietnam War, belying the claims of autonomy so central to free trade unionism.

Challenged by the Marshall Plan and the CIA, the tide of communism in Western Europe receded. As a result, pressure mounted on the WFTU, the ambitious international labor federation founded in part by the CIO to promote East-West labor accord. Incessantly depicting the WFTU as a front for Soviet designs, the AFL waged a ferocious assault against the organization. Stalin's repudiation of the Marshall Plan placed the WFTU's communist-leaning members in the unenviable position of having to attack the recovery plan and sabotage labor cooperation with the ERP. Meanwhile, the American CIO and the British TUC, both WFTU members, ardently supported the Marshall Plan and chafed at the refusal of world federation leaders to embrace it.[80]

CIO delegates also felt betrayed by WFTU lethargy in addressing questions of colonialism and third world labor movements.[81] In April 1946, a Viet Minh official, Pham Van Dong, personally lobbied the WFTU general secretary to assist in affiliating nascent Vietnamese unions begun by his organization. Demurring, the WFTU secretary general insisted that any affiliation had to be handled through the French CGT (which, though left leaning, had not yet taken a stand against French colonialism)—in a sense denying the Viet Minh claim to independence from the French. Pham, no doubt, concluded that essentially the WFTU was sanctioning Indochinese colonialism.[82] A year and a half later, the WFTU scrambled to find a suitable Indochinese representative for an upcoming regional conference in New Delhi. The organization finally turned to the French government for help—again seemingly endorsing the status quo in Indochina.[83]

Controversies surrounding the WFTU and mounting tensions between the United States and the Soviet Union finally aroused the latent anticommunism in CIO president Philip Murray. Acutely aware of the shift in U.S. public opinion and government policy, he moved to oust communists from the CIO and terminate his organization's affiliation with the WFTU. In 1948, he dispatched United Steelworkers president David McDonald to London with specific instructions to "smash" the WFTU.[84] McDonald and other CIO anticommunists, assisted by an increasingly sympathetic TUC, relentlessly pressed the issue of the Marshall Plan, bringing WFTU work to a virtual standstill. When communist delegates rejected compromise, the CIO and TUC withdrew from the WFTU—a major victory for the AFL and free trade unionism.[85]

As the WFTU disintegrated, the AFL, CIO, and TUC cooperated smoothly within the Marshall Plan Trade Union Advisory Committee. Prodded by the AFL, the committee endorsed the establishment of a new international organization of anticommunist trade unions to counter the WFTU.[86] In June 1949, CIO, TUC, and AFL delegates met in Geneva, along with other representatives of noncommunist trade unions, to lay the groundwork for what became the International Confederation of Free Trade Unions. Meany, addressing the assembled delegates, promised a pluralistic but virulently anticommunist organization that would promote neither American values nor those of any other system—save steadfast anticommunism. Later that year, in London, an international group of noncommunist trade unionists gathered for the inauguration of the ICFTU.[87]

With Europe stabilized, Meany used the London gathering to boldly announce plans to extend the work of the organization to the third world, particularly Asia. The future of the world, he told the ICFTU delegates, "will depend in large measure on the new labor movements in these Asian countries." The ICFTU should "not only welcome Asian trade unions but we must stand ready to come to their aid through concrete, specific measures."[88] Despite Meany's high hopes, the ICFTU never matched his ideal of an activist, anticommunist force promoting free trade unionism in the third world. Disputes between the CIO and AFL hobbled the ICFTU, especially when the CIO dispatched Victor Reuther to Europe in 1951. The rabidly anti-AFL brother of Walter, Victor was to oversee a CIO base of operations in competition with Irving Brown.[89] Likewise, American labor clashed endlessly with the British TUC, which the Americans viewed as soft on both communism and colonialism.[90]

Nevertheless the formation of the ICFTU underscored significant anticommunist gains in Western Europe and the increasing strength and influence of the free trade union perspective.[91] Aided by the Marshall Plan and other sources of funding such as the CIA, the AFL internationalists made great strides in the four years following World War II. Gradually the CIO and the rest of the country converted to free trade unionism's emphatic rejection of communism. By the end of 1950, the AFL had convinced international labor, at least to some degree, to join its fight against communism, a battle it intended next to take to the third world.

Encountering Indochina

As American labor prepared to extend its foreign policy activities worldwide, Vietnam was just coming onto its radar. Indochinese labor, however, shared a crowded radar screen; Vietnam was only one of many emerging nations, including several in North Africa and Latin America, vying for the attention and slim resources of the AFL and CIO in the late 1940s and 1950s. Nevertheless, the French war to maintain colonial control and mounting fears of communist incursions in the third world increasingly drew the interest of U.S. labor's internationalists. The early contact between American trade unionists and their Indochinese counterparts provides a glimpse of the intricacies and complexities that would later characterize their relationship.

American labor's first encounters with Indochina came in the context of postwar France. In October 1945, Charles Zimmerman (a veteran of the communist drive to infiltrate the Garment Workers union in the 1920s before turning against the party) and Irving Brown arrived in France to survey the labor situation for the AFL's Free Trade Union Committee.[92] The two former Lovestonites found French labor in an alarming state: communists dominated the CGT and held key positions in the government. The newly arrived American agents feared for the fate of the entire country. The FTUC quickly arranged for Brown to stay on as its permanent representative in Europe. Almost single-handedly, he began a desperate mission to reverse communist advances and mobilize anticommunists within the CGT.[93]

In the complex labyrinth of postwar France, few Frenchmen on either the Left or the Right objected to the reimposition of colonialism in Indochina and the beginning of war against the Viet Minh in late 1946. French Communist Party officials stifled their official policy of opposition to colonialism and endorsed, as members of the coalition government, the beginnings of the First Indochinese War. Even the Soviets seemed little concerned with the tumult in Southeast Asia.[94] Waging an all-consuming war against communist trade unionists, and perhaps fearing that an anticolonial position might alienate the noncommunist trade unionists he sought to cultivate, Irving Brown avoided the subject of Indochina. Neither he nor the AFL issued any public statement or private utterance of concern, despite the federation's long history of vocal enmity toward colonialism, which dated back to its call for Cuban independence in 1896. Even as the AFL assailed Dutch colonialism in Indonesia in the late 1940s, it remained silent on Indochina.

In 1947, the French Communist Party shifted its position and began openly condemning the official policy on Indochina. By May of that year, criticism of the war, among other issues, brought about the expulsion of communist ministers from a coalition government.[95] Outside the government, communists intensified their attacks on both the war in Indochina and America's growing involvement in European affairs. In his reports, Brown made his first acknowledgment of Vietnam, nervously warning of communist opportunism on the Indochina issue. Large-scale demonstrations organized by the left-leaning CGT against French policy in Southeast Asia and American aid to Greece, he feared, might undermine the Marshall Plan.[96]

Brown need not have worried, for the communist offensive backfired. The party's vociferous opposition to the First Indochinese War and the Marshall Plan alienated it from the French political mainstream and provided Brown with new leverage as he recruited anticommunists into the alternative pro-Western labor federation, the Force Ouvrière.[97]

Over the next two years, the French Communist Party and the CGT continued to lose influence. Frustrated by its diminishing status, the party launched a campaign of sabotage, *la lutte pour la paix,* targeting Marshall Plan imports and shipments destined for the war in Indochina.[98] Pressing his "peace initiative," Communist Party leader Maurice Thorez implored audiences: "Will the people of France accept the unloading and transshipment of these death machines?"[99] In April 1950, on the docks of Nice, a communist-organized mob forcibly boarded a ship destined for Indochina and rampaged throughout the vessel, eventually dumping an artillery-launching ramp into the Mediterranean.[100] In Marseille, Dunkerque, Grenoble, and elsewhere, similar acts of sabotage against shipments of men and munitions to Indochina followed. Although *la lutte pour la paix* failed to inspire rank and file support and perhaps damaged the French Communist Party's credibility, the carefully choreographed sabotage campaign confirmed American free trade union suppositions that the war in Indochina was the outgrowth of an international communist conspiracy, not a local struggle against colonialism.[101]

Brown was determined to halt the sabotage campaign. For reinforcements, he turned to the hard-edged leader of the Force Ouvrière's dockworkers, Pierre Ferri-Pisani. An arch-anticommunist, the colorful French dockworker already had survived torture at the hands of the German occupation forces and appeared determined to resist communism with the same resolve. Spurred by the AFL, Ferri-Pisani organized anticommunist maritime unions under the banner of the Comité Méditerranéen in 1950. Through this committee, he mounted counterdemonstrations and incited mob action to repel communist saboteurs on the waterfront.[102] The Comité Méditerranéen undoubtedly received financial support from Brown, presumably CIA money ferried through the AFL.[103] Ferri-Pisani's counteroffensive and Brown's funding did the trick, effectively thwarting the sabotage campaign. "In the history of European labor," waxed André LaFond, a grateful key figure in the Force Ouvrière, "Brown will be more important than all the diplomats put together."[104]

By 1950, the Force Ouvrière alternative to the CGT appeared to have been successfully launched and communist sabotage ceased. With the labor situation in France relatively stabilized, the AFL, after muffling its anticolonialism during *la lutte pour la paix,* issued its first critical words regarding French policy in Indochina.[105] No doubt mounting resistance from the Viet Minh moved the AFL. Recognizing shifting terrain, in January 1950, after his return from a trip to India, Irving Brown lamented, "Unless we break with the past in Indonesia, in Indo-China, in South Africa . . . there will be no hope for maintaining what is left of Asia."[106] A year later the FTUC echoed Brown, calling for national independence and full rights for Indochina as a French commonwealth nation.[107] By early 1952, the AFL's Executive Council weighed in with a strongly worded statement: "Resistance to communist aggression in Indo-China should be made more effective by stripping it of every appearance of a nineteenth century colonial campaign."[108] Limited independence granted by France to the Bao Dai government would not suffice. The AFL—after substantial delay—began calling for full independence.

Anxieties about Soviet strategy in Southeast Asia and its influence over the Viet Minh, however, tempered the federation's criticism of French colonialism. In late 1949, Irving Brown warned the ICFTU of a Soviet agent, F. G. Jakovlev, stationed in Siam, who had been assigned to infiltrate the emerging labor movements of Southeast Asia.[109] Increasingly, a view of the Viet Minh as puppets controlled by Moscow emerged as an unquestioned, concrete article of faith in AFL circles. "Clearly, the invasion of Indochina is being openly planned by the Soviet Union," warned the FTUC in a pamphlet on Soviet infiltration of Asia.[110] *The Free Trade Union News,* the AFL's foreign policy organ, ran a series of articles by an Indian trade unionist, S. R. Mohan Das, portraying Ho Chi Minh as "completely and totally subservient to Moscow."[111]

Trapped between its abhorrence of French colonialism and its certitude that the Viet Minh were doing Moscow's bidding, the AFL scrambled for alternatives. News of a struggling independent labor movement in Vietnam naturally caught free trade union fancies. Initially, the AFL hoped to arrange support for the nascent Vietnamese labor movement through the newly minted ICFTU, the international labor organization supported largely by AFL dollars. Irving Brown tirelessly lobbied ICFTU planning sessions for immediate aid to free labor movements in underdeveloped areas, including Southeast Asia. In 1950, an ICFTU Emergency Committee, commissioned to address the organization's most pressing concerns, voted to send an exploratory committee to Southeast Asia, a region it designated as a "top priority." Brown commended the decision, saying that he could "think of no more pressing task than organizing in Southeast Asia."[112]

French colonial officials greeted news of the ICFTU mission with some trepidation. The counselor for social affairs warned the high commissioner for Indochina that the delegation might be open to "bad impressions" spread by "French trade unionists."[113] A preliminary ICFTU task force that included Gordon Chapman, secretary treasurer of the American Federation of State, County and Municipal Employees (AFSCME), Richard Deverall of the AFL, and John Brophy of the United Mine Workers, swept through Southeast Asia later that year.[114] The team briefly visited Vietnam, where it saw evidence of a nascent labor movement. Jouan was part of the official group greeting the ICFTU delegation, and he later dined with the delegates.[115] French colonial officials worked hard to assure the delegation of plans in the works to expand trade union rights.[116] With such assurances in mind, the ICFTU delegation issued a strong call for international labor to champion the further development of a native labor movement, independent of the French. The U.S. State Department made sure to send a copy of the pointedly worded statement to French colonial officials.[117]

Nelson Cruickshank, head of the AFL's Social Security Department, on temporary assignment as the director of the Labor Division of the Mutual Security Agency (MSA, the chief U.S. agency administering foreign aid), also pursued the AFL's interest in Vietnam. In 1952, he arranged for Dr. Joseph Zisman to conduct a government-sponsored survey of the emerging Indochinese labor scene. In Vietnam, Zisman met at length with Buu and Jouan. He reported that real "opportunities exist for an MSA program" to help the Indochinese labor movement. "The existence of young and inexperienced trade unions at this time presents both a challenge and opportunity. Properly directed trade unions are among the strongest bulwarks for democracy," he advised.[118]

Conclusion

Zisman would have little trouble convincing American labor of the utility of free, anticommunist labor movements in the battle against communism. The emerging Vietnamese labor movement, modeled on Western trade unionism and leaning against communism, seemed ideally suited for those purposes. Yet American labor's resources were stretched thin even in Europe, where it depended increasingly on support from the Marshall Plan and CIA. Hopes of influencing events in Southeast Asia ultimately rested on the AFL's relationship with the ICFTU and the U.S. government. Paradoxically, such relations threatened the free trade union mandate to remain free of entangling alliances.

Meanwhile, in its struggle for survival in a country in the midst of revolutionary chaos, the CVTC faced a similar dilemma in a much more dangerous environment. As Buu later explained, "we aim at a movement which is free and independent which will avoid subversive communist domination on the left and government control on the right." Ours, Buu insisted, "is the true voice of the people."[119] Strengthening and sustaining the "voice of the people," however, would require the material and political support of outsiders. Postwar opportunities to expand the scope and influence of organized labor would come at a cost, a Faustian bargain that eventually returned to haunt both organizations.

3 "It's a Vast Jungle and We're Working on the Periphery"

By 1952, proponents of free trade unionism appeared poised to realize their ambitious national and international objectives. That year the pugnacious free trade unionist George Meany was elected president of the American Federation of Labor. Henceforth, anticommunism, internationalism, full-employment economics, and a fierce commitment to trade union autonomy would be the virtually unchallenged tenets governing the AFL. Parallel developments overtook the federation's chief rival. In 1952, Walter Reuther became president of the CIO. The polar opposite in character of the earthy, blunt Meany, Reuther nevertheless shared the AFL president's anticommunism, interest in third world labor issues, and commitment to full-employment economics. With these dynamic new leaders in place, free trade unionists anticipated swift progress on both the domestic and international fronts. For labor's internationalists, no issue was more pressing than fortifying third-world anticommunist labor movements, in particular the CVTC, whose future hung precariously as war spread in colonial Indochina.

Another election in 1952, however, boded less positively for the ambitions of free trade unionists—that of Dwight Eisenhower to the U.S. presidency. To the mounting indignation of free trade unionists, the Eisenhower administration combined a parsimonious approach to spending with what many decried as nothing short of appeasement of the Soviet Union. No single issue better exemplified the failings of the new administration than the "sellout" of Indochina at the 1954 Geneva conference. During the 1950s, in fact, Vietnam emerged for free trade unionists as a leading metaphor for the failings of modern Republicanism. Confronted with outright hostility to the goals of organized labor, Meany and Reuther moved to consolidate their organizations. However, sharp personality differences between the two handicapped the undertaking. Within a year, Meany and Reuther were openly feuding over communism and neutralism in Asia, foreshadowing deep divisions to come a decade later over the Vietnam War.

Throughout the 1950s, South Vietnamese organized labor shared with its American counterpart a sense of watching helplessly from the periphery. As American labor fruitlessly tried to secure aid for the CVTC, tumult overwhelmed Southeast Asia. With little aid available from American supporters and seeking security against the vicissitudes of life in Indochina, Tran Quoc Buu moved to make an ill-fated alliance with the Ngo Dinh Diem regime.

"We Have Missed Out on a Psychological Moment"

From its inception in 1948, the Vietnamese labor movement founded by Buu and Jouan made great strides. It quickly organized thousands of workers and drew the support and interest of key American observers. But in 1953 this progress suddenly stalled.

Among the Americans enamored with the CVTC was Dr. Joseph Zisman. In 1952, Zisman conducted an AFL-initiated study of Vietnamese organized labor, which reported tremendous potential in Buu's nascent movement. He recommended that the U.S. Mutual Security Administration inaugurate a program to cultivate and strengthen Indochinese trade unionism. Such an initiative would have delighted free trade unionists, who had few resources at their own disposal with which to aid Indochinese labor.

In Indochina, the U.S. Aid Mission to Saigon, however, split sharply over the feasibility of a labor program.[1] A mission staffer reported that key U.S. officials in Saigon "feel that industry is yet too young, that industrial development does not justify union development." Conversely, other mission advisers argued that "Indochina has, in certain cases both labor and management problems and human relations do actually exist." They urged the Mutual Security Administration to begin "gathering 'interested people' and selecting representatives to attend a trainee program in the US."[2] Presumably, American trade unionists, eager to strengthen anticommunist Vietnamese labor, would serve as instructors and mentors. But with official U.S. representatives clearly divided and the anticolonial war heating up, the mission shelved plans for a training program and systematic aid for Buu's movement.

Obstacles also frustrated free trade union hopes that the ICFTU, the international labor organization funded generously by American labor, might aid Vietnamese labor. In 1950, responding to AFL pressure, the ICFTU sent a survey team to Asia. The team, which included several American trade unionists, visited Indochina and urged further organization in the region.

But, despite the AFL's call to action, not until 1953 did the ICFTU dispatch an official mission to Indochina. It was led by a Swiss trade unionist, Lucien Tronchet, evidently chosen for his anticommunist leanings and linguistic abilities. Tronchet arrived in the summer of 1953 and spent roughly a month in Indochina.

There Tronchet found significant organizational progress since the first ICFTU junket three years earlier. Colonial law now permitted unionization, and several labor federations had been formed. Tronchet met with representatives of each of the various labor organizations, including a civil servants union and a hard-line nationalist labor federation with only a limited membership. The CVTC, Tronchet quickly concluded, already having moved beyond organizing urban workers to forming unions of agricultural laborers, offered the greatest promise. With little difficulty, he persuaded Buu—who, like Jouan, recognized the value of international leverage—to join the ICFTU. Buu eagerly signed an agreement pledging to broaden his base, affiliate with the ICFTU, and cast off the federation's religious character by renaming itself the Vietnamese Confederation of Labor (CVT). In return, Tronchet promised to procure a United Nations survey of economic potential in Vietnam, training courses in Europe for Vietnamese labor leaders, and material aid for Buu's organization.[3]

The Tronchet mission initially seemed promising; it would make the CVTC one of the most important ICFTU affiliates in Asia and provide a vital lifeline to the new organization. But the opportunity quickly slipped away. Returning from Southeast Asia, Tronchet found surprisingly little enthusiasm for his initiative in the ICFTU. The CVTC was already affiliated with the International Federation of Christian Trade Unions (the IFCTU, better known as the Christian International, not to be confused with the ICFTU) and as a result found itself snared in a bitter rivalry between the European Christian trade union movement and its largely socialist counterparts in the ICFTU. The roots of this antipathy dated from the early twentieth century, when a group of competing Christian unions developed alongside secular, socialist ones.[4] In 1920, European Christian unionists formed the Christian International (with which the CVTC affiliated in 1949). From the start, Christians and socialists regarded each other with intense aversion, resulting in fierce competition and hostility between the Christian International and the ICFTU.

The proposed CVTC affiliation immediately ignited long-standing tensions. The Christian International pressured Buu to disavow the agreement and remain solely under its umbrella. Having returned permanently to France, Gilbert Jouan, cofounder of the CVTC and a devout Roman Catholic, appealed to his Vietnamese friends to remain faithful to the Christian International; Buu—though himself a Buddhist—began to waver.[5]

Meanwhile, the ICFTU also vacillated. The Vietnamese organization seemed too Catholic, and intense American interest in the CVTC likewise concerned some at the ICFTU. To European socialists, American labor appeared to be excessively "bread and butter" oriented, wedded to a reflexive anticommunism, and not sufficiently committed to comprehensive social change. Some also suspected that with its heavily Catholic membership U.S. organized labor's sympathies leaned toward the European Christian unions.[6] Ironically, the Christian International also harbored suspicions of American labor, in part for its secular nature and role in founding and sustaining the ICFTU.

Faced with simmering misgivings, the ICFTU's Regional Fund Committee temporized. More information would be required, it claimed, before it could affiliate with the CVTC. The ICFTU promised to dispatch another agent to Indochina but moved at a glacier's pace to initiate the second mission. Officials insisted that they required the services of a French-speaking unionist, preferably an Asian, for the assignment but could find no suitable candidate. Frustrated because his earlier work had gone unappreciated, Tronchet refused to lead a second mission, lamenting that it would serve no purpose.[7] Lost in internal rivalries, international labor failed to provide aid at an hour of both great opportunity and great peril for the CVTC. In 1954, as he watched the ICFTU spin its wheels while tensions mounted in Vietnam, Lovestone angrily wrote Meany: "On Indo-China it was reported that the man who was supposed to go from Canada for the ICFTU is not going and that once again we have missed out on a psychological moment. . . . The situation is fast deteriorating and yet the ICFTU is not playing an important role in a very dangerous area."[8]

Free trade unionists continued to press the U.S. mission in Saigon to establish an aid program for the CVTC, but such plans also appeared to be permanently on hold. In 1953, newly elected President Eisenhower moved to rein in foreign aid appropriations. The Mutual Security Administration slashed its labor program. The number of U.S. labor advisers in Europe fell by almost two-thirds.[9] Free trade unionists complained bitterly that business interests controlled whatever aid remained. In early 1954, Meany resigned in disgust from a public advisory committee to the U.S. foreign aid administration, which he assailed for failing to "recognize the need of following the advice of, and working with, the representatives of labor."[10] In late 1954, a special assistant to the American ambassador in Saigon enthusiastically reported on the CVTC's ambitious social agenda, which included the construction of "welfare facilities," the resettlement of refugees, and worker training programs. But, with regret, he added that his office was "not able to assist the CVTC in the above fields of action."[11] That year an official review of American aid to Vietnam concluded that with regard to labor "little has been done. . . . The labor program for the Far East as a whole has been regrettably weak."[12]

"Another Yalta"

Organized labor's frustrations with Eisenhower hardly ended with the new president's efforts to contain foreign aid. When the former general took office, George Meany optimistically predicted that his policies would not "differ in any obvious way from that of the Truman administration."[13] Within weeks, Meany was regretting his words, for the new administration seemed almost purposefully bent on derailing free trade union activism.

Eisenhower, fearful of inflation and no friend of Keynesian economics, moved to check federal spending, infuriating full-employment devotees in the labor movement.[14] Trade unionists had already turned to military spending to fuel the American economy when Congress rejected Truman's Fair Deal spending initiatives. But the budget-conscious Eisenhower administration slashed even military expenditures. The new president announced plans to cut the annual budget by sixty billion dollars over four years and to curb defense spending by 15 percent.[15] Adding insult to injury, labor found itself suddenly stripped of influence in the new administration. Awash in New Deal sensibilities about labor-state cooperation, trade unionists had come to see themselves as valued members of a pluralistic governing coalition despite their commitment to labor autonomy. They fully expected to be consulted on policy decisions; the Eisenhower administration, however, recognized no such supposition. Arthur Burns, incoming chairman of the Council of Economic Advisers (CEA), summarily canceled the council's traditional consultations with organized labor. The CIO economist Stanley Ruttenberg blasted Burns as "belligerent" and "happy to be able to find any kind of excuse in order to avoid going through with periodic meetings with the CIO."[16]

Building on Eisenhower's efforts to restrain foreign aid, conflict quickly stirred between the administration and labor on international affairs. Although the new secretary of state, John Foster Dulles, had spoken boldly of "liberating captive nations," to labor's internationalists his "New Look" foreign policy appeared to be designed to sidestep the costly investments necessary to challenge expanding communism, especially in the third world. To many laborites, Eisenhower's drive to cut foreign aid and conventional forces in favor of a cost-saving reliance on U.S. nuclear brinkmanship and "massive retaliation" seemed like a foolish frugality, endangering national security and economic growth at home.[17] Throughout 1953, Meany watched with mounting angst as Eisenhower failed to take either the international or domestic initiative.

Nowhere was this "hands-off" policy more vexing to free trade unionists than in the emerging crisis in Southeast Asia. Since 1950, both the AFL and the CIO had grown increasingly critical of French colonialism in Indochina. From his headquarters in Paris, Irving Brown began making contacts with expatriated Vietnamese nationalists. Meanwhile, Jay Lovestone had developed a particularly strong friendship with Dr. Phan Quang Dan, a Harvard-educated physician and key Vietnamese nationalist. Both Lovestone and Brown pushed French unionists to challenge colonialism in Indochina.[18] In 1954, as the French faced defeat at the hands of the Viet Minh, the AFL reiterated its call for an end to colonial rule and for massive military aid to non-communist nationalists in Vietnam. Meany and Lovestone particularly feared that the Geneva conference, due to begin in April, would lead to Western capitulation in Vietnam. Many in the CIO shared the AFL's general concerns, if not the same immediate urgency. Touring India in the spring of 1954, Michael Ross, director of the CIO's Department of International Affairs, warned CIO vice president Jacob Potofsky that "[i]f Indochina falls the effect down here will be bad."[19]

In late April, the AFL Executive Council issued its strongest statement yet on the Indochina question. It urged immediate action: a special session of the United Nations General Assembly, free elections in Vietnam, a Pacific alliance for investment in Southeast Asia, and an Asian defense pact. Most importantly, it called for an immediate end to the French presence in Vietnam. Stopping just short of demanding American intervention, the council nonetheless endorsed strengthening the Vietnamese national army and creating an Asian military alliance to halt the advance of communism in the region.[20]

With the fate of Indochina hanging in the balance, in early 1954 Meany dispatched Irving Brown, the renowned AFL European agent, to Geneva, hoping that his "point man" might influence the conferees. In Geneva, Brown found a depressing "atmosphere of confusion and Western disunity." By contrast, the Soviet bloc moved "smoothly with confidence and iron-bond discipline." Typically, Brown saw the Soviets as dominating the Chinese and other communist bloc representatives. "The second language of most Chinese and Koreans that one meets," noted Brown, "is invariably Russian . . . proof of the extent of Soviet penetration and domination."[21] In actuality, the Vietnamese communists emerged from the sessions feeling deserted by Moscow and Beijing. Brown and his fellow free trade unionists, however, remained wedded to a monolithic view of world communism.

Distressed and despairing of "another Yalta" after only a few days at the conference, Brown returned to handle pressing issues in Paris.[22] In his place, another AFL agent, Harry Goldberg, journeyed to Switzerland with instructions to lobby for Vietnamese independence and forestall a partition. Like Brown, Goldberg quickly recognized a daunting task. "The general outlook is bad," he wrote Lovestone, "and I think we (and the world) are going to get bumped." Lovestone, he advised, should "expect the worst, and don't expect too much from our operations. . . . It's a vast jungle and we're working on the periphery."[23]

With the Eisenhower administration leaning toward a negotiated settlement and the French military in Indochina hanging by a thread, Goldberg set up what he called his "OSS operations" in Geneva. He contacted sympathetic diplomats in the American delegation and drafted the services of Swiss labor leader Lucian Tronchet, only recently returned from his ICFTU mission to Vietnam. Meanwhile, Lovestone sent Goldberg packets of propaganda material, including the AFL Executive Council statement on Vietnam and Dr. Dan's sanguine assurances that the nationalist forces could defeat the Viet Minh.[24] Lovestone directed Goldberg to distribute the "merchandise" clandestinely to delegates. He also toyed with having Goldberg issue a public statement, possibly purchasing newspaper space, to press the federation's cause. Lovestone ultimately decided against a public statement; he feared implicating Tronchet as an AFL agent and thus damaging his usefulness.[25] Nevertheless, Lovestone still hoped to interest conference delegates in the federation's proposals. If he was persuasive at Geneva, the AFL planned to press sympathetic American legislators, such as Senators Paul Douglas and Mike Mansfield, to introduce legislation directing massive military and economic aid to an independent Vietnam.[26]

By late May, however, Goldberg concluded his efforts had come to naught. Conference delegates shifted rooms daily, frustrating the delivery of the AFL merchandise.[27] The fatal blow came with the ignominious defeat of the French at Dien Bien Phu, which the AFL blamed squarely on Eisenhower's vacillations and mixed signals.[28] In the end, the conference divided Vietnam along the seventeenth parallel, turning the northern portion over to the Viet Minh. "Geneva was a dramatic revelation of the abdication of us of our natural position as world leader," Goldberg lamented. The conference settlement represented "a defeat of substantial magnitude, whose negative results will make themselves felt in the future in geometric progression."[29]

Learning of the summit outcome, Meany immediately fired off a volley of invectives wrapped in World War II analogies: the division of Vietnam was "appeasement" on "a world scale which would make Munich pale into insignificance." On Indochina, the Eisenhower administration's foreign policy was "confused, haphazard and chicken hearted."[30] The *AFL News Reporter* added that "twelve million more persons, including three and a half million Roman Catholics were added to the Red World as half of Vietnam was abandoned north of the 17th parallel. . . . As a result of the armistice the Communists gain prestige in all parts of the Far East."[31]

Later that summer, Meany again focused his gargantuan wrath at the Eisenhower administration. "During this crucial period, America's only policy was a lack of policy. We did nothing except to continue the too little, too late program of sending military supplies to the Indochina front," he told an American Legion audience.[32] The CIO echoed Meany's lamentations at its 1954 convention, deploring the administration's "impressive record for vacillating and contradictory policies" and complaining of "the loss of at least half of Indochina to the communists."[33] For free trade unionists, the "betrayal" at Geneva quickly emerged as a potent symbol of Eisenhower's passivity in the face of pressing issues both at home and abroad.

In Saigon, the CVTC shared Meany's sense of outrage and betrayal. Buu spoke passionately against the division. Banners strung across the confederation's headquarters also denounced the Geneva accords with slogans such as "Halt Moves to Divide Vietnam" and "To Divide Vietnam Is to Open the Door of Southeast Asia to Communism."[34]

Roughly a year later, Meany bemoaned a second betrayal at Geneva. In July 1955, Eisenhower and Dulles had journeyed to the Swiss city to meet the leaders of the Soviet, French, and British governments. In fact, the famed "Geneva summit" saw no substantive achievements, although the exchange of smiles between superpowers roused talk of "peaceful coexistence." But smiles alone were enough to incense Lovestone and Meany. To free trade unionists, the public relations success of the Soviets, now free of the dark image of Stalin, threatened anticommunist resolve. Before the National Press Club in 1955, Meany charged that the Soviets had "not changed their policy, they have merely changed their tactics" and "their objective of world domination was the same as it always has been."[35] In Moscow, *Pravda,* the Soviet party newspaper, scorned Meany's skepticism and chided him as the "last of the cold war Mohicans."[36] Meany, no doubt, accepted the appellation as an honor. He and his acolytes remained viscerally critical of the Soviets—and of Eisenhower, who, they insisted, had chosen the path of appeasement and capitulation. Despite tough rhetoric promising "liberation" to those behind the iron curtain, the new administration, as evidenced by its inaction in Indochina, had proven a grave and dangerous disappointment.

Uneasy Merger

Stymied by Eisenhower at every turn, mainstream U.S. labor leaders, no longer divided by the bitter rifts of the 1930s, moved to consolidate their strengths around a free trade union agenda. Those few historians who have devoted any attention to the merger of the AFL and CIO in 1955 have interpreted it as evidence of the growing bureaucratization and incorporation of organized labor. Such views have validity, but the merger—and important developments preceding it and proceeding from it—are also suggestive of a new dominant consensus among labor leaders around the issues of anticommunism, full-employment economics, and trade union autonomy. This new sense of common purpose and common enemies (in the form of both dangerous international communism and Eisenhower's perceived slothful response) led to the historic merger of the AFL and CIO, greatly strengthening and sharpening the focus of free trade unionism. But even as early as the mid-1950s bitter divisions over communism and neutrality in Asia surfaced among U.S. labor leaders, a harbinger of divisions to come over the Vietnam War.

In the years following World War II, the once bitter cleavages dividing the AFL and the CIO began to mend. While some in the CIO still dreamed of European-style, socialistic, economic planning, the defeat of Truman's Fair Deal program and the conservative resurgence in Congress forced most to accept a more realistic agenda. Increasingly, CIO leaders recognized the prudence of reasserting trade union autonomy, the central tenet of free trade unionism. In lieu of economic planning, even more radically minded sectors of the organized labor movement embraced the full-employment agenda, which prescribed heavy government investment to spur economic growth and job creation. Eisenhower's resistance to even limited Keynesian economics only added to a mounting sense of shared challenges and goals among laborites.

Seeking to revitalize the full-employment agenda, trade union leaders, in both the AFL and CIO, turned to an enterprising old friend. For two pivotal decades, Leon Keyserling had served the interests of organized labor. He coauthored the seminal Wagner Act in 1935 and the Employment Act in 1946. As chairman of the Council of Economic Advisers under Truman, he pushed growth-centered, full-employment economics with a single-minded passion, earning him scores of both friends and enemies.[37] When he left the CEA in 1953, he offered his unique services to labor. In an extended memorandum sent to both Meany and Reuther, he proposed establishing a Conference on Economic Progress, a small think tank that would weigh macroeconomic issues, prepare proposals, and generate public support for full-employment economics.

In his proposal to the AFL and CIO leadership, Keyserling sketched out a bold and massive public relations drive. New ideas would be presented in "modern and popular terms. . . .What is needed is an affirmative prosperity approach, sound yet vital, practical yet inspirational." The old-line liberal approach formulated during the Depression and war years, was "out of date and consequently inadequate and uninspiring." Through an immense program of government-sponsored pump priming, Keyserling insisted, the annual rate of growth could easily be doubled. Spending of any sort was to be applauded; government expenditures, even if they resulted in deficits, would produce jobs and fuel production. This approach, Keyserling pledged, would lift millions of economically marginal Americans into a thriving, secure, middle class. Everything lay within the potential of the American economy: full employment, a $500 billion a year economy, and the elimination of poverty.[38]

Keyserling's program also spoke directly to labor's ambitions in the developing world. He proposed generous foreign aid packages and military assistance to developing countries. Rather than stifling domestic growth, aggressive spending would provide a potent stimulus. There existed, the liberal-minded economist insisted, no necessary tradeoff between guns and butter; foreign aid and generous military and social spending promised unprecedented growth. In Keyserling's audacious program, free trade unionism found an alluring, updated economic philosophy to undergird not only its domestic agenda but also its bold international ambitions.

The great attraction of Keyserling's approach, of course, was its daring renunciation of limits; there need be no obligatory business cycle, inflation represented no threat, and waste and inefficiency were inconsequential concerns. While the vast majority of economists dismissed Keyserling as hopelessly Pollyannaish, his rabid optimism swept up the AFL and CIO leadership. Both organizations signed on as cosponsors of Keyserling's Conference on Economic Progress. His ebullience shaped labor's outlook for the next twenty years and accounted for much of the naive trust and eagerness with which the AFL-CIO approached the Vietnam War.[39]

Keyserling's views hardly resonated with the Eisenhower administration, which was dedicated to capping government spending not expanding it. Foiled by the administration and Congress, Keyserling's Conference on Economic Progress increasingly touted defense spending as the fuel that would promote economic growth. Its first report, issued in 1954, prescribed increased military expenditures to meet "gaps in our defense" programs as part of a proposed $3.0 billion spending increase linked to a $4.5 billion tax cut for low-income Americans.[40]

Heralding Keyserling's agenda, free trade unionists again seized on Indochina as a metaphor for the evils of inaction and parsimony. The "uneasy truce in Korea and Indochina," argued Meany aide George Brown in 1954, required the United States "to maintain a strong military defense program." Brown further urged the expansion of such labor-initiated programs as Defense Manpower Policy No. 4, which directed defense dollars to areas with heavy unemployment.[41] In congressional testimony, CIO representatives echoed Brown, warning that with "rumblings in Indo-China . . . [w]e must continue the military buildup that we began."[42]

Joint AFL and CIO sponsorship of the Conference on Economic Progress and their embrace of Keyserling's guns and butter outlook offered one of many signs of converging interests between the two organizations. Consensus replaced once bitter ideological divisions. Since the late 1930s, the AFL leadership had passed to a new generation of internationalists that included Meany, Dubinsky, George Harrison, and others, all of whom supported industrial organization, aggressive social legislation, and full-employment economics. More conservative elements remained, especially in the building trades, but the AFL helm was now in the hands of progressives. Likewise, the CIO had changed. Increasingly, its leaders joined free trade unionists in advocating growth-focused economics and independent collective bargaining.[43] But the most significant convergence came with regard to the issue of communism. By the late 1940s—partly out of political expedience and partly out of shifting ideologies—the CIO took decisive action against communists within its own ranks, in the process breaking with the WFTU. Seasoned anticommunists, especially President Walter Reuther and Secretary Treasurer James Carey, dominated the CIO by the early 1950s.

While a consensus around free trade union goals and antagonism toward the Eisenhower administration generated an atmosphere conducive to a merger, the growing frailty of the CIO by the mid-1950s provided the immediate motive. Key CIO affiliates, including Joseph Bierne's Communications Workers of America and David McDonald's United Steelworkers of America, resented the ambitions and ostentatious style of Walter Reuther and increasingly appeared ready to jump to the AFL. "If the CIO didn't go [into the AFL] in one piece, they would go in separately," explained one veteran observer.[44]

The merger, accordingly, occurred very much on free trade union terms, strengthening the grip of Meany and his circle. In December 1955, a special convention created the AFL-CIO. George Meany became its president, with the remnants of the CIO relegated to the new Industrial Union Department under former CIO president Walter Reuther, who also became an AFL-CIO vice president. Reuther may have hoped to revive in the new AFL-CIO some of the "old crusading spirit" of the CIO of the 1930s, but he had few resources at his disposal.[45] The new AFL-CIO represented the triumph of free trade unionism, an incorporation of the CIO into the AFL (already the larger of the two entities) rather than the creation of a new organization.

Addressing the merger convention, Meany leaped to consecrate unified labor in the language of free trade unionism. He pointedly stressed anticommunism and the essentiality of labor as an independent force. In the years to come, trade unions must assure "proper consideration of human needs along with the requirements of industry and finance. In our opinion there is no other agency—not even the government itself—that can adequately fulfill this vital responsibility." The most crucial of labor's tasks was that of combating communism. Both business and government, the new AFL-CIO president declared, must recognize the centrality of free labor movements to the cold war struggle. Labor in its "unalterable opposition to communism provides basic security for American business." Because it "has been proven time and again" that communists commence their infiltration campaigns by targeting labor unions, "a strong anticommunist free labor movement was the first line of defense."[46]

The merger raised hopes and expectations on all sides, but deeply rooted, mutual animosities could not easily be extinguished. Meany and Lovestone strongly suspected that communists remained secretly burrowed within some CIO affiliates.[47] Meanwhile, Reuther and others in the CIO, fancying themselves the progressive wing of American labor, saw the AFL essentially as a receptacle for antiquated, conservative attitudes toward organizing and social reform. Many in the CIO also remained skeptical of the AFL's campaign against corruption within its ranks, although Meany's vigorous prosecution of the International Longshoremen's Association allayed some concerns.

Foreign policy, however, proved to be the chief degenerative agent. While both organizations shared an avid anticommunism, the CIO leadership viewed the AFL as excessively strident, unsophisticated, and wedded to brute, covert operations in its opposition to communism.[48] Reuther was more tolerant of third-world neutralism and willing to engage in frank exchanges with Soviet leaders, with whom Meany steadfastly refused to meet.[49] Bitter animosity between Walter Reuther and Jay Lovestone, dating back to the bloody battle to organize automobile workers in the 1930s, compounded suspicions between the two merging organizations. By the 1950s, observers were describing Reuther and Lovestone as "blood enemies."[50]

Initially, both organizations naively hoped to transcend such tensions. To accommodate Reuther, the AFL agreed that CIO veteran Michael Ross would head the new International Affairs Department, while Lovestone was relegated to the editorship of the *Free Trade Union News* in New York (Meany, however, defiantly continued to regard Lovestone as his principal foreign policy adviser and agent).[51] Despite strong AFL reservations regarding the ICFTU, an organization it considered excessively bureaucratic and lethargic on the issue of colonialism, Meany did promise to work with the international labor federation, with the distant goal of allowing it to assume all foreign operations.[52]

The ink had barely dried on the merger agreement before foreign affairs, particularly Asian policy, began tearing the new federation apart. International issues remained George Meany's priority, and he looked for an early opportunity to fasten his new organization to his virulent anticommunism and assail what he saw as dangerous trends in Asia. To make his point, he chose to take dead aim at Jawaharlal Nehru, the Indian prime minister, who was known for his anti-Americanism, promotion of third-world neutralism, and warm relations with both the Chinese and the Soviets. Nehru's hosting of a state visit by Soviet leaders Nikolay Bulganin and Nikita Khrushchev, which culminated in the signing of a joint statement on the question of disarmament in 1955, and his high profile at the Bandung conference of nonaligned nations (considered a communist front by free trade unionists) particularly embittered Meany. To free trade union eyes, the Indian leader also appeared on the wrong side of the crisis in Indochina. In 1953, AFL vice president Matthew Woll excoriated "Mr. Nehru and his Burmese and Indonesian associates, who, for some inexplicable reason, adhere to the notion that Ho Chi Minh's Communist hordes waging war in Indo-China represent a genuine national independent movement."[53] Clearly, to those surrounding Meany, Nehru represented a debilitating threat to all of Asia. Yet despite Nehru's leanings U.S. aid continued to flow to India, and he remained a favorite figure among many American liberals, all to the consternation of free trade unionists.

Addressing the National Religion and Labor Foundation on December 13, 1955, only days after the AFL-CIO founding convention, Meany launched a frontal assault on Nehru and his supporters, an attack designed to leave no question as to the anticommunist leanings of his new organization, especially toward the developing world. As befitted the occasion (and his outlook), Meany framed his argument in moral language. International communism was an "anti-moral movement" that "sneers at our most cherished moral values." It was a "crude force" of "unlimited totalitarian terror over the individual who is denied all protection of law, religion, and free labor organization." In short, communism, Meany argued, represented the polar opposite of humanist, Western values. Nehru, whose neutralism Meany assailed as "radicalism in reverse," was facilitating this brutal system. The speech featured Meany at his most strident, blasting the Soviet Union as an "anti-social system in which there are imbedded some of the worst features of savagery, slavery, feudalism and life-sapping exploitation."[54] Alongside the Soviets and Nehru, Meany clearly aimed to repudiate the Eisenhower administration's probing of peaceful coexistence at the Geneva summit earlier that year, an exploration Meany equated with appeasement.[55]

Less extreme in tone but no less pointed was Meany's message to American liberals. "Liberals," the AFL-CIO president pressed, "should be the most consistent and energetic fighters against communism." But in their crusade for free speech and tolerance they risked missing the moral "problem of our time." Instead, Meany admonished, they were veering toward a "type of McCarthyism of their own" by being "anti-anti-communist."[56] The caustic speech blatantly betrayed early but serious cracks in the labor-liberal alliance, clefts that became insurmountable chasms during the Vietnam War.

Hoping to shame liberals, Meany charted a clear and uncompromising course for the new federation. At the very least, the National Religion and Labor Foundation speech generated a nationwide stir. *U.S. News and World Report,* numerous newspapers, and other magazines published portions of the speech. Meany's words quickly caught the attention of liberals, many of whom took umbrage. Eleanor Roosevelt branded the speech "a sad mistake" in her *My Day* column.[57] The mainstream media also expressed qualms. The *New York Times* feared the address would feed resentment and "injured feelings" in the third world.[58] The *Washington Star* urged Meany to "remember that he is now speaking not just to the U.S. and Europe but the whole world as well." Nehru's Indian supporters lodged their own protests. K. Prasas Tripathi, the general secretary of the Indian National Trade Union Congress, blasted the speech as loaded with "malicious allegations."[59]

Within the new AFL-CIO, Walter Reuther, who considered himself the voice of progressive labor, scrambled to distance himself from Meany's provocative comments. He immediately scheduled a trip to India, where he sought to carve out a separate identity for himself as a more cosmopolitan labor leader. The trip, which took place in March 1956, went well. The comparatively youthful labor leader impressed audiences with calls for social justice and equality. Always suspicious of Reuther, Jay Lovestone dispatched an agent to tail the UAW president through India. Referring to discrimination in labor unions, Lovestone's agent reported, Reuther had proclaimed that the CIO had "completely wiped out racial discrimination" while noting continuing problems in many AFL unions.[60]

The entire trip, capped by Reuther's exaggerated portrait of civil rights in the old CIO unions, enraged the trigger-tempered Meany and further drove a wedge between himself and the UAW president.[61] The two leaders increasingly viewed each other with competitive suspicion, which soon bordered on paranoia. From its foundation, foreign policy pressures related to Asia tested the shaky consensus uniting the new AFL-CIO and drove its two most prominent leaders apart. Nevertheless, however precarious, the free trade union alliance between labor leaders and between labor and mainstream liberals continued to hold—for the time being.

"Living through a Real Nightmare"

The turbulence encountered by American labor hardly matched that facing its Vietnamese counterpart. Like the AFL, the CVTC objected vehemently to the partition of Vietnam in 1954, but Buu's organization literally had to live with the division. The still-maturing labor movement had numerous affiliates in the more industrialized north. In February 1954, Buu and Jouan journeyed to Hanoi and other northern cities. There they met with members of the CVTC's northern affiliates and "a number of intellectuals who looked favorably on the trade union movement." Buu and Jouan, pleased by their warm reception, made plans to begin "study circles" in Hanoi similar to those in Saigon.[62] Jouan also met with the local chief of security, pointedly telling him that previous harassment of trade unionists had "done the greatest harm to the French cause in Vietnam."[63] Months later, possibly influenced by the earlier visit, three thousand CVTC miners launched a strike at the Cai-Da mines in northern Vietnam. Within several weeks, the mine owner caved in to union demands. The strike enhanced Buu's reputation and fed hopes for further organization in the more industrialized north.[64]

Yet all hope for further progress was imperiled by the Geneva accords. As an anticommunist organization, somewhat associated with the vanquished Bao Dai regime, the CVTC feared for the fate of its northern membership. Despite assurances of protection by the International Control Commission, the Viet Minh, upon taking control, singled out trade unionists. Northern cadres, the CVTC reported, suffered arrest and incarceration in concentration camps, where they were "brainwashed." Any sign of resistance was met with severe repression. North Vietnamese authorities executed Pham Nam, a renowned organizer of the Cam Pha mines in North Vietnam.[65] According to accounts flowing from the north, the new government had sentenced other trade unionists to forced labor on the Chinese border.[66] The CVTC was "living though a real nightmare," an unnerved Buu wrote Tronchet in July of 1954.[67]

Buu's organization hoped to evacuate those "energetically opposed to the communist regime," but it possessed few resources for such an undertaking. In July 1954, Buu penned a frantic open letter to the "workers of the world," appealing for aid to evacuate and resettle refugees.[68] Jouan, who had returned permanently to his homeland, put ideology aside and met with a representative of the ICFTU. "Under the tragic circumstances there was nothing to be gained by conflict or competition between the ICFTU and the Christian International insofar as Vietnam is concerned," he pleaded.[69] J. H. Oldenbroek, the Dutch general secretary of the ICFTU, promised aid but also privately warned of the strong "Catholic influence" on the CVTC.[70]

Marshaling whatever help could be scraped up from international labor and the U.S. government, the CVTC set about relocating the thousands of members pouring in from its 211 unions in the north.[71] For a year, homeless refugees encamped in the CVTC headquarters in Saigon, occupying nearly 90 percent of the cavernous compound.[72] In Paris, Jouan bitterly complained that the CVTC was struggling to operate twenty-five refugee camps with no help from the fading colonial government. "It would be easy for the CVTC to solve this problem," Jouan wrote the president of the CFTC, "if the government accepted the CVTC's loyal service without trying to subjugate it."[73] In Saigon, Buu sounded a more desperate alarm, writing French supporters that the government of Vietnam was "feeble and inert. The county is awash with little feudal fiefdoms, in which feudal chiefs take humiliating measures against the population."[74]

Beyond the refugee crisis and general state of emergency, Buu faced an immediate challenge—securing a place for his organization within the rapidly shifting and dangerous new South Vietnamese state. The CVTC, like its American counterpart, strove to project a public facade of autonomy, a key requisite of *doan the*. "A union leader who has very close ties with Government," warned a CVTC spokesman, "is normally suspected by trade union members as having sacrificed their interests."[75] But the emerging realities of South Vietnamese politics, even more so than those in the United States, allowed little margin for such independence. Like its American counterpart, South Vietnamese labor entered numerous potentially compromising alliances that often returned to haunt the organization.

CVTC leaders well understood this paradox. As the dangerous division of Vietnam took place, they approached the American embassy for help but asked that any aid "be provided with as little public attention as possible" for fear their organization would be labeled as "American supported." Instead, the CVTC requested that assistance be channeled discreetly through the Vietnamese Ministry of Labor.[76] If subsidies became public knowledge, then at least the CVTC would appear to be dependent on its own government rather than white foreigners.

During this period, the CVTC found another problematic source of American aid—the CIA. Lieutenant Colonel Edward Lansdale, the infamous "Quiet American," arrived in Saigon in June 1954, having recently mobilized a successful counterinsurgency and pacification campaign in the Philippines. Though known for his close ties to South Vietnamese elites, Lansdale viewed himself as a champion of the working man. "The little guys, the rice paddy farmers," he pronounced with regard to Vietnam, "know far more than the policy makers. Theirs is the simplified wisdom of the victim."[77] Working through the CIA, he quickly established useful contacts throughout South Vietnam, including Buu and the CVTC. South Vietnamese trade unionists appreciated Lansdale's patience and respectful demeanor, which contrasted sharply with the dictatorial tone emanating from other Americans. Lansdale, as one acquaintance recalled, was "more Asian than the Asians."[78]

Buu's contact with the CIA probably came through Lansdale. In the fall of 1954, two agents reported meeting with the "leader of the largest labor federation" and arranging a "propaganda and political action mechanism" with South Vietnamese labor.[79] While the precise dynamics of the CVTC-CIA relationship remain shadowy, collaboration clearly occurred. Jealously guarding his facade of independence, Buu always discreetly disguised his CIA connections, although rumors of such ties constantly surfaced. The gossip no doubt compromised South Vietnamese labor in the eyes of some, yet conversely it lent Buu's organization leverage, the aura of a hidden but mighty ally in its dealing with employers, Saigon officials, and even other branches of the American government. Ever trapped between the reality of dependence and the ideal of autonomy, the CVTC charted an awkward, expedient course that included its stealthy connection to the CIA.

As the political ground shifted dangerously in 1954, South Vietnamese labor cautiously embraced another powerful potential patron, Ngo Dinh Nhu, the political operative whose brother, Ngo Dinh Diem, had been appointed prime minister by Bao Dai in June 1954. An opium-smoking, ruthless, aspiring intellectual, Nhu clearly viewed the CVTC as an important means of broadening his brother's limited political base. In early 1953, Nhu urged Buu to join the National Union for Independence and Peace, an "opposition front capable of imposing change" and "checking the maneuvers of Nguyen Ton Hoan," a nationalist figure associated with the Dai Viet Nationalist Party. Buu, who had been allied with Hoan in the past, eschewed Nhu's entreaties and lamented that noncommunist nationalists seemed incapable of cooperation.[80]

But as Nhu accumulated more power his relationship with the CVTC deepened. In 1954, the French CFTC described him as "already for a long time having exercised a useful and discreet influence" on the CVTC.[81] When Gaston Tessier, president of the CFTC, visited Vietnam, he enjoyed a long philosophical discussion with Nhu and obviously considered the political operative a friend.[82] Initially, Nhu evinced compassion for Vietnam's workers and peasants. He furnished desperately needed support for the resettlement of refugees and other projects.[83] In return, Buu joined Nhu in forming the Can Lao Party (Personalist Worker's Party).[84] Diem and his supporters designed Can Lao not simply as a political party but also to provide the Ngos with an instrument for control and coercion as well as a disciplined, loyal cadre among South Vietnam's governing classes.

But the CVTC's relationship with the Ngo family was simultaneously laden with distrust and suspicion. At times, CVTC officials feared that the Ngo clan was intent on undermining Buu's leadership of the burgeoning confederation. On June 24, 1954, the Ngos arranged for a delegation of twenty-five CVTC unionists to attend a reception for Diem. Buu, who was conspicuously not invited to join the group, protested bitterly that only the CVTC leadership should decide who was to represent the organization. At roughly the same time, an article appeared in the French newspaper *Le Monde* identifying Nhu as the supreme head of the CVTC. Buu and his followers, suspecting that Nhu had played more than a small part in creating the false impression, announced their intention to break completely with the Ngo family and "maintain independence of all political parties and powers-that-be." In retaliation, Diem's other hard-edged brother, Ngo Dinh Can, attacked CVTC leaders, "who want to have 'a real social revolution' . . . but have no idea how to achieve it. . . . They are Mandarins in the full sense of the word."[85]

Despite tensions and lingering suspicions on the part of both parties, political expedience soon found the CVTC and the Ngo family cooperating again. Buu's affiliation with the controversial Can Lao Party shielded his organization during the volatile early days following the birth of South Vietnam. The CVTC, in turn, supported Lansdale and Nhu's successful quest to make Diem the first president of South Vietnam in October 1955. In particular, Buu exercised his still substantial influence on the Cao Dai to swing its support to Diem.[86]

Assuming the helm of leadership, Diem's survival as president of South Vietnam was far from certain. But both the CVTC and the American government watched with admiration as the new president boldly confronted competing influences in South Vietnam. In the spring of 1955, the fate of the new country hung in the balance during the "Battle of Saigon," as Diem's forces clashed openly with those of the Binh Xuyen sect of gangsters.[87] For Buu, the Binh Xuyen represented a particularly menacing enemy. Ginh Xuy, "the Al Capone of Vietnam" and a "general in the Binh Xuyen army," had a stranglehold on hiring and labor practices at Saigon's important port terminals. As "the King Contractor," Xuy sat atop an extensive system of labor subcontracting, reducing dockworkers to little more than "a starvation existence."[88] Diem's near miraculous defeat of the Saigon mob promised to open ports to labor organizers previously intimidated by Binh Xuyen violence.

As Saigon smoldered in the aftermath of the battle, CVTC members emerged to help reconstruct the city. The confederation sponsored a rebuilding day in Cholon (the ethnic Chinese city adjacent to Saigon). A parade from CVTC headquarters to the rebuilding site, with taxis and buses providing free transportation, preceded the actual work. Despite a shortage of tools, volunteers erected frames for twenty houses as young boys serenaded them and a dozen Buddhist monks bestowed blessings on the workers.[89]

The CVTC's good faith and alliance with Diem initially yielded substantial dividends. The organization grew rapidly in the first two years following the Geneva conference. The Tenant Farmers' Union, in particular, expanded dramatically under the personal patronage of Nhu.[90] By late 1955, the CVTC publicly claimed a half-million members, although it privately admitted to the still substantial figure of around 350,000.[91] Mounting militancy matched expanding numbers. In 1956, CVTC strikes shut down both the port of Saigon and the city's major electrical plant. The bus drivers' affiliate halted work to protest the beating of an elderly employee at the hands of a foreman.[92] A cigarette factory strike snowballed to include nearly 600 workers.[93] In the countryside, 13,000 members of the plantation workers' affiliate, demanding better pay and working conditions, walked off their jobs at four of South Vietnam's major rubber plantations.[94] In the summer of 1956, the CVTC even considered calling a general strike to protest the remaining resistance to unionization.[95] Meanwhile, the confederation expanded its membership services, opening several consumer cooperatives and ambitiously planning a "worker city" to provide low-cost housing and services for urban workers.[96]

Change also came for Saigon's troubled dockworkers. In May 1956, port workers, liberated by the arrest of the "King Contractor," threatened a strike to fully open the docks to CVTC organizing. The threat netted a promise from one of the major transport firms to directly hire workers rather than submitting them to potentially corrupt subcontracting schemes.[97]

These advances took place with President Diem's explicit support. Diem even moved to implement elements of the CVTC's corporatist agenda, including the formation of *chambres mixtes de métiers,* joint councils representing labor, employers, and the state convening to resolve labor issues. Weighing anxieties about maintaining autonomy against the allure of realizing its corporate ideals, the CVTC worked closely with the Saigon government on such initiatives.[98] On May Day, 1956, Diem directly addressed the workers of his country, proclaiming that his government "placed labor above capital" and recognized the right of workers and unions to participate in the "direction and progress of the country."[99] The new government's court system also appeared ready to aid labor. After several appeals, the South Vietnamese Supreme Court upheld the conviction of a French rubber plantation foreman for the beating death of a female worker. The convicted foreman quickly fled the country.[100]

Delighted by the CVTC's progress, the AFL enthusiastically embraced the new South Vietnamese government. *The AFL News-Reporter* praised Diem as a "progressive" and a "reformist," willing to fight landlords and "feudal forces." Under Diem, the AFL crowed, a "far-reaching step was taken to stimulate the democratic process in strife-torn, divided, yet strategically vital Vietnam."[101]

Despite bearing Diem's imprimatur, South Vietnamese organized labor enjoyed little real security. To thwart communist disruptions, Buu reluctantly agreed to allow plainclothes police officers to march in the confederation's 1956 May Day parade.[102] Despite support on the national level, CVTC leaders continued to protest repression and "censorship" by local officials.[103] In May 1956, the Go Cong Province chief of police arrested thirty CVTC members, and searched and closed the provincial union office. Buu managed to obtain the release of twenty-six prisoners, but the authorities brought four to trial (all eventually were acquitted).[104]

Crisis on the national level quickly overwhelmed local problems. While his membership in Can Lao brought handsome returns, Buu feared Nhu and Diem's volatility and untrustworthiness. Always guarding the CVTC's autonomy, Buu remained "reluctant to become over-obligated" to the government by "accepting outright grants from it or any of the political parties."[105]

Buu had good reason to be cautious. The controlling Ngo family did not entirely welcome the rapid gains made by organized labor. In the February 1956 General Assembly elections, Buu and the CVTC, despite its official policy of avoiding politics, endorsed a slate of candidates, some of whom had not received Diem's seal of approval. In response, government officials arrested several confederation leaders and prodded Buu relentlessly to endorse the slate approved by Can Lao. Ever the realist, Buu bent to Diem's will but not silently.[106] In a meeting with the president in February 1956, Buu bluntly told Diem that "his idea of democracy was not [Diem's] hand-picked assembly."[107] The CVTC followed up by amplifying its attacks on local officials who harassed union members. Such brazen outspokenness stoked the fires of Diem and Nhu's obsessive suspicions. The final straw, according to American embassy observers, came when the CVTC failed to pass a resolution pledging support to Diem's government.[108]

Paranoid and undemocratic by nature, the Ngos now saw little reason to maintain an alliance with South Vietnamese labor. In October 1956, the U.S. embassy reported a dramatic and dangerous shift in Diem's attitude. Government officials openly condemned the CVTC and reinstated colonial era prohibitions against large meetings without prior government approval, in effect "strangling the activity of trade unions."[109] Meanwhile, Nhu turned viciously on the Tenant Farmers' Union. Fearing that its initial successes might lead to real agrarian reform, Diem's brother transferred control of a network of farmers associations, designed to extend affordable credit to tenants, to a group of wealthy landlords. The landlords turned the associations to their own purposes. A reign of terror descended on the union. Police arrested key leaders; some languished in prison for years. Buu himself came close to arrest as tensions mounted.[110] Within months, oppression and bitterness superseded the once great promise of the Diem regime.

Diem's sudden reversal coincided with a dramatic revolt in November 1956 by Roman Catholics still living in North Vietnam. The authorities quickly and brutally broke the insurrection, but the episode excited the imagination of AFL-CIO Asian representative Richard Deverall, himself a Catholic, who had visited Vietnam in 1950. The uprising, he claimed, drew on the same spirit as the Hungarian rebellion had that same month. It "provided history," he enthused in a long telegram to Meany, "with the first authentic revolutionary protest against communist rule in Asia."[111] While celebrating the uprising, Deverall, of course, seemed blind to abundant evidence of Diem's autocratic rule in the south, where repression was already stirring revolt.

From Washington, Meany kept appraised of events in Vietnam not only through Deverall but also through his membership in various Roman Catholic organizations. As a member of the Board of Governors of the John Carroll Society, Meany was exposed to the comments of a Filipino envoy who likened the forced march of French prisoners following the battle of Dien Bien Phu to a "1954 version of Bataan."[112] Meany also sat on a committee honoring Dr. Thomas Dooley, the celebrated physician who had worked in Indochina. Yet the AFL-CIO president, in true free trade union fashion, chose his allies carefully. Noting the federation's already "close contact" with the CVTC, Meany refused an offer from the American Friends of Vietnam, an influential organization dedicated to building support for Diem and South Vietnam, to help further cement relations between the American federation and Vietnamese labor.[113]

For the AFL-CIO, the CVTC's struggles brought into further focus the continuing lethargy of the ICFTU's Asian operations. In frequent, lengthy reports to Lovestone, Deverall complained frantically of the international labor organization's inefficiency in Asia. The Indians, he insisted, who operated much of the organization's machinery in the region, were not only "hopelessly inefficient" but also resented in the rest of Asia.[114] As if to confirm Deverall's laments, in 1960 the ICFTU affiliated with the Worker's Union of Vietnam (UOV), a largely insignificant rival to the CVTC. Meanwhile, ICFTU officials continued to ignore Buu's significantly larger organization as it struggled with Diem's vicious turnabout against labor.[115] By the end of the decade, Deverall was counseling the AFL-CIO to drop the ICFTU completely and launch its own third-world activities "through its network," which presumably included the CIA and U.S. foreign aid operations.[116] Lovestone echoed Deverall's frustration, complaining incessantly of the "tragedy and stupidity of the ICFTU operations in the Far East." Increasingly he and Meany searched for other avenues through which to advance free trade unionism's Asian agenda.[117]

Disenchantment with the ICFTU only grew as the AFL-CIO watched the Christian International launch a campaign to aid South Vietnamese labor. After 1953, under the new leadership of August Vandistendael, the Christian International expanded its activities in Asia and Africa, investing increasing time and resources in the CVTC.[118] The ICFTU leadership learned with some trepidation that the Christian International had developed a "trade union centre" in Vietnam in the mid-1950s, designed to serve as a base for operations in the rest of Asia.[119] Vandistendael arranged for a series of "seminars" in Saigon, which his organization enthusiastically described as places where "Christians, Hindu, Mahommedans, and Buddhists can come to an understanding on an agreed social concept, founded on the dignity of the human person and of spiritual finality."[120] Still, the Christian International lacked the resources and political influence to truly aid the CVTC as it faced mounting threats from Diem.

Despite the official denouement of colonialism, the French government did hope to maintain its influence in Southeast Asia through, among other means, an ambitious foreign aid program. Desperately in need of funding, the CVTC looked to secure French aid, to be administered through its mentor, the CFTC. In 1955, Buu and the CVTC appealed to the French government's economic aid program for funds to expand upon its *chambres mixtes de métiers* initiatives and to open a series of "Raiffeisen Cooperatives," modeled on the rural savings and loan associations begun by Friedrich Raiffeisen in Germany in the 1860s.[121] The politically entangled French bureaucracy, however, quickly swallowed up Buu's proposal. Jouan was soon angrily lamenting the unconscionable bureaucratic tangle facing the CVTC.[122]

Nor could the Americans offer much aid. By the late 1950s, U.S. liberals had developed a sophisticated and ambitious program to promote development in the third world, an agenda some historians have labeled "liberal developmentalism." Inspired by the optimism of the likes of W. W. Rostow's "noncommunist manifesto" model for economic growth and William Lederer's indictment of the insensitivity of American diplomacy, liberals planned major development projects such as extensive dam-building projects modeled on the Tennessee Valley Authority and other enterprising nation-building initiatives. Enthusiastic supporters of liberal developmentalism, free trade unionists insisted that independent organized labor unions were necessary components of democracy and development. The AFL-CIO prescribed just such a large-scale development program for Vietnam (and elsewhere in the third world), with labor playing an essential central role. Eisenhower's frugality, however, stood in the way.[123]

Although systematic American support for the CVTC was not forthcoming, the struggling organization did have the aid of one energetic American trade unionist in the employ of the U.S. Operations Mission (USOM). Jodie Eggers, formerly of the CIO-International Woodworkers of America, arrived in Saigon in 1955 as the USOM labor adviser. He immediately made contact with Saigon's dockworkers and then journeyed into the field to connect with the CVTC's rural unions. Although the mission allotted no funds for labor programs, Eggers, obviously inspired by liberal developmentalism and free trade unionism, forged ahead on his own, establishing strong bonds with CVTC leaders. "My personal impression is that they are sincere in their desire to help the membership although they have little money nor past experiences to aid them," he concluded in his first report.[124] Inspired, he aggressively lobbied USOM for modest funds to initiate labor programs.[125] Within a year, he had founded several "labor schools" to train CVTC unionists.[126] Such was Eggers's dedication that he spent his weekends with the CVTC constructing housing for resettled workers.[127] In 1957, he managed to pry a $200,000 grant from USOM to establish training courses for trade unionists across the country that were taught by a team of twenty full-time instructors.[128]

Having bonded with the CVTC, Eggers watched with helpless anger as Diem turned against labor. "I can only say it will be a major blunder that will have far reaching effects," he reported to the State Department. Communist insurgents, he cautioned, undoubtedly planned to use the break "to their advantage."[129]

The bonds Eggers forged with the CVTC contrasted sharply with problems the confederation was having with a French adviser. After navigating a complex bureaucracy, La Mission Française d'Aide Économique et Technique au Vietnam granted funds allowing the CVTC to hire an expert adviser on agricultural cooperatives. Technical adviser Adrien Morel arrived in Saigon in 1957. By the following year, however, Buu was demanding Morel's recall, complaining that "since his arrival in Vietnam [he] has brought us vexation and tension."[130] Morel responded bitterly, complaining that the CVTC was losing its Roman Catholic orientation.[131]

But Eggers's successes hardly brought acclaim at the ICFTU offices in Europe. General Secretary J. H. Oldenbroek grumbled bitterly that the U.S. International Cooperation Administration (ICA, the successor of the MSA), by expanding labor programs in Vietnam, Thailand, and Indonesia, was "interfering with the programs and plans of the ICFTU."[132] Yet Oldenbroek appeared to have few plans of his own for that increasingly volatile part of the world.

Still largely on his own, and facing an increasingly hostile Diem government, Buu walked an ever more precarious tightrope. The CVTC had seen impressive growth in numbers and influence, but by the late 1950s every gain seemed to hang in the balance. Rumors began to swirl through Saigon of Buu's imminent arrest. Fears of communist infiltration also mounted. In 1957, the police arrested and jailed a communist agent operating in the ranks of the CVTC when they found incriminating documents in her residence.[133] The arrest drew further clouds of suspicion over the CVTC and resulted in ever tighter government restrictions.

To make matters worse, the nascent U.S. government labor program in Vietnam came to a sudden halt in 1958 when the International Cooperation Administration transferred Eggers to Pakistan. Almost immediately USOM's relationship with the CVTC collapsed. Buu, unceasingly guarding his organization's autonomy, rejected American demands for an audit of his organization's use of aid money, and USOM responded by ending both the subsidy and the labor aide program.[134]

Humiliated, the CVTC seethed with "anti-American sentiment," according to observers.[135] It had been just ten years since American trade unionists first encountered their Vietnamese counterparts, yet an awkward pattern already characterized relations between the two, replete with half-met promises, missed opportunities, and debilitating communications gaps. Still, with few alternatives, the AFL-CIO remained an important potential lifeline for the CVTC.

Conclusion

Disappointment, stagnation, and frustration plagued the free trade union agenda after 1952. In America, ambitions stalled on both the domestic and international fronts. Free trade unionists longed for action. They envisioned a rapidly growing economy, fueled by Keyserling-style full-employment economics, and the funding of bold development projects overseas such as the strengthening of South Vietnamese organized labor. Instead, they encountered Eisenhower's parsimony. But Americans would elect a new president in 1960, and labor hoped to reverse the negative trends of eight years. Ironically, the years to follow saw much of the free trade union agenda realized, with disastrous results.

4 New Frontiers

For free trade unionists, the early 1960s came like a brief Indian summer: overnight long-held hopes and ideals appeared tantalizingly within grasp. Slogging out of the discouraging Eisenhower years, organized labor embraced new frontiers thrown open by the Kennedy and Johnson administrations. Senator John F. Kennedy's 1960 "we can do better" campaign mantra, paralleling neatly labor's call for activist government at home and abroad, energized trade union activists. As president, Kennedy spent freely and aggressively pursued his foreign policy objectives. He also cultivated close personal relations with George Meany and Walter Reuther. Following Kennedy's assassination, Lyndon Johnson quickly surpassed his predecessor, thoroughly seducing organized labor. Johnson's charm assault begot an unprecedented marriage of purpose between trade union leaders and the White House.

The forthright, dynamic foreign policy practiced by the two Democratic presidents—in which social, political, and economic development ranked among top national security strategies—enraptured free trade unionists.[1] Shedding its inhibitions, the AFL-CIO enthusiastically tendered its services to the Kennedy and Johnson administrations in the form of a series of joint government-labor programs in Africa, Latin America, and Asia.

In the spirit of the times, the AFL-CIO redoubled its efforts in Vietnam; indeed, support of the South Vietnamese labor movement emerged as a priority for U.S. labor. Meany's circle envisioned Vietnamese organized labor as everything from a potential "paramilitary force" to a source of political leadership for South Vietnam. But the CVTC, though increasingly strong, remained at the mercy of a volatile and authoritarian South Vietnamese government. By the end of 1964, the AFL-CIO, like President Johnson, with whom it increasingly identified, sensed that the future of South Vietnam and its struggling organized labor movement would demand large-scale American military intervention and an ambitious nation-building program. Such a far-reaching mission, free trade unionists preached, would necessitate a vital role for American labor.

"A New Sense of Purpose"

Free trade unionists had watched impotently during much of the 1950s as conservative fiscal policies and budget-cutting measures stifled activist government. The result, they believed, had been a feeble foreign policy, anemic economic growth, and costly recessions. After a painful eight years, John F. Kennedy arrived like a knight in shining armor. In the young president, the AFL-CIO gratefully found, at least initially, a leader willing to wield the full powers of the state against the domestic and foreign problems bedeviling the country. During the 1960 campaign, Kennedy excited labor with calls for activist government, an aggressive foreign policy, and expanded federal spending.[2] His economic plan quickly won Leon Keyserling's approbation.[3] Following the Democratic convention in Los Angeles, the AFL-CIO strongly endorsed Kennedy and dedicated considerable resources to electing him. Come November, labor reveled in Kennedy's narrow victory.[4]

To treat the recession afflicting the nation in 1961, Kennedy borrowed directly from the full-employment war chest.[5] He selected Walter Heller to chair his Council of Economic Advisers. Heller, while lacking Keyserling's single-mindedness, vowed to "return to the spirit as well as the letter of the Employment Act of 1946" and arranged to meet regularly with labor leaders.[6] The new president quickly initiated retraining programs for the unemployed, targeted distressed areas for development by signing the Douglas Area Redevelopment Bill into law, increased funding for education, and raised the minimum wage to $1.25 an hour. Signs on desks and offices in the Commerce Department epitomized the new administration's priorities: "What Have You Done for Growth Today?" While Kennedy did not acquiesce to the far reaches of labor's economic agenda—which included large-scale public works and worker-training projects—compared to Eisenhower the new administration seemed swept up by Keyserling-style growth-focused economics.[7]

Labor also welcomed Kennedy's revival of military Keynesianism. Defense spending soared to the highest level since the Korean War, "the largest and swiftest buildup in the country's peacetime history," according to JFK aide Theodore Sorensen. The president directed Secretary of Defense Robert S. McNamara to launch an aggressive program, dubbed Operation

Booster, to direct defense contracts to regions with high unemployment.[8] Labor cheered the buildup and enthusiastically reciprocated with an unprecedented "no-strike" pledge in the missile industry, which was to be governed by an eleven-member Missile Site Labor Commission.[9]

Nor did the new administration's commitment to spending and full employment stop at American shores. Under Kennedy, growth-oriented economics became a foreign policy objective, another long-held goal of free trade unionists. "[A]n expanded program of long-term economic development within the Free World" was "essential to our relations with underdeveloped areas," economic development proponent and Kennedy aide Walt Whitman Rostow assured Secretary of Labor Arthur Goldberg in early 1961. Rostow's international development prescription, building on the ideals of liberal developmentalism, prescribed a massive foreign aid program coupled with full employment at home.[10] Increasingly, the virtues of free trade unionism, embraced by the Kennedy administration, appeared poised to become official national and international U.S. policy.

Suddenly infused with new life, organized labor found itself swept up by Kennedy's New Frontier. "The new administration has given the nation a new sense of purpose, urgency and hope. With forthrightness, President Kennedy has faced the unpleasant fact of recession and stagnation bequeathed by the last Administration," pronounced the AFL-CIO Executive Council only a month after JFK's inauguration.[11] Taking office, Kennedy seemed to be everything Eisenhower was not. Dismissing inflationary fears, the new president assertively attacked the economic crisis with full-employment measures. By early 1962, unemployment had fallen by almost two percentage points. To organized labor, the recovery and rising employment statistics affirmed yet again the wisdom of its guns and butter, full-employment program. In just two short years, JFK had inspired renewed confidence in the potential of activist government at home and abroad, a new spirit that in many ways led directly to the AFL-CIO's deep involvement in Vietnam.

Partners in AID

No aspect of the new administration's activism gratified free trade unionists more than Kennedy's efforts to revitalize and recast America's cold war strategy. The president's inaugural vow to "pay any price, bear any burden, meet any hardship, support any friend, oppose any foe, in order to assure the survival and the success of liberty" neatly echoed the deeply held values of free trade unionists. In the third world, Kennedy's embrace of nonmilitary "peaceful revolution" initiatives, promoting social and economic development to counter the appeal of international communism (alongside a willingness to encourage military counterinsurgency approaches), also seemed to represent the realization of labor's long-held liberal developmentalism ideals. In comparison, Eisenhower's "massive retaliation" strategy, which relied on nuclear superiority, appeared to be a cheap, sorry retreat that had failed to address the crucial socioeconomic side of the equation. Under Kennedy, the right balance seemed to have been found at last.

On November 3, 1961, the president, seeking to reorient U.S. foreign aid programs toward third-world development, revamped the International Cooperation Administration as the Agency for International Development (AID).[12] He also introduced the popular Peace Corps initiative and the Alliance for Progress, which promoted development in Latin America. Adopting a pluralistic perspective conspicuously absent under Eisenhower, the Kennedy administration eagerly sought the advice and participation of nongovernmental organizations such as the AFL-CIO. Secretary of State Dean Rusk organized a White House conference for such organizations, held on May 15, 1961, to "explore together ways of enhancing existing cooperation."[13] The allure of the young president's activism after so many years of Eisenhower stagnation elated free trade unionists, who instantly seized on the administration's offer of a partnership in conducting foreign policy and administering foreign aid.

Labor-state cooperation overseas had a precedent, of course, dating back to the Marshall Plan. During the 1950s, both the AFL and the CIO worked with the Mutual Security Administration, although the Eisenhower administration curbed labor's direct participation. For free trade unionists, the epic battle against communism and the mandate to cultivate a protective layer of anticommunist trade unions justified suspending the principle of labor-state separation and working closely with foreign aid administrators. Foreign aid spending, as Leon Keyserling taught, also fed economic growth and full employment at home. Lecturing Congress in 1963, Meany spelled out the domestic case for foreign aid: "These dollars are as important to the American economy as they are to the nations we are helping. They create jobs."[14]

Beyond economics, another factor pushed Meany and his circle toward a foreign aid partnership with the Kennedy administration. By the early 1960s, the frustrations of working with the ICFTU had grown increasingly unbearable for the AFL-CIO. Much of the mutual tension was related to issues of control. Fed by Lovestone's suspicious mind-set, Meany, imperious and intolerant by nature, chafed at any perceived challenge to his authority. The Europeans administering the ICFTU, in turn, resented Meany's bullying dictates and perhaps their dependence on American money. In early 1961, Meany vowed to withhold the federation's substantial annual allocation to the ICFTU unless the organization reorganized and redirected more of its attention toward third-world labor movements.[15] Walter Reuther sharply objected to Meany's threats, further poisoning their relationship.[16] Dependent on U.S. labor subsidies, the international labor organization eventually capitulated to Meany's demands, but the AFL-CIO president remained critical of the ICFTU and continued to press the international organization to expand its work, especially in Asia.[17]

Increasingly, Meany moved to establish his own foreign policy operations, to be funded by AID (most likely with contributions from the CIA) but independently operated by the AFL-CIO. Accordingly, the federation made common cause with Kennedy's Agency for International Development. In 1962, Kenneth Kelly, the secretary treasurer of the Massachusetts State Labor Council, became the director of labor affairs in AID's influential Office of Education and Social Development.[18] Meanwhile, Walter Reuther and Leon Keyserling took prominent positions on the AID advisory committee on economic cooperatives.[19]

Kennedy's Latin American initiative, the Alliance for Progress, designated to harness economic development as a cold war weapon, particularly appealed to U.S. labor.[20] Eager for a share of the fresh funds flowing into Latin America, Meany created a semi-independent organization, the American Institute for Free Labor Development (AIFLD), to press the cause of free trade unionism in Latin America. Labor and AID jointly funded AIFLD—a sort of labor version of the military-oriented School of the Americas. Under the program, Latin American trade unionists came to Washington for education and training with a particularly anticommunist orientation.[21] On August 8, 1962, Kennedy personally greeted the first AIFLD class on the south lawn of the White House. "I don't think there is any effort which could be made at this time which can be more fruitful than this common effort by the American labor movement working with the labor movements of other countries," the president told the gathering.[22]

In late 1963, Kennedy named Meany to head a permanent labor advisory committee for AID, which had evolved from an ad hoc labor committee attached to the Alliance for Progress.[23] In 1964, the AFL-CIO, in cooperation with AID, established the African Labor College (ALC), an African version of AIFLD, to be directed by the ubiquitous Irving Brown. Fearing their own obsolescence, ICFTU officials complained bitterly of the growing relationship between the AFL-CIO and the foreign aid community. Meany, Lovestone, and Brown, however, clearly preferred a closer and potentially more productive relationship with the U.S. government in contrast to maintaining a frustrating partnership with the ICFTU. With AID-sponsored labor institutes, operated by the AFL-CIO, chartered in both Latin America and Africa, free trade unionists naturally began toying with the idea of establishing similar operations in Asia, where the ICFTU had proven particularly resistant to aiding the CVTC in Vietnam.

The growing labor-state foreign aid partnership posed numerous dilemmas for U.S. labor, however. Questions of cost effectiveness plagued the aid programs. Adopting Keyserling's "all spending promotes growth" position, complaints about waste and inefficiency never troubled the AFL-CIO. But large segments of the public—and no doubt many trade unionists—viewed foreign aid programs as wasteful diversions from pressing domestic problems and as costly contributors to the nation's negative balance of payments.[24] Seeking to counter public skepticism, Kennedy commissioned a study of U.S. foreign aid to be overseen by retired general Lucius Clay. The president appointed Meany to represent organized labor on the committee. Kennedy and Meany expected Clay's committee to arrive at supportive conclusions, solidly justifying foreign aid expenditures. The Clay committee's findings, released in the spring of 1963, shocked its sponsors. The committee sharply criticized the AID administration and called for cuts and a fundamental reorientation. "There is a feeling that we are trying to do too much for too many too soon . . . [and] new countries value their independence and do not want to acquire a new master plan in place of the old one," it warned. These assertions directly challenged the AFL-CIO's sense of urgency and supreme faith in its agenda. Despite having missed every committee meeting, Meany issued a blunt dissent, the only committee member to do so.[25] "AID and our military assistance programs wisely administered are insurance against possible vast military expenditures and sacrifices of American lives, so great as to overshadow completely the cost of this insurance," he proclaimed.[26] "The AFL-CIO is the only true friend and supporter of AID," a grateful foreign aid staffer wrote Meany.[27]

Later, to counter the damage of the Clay report, the Johnson administration, with the cooperation of organized labor, launched a public relations campaign, culminating with a highly publicized trip by Vice President Hubert Humphrey to Africa.[28] The Clay committee report, however, offered an ominous reminder to free trade unionists that the public, including many rank and file workers, viewed foreign aid with very mixed feelings. Likewise, it contained an admonition that recipient nations might not always welcome American initiatives, even those undertaken with the best of intentions.

Beyond the public relations dilemmas lay the issue of labor's compromised autonomy, both real and perceived, when it accepted generous government subsidies to operate its overseas programs. Dismissing ideological inconsistencies, Meany and his acolytes maintained that they could accept AID money and still maintain autonomous international operations—have their cake and eat it, too. But within a few years, as public awareness grew of labor's extensive involvement with the Alliance for Progress, AID, and the CIA in Europe, Meany found his organization's reputation severely tarnished. And none of labor's extensive overseas undertakings proved more controversial than those soon to develop in Vietnam.

"It Is Still Possible to Avoid a Second Laos"

Roused by Kennedy's call to action and the burgeoning AID-labor alliance, the AFL-CIO redoubled its efforts to strengthen anticommunist labor movements in the third world. Such a campaign, Meany and his supporters insisted, remained integral to thwarting international communist designs. With the swelling support of the Kennedy administration, from Central America to Africa to Asia, the federation moved to cultivate and empower anticommunist trade unions. But the CVTC, facing a mounting political crisis in South Vietnam, increasingly took center stage for free trade unionists.

With Buu's movement continuing to struggle against Diem and communist guerrillas forming the National Liberation Front (NLF) in 1960, the AFL-CIO decided that the time had come to intervene more forcibly in South Vietnam. In the fall of 1961, Meany dispatched Irving Brown, the federation's capable European agent, to Saigon to evaluate the tense Indochinese situation. By the early 1960s, Brown's reputation had spread worldwide. His rumpled demeanor and crooked smile belied a resourceful ruthlessness. Communists saw him as a menacing agent provocateur working in league with the CIA. To his admirers, Brown was a sheer force of nature, who moved mountains for the anticommunist cause through tenacious persistence and an elaborate network of connections. The Paris-based American agent focused primarily on European labor issues, but in the face of perceived ICFTU incompetence he gradually expanded his jurisdiction worldwide. Brown had friends and benefactors at the highest levels, including the CIA. Virtually every American ambassador knew of Brown and willingly arranged meetings and support services for him. Typically, Brown arrived equipped with ample sources of cash and counsel, which he readily doled out to friendly clients; to any he suspected of communist sympathies, he showed little tolerance.[29]

In November 1961, Brown arranged a brief trip to South Vietnam. Officially, the AFL-CIO billed the visit as a humanitarian mission to deliver relief to flood victims along the overflowing Mekong River.[30] The cover allowed Brown to circumvent the troublesome ICFTU, which worked with a smaller, less-influential labor federation in Vietnam. The American agent's real concern was the CVTC and its ongoing struggles with Diem.

Brown's visit coincided with the darkest period of Diem's rule in South

Vietnam. The Ngo family's repressive policies alienated ever increasing numbers of their countrymen. CVTC cadres found themselves the targets of both Diem's South Vietnamese police force and Viet Cong (VC) guerrillas. Diem sent scores of unionists to the Poulo Condore prison (the site of Buu's imprisonment by the French in the early 1940s, now revamped for Saigon's use) and had numerous others tortured or killed. In 1960, Dr. Phan Quang Dan, a Lovestone associate and frequent contributor to *The Free Trade Union News*, was denied a seat he had won in the National Assembly. Diem then charged Dan with complicity in a coup plot and slapped the reform-minded doctor into prison. Part of his incarceration was spent at the Saigon zoo, which had been converted into a prison for Diem's enemies.[31] Meanwhile, rumors swirled throughout Saigon that Buu was next in line for arrest.

Under constant threat, union membership, especially among the CVTC's rural affiliates, steadily declined. Surrounded by hostile forces, one union official metaphorically described his organization's struggles as equivalent to being "pinched between a mountain and a river."[32] On one side lay the oppressive Diem, on the other the totalitarian Viet Cong. To counterbalance the volatility of life under the despotic Diem, the CVTC assiduously avoided direct confrontation with the South Vietnamese authorities. Meanwhile, it sought to strengthen ties to the AFL-CIO and U.S. government.[33] The CVTC hoped that Brown's visit would send the message that Buu's movement still had politically influential friends in the United States.

Arriving in Saigon on November 15, Brown immediately sized up the Vietnamese labor movement. As he traveled throughout the city, he could not shake the sense of a country in a deep morass. Particularly disturbing was the vast gap between rich and poor. The "poverty and misery of the masses" moved the American agent as he walked through the slums of Saigon. The Viet Cong, he grasped, had managed successfully to "identify itself with the thinking and actions of the masses and the reality of daily existence." Meanwhile, Diem's government remained mired in corruption, incompetence, and repression. "Unless there is a cleansing of the Augean stables and an introduction of new, hopeful political elements into the regime, the masses, especially the peasants—will not defend the regime no matter what this government or the USA says," Brown concluded in his official report to Meany.[34] Despite the myriad problems he witnessed, Brown, buoyant by nature, remained optimistic. Pointing to Vietnam's embattled neighbor, which was on the brink of defeat at the hands of communist guerrillas, he concluded, "It is still possible to avoid a second Laos [in Vietnam]."[35]

Many of Brown's hopes lay in South Vietnam's maturing labor movement and its leader, Tran Quoc Buu. He met with representatives of the ICFTU-affiliated Vietnamese labor federation but found it weak and divided. Only the CVTC, under Buu, constituted "a moral or social side of what must be a total fight against a total enemy." Brown admiringly noted how Buu inspired public confidence at a time when other leaders appeared corrupt and ineffectual. The two conferred closely during the visit, forming a lasting bond. Buu described his struggles with Diem and his fears for his movement's future. He explained his ambitious plans for expansion and impressed Brown with his ardent anticommunism.[36]

In short, Buu wowed his American guest. Brown wrote he was "so impressed with Buu that I believe he should be considered in terms of any possible reshuffling of the political control of the government." The CVTC, Brown ebulliently proclaimed, was not only a potential political and social weapon but also "a possible para-military" force.[37] Buu apparently encouraged such thinking. He told Brown that both Emperor Bao Dai and Diem briefly had enlisted the CVTC for paramilitary purposes. Both leaders, however, later turned against the CVTC, fearing the potential of armed political opposition to their own governments.[38]

Despite the hardships he witnessed in Saigon, Brown left the city intoxicated with the potential of the CVTC, a force he believed capable of inspiring and sustaining a grassroots struggle against communist invaders. Brown's was an imaginative leap given that Buu's movement was struggling for its very survival under Diem. Realistic or not, the mission of the AFL-CIO's top agent ushered in a new level of intimacy between American labor and its South Vietnamese counterpart, though it was one marked as frequently by communications gaps and tensions as by cooperation. Yet before closer relations could be forged there remained the problem of the repressive and mercurial Diem.

"We Must Insist on a New Line of Approach"

Following Brown's warnings about Diem, the AFL-CIO grew increasingly impatient, as the South Vietnamese leader resisted even modest reforms. In Paris, Brown consulted frequently with leaders of the Vietnamese exile community. His contacts urged him to use his influence against Diem and to support the "real" nationalists operating in South Vietnam.[39] In 1962, as repression mounted in Saigon, Meany appealed personally to Kennedy and Rusk to protect Buu and address the worsening situation.[40]

Despite the brewing crisis, the ICFTU continued on its plodding, ineffectual course in Asia. The organization, commented labor journalist John Herling in 1960, "remained an area of rancorous infighting, personality conflicts, and raging national feuds."[41] Tension and resentment, especially over Asia, multiplied between the AFL-CIO and the ICFTU. In 1962, responding to American prodding, the ICFTU finally dispatched an agent, Luigi Turconi, to Vietnam. Turconi was to supervise a project designed to strengthen the ICFTU's small Vietnamese affiliate, the Worker's Union of Vietnam (UOV). The UOV had appealed to the international labor confederation for funds to pay the salaries of six full-time organizers and to publish a monthly bulletin. Arriving in Saigon, Turconi found that the UOV had squandered an initial grant of ten thousand U.S. dollars and greatly exaggerated its membership rolls and activities. To Turconi's dismay, the UOV, which aspired to compete with the CVTC, appeared to be little more than a paper organization. The Italian returned to Europe complaining that "our affiliate in Vietnam did not possess either the will nor the capability to implement our programme." In December of 1962, the ICFTU discontinued aid and suspended the UOV.[42] Ironically, while uncovering the distressing truth about its Vietnamese affiliate, even ICFTU staffers recognized the potential of the CVTC, particularly its plantation workers' affiliate. "Despite tremendous difficulties created by both a semi-fascist government and communist guerillas," noted an ICFTU committee report, "this organization is extremely well-run and efficiently led."[43] Yet the ICFTU's antagonism toward the Christian International remained such that it ruled out any question of building relations with the CVTC.[44]

Frustrated, Meany continued to press the ICFTU for action in Asia. At one point in 1963, he dispatched Edwin Wilson, a foreign relations representative for the Seamen's International Union, on a fact-finding mission to the region. Wilson, "in cooperation with the ICFTU," was to seek ways to revitalize free trade unionism in Asia.[45] The mission proved fruitless, however, and by this time Meany had given up on the ICFTU. Instead, shelving concerns about free trade union autonomy, the AFL-CIO moved to expand its partnership with AID and other U.S. government agencies.

In the summer of 1963, the smoldering crisis in South Vietnam erupted into an inferno. Buddhist uprisings in Saigon and Viet Cong attacks paralyzed the country. Fearing that the Viet Cong would capitalize on the chaos, the AFL-CIO sent agent Harry Goldberg to Saigon to assess the worsening situation. Goldberg, the AFL lobbyist assigned to the Geneva conference in 1954, found a crisis spiraling out of control. Corruption and political decay polluted every level of the South Vietnamese government. The Ngo family was perilously isolated from the rest of the country. Madame Nhu, the president's sister-in-law and wife of the labor-benefactor turned CVTC oppressor, according to Goldberg, was "the real power in the nation." The Viet Cong had the initiative, and no popular support could be mustered for Diem's government. "The US cannot get out, of course, and must stay," concluded Goldberg, "but we must insist on a new line of approach. All of our power must be used to bring pressure upon Diem and his family to change course, or else!"[46]

In September, following his return to Washington, Goldberg met, at the suggestion of the CVTC, with Vietnamese exiles representing the Democratic League of Vietnam. Leading the delegation was Dr. Nguyen Ton Hoan, a physician and veteran political operative, who had been exiled to Paris in 1955 after supporting a failed attempt to unseat Diem. Hoan had worked with Buu on nationalist causes in the 1940s and 1950s, and he claimed that recently the CVTC president had secretly journeyed to Paris to build support for a coup against Diem. Hoan urged U.S. labor to lobby aggressively against Diem. He claimed to have already earned the sympathies of Michael Forrestal, a key aide to National Security Adviser McGeorge Bundy. The Hoan group proposed to replace Diem's regime with a "broad-democratic, anti-communist coalition."[47] The next month, Irving Brown arranged a meeting between an aide to the Joint Chiefs of Staff, General Victor Krulak and Ho Thuong Minh, a former defense minister of South Vietnam, who had been forced into exile by Diem. Ousting Diem, Minh stressed, represented the only hope for his troubled country.[48]

Meanwhile, the Kennedy administration scrambled for a solution to the mounting chaos in Saigon. Desperate to stabilize Diem's collapsing regime, Roger Hilsman, the State Department's director of intelligence and research, urged the immediate reorganization of the Saigon government to include Buu and other popular civilians.[49] Yet by late summer and early fall Buu wanted nothing more to do with the Saigon government. Instead, he joined the ranks of those plotting to remove Diem.[50]

Alongside his covert scheming, Buu adopted a more public posture in opposition to Diem. In the fall of 1963, he sharply criticized Diem before a United Nations committee investigating the situation in Vietnam.[51] Buu also bitterly complained to allies in the CIA of recent arrests of CVTC officials designed to "intimidate labor" and warned that workers were growing "restive." Some were responding to Buddhist calls for a general strike against Diem.[52] Seeking Buu's counsel and perhaps hoping to shield him from arrest, the AFL-CIO invited the CVTC president to its mid-November 1963 biannual convention. President Kennedy also planned to attend, providing Buu with an opportunity to meet the popular American leader.

Just prior to the convention, however, a circle of high-ranking South Vietnamese generals launched a coup that was tacitly supported by U.S. authorities. The military leaders assassinated Diem and his brother Nhu, ending their repressive regime. Although sympathetic to the coup, Buu quickly found himself in trouble. Unsure of the CVTC president's ultimate leanings, the coup leaders took him into custody. The AFL-CIO immediately demanded to know his whereabouts. The new Saigon leadership demurred, claiming that the labor leader had been kidnaped by unknown persons. Finally, with the personal intervention of Ambassador Henry Cabot Lodge, Buu's release was secured.[53]

Within weeks, chaos also enveloped American politics. John F. Kennedy's assassination devastated organized labor, which had developed a strong emotional attachment to the dynamic, young president. Just before his death, Kennedy addressed the AFL-CIO's convention. He reviewed his administration's activism, its anticommunism, unprecedented defense buildup, and 600 percent increase in counterinsurgency forces. "America is stronger today than ever before in our history," Kennedy told the cheering delegates.[54] The loss of the activist, personable president in the midst of labor's Indian summer left trade union leaders yearning to forge a relationship of equal intimacy with his successor.

"I'm a Christian Now"

In the 1950s, few could have foreseen anything beyond a reserved, distant relationship between Lyndon B. Johnson and organized labor—and none would have predicted that LBJ would one day forge the strongest bond ever between a president and trade union leaders.[55] Johnson, after all, hailed from the conservative state of Texas. Although a New Dealer, he showed little sensitivity toward organized labor, nor could he afford to, given the antilabor leanings of his state. As a congressman, Johnson had voted for the Taft-Hartley Act and clashed repeatedly with local organized labor in Texas. When he was the majority leader of the Senate, the United Auto Workers had considered Johnson an "enemy." Informed of Kennedy's intention to tap the Texan as his running mate, Meany had threatened to renounce the Democratic ticket and pitched one of his legendary temper tantrums, lasting hours.[56] Johnson managed to further alienate labor leaders when, during the 1960 campaign, he thoughtlessly crossed a picket line set up by Continental Airlines flight engineers.[57]

As vice president, however, Johnson moved with single-mindedness to repair his rocky relationship with union leaders. Organized labor became the object of a classic LBJ courtship. The vice president threw himself into the pursuit, learning the language of free trade unionism, frequently addressing labor gatherings, and lavishing attention on union officials.[58] Astutely aware of labor's interest in foreign policy, Johnson invited James A. Suffridge, president of the retail clerks' union, to accompany him on his 1961 state visit to Asia.[59] In Saigon, Suffridge conferred with Buu and other CVTC leaders, who expressed thanks for AFL-CIO aid and left "the impression" that they "were very unhappy" with Diem.[60] Throughout Asia, LBJ met with local labor leaders and strove to show sensitivity toward labor-related issues. Reporting on his junket, Johnson was careful to make numerous references to Asian trade unionism. Among his specific recommendations for Vietnam, the vice president stressed industrial aid, urged the expansion of public education, and advised that local governments "enforce existing labor laws and work toward social reforms." Overall, he endorsed a more "liberal official attitude" toward the nascent trade unions of Asia and generous American financial assistance for the training of union leaders—recommendations doubtless designed for the specific consumption of Meany and free trade unionists.[61]

As president, Johnson intensified his pursuit of labor, consulting closely with union leaders on all manner of issues. The new president made sure to give Meany a courtesy phone call on November 22, 1963. In a follow-up conversation a few days later, Johnson assured Meany of his commitment to organized labor and solicited advice for a planned expansion of the Alliance for Progress program.[62] Throughout his presidency, Johnson habitually touched base with Meany; the two spoke on the phone an average of two or three times a week.[63] Chatting with the former plumber, Johnson assumed a thoughtful and attentive air rather than the aggressive, arm-twisting persona he adopted with others. Under the radiant light of presidential attention, Meany and LBJ became confidants. White House adviser Walt Whitman Rostow remembered the two as sharing "the same general intellectual mind set," including a distrust of intellectuals and sympathy for "underdogs."[64]

The rest of organized labor quickly followed Meany in succumbing to Johnson's legendary charm. After just six months under Johnson, the president of the Amalgamated Clothing Workers of America, Jacob Potofsky, remarked that he "had never seen such enthusiasm before" between labor and a president.[65] Reminded by AFL-CIO vice president Joseph Keenan of the earlier coolness between labor and the president, Johnson smiled and explained: "But I'm a Christian now."[66]

No doubt the remarkable speed with which organized labor bonded with the new president was related to emerging doubts about his predecessor. Despite the warmth between Kennedy and the leadership of organized labor, after the first year of his administration the young president often seemed to retreat. Secretary of Defense Robert S. McNamara, a former automotive executive, annoyed organized labor with initiatives intended to rein in military Keynesianism. He instructed procurement officers to "buy only what we need . . . at the lowest price possible."[67] Not only at the Pentagon but throughout the Kennedy administration organized labor complained about a lack of representation on key decision-making bodies.[68] By 1963, American labor was no longer hiding its frustrations. Concerned that "government expenditures are not rising nearly fast enough to make up for the deficiencies of tax and monetary policies," UAW economist Nate Weinberg warned Walter Reuther that full employment no longer appeared to be a Kennedy administration priority.[69] On August 15, 1963, the AFL-CIO Executive Council ominously forecasted a "recession in 1964 unless decisive government actions are taken, immediately, to lift sales, production and employment."[70] A columnist for the *AFL-CIO News*, Edward P. Morgan, lamented that "Kennedy, like Ike, hasn't yet gotten the U.S. moving again."[71] Meanwhile, Kennedy's incipient interest in détente, most evident in his 1963 call for Americans to "reexamine our attitude toward the Soviet Union," seemed almost a direct repudiation of the uncompromising free trade union line on the Soviets. Increasingly, the bloom was off the rose.

Johnson offered just the antidote. In the wake of Kennedy's tragic death, the new president seemed to clasp in his large hands the entire federal government and shake out its lethargy. In his first meeting as president with the AFL-CIO Executive Council, LBJ impressed the gathering by vowing to create seventy-five million new jobs.[72] He aggressively and skillfully pushed forward many of the programs long on labor's wish list, including Medicare, Medicaid, civil rights provisions, and a series of programs designed to address persistent poverty.[73] After a decade of inaction, an American president seemed fully prepared to embrace the free trade union program and—better yet—to possess the legislative skills and momentum required to push his agenda through Congress. Johnson appeared to be almost the embodiment of Keyserling's long-maintained claim that the state had within its resources all it needed to address social problems, vigorously expand the economy, and meet international commitments.[74] Johnson's War on Poverty also exhilarated laborites. Jack Conway and Brendan Sexton of the UAW eagerly left their union jobs to join Great Society agencies. Johnson matched his domestic activism with action overseas, renewing the nation's commitment to aggressive anticommunism and a comprehensive approach to international development, particularly in Vietnam. To labor, LBJ seemed to represent the fulfillment of Kennedy's early promise. Thanks to the new president, the sun shone again over labor's briefly deferred Indian summer.

Vietnam, 1964

As Johnson cemented his relationship with organized labor, both he and the trade unionists he so aggressively courted faced a renewed crisis in Vietnam. The pivotal events and developments of 1964, which led to direct U.S. military intervention in Vietnam, have both intrigued and confounded historians. Fredrik Logevall recently argued that in 1964, far from blindly entering the quagmire, U.S. policymakers waded through a swamp of contingencies and forewarnings before deciding to intervene, despite abundant evidence of the trials to be faced in Southeast Asia.[75] In microcosm, American labor underwent a similar test in 1964. The year laid bare all the painful challenges that would confront U.S. labor's Vietnam agenda: a recalcitrant South Vietnamese state, the CVTC's ambivalence toward U.S. aid, deep cultural and communications gaps, and a resourceful communist enemy. But, like President Johnson, with whom it so closely identified, the AFL-CIO trudged through the swamp of 1964 and emerged as confident of its mission as ever.

Despite Buu's brief incarceration after Diem's assassination, he and his fellow trade unionists welcomed the November 1963 Saigon coup. For over a decade, the CVTC had struggled first against the French and then against the Diem regime, all the while regarding the Vietnamese communists as an equally dangerous alternative. Absent Diem, South Vietnamese labor hoped at last to escape the sense of constraint that had haunted the movement from its inception.

The coup leaders, however, proved unable to secure a hold on power. Locally, many of the same Diem era officials continued to harass the peasantry, local farmers, and labor organizers.[76] Meanwhile, Saigon collapsed into disarray. When a second coup was launched in January 1964, Buu, fearing arrest, slipped into hiding. Ironically, even as he went underground the State Department was considering him, along with others, as a possible candidate for the South Vietnamese premiership. Secretary of State Rusk advised Ambassador Henry Cabot Lodge that should General Nguyen Khanh, the primary coup leader, falter the Americans might "consider the possibility of Tran Quoc Buu, president of the CVTC, as [a] personality with political savvy and ability to attract popular support."[77]

Khanh, however, managed to consolidate power. In his drive to eliminate his rivals, the general ordered Buu's arrest on the trumped-up charge of favoring neutrality. The American embassy, as quickly became the pattern in Vietnam, interceded on behalf of Buu. Khanh, it insisted, must drop the charges and learn to live with Buu and active trade unionism. Fully cognizant of the fate of the last South Vietnamese leader who dared resist U.S. pressure, Khanh chose to accede. He met with Buu in early February. Under watchful American eyes, the two worked out a preliminary arrangement granting the CVTC room to breathe.[78]

The U.S. embassy's intercession clearly stemmed from the American campaign to promote a semblance of democracy in strife-ridden South Vietnam. Seizing on U.S. nation-building initiatives, Meany began aggressively lobbying on behalf of South Vietnamese labor, seeking to set in motion Brown's ambitious plans for the CVTC.[79] First he invited Buu to the United States to address the May 1964 AFL-CIO Executive Council meeting. He then leaned on his White House contacts to arrange a personal meeting between Buu and President Johnson.[80] Johnson, of course, viewed the meeting as part of his continuing courtship of labor. But the visit also served the administration's public relations agenda for Vietnam. White House staff assistant Michael Forrestal described it as an opportunity to counter "the image of a U.S., which all too often is believed to be preoccupied in Vietnam solely with military solutions." He also anticipated the meeting as "helpful in getting across to the American public that the Khanh government is not a military dictatorship."[81]

Ushered into the Oval Office on May 20, Buu, apparently unintimidated by his surroundings, seized the moment. South Vietnam's peasant class, he told the president towering over him, had "tired of empty promises . . . [and] the new government must live up to its assurance of economic and social progress."[82] The "missing link in the present Vietnamese chain of events," he explained, was a free labor movement capable of addressing the "daily hardships" suffered by Vietnamese workers "and creating an almost para-military type of civilian organization to . . . transform the indifferent and neutral mass of people into an active barrier against the communists."[83] American support for democratization and free trade unions, Buu emphasized, offered the only hope of making these goals a reality. Johnson concurred, assuring his guest that he saw the conflict in Vietnam as much in political as military terms and recognized the importance of trade unions to strong democracies. He urged Buu to help him convince the American people of what was at stake in Vietnam.[84]

Buu made a "tremendous impression" on both U.S. government officials and trade union leaders. In sessions with the CVTC leader, Meany, Irving Brown, and Jay Lovestone pressed Buu to commit to a formal mentoring relationship with U.S. labor. The ever cautious Buu finally agreed to accept aid for training cadres operating in areas "controlled" by the Viet Cong, as well as for the creation of welfare centers and propaganda programs. He insisted, however, that AFL-CIO subsidies remain modest and discreet. American aid, Buu well understood, came at a premium. Dependence on outsiders, or the perception of such dependence, implied weakness and illegitimacy, imperiling claims to *doan the*.[85] Yet Buu needed and reluctantly accepted the aid. South Vietnamese trade unionists found that their ambitions required difficult choices, which often jeopardized the very "freedom" central to free trade unionism.

While Buu feared the tainting impact of his developing relationship with the Americans, paradoxically his White House visit endowed him with a new aura of power and influence in Vietnam. More sensitive to the importance of his relationship with Washington than Diem, General Khanh recognized Buu's growing clout and eased restrictions on labor. Seizing on the newly liberalized atmosphere, the CVTC embarked on a flurry of new organizational activity. The plantation and tenant farmers unions, virtually decimated by Diem, rebounded as tens of thousands of Vietnamese farmers and workers joined CVTC-affiliated unions and Buu established new welfare centers around the country.[86] Seeking to broaden international support, Buu's federation dropped the term *Christian* from Western translations of the confederation's title (Vietnamese use the same word for *Christian* and *worker*), although it retained its affiliation with the International Federation of Christian Trade Unions.[87] Buoyed by its success, in mid-1964 a CVT cadre ecstatically declared at a Singapore labor conference that "[t]hanks to the theory of free trade unionism . . . the activities of our syndicate are not like a thatch fire, burning for a short time and often dying out. But in the contrary, her activities persist like a coal fire under a layer of ashes."[88]

Sensing that the "coal fire" might ignite the anticommunist campaign, Lovestone asked Arnold Beichman, a globetrotting journalist with solid anticommunist credentials, to tour Vietnam and assess its reemerging labor movement. The diminutive journalist, with a talent for making quick friends, spent several days with Buu, traveling through Saigon and into the countryside. He found a vibrant labor federation, one rife with young activists ready for action. Buu particularly impressed him. The "Eighth Brother," as Buu was known, evoked an unassuming "air of gaiety and spontaneity about him." Beichman, who had toured South Vietnam with President Diem in 1959, found Buu, whom the people held in respect but not awe, a refreshing contrast to the former South Vietnamese president. Touring the slums of Saigon, the CVT president's compassion particularly struck Beichman. Buu's "feelings of anger and frustration came to the surface easily, as we wandered around the slums of Saigon. 'How can one talk to these impoverished peoples about the struggle against communism and the significance of liberty?'" the Eighth Brother wondered aloud.[89]

Seeking an independent perspective, Beichman slipped away from one tour and wandered into a union hall, where he gratifyingly found a bustling, vibrant meeting of thirty-five Lambretta (motor scooter taxis) drivers debating tactics in their campaign to decrease daily bike rental fees. The CVT, he reported to Lovestone, amounted to "more than just a union in an economic sense" and, echoing Brown's earlier impression, "could be transformed under proper guidance into a para-military organization of high value to the present emergency."[90]

Notwithstanding the strengths Beichman found in the CVT, he recognized its vulnerabilities. Buu remained a "target" of the military, political parties, and rival unions. His organization had no real blueprint or plans for the future and remained subject to the capricious whims of local officials.

The situation required American intervention, especially if Brown's goal of transforming the organization into a social and military bulwark against communism was to be achieved.

The AFL-CIO, Beichman advised, should establish a permanent office in Saigon to develop the "paramilitary" and informational potential of the CVT. American trade unionists, he recommended, must help fund the construction of union halls, establish confederation welfare centers, purchase Lambrettas for operators, and provide much needed education for union leaders, who had "been cut off from the rest of the world for such a long time."[91]

Perhaps urged on by Lovestone, Beichman personally spelled out for Meany what he saw as at stake in Vietnam. In a handwritten note included with his official report, the journalist reviewed Buu's personal selflessness and dedication to free trade unionism. Then he cut to the chase: "George, this is going to be a long, long war, maybe as long as 10 years because there's so much to do, so much which went undone for so long. But the stakes are high and I suppose it's better to fight here than in Staten Island or the Golden Gate."[92]

In early August, Irving Brown returned to Vietnam to put in motion Beichman's plans for a permanent U.S. labor presence in South Vietnam. Step one involved a visit to the offices of General Khanh to attain assurances of official cooperation. With Buu present, Brown pressed the general to open his government further to CVT participation. Khanh seemed to acquiesce, but Brown pushed further. "What about the implementation in the villages? In the districts? In the provinces?" Brown prodded. Pressured, Khanh promised full consultation and collaboration on every level. Such assurances were perhaps more than the general could deliver, but his commitment endowed South Vietnamese labor with a novel sense of official backing.

By mid-1964, American military and economic aid began to pour into South Vietnam in ever greater volume. Brown hoped to siphon off some of the flow for his planned CVT initiatives.[93] Therefore, he next arranged a meeting with James Killian, chief AID officer in Vietnam. Pressed to make AID dollars available for a labor program, Killian "indicated a great willingness to work directly with us" and, to Brown's relief, seemed to offer American labor relative autonomy in the spending of AID money, thus preserving a facade of trade union independence.[94] Even as he negotiated with Killian for funding, Brown apparently had other sources of money, most likely from the CIA. During his trip, he passed along ten thousand dollars to the CVT, which Buu quickly exchanged on the black market to mask its origin.[95]

As in 1961, Brown again emerged transfixed by South Vietnamese trade unionism. "As a result of my contacts with the CVT both inside and outside of Saigon, I am more convinced than ever that Brother Buu and his organization constitute the only real civil mass organization. It is the only body which in terms of people and power can implement or stand up to the army as a real, genuine, distinct movement," he waxed. Once more he raised the alluring possibility of molding South Vietnamese labor into a paramilitary organization in which members might have "contact with the village military guards and with the local authorities in order to have the arms, mostly defensive, necessary to protect the organization and those supporting the official war effort."[96] Brown's ambitious plans, however, took little account of formidable obstacles still impeding South Vietnamese labor and the CVT's own determination to avoid overreliance on outsiders, including the AFL-CIO.

While its long-term agenda remained the source of some debate, by mid-1964 the CVT was yearning to make up for lost time. As in the previous year, autumn in Saigon brought demonstrations and demands for further political reforms. And as with the uprising against Diem, Buddhists led the agitation. Although Buu, like the majority of CVT members, identified himself as a Buddhist, the organization feared the expansion of Buddhist power, especially as the influential Buddhist Institute in Saigon began exploring the formation of its own labor federation.[97] Likewise, despite Khanh's promises, segments of the military and government remained hostile to the CVT. In July, a clique of Army officers organized a rival longshoremen's union, composed of poorly paid women and children. Labor friendly U.S. ambassador Maxwell Taylor attempted to intercede on behalf of CVT dockworkers, but the best he could arrange was a compromise, dividing work between the two unions.[98] Facing what he saw as a decisive hour, Buu sought an opportunity to assert his organization's presence and power. Buu put the country on notice in late August, lamenting mounting violence in South Vietnam and declaring: "The time has come when humanity and love must conquer the bloody instincts of man."[99] He found such an occasion in the CVT's drive to organize a textile mill in Saigon. Owned by an American-born Chinese textile magnate who had purchased the factory with a loan of six million dollars from the U.S. Operations Mission, the Vimytex mill was the largest producer of textiles in Vietnam. Typical of the Asian textile industry, Vimytex had a reputation for dismal labor conditions. With the U.S. president and labor movement committed to protecting Vietnamese workers, the plant, purchased with U.S. dollars, offered an ideal target: American officials could pressure the Vimytex ownership behind the scenes, while the CVT could play the role of an aggressive and autonomous agent for South Vietnamese workers. But the mill owner, a Mr. Jen, proved resistant. He locked out three-quarters of his workers, roughly 120 employees, and transferred others to a military camp.[100]

As the CVT mobilized, General Khanh suddenly threatened the campaign. On August 19, amid growing political chaos, the general declared a state of emergency, ostensibly in reaction to the Gulf of Tonkin incident. Assuming total authority and jettisoning his promises to Irving Brown, made only days earlier, Khanh banned all strikes and mass meetings.[101] Seizing the moment, Buu upped the ante by announcing a general strike that would involve all the labor unions in Saigon. Constant protests against the state of emergency by students and Buddhists already had brought Saigon to a near standstill. But to Buu these groups were undisciplined and unfocused, the CVT was the true voice of the disenfranchised populations of South Vietnam, and he longed to assert its voice. An effectively mounted but brief general strike could increase the visibility of the CVT, positioning organized labor as an alternative to the authoritarian military dictatorship, the perennially protesting Buddhists, and the subversive Viet Cong. The event might also help Buu overcome his lingering association with the Diem regime. A general strike, even one the Viet Cong might try to hijack for its own purposes, would demonstrate to all of Vietnam the independence and potency of the CVT.[102] "We have arrived at a point where we must take chances. We are taking this one now with the conviction that for the world of labor we represent the only solution outside communism," Buu explained to French journalist Jean Lacouture.[103]

As the CVT prepared for the general strike, Buu and his lieutenants disingenuously insisted that their sole motive was to draw attention to the Vimytex dispute and protest the general emergency provisions against labor. But, with students and Buddhists marching daily against the ruling regime and a recent coup nearly ousting Khanh, a general strike could not help but have political reverberations, as the fate of the state hung in the balance.

Seeking to commandeer the event for its own cause, the National Liberation Front called for a popular uprising in all southern cities just days before the planned CVT strike.[104] Some also worried about the prominent role in organizing the general strike played by Vo Van Tai, the lean, hard-driven leader of the CVT Saigon labor council, who was frequently, though falsely, imputed to be a communist agent. To observers, the CVT left itself wide open to charges of Viet Cong infiltration. Ideally, Buu would have preferred to work behind the scenes with a strong South Vietnamese government capable of preserving domestic calm and fending off the National Liberation Front. But no such leadership existed.[105] As the forces of chaos closed in, Buu moved his organization into a more public, exposed position. "We are aware and concerned about the critical situation in our country, but we do not see why the government will not satisfy the reasonable demands of the working-class," declared Vo Van Tai.[106]

To journalist Jean Lacouture, the moment resonated and the strike embodied a definite "political aspect, in fact a clearly revolutionary one."[107]

Indeed, Buu did appear to be seizing the moment to assert the CVT's vision of *doan the*. The French newspaper *Le Figaro* echoed Lacouture: "In reality the political implications of the strike amount to a clear challenge to the regime."[108]

On September 21, the CVT shut down Saigon. Buu contacted Lovestone, seeking AFL-CIO support to deter overreaction by the South Vietnamese authorities. Meany immediately wired Buu, offering "our all-out unstinting support to the free and independent workers organized in the CVT under your great leadership."[109] U.S. embassy officials, however, shared none of Meany's enthusiasm. They fretted that the "general strike was an extreme reaction and another example of national indiscipline."[110]

When the city's electrical workers joined the strike, South Vietnam's capital city sat in darkness for a full day, without water, electricity, phone service, or bus transportation. Organized and unorganized laborers rallied to the cause. Sixty thousand CVT members joined in the work stoppage. Buu led a parade of several thousand strikers through Saigon to Khanh's offices, where they presented their demands. With the general conveniently out of town, his aides negotiated with the strike leaders.[111] Thousands of workers waited outside for news of the deliberations. Tensions mounted when the crowd turned against an "alleged Viet Cong" spy, who was supposedly trying to incite violence.[112] Finally, to great fanfare, Buu appeared, announcing a tentative settlement easing labor restrictions.

To Lacouture, the one-day mobilization marked the emergence of a potential third force: "A mass, whose roots were deeply anchored in the people of the countryside, was on the move . . . [and] for the first time a force arose that could be either a possible replacement for the present regime or a link to the enemy regime or the first pillar of a regime to come."[113] The general strike, in fact, was only the most dramatic of a wave of strikes, sixty-nine in all, sweeping through South Vietnam in September 1964. Working-class frustrations pent up during the Diem era erupted, and the CVT emerged as a leading vehicle for channeling working-class anger.[114]

Buu's organization was badly overextended, however. In dramatically asserting itself, the CVT had created new enemies and infuriated old ones. Buddhists as well as Buu's foes within the labor movement now viewed the confederation as a surging threat. More seriously, the CVT moved to the head of General Khanh's list of enemies. On one hand, the general could recall that Buu had been associated with Diem, against whom Khanh had once conspired; on the other, he heard constant rumors of VC infiltration of the trade unions.[115] Whatever the case, Khanh hardly welcomed the addition of another active political force aligned against him.

Complicating matters, rumors swirled through Saigon identifying Irving

Brown as the mastermind behind the general strike. While the street chatter had no validity, Brown's recent visit to Vietnam and his ready sources of money fueled suspicions. The U.S. embassy traced the rumors back to a colonel who worked directly for General Khanh.[116] The tottering Saigon regime perhaps sought to discredit its latest political threat with a whispering campaign. The episode no doubt confirmed to Buu what he had long suspected: U.S. aid, while indispensable and seductive, jeopardized the organization's delicate claims to legitimacy in the perilous world of South Vietnamese politics.

That autumn Buu could feel forces conspiring against him, both from his competitors within the Vietnamese labor movement and from within the army and government. In early October, John Condon, the U.S. embassy's labor attaché, gave Buu only even odds of survival. Told by an American friend that he hoped to see him soon in America, Buu half joked, "Yes, as a refugee."[117]

Buu's fears quickly crystallized. The first sign of trouble came in early October, when the Ministry of Labor, insisting that communist agents lay behind the recent spate of strikes, issued a tersely worded plea for labor peace that was interpreted by many in the labor movement as a threat.[118] Then, on October 10, General Khanh included Buu's name on a list of thirteen military officers and seven civilians to be arrested on charges of conspiring against him in the failed September 13 coup.[119] Accusations focused on a meeting between Buu and the conspiring coup leaders after the uprising had turned sour. Khanh insisted that the conspirators, Generals Lam Van Phat and Duong Van Duc, had sought Buu's help in arranging a meeting to discuss the coup with American ambassador Alexis Johnson. Buu, he claimed, had acquiesced.[120]

Upon learning of the charges, Buu turned immediately to the U.S. embassy and the AFL-CIO.[121] Infuriated at the arrest, Meany drafted a caustic statement denouncing the South Vietnamese authorities for their "inhuman and destructive action in trumping up treason charges against Buu" and contending that whatever actions Buu took came "with full knowledge and agreement of the U.S. government." Given its close relations with the Johnson administration, the AFL-CIO first vetted the statement through the State Department, where Secretary of State Rusk deemed the draft too "harsh." He dispatched George Delaney, a former AFL-CIO official who oversaw international labor affairs for the Department of Labor, to dissuade Meany from releasing his condemnation of the Saigon government. Reluctantly, Meany removed the most inflammatory language, but he insisted on making a statement that Rusk admitted was "as mild as we could expect." In the end, Meany publicly prodded both Rusk and Khanh to make "personal assurances that our colleague Buu will be provided every opportunity to refute the allegations made against him."[122] In Vietnam, Buu read Meany's statement at a press conference, where he declared his innocence and decried the recent "campaign of slander" against him.[123]

The U.S. embassy fully recognized the political nature of Buu's arrest and that the CVT chief had had nothing to do with the coup other than acting as a go-between. Ambassador Maxwell Taylor provided Buu with a letter "summarizing in agreed form" events on the date of the coup. Buu, again fearing that he would publicly appear beholden to the Americans, resisted using the letter in his trial before a military court.[124]

Both the Americans and the South Vietnamese had staked much on the promise that a civilian government would soon be elected in the turbulent nation. Under the tense circumstances, with the Americans moving toward full-scale intervention, neither the U.S. nor the South Vietnamese government relished the specter of convicting a labor leader who only months before the American president had greeted warmly at the White House. Khanh also faced mounting international pressure. In Europe, the Christian International urged its member organizations to come to Buu's defense. Letters of protest arrived in Saigon from as far away as the Congo.[125] At the United Nations, a Costa Rican delegate and acquaintance of Buu pressed the American ambassador, Adlai Stevenson, on the CVT president's behalf. Buu, the Costa Rican told Stevenson, provided the South Vietnamese people a unique "mystique to fight for against Communism."[126]

To the relief of all parties, a military court on October 22 found Buu innocent of all charges; loud cheers reverberated through the courtroom with the announcement of the acquittal.[127] The CVT chief immediately cabled Meany to offer his thanks. While not directly critical of Saigon officials, Buu expressed his hopes the verdict signaled new openness to democratic governance and that Khanh at last was "ready to show sincere comprehension and cooperation with a free and independent labor organization in the national struggle."[128] Several weeks later Buu again cabled Meany, offering his congratulations on the landslide election of Lyndon Johnson, for which the AFL-CIO had worked so hard.[129]

In December, Meany dispatched George Baldanzi, president of the Textile Workers Union, and AFL-CIO staff assistant Thomas Altaffer to Vietnam. Their mission, in the wake of the tumult of 1964, was to lay the groundwork for a permanent American labor presence there—an AFL-CIO Saigon bureau to provide expert advice and act as middleman between both the CVT and American government and the CVT and the South Vietnamese government. Recent events had persuaded Meany of the necessity of such an undertaking, although the CVT remained ambivalent. Baldanzi's trip was the first of several American labor missions to Vietnam, which eventually resulted in the creation of the Asian American Free Labor Institute, an undertaking not unmarred by significant misunderstandings and confusion. By sending two trade unionists with CIO backgrounds (Altaffer began his career with the steelworkers), Meany obviously sought to build broad support for his Vietnam initiative within the federation.[130]

Baldanzi immediately connected with Buu, whom he approached as a fellow union leader, sharing similar burdens and perspectives. Soft-spoken and willing to listen, the textile workers president also impressed his hosts.[131] Altaffer and Baldanzi ventured into the countryside "under difficult and at times risky conditions" to meet with the federation's rural affiliates, which remained very much under threat from the Viet Cong. Only days after the Americans visited a CVT agricultural center, VC guerillas attacked it, harassing and threatening union cadres.[132]

Notwithstanding the many positive developments of 1964, Baldanzi believed conditions were grave. The Viet Cong, he explained, was in it for "the long pull" and had "clear-cut programs around which peasants could be rallied." Urban workers, though not aligned with the communists, remained largely neutral in the struggle over the fate of South Vietnam. Indeed, the CVT admitted to a decline in its paying membership. Meanwhile, Buu remained in an exposed position both politically and personally. During Baldanzi's visit, several local railroad unions, attacking Buu as "Diemist Can Lao remnant number one," angrily disaffiliated themselves from the CVT. Meanwhile, Bui Luong, a longtime adversary of Buu, publicly charged CVT officer Vo Van Tai with accepting $200,000 from the North Vietnamese to build a house and "Emperor Buu" of receiving $45,000 from the U.S. embassy.[133] "The Vietnamese labor movement is without any hope today," Baldanzi sadly concluded. Free of Diem and with expanded opportunities, the CVT was still pinched between a river and a mountain.

Paradoxically, despite his discouraging assessment, Baldanzi remained eager to move ahead with the proposed AFL-CIO Saigon office. He strongly endorsed U.S. aid for CVT projects such as the construction of welfare centers and the distribution of fertilizer and insecticide to the confederation's tenant farmers.[134] Baldanzi and Meany proposed that Buu appear before the January 1965 AFL-CIO Executive Committee meeting in Miami, where they planned to formally present the mentoring and aid program.

U.S. labor was preparing to initiate its Vietnam program at precisely the same hour as the Johnson administration was weighing the options for a greater military commitment to Southeast Asia. Neither Johnson nor the AFL-CIO could claim ignorance of the labyrinth each seemed determined to enter. The troublesome events of 1964 clearly manifested the ominous challenges to be faced, in particular the burden of an ally struggling with democracy and deeply ambivalent about its dependence on U.S. support. Surprisingly, neither Johnson nor the AFL-CIO seriously considered turning back. For Johnson, the exigency of appearing strong and undeterred in the face of communism overrode all caution. And for his political soul mates in organized labor the mandates of free trade unionism propelled the AFL-CIO into Southeast Asia with equal force.

5 Into the Quagmire

"To a greater degree than ever before in the history of this country," crowed George Meany in early 1965, "the stated goals of the administration and of Congress, on the one hand, and of the labor movement on the other are practically identical." That year, eight hundred union leaders polled by *U.S. News and World Report* "almost unanimously praised LBJ."[1] Union leaders had reason to savor the hour, for the years between 1965 and 1968 in many ways marked the apex of postwar American labor. The economy soared to near full-employment levels, and a sympathetic, activist president sat in the White House. Internationally, the United States matched its military offensive against communism in Southeast Asia with an unprecedented campaign of nation-building in South Vietnam, an undertaking in which Vietnamese organized labor was slated to play a major role.

Yet, even as labor celebrated, its heyday proved unfulfilling. Almost immediately, the war in Vietnam, increasingly a testing ground for the defense of free trade unionism, proved corrosive. Growing antiwar sentiment within the labor movement belied AFL-CIO efforts to present a united front on the war. Tensions surrounding the war exacerbated the Reuther-Meany feud and led to the exposure of labor's dubious dealings with the CIA. As the conflict in Southeast Asia divided the nation, the labor-liberal anticommunist consensus also badly frayed.

In Saigon, Buu's movement remained under duress despite the U.S. military intervention. The Saigon government continued to be a vexing source of peril, and cultural differences between South Vietnamese and U.S. trade unionists scuttled AFL-CIO plans to establish a formal mentoring relationship between American labor and the CVT. In the first several weeks of 1968, all this was overshadowed when a strike by Saigon's electrical workers spiraled into open warfare between the CVT and the South Vietnamese government. The bloody Tet Offensive followed quickly on the heels of the labor strife, as chaos enveloped U.S. labor's carefully laid plans for the CVT and increasingly threatened the entire free trade union mission.

Kirsch, Ky, and the CVT

Throughout 1964, U.S. officials hoped General Khanh might provide leadership for the strife-torn country of South Vietnam. In August, President Johnson, seeking to stem communist advances, won congressional approval of the Gulf of Tonkin Resolution, providing him with a free hand in Vietnam. After his overwhelming reelection victory in 1964, Johnson unleashed the so-called Rolling Thunder bombing campaign early in 1965, seeking to force North Vietnam to capitulate.

Stability, however, remained elusive in South Vietnam. Large-scale Buddhist protests, in particular, continued to test Saigon's leadership and its labor movement. In early 1965, the Buddhist Institute for Secular Affairs began organizing workers. On February 11 of that year the institute launched general strikes in several cities, including Hue, Quangtri, and Danang.[2] To the CVT, the uprisings were a dangerous fraud, possibly initiated by the Viet Cong, and a serious threat to legitimate labor organizing.[3] Increasingly, Khanh appeared to have lost the confidence of both his people and his supporters in Washington. In a last ditch effort to save himself, the general forged an alliance with Buddhist radicals, an act that only further undermined his leadership.[4]

Despite the deteriorating scene in Saigon, the AFL-CIO moved ahead with its plans for Vietnamese labor. In December 1964, its agent, George Baldanzi, reported from Saigon that the CVT desperately required large-scale support. Meany quickly moved to arrange U.S. government funding for an AFL-CIO initiative in Saigon similar to the federation's AID-sponsored programs in Africa and Latin America. In February 1965, he aggressively prodded AID officials at a meeting of the Labor Advisory Committee on Foreign Assistance. Properly supported, he assured the gathering, the CVT would be an invaluable force capable of mobilizing the Vietnamese people against the Viet Cong.[5]

Meanwhile, Meany stage-managed what was to be a grand appearance by CVT president Buu before the AFL-CIO Executive Council meeting set for Miami in late February. There Meany expected Buu to personally make the case for the planned Vietnamese labor program.[6] Thomas Altaffer, Baldanzi's aide, was to accompany Buu from Saigon to Miami. On February 21, only hours after Meany sang the praises of the CVT before the AID advisory committee, Buu and Altaffer arrived at Tan Son Nhut airport to board an Air France flight to Miami. As they took their seats, military police stormed the plane to block Buu's departure. A troika of military leaders had staged a coup against Khanh. Chaos reigned in Saigon. It was days before Buu realized that not just he but all prominent South Vietnamese citizens were barred from international travel.[7]

With Buu detained and chaos once again enveloping Saigon, the AFL-CIO's Vietnam program went on hold. As South Vietnam tottered, Undersecretary of State George Ball, a supporter of the AFL-CIO's plans, deemed the situation too volatile to risk initiating long-term labor projects.[8]

After several months of instability, Air Marshall Nguyen Cao Ky emerged in May as prime minister of a military government.[9] Initially, the airman appeared to threaten the CVT's precarious hold on post-Diem gains. Described by British observers as "flamboyant, impulsive, direct and impatient," with an outlook bordering on an "old warlord mentality," the thirty-four-year-old newly minted leader immediately resurrected a decree from the Diem era, requiring official sanction forty-eight hours in advance for all union meetings.[10] Buu and the CVT concluded that the new prime minister considered them an enemy. Ky, they feared, meant to "thwart, if not destroy, the CVT."[11] To draw attention to Ky's dangerous attitude, journalist Arnold Beichman prepared an article for the *New York Herald Tribune* protesting Ky's regressive labor policies. American embassy officials in Saigon, arguing that its publication would be "counterproductive for the CVT," persuaded Beichman to hold off.[12] Meanwhile, the embassy, as it had with Khanh, pressed Ky hard to liberalize his policies toward labor and personally meet with Buu.

As the CVT struggled in the early months of 1965, the U.S. military greatly expanded its presence in Southeast Asia. In early March thirty-five hundred Marines landed in Danang to protect an airbase. By the summer, a full-scale U.S. ground intervention was under way. Alongside the military initiatives, the nation-building program for South Vietnam was kicked into high gear. Aid money flowed in at a rate of two million dollars a day.[13] Endorsing the intervention wholeheartedly and seeking to harness aid money for the CVT, the AFL-CIO moved to revive its recently postponed plans for a Saigon mentoring project.

As U.S. troops flooded into South Vietnam in large numbers, two AFL-CIO agents landed in Saigon in the summer of 1965, confident of their mission to set in motion U.S. labor's program for the CVT. Thomas Altaffer, who already had spent several months with Buu in Vietnam, and veteran agent Henry Kirsch were to lay the groundwork for the program.[14] But despite high hopes the mission immediately floundered. Kirsch angrily objected to his pairing with Altaffer, whom he insisted, without elaboration, "had previously been identified as a CIA man." With Altaffer on board, Kirsch complained, his work "was subject to the suspicions of the CIA and U.S. government involvement," hence compromising the principles of free trade unionism. While available sources offer no guidance as to Altaffer's ultimate loyalties, the AFL-CIO, through its close work with AID, the American embassy in Saigon, and other official U.S. government agencies in South Vietnam, clearly left itself vulnerable to such suspicions.[15]

In any case, it was Kirsch who proved the mission's undoing. He refused Buu's invitation to journey to the countryside to inspect the CVT's rural unions. Instead, he insisted on remaining in Saigon to focus solely on urban affiliates. Buu and others approached him regarding aid for the CVT's ancillary business operations, which included warehousing, insurance, and a print shop. As was common practice among Asian trade unions, profits from these enterprises provided the CVT with supplementary income and subsidized sporadic dues payments. Kirsch undiplomatically lectured Buu that such business pursuits only distracted from real union work. Instead, he proposed a program of direct U.S. financial aid.

Kirsch's personality also alienated Buu and the CVT leadership. His prickly, dictatorial style breached the patience and respect mandated by Asian customs. In particular, he seemed deaf to the CVT's anxieties regarding the implications of overt U.S. aid. However lucrative, direct grants from U.S. labor left an impression of subservience. It compromised the CVT's tenuous claims to *doan the*. Already rumors buzzed in Saigon of lavish cash gifts bestowed on CVT officers by U.S. benefactors. Even as Buu dealt with Kirsch, the city's gossip mills had him personally pocketing a million dollars of American money.[16] Given the AFL-CIO's own ideological preoccupation with autonomy, more sensitivity might have been expected. Instead, Kirsch seemed obsessed with suspicions that the CVT sought to profit from its outside enterprises.

Tensions quickly mounted between Kirsch and Buu. Soon the two found it impossible to discuss substantive issues. Meanwhile, Buu remained on good terms with Altaffer.[17] When his frustrations boiled over, Buu angrily canceled all plans for joint work with U.S. labor. Incensed and insulted, Kirsch departed Saigon in a huff two weeks earlier than planned.[18]

When Altaffer returned to Washington, he filed a separate report trying to contextualize the failed mission. He described Buu's worsening relations with Ky and his struggle to preserve some measure of autonomy for his organization. In spite of Buu's stubbornness, Altaffer believed the CVT was in trouble and needed American help. Danger surrounded the organization on all sides: from the Viet Cong, the Buddhists, the new Ky government, and Buu's enemies in the labor movement. "In the final analysis, it is only American trade unions which can effectively help the trade unions of Vietnam," concluded Altaffer.[19]

By late summer, Buu appeared to be less and less in control. The Buddhist Institute moved to challenge CVT unions in the textile and transportation sectors.[20] Serious infighting within the CVT suggested an organization on the verge of collapse. Early in June, a dispute over union jurisdictional rights among transportation workers escalated into a small riot, with rocks and clubs wielded as weapons. The battle took place directly outside AID's Saigon headquarters. Eventually, Vietnamese soldiers arrived to break up the fight and arrest fifteen unionists.[21] Amid such tensions, it seemed clear that AFL-CIO aid would only complicate an already tangled situation.[22]

As the CVT wobbled, Buu's relations with the South Vietnamese authorities went from bad to worse. Frequent police interrogations of union officials and government surveillance of the CVT were "obvious even to visitors."[23] In late summer 1965, John Condon, the U.S. labor attaché, described Buu as "pessimistic," seeing "conspiracies" all around him, from the government, the Buddhists, and rival unions.[24]

The failure of the Kirsch mission, Buu's rebuff of American aid, and the apparent chaos in the ranks of South Vietnamese labor disheartened observers at the AFL-CIO. In early August, Ernest Lee, a staffer with the federation's International Affairs Department, proposed placing both the CVT and the South Vietnamese government in "caretaker" status, under American supervision, until the U.S. military mission in Vietnam achieved some level of stability. This offered the only chance, Lee argued, of preserving the CVT's "economic, social and para-military" capabilities. "Under such circumstances," he wrote, "an AFL-CIO representative might well be included in the ranks of civil government much as Henry Rutz and Joe Keenan performed such functions following WW II in Germany."[25]

Lee's proposal, of course, would have immensely complicated the U.S. mission. It would essentially belie Johnson's claim that South Vietnam represented a viable, free state, worthy of defense in its battle against communism. An American occupation would revive ugly memories of Vietnam's colonial past. Despite the appeal of a receivership, U.S. officials were stuck with an ally of questionable competence that both needed and resented American support.

Faced with CVT resistance to its offers of direct aid, the AFL-CIO sought other ways to help. In October, George Meany issued a stern public statement demanding that the Ky regime halt its "hostile attitude and acts against the CVT and peasant organizations."[26] Meany's admonishment marked a sharp break at a time when the Johnson administration desperately sought to promote a prowar unanimity. The federation also remained in close contact with AID's labor adviser in Saigon, Emil Lindahl, a Long Island native and former member of the International Union of Electrical and Machine Workers of America (IUE). Very much a free trade unionist before joining AID, Lindahl was a veteran of the fight to rid the IUE of communist influences. His specific assignment in Saigon was to evaluate potential training programs that in time could operate in conjunction with U.S. labor.[27]

In the wake of the failed Kirsch mission, Meany recognized the necessity of dispatching an agent more attuned to the sensitivities of South Vietnamese labor. In the fall he sent to Saigon Harry Goldberg, who a decade earlier had represented the AFL at the Geneva conference. Goldberg's instructions were to repair relations between the federation and South Vietnamese labor—and between Buu and the Ky regime. In Saigon, Goldberg sat through long meetings with Buu. He allowed the CVT leader to vent his frustrations with Kirsch and Ky. Buu explained that however desperately he needed American help he feared appearing in public with Americans and being labeled a stooge by the Viet Cong. Unlike Kirsch, Goldberg endured the CVT's "incredibly full, but exceedingly worthwhile" agenda, which involved long trips into rural areas to visit union affiliates. Meanwhile, despite Buu's reservations, Goldberg "pulled strings" to arrange a meeting with Prime Minister Ky.[28] Behind the scenes, General Edward Lansdale, an old friend of South Vietnamese labor who had returned to Vietnam as a special adviser on pacification and counterinsurgency, leaned on Ky to cooperate.[29] Goldberg accompanied Buu to the meeting and, as Irving Brown had done the year before, aggressively pushed the CVT's agenda and prodded Ky to develop specific policies for labor. Thrown on the defensive, the aviator turned prime minister insisted that his government was both "pro-worker and pro-peasant."[30]

Goldberg's pressure evidently made an impression on Ky. Several days later the prime minister hosted a seven-hour get-acquainted session with the CVT leadership, highlighted by a lavish buffet lunch. Ky vowed that he had no intention of exploiting divisions within the labor movement to "divide and rule." He apologized for the problems with exit visas for CVT officials seeking to attend international conferences. Should trouble again arise, he assured the group, they could contact him anytime, "including Sundays and Holidays." Buu was pleased. He told the U.S. embassy's labor attaché that if not "for age and experience" he would have "shown unrestrained elation."[31]

Throughout 1966, despite occasional conflicts with local officials and the Saigon police, the CVT's relations with Ky continued to improve. At a briefing for AFL-CIO officials, General Lansdale touted "a growing rapport between Ky and Buu. Each hoping that the other will sustain the other's efforts."[32] In private meetings with Buu, Ky waxed eloquent about his plans for a "social revolution on behalf of workers and peasants." The prime minister consulted Buu on cabinet appointments.[33] When police in Giadinh Province broke a sit-down strike by women workers at a textile factory, the CVT demanded action against the offending officers. When none was forthcoming, Buu threatened a general strike in all trades except those associated with public utilities and hospitals. Almost immediately, Ky intervened and suspended the army major who headed the national police in Giadinh Province.

Ky's personal intervention came at a tense time. He was about to move militarily to squash a Buddhist-inspired coup in Danang.[34] While upsetting many Americans, Ky's harsh anti-Buddhist crackdown impressed laborites, who regarded the Buddhist activists as little more than VC agents.[35] The Buddhist Institute's drive to organize workers of course helped persuade trade unionists of the need for Ky's hard line. In August 1966, following decisive anti-Buddhist raids in Danang and Hue, the CVT invited Ky to its headquarters as an honored guest. There, five hundred unionists greeted the prime minister as a hero, interrupting Ky's speech with applause ten times.[36] Even as American officials lost faith in the often erratic Ky, many in the CVT appreciated the airman's "straight talk" and accepted his cowboy image more as an indication of independence and strength than of immaturity and flamboyance.[37]

Buu's improved relationship with the national government gave the CVT an opportunity to expand. In particular, the Tenant Farmers' Federation, a key CVT affiliate, flourished, expanding to nearly one hundred thousand members. At times, the Tenant Farmers competed directly with the VC. In early 1965, Viet Cong guerrillas, relying heavily on violence and intimidation, drove away the French management of South Vietnam's largest rubber plantation in Binh Duong Province. The VC, however, quickly proved unable to pay or feed the workers. A "delegation of workers therefore made their way to Saigon," where the CVT tenant farmers took up their cause, successfully negotiating a new contract with Michelin.[38] The "only place the peasants can go now is the union movement; not the dictatorial government, or the cruel Viet Cong," contended Vo Van Giao, president of the Tenant Farmers' Federation, in 1966: "The union cannot put them in prison, and will not call upon them for contributions and forced labor."[39]

But in spite of its entente with Ky the CVT faced a myriad of challenges. As U.S. soldiers swept into the country, so, too, did painful inflation. The meager wages paid to South Vietnam's workers, especially in rural areas, lagged behind rising prices, soaring at an annual rate of 124 percent in 1966.[40] The CVT also remained at the mercy of local police. Buu openly worried that General Nguyen Ngoc Loan, the near psychotic head of the national police, would kill him and blame it on the Viet Cong.[41] At times in 1965 and 1966, Buu relied on the services of Lutz Baehr, a young German working for an international relief agency, to pass warnings to CVT members facing arrest.[42] Most seriously, Ky, despite his cooperation with labor, remained mercurial. By early 1967, the prime minister apparently had grown jealous and suspicious of Buu's close ties to certain Americans. According to U.S. reports, the South Vietnamese leader planned to weaken the CVT by spreading rumors about Buu's wife, a woman with a reputation for controversy and ambition. Warned by American officials, Buu threatened to retaliate with stories about Ky's wife.[43] Despite the apparent labor-state rapprochement, the South Vietnamese political scene remained treacherous.

Challenges also came from other sectors of the South Vietnamese labor movement. While the CVT remained by far the largest, two rival federations and numerous unaffiliated unions constantly sniped at it. The American aid supposedly flowing to Buu's organization particularly stirred jealousy among its competitors. Bui Luong, a former CVT official who had organized a small labor federation after a falling out with Buu, never tired of charging his former colleagues with corruption and servility to Americans (even as he openly sought U.S. aid for his own organization).[44] Elsewhere, the president of the non-CVT motor cyclo drivers' union publicly accused the CVT of pocketing some three hundred thousand dollars given to it by the International Union of Electrical and Machine Workers for the construction of a refugee center. The actual IUE donation amounted to merely fifteen thousand dollars, but Buu's refusal to disclose the details of contributions or account for his use of funds—byproducts of his organization's obsession with autonomy and independence—clearly fueled the rumors.[45]

Even within his own organization Buu faced hazards. In late 1966, Vo Van Tai, the young, gaunt, and aggressive general secretary of the CVT's Saigon Labor Council, launched a strike, without Buu's permission, against government plans to ban civilian workers from Newport, a newly constructed military port near Saigon. Tai's work stoppage achieved little and lasted a mere five days, during which American soldiers replaced picketing workers. Still, the U.S. embassy concluded Tai had emerged from the strike with the reputation of a "fighter," inspiring a younger, militant generation of unionists. Meanwhile, Buu projected the image of an "international statesman hobnobbing often with Americans—and far too much under our influence."[46]

Seeking leverage against his opponents, Buu cautiously moved to revive relations with the AFL-CIO. American intervention was in full gear, resulting in unprecedented mobilization and construction in a country previously only teetering on the edge of modernity. The U.S. army contracted, for instance, with Meadowgold Dairies to build forty "in-country" ice cream plants for American troops. The RMK-BRJ construction firm (whose close connections to the Johnson administration raised eyebrows) undertook the massive job of building military bases in South Vietnam, eventually employing some fifty thousand Vietnamese workers.[47] The construction balloon created, as the AFL-CIO and Johnson administration fully recognized, a "tailor made set up" for South Vietnamese labor to augment its ranks and influence; Buu and the CVT would appear to operate independently, and the U.S. government could claim the thriving labor movement in South Vietnam as evidence of an emerging democracy.[48] Given the potential windfall, AFL-CIO staffer Ernest Lee implored: "Every effort should be made to organize workers in the building trades of the large U.S. firms and Vietnamese employees of the U.S. military within the CVT."[49]

Still sporting ambitious designs for South Vietnamese labor and pleased by signs of a new stability in South Vietnam, the AFL-CIO dusted off its plans to set in motion a Vietnam labor program.[50] It planned a new organization modeled on the federation's other international institutions, the American Institute for Free Labor Development and the African Labor College, which provided training and support services for anticommunist trade unionists and were administered by the federation yet funded largely by AID.[51] Eager to mold South Vietnamese labor into a social, political, and military force, the AFL-CIO gladly sought help from the U.S. government, even when such plans violated free trade union tenets mandating separation between labor and the state.

"Will the Sergeant-at-Arms Clear Those Kookies"

The federation's determination to aid the CVT sprang, of course, from a virtually all-consuming anticommunism. So unyielding was this ideological mandate that it often left little room for thoughtful discussion or dissent. Bordering at times on paranoia, the secrecy and intrigue that enveloped Meany's circle derived largely from Jay Lovestone's roots as a communist agent, replete with spying, blood enemies, traitors, and secret cells. As dissent erupted over the Vietnam War, free trade unionists refused to see opposition as anything less than the sinister workings of Moscow—treasonous machinations not to be tolerated.

In early 1965, with the inauguration of Johnson's bombing campaign against North Vietnam, antiwar protests broke out on college campuses across the country. A small but committed group of antiwar unionists joined the protest movement. Meany's fierce anticommunism and dictatorial control of the federation no doubt contributed to driving some into the opposition. Emil Mazey of the UAW and Patrick Gorman of the Amalgamated Meat Cutters, for instance, openly impugned Meany's foreign policy line at every opportunity. Relations between Meany and Reuther also remained strained, and the UAW chief often took shots at the AFL-CIO's dogmatic anticommunism. Even among labor leaders who generally sided with Meany, occasional murmurs of dissent could be heard. In 1964, Jacob Potofsky, president of the ACWA, confided to an interviewer that Lovestone was "living in the past" and that the "kind of verbiage and the old communist terms" he employed in speeches written for Meany was "not up-to-date."[52]

While the core of the organized labor leadership stood firmly behind Meany's pro-war pronouncements, protests on college campuses and antiwar activism by some liberals needled the former Bronx plumber. Halting the spread of communism and preserving freedom, Meany insisted, must be the bedrock of progressive politics. As campus protests spread, Meany blasted the teach-ins and sit-ins as infantile, futile, and counterproductive. The Soviets and Chinese communists, he argued, bore ultimate responsibility for the war. On August 31, 1965, Meany reiterated this theme in a speech berating campus protests. "The record is clear," he pronounced. "Every university professor seeking the truth can see it clearly. No student really thirsting for knowledge can fail to see it."[53]

With relations between the AFL-CIO and CVT back on track and mounting evidence of an improvement in Ky's treatment of labor, Meany decided to turn the federation's December 1965 convention in San Francisco into a showcase of support for Johnson's Vietnam policies. He lined up an impressive group of speakers, including the president, vice president, and secretary of state. He also invited a large delegation of South Vietnamese trade unionists and an array of other international visitors. A special breakfast session for all the foreign visitors focused entirely on the Southeast Asian crisis.[54]

Meany's pro-Vietnam rally reached its zenith with an address to the convention by Lyndon Johnson via telephone, in which the president portrayed the goal of the U.S. mission in Vietnam as simply "the pursuit of freedom." Aware that the federation's critics might cynically link its strong support of the war to jobs produced by the administration's guns and butter orientation, Johnson painfully explained: "Everyday someone asks why are we in Vietnam, and every day I want to answer: Not for economic reasons. We are spending our treasury, not producing it there."[55]

Later in the convention Vice President Hubert Humphrey, equating Vietnam protesters with pre–World War II isolationists, earned a standing ovation.[56] Deputy Secretary of State U. Alexis Johnson then credited Prime Minister Ky with inaugurating agricultural, educational, and social reforms.[57] Adopting the free trade union economic line, Sargent Shriver, of the Office of Economic Opportunity, directly tackled the guns and butter issue. "We say we have got to fight both wars and win both wars at the same time," he proclaimed to cheering delegates.[58]

Meany's hopes for an uninterrupted display of support for the war ended abruptly when Secretary of State Dean Rusk took the podium. Student protesters, who had quietly slipped into the convention gallery, suddenly exploded with boos and catcalls. Provoked, delegates on the floor responded with "a thunderous reception" for Rusk. After the speech, in which the secretary echoed Humphrey's Munich analogy, demonstrators and delegates turned on each other. Verbal volleys of "labor fakers" and "Get out of Vietnam" cascaded from the gallery. From below flew rejoinders of "Get a haircut" and "Go back to Russia." Walter Reuther's voice joined the chorus. "You are demonstrating in the wrong place. Why don't you tell Hanoi and Peking?" he shouted.[59] A burly protestor assaulted Rusk as he tried to exit the arena. Incensed as he watched chaos threaten his carefully scripted affair, Meany seized the podium and bellowed, "Will the sergeant-at-arms clear those kookies out of the gallery." With that, the protesters were removed.[60]

As a capstone to the convention, Meany had scheduled the resounding adoption of a pro-war resolution drafted by Lovestone. When the draft came before the resolution committee, however, Walter Reuther, Lovestone's "blood enemy" since the 1930s, cried foul. As written, he protested, the resolution "gave the impression of an American objective to encourage expansion of the war and to goad the Chinese and Russians." Not wishing to embarrass President Johnson, Meany and Reuther, in a rare display of cooperation, jointly worked to revise the document. They removed what Reuther deemed unsophisticated, "chauvinistic language" and added mention of the administration's "persistent efforts to hasten the end of military operations."[61] In its final form, however, the resolution contained an emphatic declaration of "unstinting" support for the war. On the convention floor, David Sullivan of the Service Employees International Union introduced the resolution as proof that in spite of "protests and demonstrations which have been lodged against U.S. policy . . . the nation's working men and women do support the Johnson administration in Vietnam." Walter Reuther immediately rose to second the motion, proclaiming, "Our government is doing what must be done."[62]

One of Reuther's key UAW lieutenants, Emil Mazey, resolved to buck the consensus. Furious at Meany's dismissive treatment of the protesters and disgusted by the resolution, Mazey rose to demand that labor "take the lead and . . . demonstrate and fight for the right of people to disagree." American support for colonialism and the subversion of promised elections in 1956, not expanding communism, had brought on the current crisis in Vietnam, he insisted. Hardly a democracy worth defending, the Ky government was "a corrupt military dictatorship." Finally, turning the Munich analogy on its head, Mazey noted Ky's recent comments praising Adolf Hitler.[63] Despite his passion, Mazey found virtually no support among the crowd; "no audible dissent" could be heard as the "unstinting" resolution passed overwhelmingly.[64] Still, Meany's convention hardly provided the unabated procession of support for the war the ex-plumber had planned. His authoritarian handling of the protesters, the generational and cultural gap exposed by the protests, and emerging doubts about the war among some unionists all augured crises soon to come.

In spite of the AFL-CIO's pro-war declaration, Mazey's dissent attracted support from some laborites. In late 1965, a group called the Detroit Women for Peace, quoting Mazey's unexplained insistence that "there is no free trade union movement in South Vietnam," urged the AFL-CIO to rescind its pro-war position. In February 1966, the Executive Council of the Amalgamated Clothing Workers of America officially questioned the "burden of expense" of the war and complained that "the sons of workers . . . are being drafted first for military duty."[65] A few smaller unions followed the ACWA's lead. In New York City, Local 1199 of the National Union of Hospital Health Care Employees, under the radical Leon Davis, quickly joined the peace movement and helped establish the Labor Committee for Peace in Vietnam, along with members of the leather and machine workers, the Amalgamated Meat Cutters, and the Actors Equity and Screen Actors Guild.[66] Harry Bridges' International Longshoremen and Warehouse Workers on the West Coast also took a strongly antiwar stance and even dispatched a fact-finding team to Southeast Asia.[67]

Meany and his circle found themselves ill-equipped to understand the nascent antiwar movement among trade unionists. Lovestone, characteristically, saw a plot. "The drive in the unions against the AFL-CIO position is being stepped up by the Commies throughout the country. They are putting plenty of money into this drive," he warned Meany.[68]

"It's Mostly Foreign Policy"

If the emerging antiwar sentiment enraged Meany, it deeply anguished Walter Reuther. As the leader of the progressive wing of the labor movement, he had long resented Meany's heavy-handed control of federation foreign policy, a subject that had first publicly divided the two in 1956, when Meany denounced Jawaharlal Nehru. Reuther's hopes of replacing Meany as federation president faded as the Bronx plumber resisted retirement and tightened his control. While the developing war in Vietnam deeply troubled Reuther, his intimate relationship with Johnson impeded him from acting on his instincts. Reuther watched the peace movement mobilize with a painful sense of divided loyalties and a nagging feeling that he should be molding and guiding the youthful activists.[69] Sidelined, the UAW president, as his biographer suggests, felt that "history had passed him by."[70]

Reuther directed much of his discontent at Meany.[71] Long rivals, the two were becoming bitter enemies, and increasingly, international issues rather than domestic policy differences exposed the raw resentments that divided the labor titans. About his frustration with Meany, Reuther told an aide, Douglas Fraser, that "there's hardly a domestic issue where we have a disagreement anymore, it's mostly foreign policy."[72] Intent on creating a separate identity, Reuther moved subtly to differentiate himself from Meany's hard line, as when he insisted on softening the 1965 AFL-CIO Vietnam declaration. Much to the consternation of Meany, Reuther also began pressing for liberalized contacts between communist and noncommunist unions, thus treading on free trade unionism's sacred policy of quarantining communist labor organizations.[73]

Small gestures, however, failed to satisfy a radically minded segment within the UAW leadership, a group that included Executive Council members Emil Mazey, Paul Schrade, and Victor Reuther, Walter's brother, who handled foreign policy issues for the auto workers. The radicals pressed Walter Reuther to speak out against the war. At a 1966 UAW Executive Council meeting, Schrade sharply questioned the vacuous nature of a UAW statement on the war. "You're for the good things and against all the bad things, but you're not really saying you're against the Johnson policy, which is to continue the war," he bluntly harangued Walter Reuther. Later, when the UAW printed the minutes of the session, Schrade's criticisms were deleted. Confronted on the matter, Walter Reuther sheepishly explained he had decided to consider Schrade and Mazey's antiwar comments as "off the record."[74]

Victor Reuther, whose disdain for Lovestone had begun when the two served as organizers for competing auto workers' unions in the 1930s and hardened when Victor headed CIO foreign operations in Europe after World War II, decided to take matters into his own hands and precipitate a full-scale break between his brother and the AFL-CIO. In May 1966, in an extended interview with a *Los Angeles Times* reporter, he denounced the AFL-CIO International Affairs Department under Jay Lovestone as a virtual subsidiary of the CIA. In particular, he asserted, the federation's American Institute for Free Labor Development amounted to little more than a front for official U.S. intelligence activities. Similar allegations long had circulated in left-wing circles, but Reuther's claims put the rumors in the mainstream press. Nor could Victor resist a shot at his old nemesis. He added that "Lovestone seems to have brought into the labor movement the working habits and undercover techniques which he learned when he was in the highest echelon of the Communist Party . . . it's awfully hard to break old habits."[75] When confronted, Meany obfuscated, angrily denying any direct CIA connection. But the disavowals rang hollow. Victor Reuther had dealt a sharp initial blow to the previously unchallenged pillars of free trade unionism and placed his brother in a difficult position.

Over the next several months, relations between Meany and Walter Reuther continued to unravel.[76] Vice President Humphrey, fearing the political impact of the increasingly open battle between the two, approached both. He asked that they resolve their differences before Johnson's foreign and domestic programs suffered damage. Cord Meyer, the CIA liaison to the labor movement, also warned the feuding labor chiefs to keep their accusations out of the press lest the agency suffer in the process.[77]

Once out of the bottle, however, the CIA issue proved impossible to contain. The August 1966 AFL-CIO Executive Council meeting opened with members angrily assailing Victor Reuther's allegations. Pressured, Walter Reuther acknowledged that his brother had erred. "The CIA is something which you do not discuss publicly," he conceded. But Victor, he insisted, as he glanced around the table, "had no monopoly on mistakes."[78]

The council then took up Vietnam. With Walter Reuther temporarily absent, the assemblage approved a statement supporting the war and condemning antiwar demonstrations as threatening to "poison the bloodstream of democracy."[79] Despite apparently having approved an earlier draft of the statement, Reuther, upon his return, rejected the resolution as "intemperate, hysterical, jingoistic and unworthy of a policy statement of a free labor movement."[80]

As word of the tense meeting circulated, Secretary of Labor Willard Wirtz alerted President Johnson that the "split between George and Walter is real, and probably permanent." Its ramifications, he warned the president, "will not be pleasant."[81] Although Reuther still shrank from openly joining his brother and the UAW doves, he decided by the end of 1966 to declare his independence from the AFL-CIO. The UAW, in December, issued a statement assaulting the federation for "lack of the social vision, dynamic thrust, the crusading spirit that should characterize the progressive, modern labor movement."[82] With that, Reuther announced his resignation from the AFL-CIO Executive Council.[83]

The repercussions of the CIA revelations were far from over, however. In May 1967, journalist and former CIA agent Thomas Braden divulged that, while working for the CIA in the early 1950s, he had passed agency money not only to Irving Brown and Jay Lovestone but to Victor and Walter Reuther as well. In an article in the *Saturday Evening Post,* Braden vividly recalled going to Detroit with fifty thousand dollars in neat piles of fifty-dollar bills for the Reuthers. "Victor Reuther ought to be ashamed of himself" for his supposed whistle-blowing on the AFL, wrote the ex-agent. Although substantial funds had been paid to the AFL, Braden revealed that the federation had refused to provide accountings for them, which led to a confrontation with the agency and the eventual termination of the subsidies.[84]

Braden's revelations again painfully exposed the issue of American labor and CIA money. As he had with Victor Reuther, George Meany branded Braden a "damn liar."[85] For his part, Reuther sheepishly admitted that the UAW had accepted Braden's money in "an emergency situation." Again free trade unionism appeared to have been compromised. Blistering editorial reaction reinforced the point. The *Washington Post* complained that "a union which does secret government work is not the kind of 'free trade union,' responsive to its members' will, which American ideals enshrine." The *New York Times* saw the affair as having "blurred the lines between separation and mortgaged confidence in labor's independence."[86] No longer could free trade unionists portray themselves unchallenged as autonomous actors driven only by the ideals of an independent labor movement.

The fallout from the CIA charges reached as far as South Vietnam, where Buu's political rivals had long maintained a drumbeat of attacks on his close relationship with Americans. In its union newspaper, the Vietnamese Federation of Railroad Workers, an independent union often at odds with the CVT, reviewed the CIA charges and rhetorically asked: "This makes one wonder about the aid which the CVT has received from the AFL-CIO. Is this CIA money?"[87]

Dump LBJ?

President Johnson's courtship of labor represented one of the most successful undertakings of his prodigious political career. But even as most trade unionists sang his praises, high expectations on one hand and growing divisions within organized labor over the war on the other complicated the relationship. Free trade unionists long had called for precisely the foreign and domestic policies embraced by Johnson: activist anticommunism abroad and generous spending at home. As long-sought ideals became reality, laborites were in no mood to compromise. While historians have rushed to conclude that fears of a right-wing "Who lost Vietnam?" attack cemented the president's firm stance in Southeast Asia, the anticommunist Left, and organized labor in particular, also may have influenced a president determined to preserve a delicate liberal coalition. The politically driven Texan clearly recognized that any signs of "weakness" on Vietnam, any openness to "premature" negotiations, any tolerance for neutrality or retreat from guns and butter economics might imperil his hard-won relationship with Meany and the free trade unionists. Johnson fully understood that the ideological rigidity of Meany and his circle would supersede personal loyalties should the president backtrack on Vietnam.

In fact, as a growing peace movement coalesced, some in organized labor pressed Johnson to take an even stronger stance on Vietnam. Pro-war members of the maritime unions, which were often involved in shipping military supplies to Vietnam, deeply resented countries such as Sweden, which, in spite of the war, continued trading with communist North Vietnam. The Johnson administration disregarded such transgressions for fear of creating further international tensions, but they deeply embittered maritime trade unionists. On February 15, 1966, the presidents of the three major AFL-CIO maritime unions sent Johnson a blistering letter, declaring that "the time for pussyfooting is long past." Their respective unions would soon commence boycotting and picketing vessels of foreign nations that traded with North Vietnam.[88] A week later, five hundred longshoremen picketed British ships along the Hudson River pier known as Luxury Liner Row. Brandishing signs reading "We Have Sons in Vietnam—Don't Want British Ships to Help to Kill Them," the picketers, members of the International Longshoremen's Association (ILA), called the protest a "warning to all foreign-flag lines."[89]

President Johnson immediately dispatched veteran diplomat Thomas Mann to pacify the leaders of the boycotting maritime unions. Mann assured the union heads of the administration's dedication to curbing trade with North Vietnam and pleaded that such matters were best handled through less public channels. The labor leaders remained dubious but agreed to shelve plans for future protests.[90]

Beyond demanding a vigorous prosecution of the war, the AFL-CIO also pressed the Johnson administration to maintain its guns and butter economic policy of generous domestic and military spending. Echoing Leon Keyserling's teachings, the federation contended that the U.S. economy would thrive on such a diet.[91] In fact, the early years of the Vietnam War appeared to be a resounding affirmation of Keyserling's full-employment economics. In March 1966, the unemployment rate fell a full point, to 3.7 percent, the closest the country had come to full employment since the Korean War. Meanwhile, poverty declined and the gross national product soared.[92] As labor grew scarce, the power of trade unions grew proportionally. A Boston construction worker remembered the era as "one of those rare periods when individual workers held the upper hand as employers competed for a limited pool of skilled labor."[93]

The AFL-CIO credited the strong economy to Johnson's free-spending policies and sought to keep the ball rolling. Federation lobbyists pressured the White House to refrain from tax hikes or cuts in domestic spending. In the early months of the war, the AFL-CIO legislative director, Andrew Biemiller, warned White House aide Joseph Califano of the federation's fears that Great Society programs might be "gutted" due to the demands of the war. Califano assured Biemiller that there would be no major cuts.[94] The following year, Leon Keyserling, arguing that inflation resulted from inadequate rather than excessive growth, cautioned the White House against raising taxes.[95] In meetings with Johnson's staff, Meany also communicated his "lack of enthusiastic support for a tax increase."[96] He reiterated labor's views in a July 1967 letter to the president that forcefully assailed "the false cry of guns or butter raised from opposite ends of the political spectrum."[97] Later that year twenty economists working for AFL-CIO unions met with the Council of Economic Advisers and sternly warned that any tax hike would hurt working people.[98]

Johnson sided with labor's guns and butter approach through most of his presidency. In his 1966 annual budget message to Congress, the president assessed the costs of the war: "The true costs of this conflict are death, pain and grief. . . . But the economic costs of Vietnam impose no unbearable burden on our resources."[99] Yet in private the White House was not so sanguine. Joseph Califano worried, in the summer of 1966, that if the current high levels of employment were to be maintained the result would be a level of inflation that would not be "tolerated domestically." But with unions demanding wage increases and the Johnson administration unwilling to challenge labor and risk offending a supporter of its Vietnam policy, Califano lamented: "Maybe things have to get worse before they get better."[100]

As inflation edged upward in 1966, Johnson came under increasing pressure to propose a tax increase. Not until late summer 1967, however, did he offer a concrete plan to raise taxes. Congress, thereupon, took almost a year to grant the tax hike, a painful delay that many scholars charge allowed "the inflationary spiral to take hold" and commenced an economic collapse that culminated in thc 1970s.[101] LBJ aide Bill Moyers labeled the delay "the single most devastating decision in the Johnson administration."[102] The AFL-CIO, with its intense lobbying campaign on behalf of its guns and butter agenda, almost certainly hardened the president's reluctance to raise taxes. Johnson, hesitant to alienate one of the few liberal constituencies strongly in support of his Vietnam policy, clearly wished to avoid jeopardizing his special relationship with labor.

While the AFL-CIO leaders saw no necessary tradeoff between guns and butter and remained vigorous supporters of the war in Vietnam, rumblings of discontent became hard to ignore among the rank and file and some segments of labor's leadership. In the spring of 1966, Johnson's secretary of labor, Willard Wirtz, attended the annual conventions of four unions, the UAW, the ACWA, the Hotel Employees and Restaurant Employees International Union, and the Retail, Wholesale and Department Store Union. While the unions had reputations for independence on foreign policy issues, what Wirtz found shocked him. "It is clear in a dozen ways, that the one thing on everybody's mind is Vietnam, and that the general reaction of these unions and their leaders is pretty critical," he reported to the president. At each convention, union officials had advised Wirtz to avoid "entirely" the subject of Vietnam. Labor leaders, he warned LBJ, were "having a hard time keeping elements within the union from precipitating a large-scale debate."[103]

Even among the pro-Meany Communications Workers of America (CWA), whose president, Joseph Bierne, was a hawkish, influential AFL-CIO vice president, dissent was palpable. An internal poll commissioned by the union in the summer of 1966 showed 56 percent of respondents favoring withdrawal or negotiations, while only 40 percent supported the status quo or escalation. The pollsters concluded that "an excellent Administration record in domestic affairs is completely overridden by what is happening in Southeast Asia."[104]

Such dovish sentiments spurred the nascent peace movement among trade unionists. On March 26, 1966, following a New York City peace march, antiwar trade unionists founded a Trade Union Division of the National Committee for Sane Nuclear Policy (SANE). By the end of the year, the SANE Trade Union Division had grown modestly to four chapters nationwide.[105] Still, in the early years of the war labor's peace factions remained small and uncomfortable with many of the tactics adopted in more radical antiwar circles.

The more immediate concern for AFL-CIO leaders was their liberal allies and early signs of serious fissures in the labor-liberal coalition. Alongside doubts about the geopolitical wisdom of the war, many liberals feared that the expanding conflict would soak up funds earmarked for social and welfare programs. In May 1967, Leon Skull, the national director of the Americans for Democratic Action (ADA), an organization whose membership included many influential trade unionists, loudly voiced his concerns that the costs associated with the war were imperiling social progress at home, a sharp rejoinder to the AFL-CIO guns and butter, more is better outlook. Unless Johnson sought an immediate end to the war, Skull warned, the ADA would consider endorsing another candidate for president in 1968. This marked the beginnings of the "dump Johnson" movement.

Repudiating Skull, in an article entitled "The Coalition Must Remain," Meany ally and ILGWU education director Gus Tyler decried the growing gulf between labor and liberals. He ardently defended Johnson, the war, and guns and butter economics. "It would be monstrous to advocate war as a way to continue the war on poverty, to make mass murder a measure for mass uplift," Tyler acknowledged, but liberals must admit the "bitter facts, the ironic logic" that war often brought both social and economic advances. He noted the gains made by women and blacks during World War II, which had been "due in no small degree to the war itself." Opposition to war might be commendable, he wrote, but to "make a sweeping rejection of the Administration on the grounds that in Vietnam we are losing not only our boys and our good name but also our social programs and our hopes for Negro progress is not permissible."[106]

Tyler's impassioned, although strained, defense of guns-and-butter economics failed to resonate with the ADA. The next year the liberal organization refused to endorse Johnson. The rebuff reflected the growing corrosiveness of Vietnam; the war exposed and aggravated longstanding divisions in the liberal coalition, in the process weakening causes such as full-employment economics and anticommunism—issues at the heart of free trade unionism, but no longer at the heart of liberalism.

"We Are Somewhat Reluctant to Kick off Our Drive"

Facing growing resistance from Walter Reuther, antiwar trade unionists, and dovish liberals, Meany attempted to counterattack. He moved to broaden and better publicize labor's work in South Vietnam. He pushed federation affiliates to establish high-profile mentoring relationships with Vietnamese unions in corresponding trades. The Communications Workers of America responded with a program of exchanges and collaborative work with the Vietnamese Telecommunications Union.[107] The CWA also sponsored "Call Mom," a free telephone program for American soldiers in Vietnam.[108] The steelworkers' union sponsored a chocolate milk drive for South Vietnamese youth, and the IUE funded construction of a resettlement village for refugees.[109] Building on Victor Reuther's trip to Vietnam in early 1965, the auto workers sent three tons of medical supplies to "fully equip an out-patient pediatric clinic which will be one of several to be established by the CVT."[110] A Milwaukee local of the International Union of United Brewery, Flour, Cereal, Soft Drink and Distillery Workers arranged with the Schlitz Brewing Company to ship three thousand dollars' worth of beer to American soldiers in Vietnam, an offer the Pabst Brewing Company immediately matched. General William Westmoreland, commander of U.S. forces in Vietnam, however, deferred the beer shipment due to a dangerous backlog at the port of Saigon.[111]

The backup on Saigon's overwhelmed docks provided another venue for U.S. labor's good works campaign. In early 1966, Thomas Gleason, president of the International Longshoremen's Association, journeyed to Saigon to redesign and modernize the city's antiquated harbors. Using busy U.S.

ports as his model, Gleason reorganized the overwhelmed system. For Vietnamese dockworkers, who had long suffered under the influence of corruption and organized crime (like their American counterparts), he designed an American-style hiring hall. Following Gleason's departure, the ILA stationed three veteran stevedores in Saigon for six months to oversee a training program for dockworkers.[112] Gleason's labors drew favorable publicity, but the entangled realities of South Vietnamese life undermined his work. Government officials ignored his proposals, and within a year corruption, ever a lurking presence, regained its stranglehold.[113]

The emerging antiwar movement also frustrated Meany's public relations campaign. The Los Angeles CWA Local 9578 had planned an extensive "soap drive" for Vietnam as part of the war effort. But a local official warned President Joe Bierne that, with growing controversy over the war, "we are somewhat reluctant to kick off our drive for fear of inadvertently receiving unfavorable publicity in local and state newspapers." National CWA leaders pushed the reticent local ahead and promised to dispatch visiting members of the Vietnamese Telecommunications Union to generate positive publicity.[114]

Growing skepticism about the value of the foreign aid pouring into Vietnam also hampered Meany's campaign to broaden support for the war. In 1966, AID officials acknowledged that roughly 40 percent of U.S. aid to South Vietnam evaporated into a cloud of theft and corruption.[115] "AID Saigon," an official stationed in South Vietnam confidentially told Meany, is "so internally snarled that they accomplish almost nothing in relation to the money spent."[116] Stories about the severe corruption in Saigon began appearing in the American media. Yet Meany and the AFL-CIO remained resolutely undeterred, still wedded to their Vietnam program.

The Keenan Mission

From the outset, the federation's Vietnam program centered on the proposition that victory required political, social, and economic reform as much as military success. Political democracy and a strong, independent labor movement, according to the federation, were indispensable to winning the "hearts and minds" battle. In Saigon, Buu shared such goals, telling the British embassy in 1967 that too often the working class and peasants were simply not involved in the political process, and hence his country "lacked a genuine political understanding at the 'base.'"[117] Free trade unionists thus welcomed the national plebiscite scheduled for the fall of 1967, the final step in the long-anticipated shift to a civilian government.[118]

The CVT shared its American supporters' hopes and cautiously moved to exert its influence. Under political pressure from Americans, Prime Minister

Ky agreed to serve as the vice-presidential candidate on a slate headed by the ambitious General Nguyen Thieu, although the two disliked each other. Fearing that the Thieu and Ky ticket appeared, as Buu explained, "too military," the CVT broke from its policy of political neutrality, allowed its officers to run for office without resigning their union positions, and endorsed a slate of candidates to the upper house (Senate) of the National Assembly.[119] The government immediately responded to the challenge. It disqualified the CVT's slate on a technicality, a familiar tactic of South Vietnamese rulers.[120] Undaunted, Buu joined forces with General Tran Van Don's Farmer-Worker-Soldier (Nong Cong Binh) slate. The coalition hoped to unite a diverse set of working-class interests into a political force.[121] As election day approached, Buu shifted his posture somewhat and personally endorsed Thieu and Ky, by that point the sure winners (although Thieu won with only an embarrassing 35 percent of the vote). The last-minute endorsement kept Buu in relatively good standing after the military ticket's victory.[122]

American supporters of the war touted the election, despite allegations of corruption, as evidence of a rising democracy deserving of U.S. support. Eager to endorse the process, Meany dispatched federation vice president David Sullivan to Saigon as part of the official U.S. delegation that would observe the balloting. Predictably, Sullivan enthusiastically sanctioned the election results and endorsed the new South Vietnamese constitution, which would implement a civilian government. He reported to the State Department his pleasure at "the positive role that the CVT and its members throughout the country have taken in assuring full, intelligent participation of all the people in the critical elections." He added an appeal, urging that Vietnamese civilian employees on U.S. military installations be given full rights to organize.[123]

Sullivan had reason to be pleased. While the CVT had avoided formally endorsing any particular presidential ticket, the Worker-Farmer-Soldier slate managed to carry some twenty-three of fifty provinces and autonomous cities, enough to deem the election a success.[124] Evaluating the recent plebiscite, the CVT's Civic Action Committee saw "reason for hope, even in the political sphere, that the working class in Vietnam will receive all-out support."[125] When Vice President Humphrey sent a list, ordered by preference, of possible Americans to attend President-Elect Thieu's inaugural, George Meany was his first choice.[126]

The CVT, despite the relative success of its political debut, recognized the dangers inherent in assuming a larger civic role. The South Vietnamese government teetered dangerously between autocracy and a struggling democracy. Only American pressure seemed to counterbalance the undemocratic impulses of South Vietnam's leadership. More than ever, Buu and his lieutenants recognized that their ties to U.S. labor proffered a valuable shield as the organization moved tentatively into politics. Meanwhile, the AFL-CIO remained determined to play a greater role promoting the war into which it had poured so much political capital. It continued to push its plans to establish a U.S. labor office in Vietnam, through which it would guide and promote free trade unionism in Southeast Asia. Like the federation's other international programs, AIFLD and ALC, the Asian labor organization would be heavily funded by U.S. tax dollars but administered by American labor. While accepting AID support on such a large scale seemed like a violation of free trade union ideals, the AFL-CIO insisted that it—not the U.S. government—ultimately would control the joint projects.

The federation's belief that victory lay just around the corner heightened its eagerness to work with the CVT. Buu's constant assurances of progress against the Viet Cong, combined with positive official U.S. appraisals, convinced free trade unionists that militarily all was going well.[127] With military victory secured, both Buu and his U.S. supporters believed, the equally crucial second half of the war would begin—the job of nation-building and achieving real social, economic, and political stability for South Vietnam. With much at stake, Buu, despite his reservations, moved to embrace the formation of an Asian-American labor institute to be operated by the AFL-CIO in Saigon.

Following the election of Thieu and Ky, AFL-CIO vice president Joseph Keenan and a delegation drawn from the federation, the Department of Labor, and AID journeyed to South Vietnam. Their objective was to set in motion plans for the new American-Asian labor organization. Keenan, while very much a free trade unionist, shared none of the curt impatience or blunt style of a Kirsch or a Meany. Tall and sporting a permanent smile, the Chicagoan was a respected senior figure among trade unionists, known for his warm, diplomatic demeanor. With such talents in play, there appeared to be little danger of repeating the sequence of misunderstandings that had marred the Kirsch visit two years before. Arriving in October 1967, the Keenan entourage conducted extensive interviews with Buu and other members of the CVT, journeyed into the countryside, and even took an "exhilarating" helicopter ride to the battle front.

Through extensive formal and informal talks with CVT leaders and rank and file unionists, the delegation came to recognize an overburdened organization on the brink of bankruptcy. The confederation had fallen months behind in paying its staffers, and its finances were deeply in the red. Meanwhile, inflation was eating voraciously at CVT resources. When approached regarding aid, Buu, as he had done with Henry Kirsch in 1965, "mystified" the Americans by requesting funding solely for the CVT's small business projects. Slowly, the Americans came to realize that "the CVT does not want to turn to the direct aid approach (even through it needs it) because it does not want to be beholden to either the AFL-CIO or USAID. In Vietnam, one who takes another's money is considered a kept man." While the CVT might accept an AFL-CIO training program, Keenan grasped, it would continue to resist offers of direct aid.[128] On a larger scale, this dilemma haunted and hampered the overall U.S. mission in Southeast Asia, as the crushing American military and foreign aid presence overwhelmed South Vietnam, leaving its citizens little more than bystanders, watching the fate of their country unfold.

As Keenan prepared to leave Vietnam, Buu presented him with a memo requesting aid for training and help developing a permanent "Civic Action Committee" to promote the CVT's political agenda. He cited the AFL-CIO's political action committee, the Committee on Political Education (COPE), as his model.[129] Despite the dangers involved, the recent elections apparently motivated Buu to expand his political work and seek more American help. This was welcome news to his allies in the American labor movement, who had long envisioned the CVT as a political force. Despite the cleavages already exposed by the war, the Keenan mission revived hope. According to both South Vietnamese and American labor, the actual fighting would soon end, allowing the real work of democratizing South Vietnam to begin, guided by a politically active and influential CVT and strengthened by a permanent AFL-CIO presence.

"Planned in Hanoi"

At home, however, free trade union ambitions in Southeast Asia continued to run afoul of a growing antiwar movement among American laborites. On Veteran's Day, November 11, 1967, the Chicago branch of the SANE trade union division hosted the National Labor Assembly for Peace, a national conference of trade unionists opposed to the war. Held at the University of Chicago, attendance surpassed five hundred. Speakers included Victor Reuther, Emil Mazey, Dr. Martin Luther King Jr., Senator Eugene McCarthy, and Harry Bridges. Victor Reuther used the occasion to rail against the labor-CIA nexus and blast what he termed the "fascist corporate unions" sponsored worldwide by the AFL-CIO.[130] Reuther, who during his 1965 trip to Saigon had established and maintained warm relations with the CVT, also angrily denounced the AFL-CIO position on the war.[131] John Kenneth Galbraith then spoke, decrying the growing gulf between labor and "we intellectuals." In the corridors, delegates chattered candidly about "dumping LBJ," but when push came to shove the assemblage stopped short of abandoning the president, who had so cultivated and captivated labor.

Still, a final statement declared the war "immoral" and urged "an immediate and unconditional end to the bombing of North Vietnam."[132]

Several speakers in Chicago invoked the bitter guns or butter debate that was increasingly dividing liberals and labor. Recognizing labor's divided view on the issue, Dr. King treaded lightly when discussing the economic impact of the war. "Theoretically the U.S. has the resources for both [guns and butter]," King diplomatically acknowledged. But the "logic of war" resulted in an "inescapable contradiction between war and social progress at home."[133] Increasingly, however, antiwar liberals were reluctant to grant even King's concession that the economy could support both guns and butter. Claims that the war in Southeast Asia was draining desperately needed funds from social programs became a leading mantra of the antiwar movement. Such rhetoric resonated with many liberals and some laborites, but it also contained an implicit rejection of Keyserling-style expansionist economics. Arguing that the country could not afford both social and military spending, antiwar liberals repudiated the underpinnings of full-employment economics and expedited the rise of a new outlook emphasizing finite resources and limits.

While relatively few unionists attended the Chicago meeting, its spirit managed to infect the biannual AFL-CIO convention, which was held a month later. There, as twelve guest delegates from the CVT, about to receive an education in the bitter politics of the Vietnam War, looked on, Charles Cogen of the American Federation of Teachers stood to propose that the federation refrain from taking an official stance on the war. Leon Davis, president of Local 1199 of the National Union of Hospitals and Health Care Employees, next rose to blast the South Vietnamese government, passionately arguing that Thieu and Ky bore a greater resemblance to Adolf Hitler than Thomas Jefferson (again commandeering the Munich analogy). Another speaker then stood to read the antiwar resolution produced at the peace assembly in Chicago.[134]

The delegates greeted the resolution with a chorus of loud boos. Nonetheless, the reading of the Chicago assembly resolution and the twisted reference to Hitler sent Meany over the edge. As the Vietnam debate drew to a close, Meany, temper boiling over, took to the podium. Branding the antiwar speakers "isolationists," he launched into the history of labor's early opposition to fascism in Germany. Growing irate, Meany then turned to the Chicago peace gathering. "That meeting was planned in Hanoi by a special assembly that went there," he charged. There was no need to hear the resolution read because he had "seen that resolution, every word of it, every line of it, in the *Sunday Worker* two weeks before the meeting was held in Chicago."[135] Meany was hardly alone in his conviction that the antiwar demonstrators were part of a communist plot. His close friend President Johnson had ordered the CIA to conduct "Operation Chaos" to investigate foreign backing of the peace movement. In private conversations, president and plumber freely indulged in their shared suspicions, reinforcing each other's paranoia.[136]

Reaction to Meany's blowup was swift and condemnatory. The *New York Times* asked if, with polls showing increasing numbers of working people opposing the war, Meany wished to label them all "enemy agents."[137] "To put it in extreme charity," wrote liberal columnist James Wechsler in the *New York Post,* "his statement reflected an inordinate capacity for digesting and disseminating falsehoods transmitted by his unscrupulous aides."[138] The National Labor Leadership Assembly for Peace, in its new publication, *Labor Voice for Peace,* demanded an apology.[139] Emil Mazey wrote to Meany directly. "Your conduct in this matter raises serious questions as to your personal integrity and your capacity to lead in the American Labor Movement," he charged.[140]

In fact, Meany's rambling diatribe not only suggested a leadership deeply out of touch but probably energized the peace movement within organized labor. Yet even as the trade union doves grew in numbers they remained outside the mainstream of the general peace movement. Considered radicals within the labor movement, labor's doves were often disconcerted by the unpatriotic excesses of the antiwar movement and disquietingly aware of the growing generation and cultural gap that separated the typical labor union member from the youthful protesters. Emil Mazey, the UAW antiwar activist, bemoaned the antiwar movement's tolerance for "flag burners," whom he saw as part of an unwanted "lunatic fringe." The Labor Leadership Assembly for Peace, unwilling to break completely with LBJ, avoided endorsing any candidate for president in 1968. Nor were there efforts to merge labor's peace movement with any of the larger antiwar organizations.[141]

Culturally, socially, and politically, the late 1960s witnessed the opening of an increasingly painful divide between the middle class and so-called blue-collar workers. Hardly the agents of change, workers seemed increasingly conservative, resenting national discord and embracing a defensive patriotism. Vietnam exacerbated the cleavages. College deferments, more readily available to the middle class, rendered Vietnam a working person's war. Trade unionists more often than their middle-class counterparts had immediate contact with people fighting in Vietnam. During the 1967 AFL-CIO convention debate on Vietnam, for instance, Joseph Curran, president of the National Maritime Union, rose to defend his own son, then fighting in Southeast Asia.[142] When peace activist and UAW executive board member Paul Schrade attempted to make the case for peace at a California union meeting, a member of the audience who had lost a son in Vietnam passionately challenged him. Schrade recalled the confrontation as "very difficult."[143]

Even as the fault lines grew between labor's hawks and doves, both camps felt increasingly alienated by the social, political, and cultural winds sweeping through the country. Soon those winds would take on gale force.

Vietnam, 1968

Throughout the early years of the war, free trade unionists, dismissive of all obstacles and opposition, remained faithful to their Vietnam agenda. Military victory, they believed, lay just around the corner, as did democratization and a brighter future for the struggling labor movement of South Vietnam. However, in the early weeks of 1968 a series of successive blows—beginning with a brutal clash between the CVT and the Saigon government and culminating with the Tet Offensive—shattered the illusions undergirding the federation's commitment to Johnson's war. The ramifications of these events profoundly shook the foundations of free trade unionism.

While the CVT often conducted its affairs with a remarkable militancy—energetically organizing and calling for frequent strikes—it carefully avoided direct confrontation with the South Vietnamese state.[144] Buu realized he was treading a fine line in his dealings with government officials. The fragile edifice of South Vietnamese democracy, he reasoned, was best left untested, especially during wartime. Beginning in mid-1967, however, circumstances set the CVT on a collision course with South Vietnamese officials. That summer, the French-owned Compagnie des Eaux et de l'électricité (CEE) agreed to transfer the operation and control of a large power plant serving Saigon to the South Vietnamese government.[145] The U.S. Agency for International Development, eager to modernize and expand Saigon's antiquated power-producing system, funded the transfer with a grant of thirty-two million dollars. But American good intentions (as had become a pattern by that point) had unexpected consequences.[146] Plant employees anticipated job losses, and the CVT-affiliated Water and Electricity Workers Union demanded a fair severance package for any left unemployed, including several months pay for workers with more than twelve years of experience. For employees who would remain, the union demanded a 12 percent pay hike. According to the South Vietnamese minister of labor, some employees also hoped to assume management positions that had previously been barred to them. When neither severance concessions nor promotions materialized, the workers threatened to strike. Vo Van Tai, the leader of the CVT's militant "young turks," who headed up the

Saigon labor council, aggressively pushed the electrical workers to take a strong stand. Buu obviously preferred moderation but feared stifling the ambitions of militants in his ranks.[147]

The threat of a strike alarmed the South Vietnamese government. Not only might a work stoppage disrupt power distribution during war, but it also threatened chaos as South Vietnam moved toward elections in September 1967. The authorities suspected that VC infiltration lay behind the brewing crisis. Attempting to defuse the situation, Prime Minister Ky promised a fair hearing after election day if the union held off on its strike plans. The electrical workers accepted the offer. But prior to the election, on August 22, a massive daylong power failure struck Saigon. The government held the union responsible. Electrical workers blamed a technical problem, while privately insinuating that national police chief General Nguyen Ngoc Loan had rigged the interruption as part of his campaign to discredit labor. The episode passed, but tensions smoldered.[148]

In December, with the elections over, the electrical workers renewed their demands for a cost of living raise, a Tet (the Vietnamese New Year) bonus, and immediate payment of severance packages. When the plant's new director demurred, the electrical workers scheduled a strike. A work stoppage was a dicey proposition. Militants such as Tai wished to put Vietnam's new leadership on notice and push the country toward democracy. But the South Vietnamese government, with the police and army at its disposal, would be the adversary. A strike by electrical workers, in the midst of a war, with the VC eager to foment chaos, also might cast suspicion on the loyalties of union leaders. The CVT confidentially acknowledged that both VC and Buddhist elements had infiltrated the water and electricity union but insisted the infiltrators had been identified and were under close surveillance.[149] Such assurances hardly satisfied the government.

As tensions simmered, other strikes flared throughout the country. In late 1967, CVT-affiliated workers at Pan American Airlines and Air America walked off their jobs, as did workers at the Brasserie et Glaciers de l'Indochine (BGI), Vietnam's primary beer-brewing operation.[150] To Saigon officials, the confluence of events portended anarchy and possibly a VC-initiated drive to undermine the new government. On December 30, 1967, General Loan issued a communiqué decreeing that the National Police would "no longer refrain from intervention in the growing number of strikes." He ordered his officers to "remove all banners and slogans and to disperse and prevent all gatherings on the streets and sidewalks." He ordered "all workers presently on strike to return to their jobs immediately."[151] An alarmed U.S. embassy warned Washington that while labor friction "is evidence of democracy," the burgeoning crisis "has gone beyond the desirable stage."[152]

General Loan, the CVT had long recognized, was a dangerous and unpredictable character. A former air force pilot and a classmate and close associate of Ky, Loan had assumed near total control of South Vietnam's intelligence and policing agencies. He cracked down ruthlessly on communist infiltrators, regarded democracy as an impediment, and, like so many South Vietnamese officials, was no stranger to corruption. He particularly despised the democratic aspirations of the CVT and harassed trade unionists mercilessly. Laborites delighted in recounting the story of a CVT cadre who defiantly urinated in front of Loan. "This is my territory; this is a free country. I can pee anywhere I want," insisted the instigator as the general violently upbraided him.[153]

Despite Loan's threats and reputation, Tai and the electrical workers refused to back down, perhaps hoping they could rely on the leverage of the American embassy and the AFL-CIO to forestall a clash with police. When the government refused to compromise, on January 11, 1968, one thousand power plant employees walked off their jobs.[154] But there would be no dissuading Loan from a confrontation. In the same way that his ally Prime Minister Ky had cracked down on Buddhist agitation in 1966, Loan was determined to thwart the strike and restore order at all costs.

A few hours after declaring the strike, the CVT Saigon Labor Council arrived at the labor ministry's offices to open negotiations. Suddenly Loan's men burst into the room and arrested six labor leaders, including Vo Van Tai.[155] Word of the arrests spread rapidly, and sympathy strikes broke out all over Saigon. Bus drivers quit their routes and longshoremen abandoned the ports.[156] As workers walked picket lines, South Vietnamese troops took over the power plant and U.S. soldiers unloaded ships.[157]

With tensions boiling, the confrontation lurched toward a climax. Both sides felt their credibility was at stake. Striking workers viewed compromise as tantamount to abandoning democracy. Government officials, conversely, saw a restoration of order and control as essential to the new government and national preservation. Buu, never comfortable with the aggressive tactics of the young turks, met with Vice President Ky (second in command since the recent elections). The CVT president rejected any conditional release of the prisoners. If the government meant to handle the situation in an authoritarian manner, he insisted, it should arrest him as well. Making his point, Buu extended his arms to Ky for handcuffs. Laughing off the gesture, Ky joked: "Enough of your provocations." The vice president turned to his labor minister and asked if there was not some way to resolve the situation. The minister signaled a willingness to compromise.[158]

Neither Ky nor his labor minister, however, seemed able to control Loan and the national police. On January 13, the day after Buu's meeting with Ky, a government decree ordered all electrical workers back to their jobs. When workers ignored the mandate, General Loan moved to end the strike his way. He loaded five garbage trucks with police, directed the convoy to CVT headquarters, and personally delivered "requisitions," ordering workers to go back to their jobs immediately or face arrest. Police ripped down strike banners and arrested any who dared resist. Loan's violent reputation persuaded enough workers to return to their jobs to allow the electrical plant to reopen at full capacity. In the wake of the crackdown, sympathy strikes petered out.[159]

As the police rampaged through Saigon, Buu's second in command, CVT General Secretary Tran Huu Quyen, held a news conference with Buu noticeably absent. While a virtual brother to Buu since their days together in Poulo Condore prison, Quyen was known to be more militant and to sympathize with the CVT's young turks.[160] Before the crowd of reporters, he vowed to sue the government over the strikebreaking and threatened a retaliatory general strike. A new banner strung across CVT headquarters read "Release Our Jailed Leaders Immediately."[161]

Meanwhile, pressure was building on Buu and his organization. With the upcoming Tet festivities, the CVT feared a public backlash from city residents with little appetite for a protracted strike and its accompanying power outages during their holiday.[162] Ominously, Radio Hanoi began broadcasting support for the strikers. The South Vietnamese government and "capitalist" employers, according to Hanoi, "resorted to most brutal tactics to thwart the very legitimate struggle of the workers."[163] Despite the determination of Quyen and the young turks, Buu sensed that the strike was spiraling out of control. Seeking to resolve the crisis before the Tet holiday, on January 16 he ordered remaining strikers back to work. In return, the Saigon government agreed to a 12 percent pay increase and General Loan released the labor leaders still in his custody, including Vo Van Tai.[164] Still, while the government dropped the charges against five of the six, Tai, temporarily free, remained subject to trial.[165]

Watching from the sidelines, AFL-CIO leaders felt intense discomfort and helplessness. They were furious—"mad as hornets," according to labor journalist John Herling—over Saigon's handling of the strike. But federation leaders worried that a public denunciation would only lend credence to the antiwar movement's portrait of South Vietnam as a brutal, corrupt autocracy.[166] Likewise, Meany feared compromising the CVT at a time when, if nothing else, it appeared to be acting autonomously. Given its uneasy relationship with the CVT, the federation resisted overstepping its boundaries by publicly coming to the aid of its Vietnamese counterpart.[167]

The AFL-CIO's silence provoked its critics both on the Left and the Right. *Business Week* ran an article on the Saigon strike, noting that for once Meany had remained "publicly silent" on an issue related to Vietnam in spite of his frequent declarations that freely operating labor unions represented the essential distinction between north and south. Meanwhile, the left-leaning *Missouri Teamster,* a mouthpiece for Teamster vice president Harold Gibbons, observed acidly that "the latest suppression of the labor movement in South Vietnam is a unique expression of how freedom operates in Vietnam."[168]

While awkwardly silent in public, behind the scenes Meany pressed his allies in the Johnson administration to intervene. Seeking to appease his friend, Secretary of State Rusk ordered Ambassador Ellsworth Bunker to confront Nguyen Van Thieu, the new president of South Vietnam, regarding the strike and labor relations. At a tense meeting on January 25, 1968, Bunker stressed to Thieu the importance of both U.S. and South Vietnamese labor to the war effort. American labor, the ambassador explained, had been a consistent supporter and "it was important to keep it that way." Thieu acknowledged that he had been flooded with complaints about recent events but blamed the strike on young militants in the CVT and claimed that communists had infiltrated some trade unions. He added that he remained particularly suspicious of Vo Van Tai, who was widely rumored to be a Viet Cong agent. The president expressed respect for Buu and promised to establish a "labor and management consultative committee" to resolve future differences. Reporting his meeting to Rusk, Bunker added, "Thieu's private assurance and indication of attitude will be useful to you with the AFL-CIO leadership."[169] The reassurances of Thieu and Bunker may have brought some solace to the AFL-CIO, but behind the scenes diplomacy did little to erase the image of a paralyzed American labor federation, dogmatically bound to support the war while democracy in South Vietnam seemed to be unraveling.

Forever optimistic, Ambassador Bunker also assured Rusk that despite the strikes and arrests the CVT, by demonstrating that it was no "puppet of the government," would emerge stronger. He advised Washington to disregard a recent VC broadcast warning that "[o]n the eve of Tet, the stormy fire of revolutionary struggle of our workers and laborers will kindle fiercely right in the cities." There existed, he confidently assured his superiors, no evidence of a "fire raging."[170] In terms of the recent labor strife, he advised: "There is time for healing, to occur before, during and after the festive days that mark Tet."[171]

Five days after his meeting with Thieu, U.S. marines awoke Ambassador Bunker at 3:00 a.m. with the news that his embassy was under attack. With no time to spare, the ambassador fled in his bathrobe. Tet, the Vietnamese New Year, proved anything but a "time for healing." Under the cover of the holiday, the Viet Cong launched a massive push into South Vietnam's urban centers. During the attack, VC agents specifically targeted working-class neighborhoods for propaganda campaigns and singled out CVT officers for assassination.[172] The homes of more than a thousand trade unionists were destroyed. In the midst of the battle, the entire world glimpsed the brutality of Police Chief Loan, when he summarily executed a suspected terrorist in front of cameramen.[173]

As Saigon came under fire, Buu briefly considered going into hiding and closing down the CVT headquarters. Militant CVT members argued that in light of the government's recent strikebreaking the confederation should assume a stony silence, sending the authorities a pointed message. But Buu and the CVT leadership decided to focus on the immediate terrorist threat. The organization issued a sharp condemnation of the "criminal action of the enemy."[174] Buu offered to organize his most trusted men into an armed civilian commando unit. To his consternation, the government refused.[175]

After absorbing the initial onslaught, the CVT sent the AFL-CIO a short telegram: "We at the CVT are safe and sound. We appeal urgently to the free world union organizations to aid the workers and other Vietnamese who were savagely attacked by the communists."[176] As the siege lifted, Secretary of State Rusk, hoping to use the CVT for political purposes, asked Bunker to secure from Buu a "circular letter to his contacts here and elsewhere in which he would describe the improved situation in Vietnam and his somewhat optimistic view of the immediate future for Vietnamese labor."[177] But, as sporadic VC attacks continued and with memories of government strikebreaking still fresh, Buu demurred.[178]

In the days following the attack, the AFL-CIO strove to put the best face on the reversals suffered by Saigon and the CVT. The federation issued a statement insisting that "the terrorist campaign has only hardened the resolve of Vietnamese labor to resist terror and oppression," and vowing to "pledge our full support to the President in his determination to halt Communist aggression against the people of South Vietnam."[179] Answering Buu's pleas for support, Meany pledged substantial AFL-CIO resources to rebuild the facilities destroyed by the Tet Offensive.[180]

Jay Lovestone and Irving Brown, however, recognized that while the VC maneuver had fallen short of cracking the South Vietnam regime the tide had shifted. Characteristically comparing the New Year's offensive to "the Bolshevik call for the overthrow of the Kerensky government," Lovestone lamented that the Americans had "underestimated the strength of the enemy." He acknowledged that "[w]hat has happened is no doubt a political blow to us."[181] In March, the AFL-CIO dispatched Irving Brown to Saigon to help the CVT rebuild. The veteran agent tried to cast the Tet Offensive as heartening proof that in spite of the attack "the government existed, it withstood the betrayal and its stability was reaffirmed." But in the wake of the offensive he admitted Saigon had lost the "initiative" to the Viet

Cong. "Everyone talks about preparing for the VC," he lamented. "No one talks about taking the war to the other side."[182] Like many Americans, Lovestone and Brown concluded that the Tet Offensive represented a setback.[183]

During the communist attack, Buu and the CVT had remained loyal to the government.[184] Yet, in the suspicious atmosphere following Tet, the South Vietnamese police struck out again at the CVT. Roughly two weeks after the initial uprising, General Loan rearrested Vo Van Tai, whom the police chief always insisted had communist leanings. Loan also arrested Buu's close associate and cofounder of the CVT, Tran Huu Quyen, no doubt in retaliation for his recent public condemnation of police strikebreaking. Ostensibly, the arrests were meant to protect the pair from assassination or kidnaping at the hands of the VC, but the police action mystified Buu, who could only speculate that Loan "must be insane."[185] He sent a long formal protest to President Thieu, recounting the CVT's anticommunism and noting that while "all of us were working for the salvation of the nation, the National Police arrested Messrs. Quyen and Tai."[186] Still, with a citywide nighttime curfew and other restrictions in effect in the wake of continued fighting, Buu had little leverage.[187] Privately, he complained bitterly to his friend General Lansdale. South Vietnam's workers and peasants, he claimed, had reacted with "white hot" anger at the bloody communist attacks during the Vietnamese New Year. Workers were like "hot iron ready to be shaped by the government." Arresting the labor leaders had effectively "doused them with cold water."[188]

The detention of Tai and Quyen increasingly emerged as a public relations problem for Washington, already reeling from the Tet Offensive. Stories about the arrests appeared in the *New York Times, Washington Post,* and elsewhere. The AFL-CIO also applied pressure, threatening the State Department with a public denunciation of the South Vietnamese government.[189] Meanwhile Assistant Secretary of State William Bundy, preparing for a scheduled television appearance on *Meet the Press,* worried that he would be "heckled" by journalists about the jailed labor leaders. "You can't run a war on TV deadlines, but this one is hitting rather hard in some quarters," he cabled the Saigon embassy. "It would be particularly helpful if [the] labor leaders were released by then."[190]

Again Ambassador Bunker moved to intercede "forcibly" with Thieu. In a private meeting, he explained "the unfortunate consequences the detention of the labor leaders can have in the U.S." and reminded Thieu of the CVT's loyalty during the Tet Offensive. The ambassador's direct appeal brought Quyen's release (meeting Bundy's TV deadline).[191] But Tai, whose severe demeanor and grim determination had aroused particular disdain and rumors of links to the VC, languished in jail. Pouring salt on the wound, only days after Quyen's release General Loan suddenly arrested Saigon CVT chairman To Thanh Tuyen along with another important CVT official. At a complete loss, Buu could only postulate that the arrests were an act of revenge for the American intervention to gain Quyen's release.[192] Behind the scenes, the arrests most likely related to a power struggle between newly elected President Thieu and the powerful internal security chief Loan, whose loyalties lay with his fellow airman, Ky, who had been demoted to vice president.[193]

In Washington, the AFL-CIO continued to mobilize its resources on behalf of Tai and the other imprisoned labor leaders. At a meeting of the labor advisory committee to AID, Lovestone and Joseph Keenan angrily protested General Loan's harassment and the continuing incarceration of CVT leaders. When Philip Habib, deputy assistant secretary for East Asian affairs, suggested that the solution lay with President Thieu and tried to change the subject, Keenan strongly objected and turned the discussion back to the arrests.[194]

Fearing for the fate of its entire Vietnamese agenda, the AFL-CIO again dispatched its "point man," Irving Brown, to Saigon. Brown wasted little time, meeting with Ky, Prime Minister Loc, and President Thieu, whom he pressured "hard but politely on the Tai matter."[195] He then held an hour and a half meeting with General Loan. No doubt, the American agent was characteristically blunt—probably threatening. Forty-eight hours after his encounter with Brown, Loan released Tai, fifteen pounds lighter following his ordeal. The freed Saigon labor leader immediately sent personal thanks to both Meany and Brown and seemed sincerely grateful.[196] But Tai's lean frame was almost a physical embodiment of the damage done to both his country and the CVT's cause over the previous weeks.

The Saigon electrical workers' strike in January 1968 had abruptly snapped several years of optimism about South Vietnam. In the course of a few short weeks, the facade of democracy, so carefully cultivated by U.S. officials, lay in shreds. The CVT appeared to be at the mercy of a draconian and autocratic state and a dangerous Saigon police force. Meanwhile, the Tet attack, while a tactical defeat for the Viet Cong, portended a dire military situation. No longer would it be a neat, organized, limited war nearing a satisfactory conclusion. Most serious was the profoundly disillusioning impact of these events on the American public. Before 1968, the AFL-CIO had faced a membership with little enthusiasm for the war. After 1968, its twin tasks of helping the CVT and supporting the war effort would prove an ever greater challenge.

6 Free Fall, 1968–69

If the mid-1960s, despite unprecedented prosperity and political power, proved unfulfilling and anxiety ridden for organized labor, a downward spiral following the Tet Offensive quickly confirmed that all was not well with the free trade union agenda, neither in Vietnam nor at home. Indeed, over the course of roughly a year, the fortunes of free trade unionism went into free fall. In quick succession, the Democrats lost the White House, Walter Reuther pulled his UAW out of the AFL-CIO, and Meany finally divorced his organization from the ICFTU. The repercussions of these painful events reverberated through national and international labor, leaving wounds that would linger for decades.

Defying bad omens everywhere, Meany remained wedded to his agenda in Vietnam. But even there he suffered setbacks. The CVT, just as determined to maintain a proud facade of independence as American labor, reacted with deep ambivalence to the creation of a permanent AFL-CIO labor advisory office in Saigon. Soon relations between U.S. and South Vietnamese labor grew strained, adding to the mounting woes faced by free trade unionists.

Losing Ground

For free trade unionists, the tumult surrounding the Saigon electrical workers' strikes and the subsequent Tet Offensive in the early weeks of 1968 opened a year of unnerving setbacks. At the causal center of this annus horribilis lay the Vietnam War. By the end of 1968, the war had poisoned the Democratic Party coalition, fomented the first serious challenge to U.S.

labor unity since the formation of the CIO in the 1930s, and driven a wedge between the AFL-CIO and international labor. Over the course of roughly eighteen months, the AFL-CIO went from an organization at the center of national and international power to one increasingly isolated from its former liberal allies, international labor, and key segments of the American trade union movement.

From the beginning, the 1968 presidential campaign portended trouble. Frayed and divided by the Vietnam War, the liberal coalition, which had elected LBJ so overwhelmingly in 1964, veered toward collapse. While the core of organized labor stood solidly behind the president, a growing group of liberal antiwar activists frantically searched for an alternative. In late 1967 came the first signs of serious, Vietnam-induced fissures in the Democratic coalition. The leadership of Americans for Democratic Action, whose membership included numerous high-ranking union leaders, announced that short of immediate negotiations to end the war it would abandon LBJ and back an antiwar candidate. When requisite developments failed to materialize, the ADA threw its support to Senator Eugene McCarthy. Refusing to abandon the president and his war, one by one, led by Vice Chairman Leon Keyserling, trade unionists resigned from the ADA in protest. Board members I. W. Abel, president of the United Steelworkers of America; Louis Stulberg, president of the ILGWU; and Joseph Bierne, president of the CWA, all resigned. Calling it "one of the saddest days of my life," ILGWU lobbyist Evelyn Dubrow, a founding member of the ADA, also withdrew. Walter Reuther remained on the organization's board but suspended the UAW's yearly contribution of twelve thousand dollars.[1]

Through the jolt of the Tet Offensive and the president's near defeat in the New Hampshire primary, mainstream trade unionists stayed loyally beside Johnson, even as liberals jumped ship in droves. The president's sudden withdrawal from the presidential campaign on March 30, 1968, shocked the AFL-CIO leadership. "I don't know how long it will take me to recover from the atomic bomb which President Johnson hurled," wrote Lovestone to Meany. "Frankly, I am at a loss to understand the move."[2]

Stunned, labor leaders scrambled to find a new candidate. Some, including key members of the UAW's Executive Board, lined up behind Robert F. Kennedy, and several joined the New York senator's campaign staff.[3] But to free trade unionists Kennedy was suspect as a dove. And Eugene McCarthy offered even slimmer pickings; the Minnesotan was both a dove and a moderate on many social and economic issues.[4] Desperate, Meany begged Vice President Hubert Humphrey, the only Democratic candidate he saw as committed to the AFL-CIO's agenda in Vietnam, to enter the race. When Humphrey temporized, Meany, bucking the federation's tradition of neutrality during the primary process, personally walked the two blocks from his office to Humphrey's to urge the vice president to run.[5] Seeking to further press his choice, Meany publicly declared his support for Humphrey on April 4, in advance of the vice president's official announcement.[6] Antiwar trade unionists, angered by Meany's undemocratic rush to endorse Humphrey, warned that his action would alienate former allies and box organized labor into a corner should the vice president fail to garner the party's nomination. The Bronx plumber remained characteristically unapologetic.[7]

With the assassinations of Martin Luther King Jr. and Robert Kennedy, by June the campaign took on an increasingly nightmarish quality. Nonetheless, at the violence-marred Chicago convention Humphrey pulled together enough delegates to win the party's nomination. Still, his candidacy aroused little excitement in the Democratic Party. Only organized labor, inspired by Humphrey's commitment to uphold Johnson's Vietnam policy abroad and social activism at home, enthusiastically rushed to the vice president's corner.

Besides Humphrey's lethargic support among liberals, another factor deeply disturbed organized labor. Polls showed significant rank and file support for the populist, backlash candidacy of Alabama governor George Wallace. Late in the campaign, surveys showed Wallace taking 25 percent of the labor vote in Pennsylvania, 32 percent in Connecticut, and close to 50 percent in Maryland. Wallace's appeal clearly sprang from his opposition to civil rights reform, an increasingly touchy issue for organized labor.[8] But the governor's hard line on Vietnam—reflected in his selection of ultrahawk General Curtis LeMay as his running mate—posed an equally troublesome dilemma for the AFL-CIO. Wallace's hawkish agenda, which called for an unlimited war against North Vietnam, including the use of nuclear weapons, clearly appealed to unionists who were frustrated by the pace of the conflict. Like Meany, the Alabamian seemed to revel in bitter, mocking attacks on antiwar protesters, intellectuals, and liberals. To free trade unionists, Wallace seemed to be stealing their best rhetoric and fusing it with a combustible populist poison directed against civil rights, big government, and liberalism.

Recognizing a serious threat, Meany and the AFL-CIO unleashed a massive public relations drive to forestall the Wallace candidacy and elect Humphrey. Meany poured AFL-CIO funds and organizing efforts into the Humphrey campaign and pressed affiliates to do the same. President I. W. Abel of the Steelworkers sent anti-Wallace letters to 1.2 million members.[9] All told, labor spent an unprecedented sixty million dollars on the presidential election. The AFL-CIO public relations director, Albert Zack, described the federation's campaign as "the most all-out effort that the labor movement has ever made."[10] Against all odds, Humphrey staged a startling comeback in the final days of the campaign.

The federation's pro-Humphrey drive, however, proved as much a burden as a blessing to the Minnesotan. While AFL-CIO sponsorship kept Humphrey in the race, his dependence on federation support deterred him from softening his stance on Vietnam. With every move to distance himself from the Johnson administration's Vietnam policies, the vice president's poll numbers rose, yet he simultaneously risked alienating his primary, most loyal supporters. In November, Humphrey lost and Nixon prepared to move into the White House. While Wallace also went down to defeat, the Alabamian received nine million votes.

The agonizing campaign of 1968 exposed deep fissures in American politics. Organized labor enthusiastically backed Humphrey while many liberals remained indifferent. The dissolution of the civil rights movement and demands for "black power" alienated many whites prone to voting liberal. Meanwhile, in the wake of Vietnam, large segments of the old Democratic coalition abandoned anticommunism. In their insistence that the American economy could not afford the war in Vietnam, antiwar liberals also deserted the principles central to full-employment economics, the tenet that *all* public spending generated growth. Besides buoying the Wallace candidacy and ravaging Humphrey, the war in Southeast Asia crippled the Democratic Party. The AFL-CIO was alone in holding down the fort in 1968. And even within the fort there were disgruntled soldiers.

Politics was hardly the only arena infected by the corrosiveness of Vietnam. Tormented by the unpopular war, Walter Reuther, long discontented within the AFL-CIO, moved to go his own way. During the 1968 Democratic primary, Reuther first supported Johnson and then, after flirting with Robert Kennedy, shifted his support to Humphrey.[11] But the war ate at the UAW chief. "I am not sure it isn't as important to win the war at home than it is to win the war in Vietnam," he ruminated early in the presidential campaign.[12] As Reuther wavered, many on his UAW staff, propelled by antiwar sentiment, defected to Kennedy's antiwar campaign. UAW board member Paul Schrade was at Kennedy's side when the senator was killed in June.

While Reuther vacillated and searched for a new relevancy in changing times, he became convinced that his continuing relationship with the AFL-CIO and its obstinate support for the war was holding him back from his yet to be realized destiny. In March 1968, he demanded a special AFL-CIO convention to "modernize and revitalize" the labor movement. Without such a convocation, Reuther vowed, the UAW would exit the federation. Meany—for whom acceptance of Reuther's demand would represent an acknowledgment of the deficiencies of his leadership—slyly offered to hold the special convention but only if the UAW agreed to attend and support any "democratically arrived at" decisions.[13] Knowing full well that Meany would control the majority of delegates, Reuther quickly dropped the idea and pulled his UAW out of the AFL-CIO.

Initially, Reuther hoped to weld together an alliance of former CIO unions to challenge Meany's leadership. But even among his allies he found little support.[14] Outside the federation and increasingly isolated, he contacted the Teamsters. In the late 1950s, in the wake of revelations of immense corruption, Meany had ousted the renegade two-million-member Teamsters union from the AFL-CIO and it had remained very much a pariah. With its reputation for hawkishness on Vietnam, conservatism, and vice, the Teamsters seemed a strange bedfellow for the progressively minded UAW. Still, liberal elements lay within the ranks of the Teamsters, and, with the Meany-Reuther feud grounded in personal animosity, a UAW-Teamsters alliance offered the added incentive of being sure to infuriate the temperamental ex-plumber.

In the summer of 1968, Reuther and Teamster president Frank Fitzsimmons announced plans to form the Alliance for Labor Action (ALA). Although from the beginning it proved a troubled affair, during its brief life the ALA put forth a serious agenda and articulated a broad, updated vision of labor as a social and economic force. In May 1969, at its founding convention, the ALA—armed with a large grant from the UAW and a membership of roughly 3.5 million—called for a massive push to organize the unorganized, expand the War on Poverty, and promote social and economic justice.

The ALA could not escape the divisiveness of the Vietnam War, however. Reuther might have preferred a more staunch antiwar position, but he was determined to preserve his uneasy coalition, which meant that he must pacify hawkish elements within both the UAW and the Teamsters. At its founding convention, the ALA called for an end to the war but avoided elaboration; hawks and doves alike, interpreting it their own way, embraced the vacuous statement.[15] Yet divisions between the two allied unions remained palpable. When representatives from both organizations gathered to plan Vietnam Moratorium Day activities, UAW staffers wore peace buttons while the Teamsters sported American flag pins.[16] As they attempted to craft an antiwar resolution, deep divisions quickly surfaced, assuaged only when UAW representatives appeased the Teamster hawks by agreeing to add a denunciation of violence by antiwar demonstrators.[17]

Despite the entrenched pro-war elements, Reuther managed to work closely with dovish Teamsters such as Vice President Harold Gibbons to coordinate ALA activism. Reuther played on the Teamster leadership's desire for respectability to rally support for progressive initiatives that included an organizing drive in the South and an anti-drug-abuse campaign. Nevertheless, the Teamster-UAW marriage remained strained.

In addition, the ALA faced an angry, spurned Meany, who was outraged by the challenge to his authority and the threat of a return to the labor wars of the 1930s. Meany and other federation officials also worried about the impact of the bitter feud on their operations overseas. Robert Walkinshaw, the Asian labor adviser at the State Department, had roots in the UAW and close ties to the Reuthers. Officials in the AFL-CIO fretted that he would undermine their Vietnam initiatives.[18] Frantic to halt the ALA, Meany threatened any AFL-CIO union joining the new organization with immediate disaffiliation.[19] When the small Chemical Workers Union joined Reuther's alliance, the AFL-CIO quickly expelled the group.[20]

With Meany on the warpath and the ALA divided over Vietnam, the future of the alliance was precarious. Walter Reuther's death in an airplane crash on May 9, 1970, robbed the ALA of much of its ambition and energy, and the awkward alliance quickly collapsed. While fleeting and hampered severely by Vietnam War politics, the ALA had, in many ways, presented a real threat to the AFL-CIO and free trade unionism by charting a fresh, innovative course for organized labor during difficult times.

As 1968 wore on, the AFL-CIO also faced significant challenges abroad. Again the war in Southeast Asia proved the corrosive agent. By the late 1960s, the ICFTU, the international labor organization heavily subsidized by the AFL-CIO, had grown increasingly critical of the Vietnam War. In the fall of 1967, the ICFTU Executive Board issued a statement "deploring the grave loss of life and the material destruction" caused by the war. It called for negotiations and the withdrawal of foreign troops.[21] Already tense, relations between the AFL-CIO and the ICFTU collapsed under the stress of the increasingly controversial war.

As the ICFTU took a more critical line on Vietnam, its Soviet bloc rival, the World Federation of Trade Unions, whose membership included the North Vietnamese-dominated Vietnam Trade Union Federation, launched its own well-coordinated attack on U.S. involvement in Southeast Asia. In April 1968, the WFTU convened for an "extraordinary session" in Moscow to promote the "intensification and extension of solidarity with the people of Vietnam and condemnation of this aggression." Despite previous indifference to the plight of labor in Vietnam, the WFTU's General Council announced "a world-wide collection . . . for the benefit of the working men and women of Vietnam" and plans to publish a biannual bulletin entitled *The World Federation of Trade Unions and Vietnam*. The banner headline across the premier edition of the new publication read "Americans Out of Vietnam! Vietnam for the Vietnamese!"[22]

Incensed by weakening international support and the WFTU's new activism on Vietnam, the AFL-CIO grew ever more impatient with the ICFTU. Since the Russian revolution, the AFL had persistently stood against communication between free, democratic trade unions and the state-controlled unions behind the iron curtain. Since its founding in 1949, the ICFTU and most other major trade union organizations in the West had honored Meany's boycott, perhaps more out of economic necessity (dependence on AFL-CIO funding) than ideological commitment. But, as its protracted engagement in Vietnam continued to discredit the United States, labor leaders in both America and Europe began advocating liberalized contact between Eastern bloc nations and the West.[23] In West Germany, newly elected chancellor Willy Brandt began pursuing "Ostpolitik" initiatives aimed at reconciliation with East Germany. Following the chancellor's lead, the German Labor Federation seized on early signs of détente and established relations with the Soviet-controlled WFTU and trade unions in East Germany.[24] Much to the consternation of free trade unionists, pressure built within the ICFTU to pursue such contacts.

Walter Reuther had never been comfortable with the AFL-CIO quarantine of Eastern bloc unions. As early as 1959, he had defied Meany by meeting with visiting Soviet premier Nikita Khrushchev. Free at last from AFL-CIO constraints, Reuther now moved to openly explore trade union exchanges across the iron curtain.[25] In the fall of 1968, he announced that he would independently affiliate the 1.3 million members of the UAW with the ICFTU. Presumably the autoworkers would bring to the ICFTU an independent American perspective critical of the Vietnam War and comfortable with East-West labor contacts.[26] Meany reacted to the news with predictably unbridled fury. He threatened to withdraw the 13.8 million members of the AFL-CIO from the international organization should it accept the UAW into its ranks.[27]

When the ICFTU defied his threat, Meany, on February 20, 1969, spitefully withdrew the AFL-CIO from the ICFTU.[28] Several weeks after the announcement, the UAW broke the twenty-five-year-old no-contact policy between American and Eastern European unions when Victor Reuther led a UAW delegation on an official visit to Czechoslovakia.[29] By the early 1970s, interaction between unions from Eastern and Western Europe had become commonplace. While free trade unionists remained wedded to a primal, uncompromising cold war, the Reuthers, along with growing numbers of U.S. trade unionists and policymakers, embraced détente, seeking new international arrangements beyond the East-West struggle. Increasingly, the AFL-CIO found itself alone at home and abroad.

Meany's withdrawal from the ICFTU, a byproduct of American involvement in Southeast Asia, quickly had repercussions in Vietnam itself. Meany had acted partly in defense of the Vietnam War, but in Saigon, when Buu was informed of the federation's decision, he reacted with "dismay" and fretted that his organization, along with the AFL-CIO, was becoming isolated from world labor.[30] In the late 1960s, Buu had more than enough cause for concern. On every formerly secure front—internationally, within the Democratic Party, and within a once unified domestic labor movement—his free trade union allies seemed to be losing ground.

"Whatever You Do in Vietnam, Do Not Compromise the Autonomy of the AFL-CIO"

In 1968, American organized labor was divided and in disarray. But this was a modest crisis compared to what the CVT faced in Vietnam in the aftermath of the Tet Offensive. For the first time the Viet Cong had attacked urban centers, specifically targeting the CVT in the process. With the initial assault, military commanders pulled U.S. and South Vietnamese forces from the countryside to defend the cities, exposing in turn the CVT's peasant-based organizations to Viet Cong intimidation. Even after the first wave of attacks on the cities, sporadic Viet Cong violence in Saigon and continuing friction with the South Vietnamese government "paralyzed the CVT movement during the first six months of 1968," according to the organization's official newspaper. Violence forced unionists to shelve long-standing projects and focus on relief and rebuilding.

Despite the havoc it wreaked in South Vietnam, the Viet Cong had nearly destroyed itself with the unprecedented offensive. In later years, North Vietnamese contingents were forced to take over fighting in the south for their fallen VC comrades. By mid-1968, the VC had retreated, and once again U.S. and government of South Vietnam (GVN) forces expanded into the countryside. During this time, the CVT found its relations with Saigon authorities improving. Following his controversial execution of a suspect at the height of the Tet Offensive and a severe injury suffered during a Viet Cong rocket attack, General Loan retired as Saigon police chief. A tremendous relief to the CVT, Loan's exit removed one of its most dangerous and persistent enemies.[31] With the VC severely weakened and stability returned, the CVT found new opportunities for organizing and expansion. "The sky was bright again after several months of tempest," a CVT official explained.[32] The South Vietnamese economy entered its most productive period in history, and the CVT enjoyed corresponding success.

Despite its trials at home, the AFL-CIO eagerly sought to help the CVT regain momentum. Free trade unionists, defying mounting public pessimism about Vietnam, moved to launch the long-awaited Asian-American Free Labor Institute (AAFLI), a permanent AFL-CIO advisory office in South Vietnam. Yet this initiative, like virtually everything else during U.S. labor's plague-ridden year of 1968, rapidly backfired.

An outgrowth of Joseph Keenan's 1967 mission, AAFLI initially was to focus on Vietnam and eventually expand to all of Asia. The aim was to provide training seminars, support services, and expert advice to Vietnamese trade unionists—in short, to guide the CVT toward the free trade union ideal. Through a special agreement with the Johnson administration, USAID agreed to subsidize roughly 90 percent of AAFLI expenses.[33] Thus, USAID and U.S. labor were now full-scale partners in Vietnam.

On February 29, 1968, Fernand Audie, formerly the Asian representative of the Federation of Commercial, Clerical and Technical Employees, arrived as AAFLI's Vietnam "country director." His initial instructions from the AFL-CIO reflected the federation's unease in the role of partner with the U.S. government. "Whatever you do in Vietnam, do not compromise the autonomy of the AFL-CIO," he was told.[34] Employed by an organization preoccupied with maintaining a facade of independence, despite its dependence on government funding, and charged with aiding an organization that—despite its need—often eschewed outside help, Audie faced a daunting assignment. In Saigon, he hired a staff of ten (one American and nine Vietnamese) and set up the AAFLI offices inside the CVT headquarters compound. Within several months, he had established training programs for CVT cadres and, in a highly publicized ceremony, distributed the first of ten tractors to CVT farmers.[35]

While the CVT and Buu initially welcomed AAFLI, strains quickly developed. The AFL-CIO intended AAFLI to be a permanent and independent source of support and expert advice to the CVT. Early on, its most experienced agents—Irving Brown and Harry Goldberg—had proven indispensable to South Vietnamese labor in times of crisis. Both had forged close bonds with Buu and other CVT officials. But American labor struggled to find representatives with comparable skills. Buu and the leadership of the CVT were deeply sensitive to the protocols of patience and respect inherent in Asian culture, sensitivities that were intensified by Vietnam's painful colonial past.

At times, Buu could exhibit signs of the xenophobia quite common among Vietnamese. He particularly resented foreign encroachments on his organization's independence. His interpreter and aide Nguyen Duc Dat counseled Americans meeting Buu for the first time to simply listen and learn rather than dictate. Few, Dat lamented, took his advice. Those who connected most effectively with Buu, including Irving Brown, Harry Goldberg, General Edward Lansdale, and USAID labor counselor Emil Lindahl, seemed instinctively conscious of Vietnamese etiquette and customs.[36] Others, such as Henry Kirsch (during his 1965 visit), proved too abrasive to suit Buu.

With a limited pool of qualified candidates and the most talented assigned to Europe, the AFL-CIO hardly could hope to find a perfect match for each mission. Language requirements further narrowed the candidates. Fernand Audie quickly proved to be the wrong choice to lead the sensitive mission of establishing the AAFLI in Vietnam.

Long before Audie's arrival, Buu and the CVT had established close working relations with USAID's labor division (AID/LAB) in Saigon. The AID/LAB staffers generally came from trade union backgrounds and received commissions on the recommendation of the AFL-CIO. Its Saigon headquarters sat conveniently across the street from those of the CVT. Buu customarily turned to his contacts in AID/LAB for advice. In addition, AID contracted with the CVT to conduct its manpower training programs in South Vietnam. Such arrangements provided the CVT with much needed sources of cash. South Vietnamese organized labor and USAID were further intertwined when the CVT organized Vietnamese workers employed by AID.[37]

Audie's arrival disrupted this relationship. It imposed a new layer of bureaucracy between Buu and his contacts at AID/LAB. A stickler for regulations, Audie insisted that Buu go through AAFLI for money or assistance. Buu resented the intrusion. "Considerable time and effort has been expended by the AAFLI-Vietnam Country Director [Audie] in obtaining the necessary cooperation of the CVT president," admitted Audie in his first report.[38] Buu clearly preferred his familiar contacts in the labor division of AID. While the AFL-CIO regarded AAFLI as an independent body free of government interference and focused solely on supporting and servicing Vietnamese organized labor, Buu, fully cognizant of the financial arrangements involved, saw AAFLI more as a subsidiary of AID. While appreciating the AFL-CIO's interest and the promise of additional support, Buu hardly viewed AAFLI as an autonomous entity.[39]

Audie's demanding attitude and cold personality also annoyed Buu and other CVT officers. The American insisted on sticking closely to his job description. He would deal strictly with trade union activities, a narrow mandate compared to Irving Brown's eagerness to dabble in everything from politics to military planning. When two of AAFLI's Vietnamese staffers began organizing for a political alliance endorsed by the CVT, Audie feared his organization would attract accusations of interference in the internal politics of South Vietnam and summarily fired the pair. Buu was incensed. He went immediately to USAID with his complaints. Eventually Deputy Ambassador Samuel Berger had to mediate the dispute.[40] Relations between the CVT and AAFLI then further deteriorated. Audie was accused of "speculating in the market and having an affair with a Vietnamese woman."[41] In his summary of CVT activities in 1968, General Secretary Tran Huu Quyen avoided all reference to AAFLI, an omission Berger ascribed to Quyen's "antipathy toward the AFL-CIO's regional organization, an antipathy which is common knowledge within the CVT and amongst the CVT's many foreign and Vietnamese observers."[42]

Audie not only clashed with Buu and the CVT, but he also managed to alienate AID/LAB. In dispatches from Vietnam, Audie bitterly lamented the absence of a sharper delineation in responsibilities between AID/LAB and the AFL-CIO's AAFLI. The labor division, he bristled, should be confined to working only with the South Vietnamese labor ministry and "should keep the h—l out of CVT activities and let us work with the CVT exclusively." Audie fumed that AID/LAB had waged a campaign of harassment against AAFLI and himself. Citing the AFL-CIO's policy of not accounting for grants of government money, Audie refused AID demands for audits, further exacerbating the tension.[43]

Finding the AAFLI representative a prickly personality, AID/LAB followed Buu's lead and essentially ostracized him. In response, an enraged Audie accused AID/LAB of stealing AAFLI's initiatives for its own use. "Pass us all your ideas on paper and we'll use them for our own projects and cut your budget," ranted Audie of his colleagues at AID/LAB.[44] He also brazenly dismissed Buu's coolness to the AFL-CIO Saigon mission. The CVT chief, Audie speculated, was "protecting his flanks just in case" AAFLI folded under the pressure of AID budget cuts.[45]

The AFL-CIO had commissioned AAFLI (along with its African and Latin American labor institutes) as an independent body charged only with promoting the virtues of free trade unionism. Yet, as was no secret, the U.S. government—not the AFL-CIO—provided the primary funding for the operation. The arrangement proved perplexing even to a veteran trade unionist like Tran Quoc Buu. If not confused, Buu, despite his own sensitivities, perhaps simply had no patience with the veneer of independence so important to AAFLI. A combination of bad personnel decisions and administrative chaos hobbled the Asian labor institute from the beginning. The AFL-CIO's goal of establishing an independent support system for Buu and the CVT remained elusive. Good intentions, it seemed, would only go so far. Unaccompanied by good administration and thoughtful sensitivity toward cultural and political pressures in host countries, initiatives such as AAFLI were doomed to failure. Yet, even had Audie been more sensitive and the delineation between AAFLI and AID/LAB better clarified, the very presence of Americans, even on the periphery, advising and funding South Vietnamese labor left a taint that in Vietnam could be lethal.

"Awakening the Conscience of the Masses"

Buu and the CVT's ambivalence regarding outside help was best exemplified by his embrace of the new American policy of Vietnamization—the promise that the South Vietnamese would take up a greater share of the defense of their country. Following the Tet Offensive, Johnson had moved in the direction of this policy, and Richard Nixon, in 1969, proclaimed it as his objective. To Buu, Vietnamization offered an opportunity. A U.S. withdrawal, he optimistically forecasted, would inspire an "awakening of the conscience of the masses."[46] The peasants and workers of South Vietnam, freed of humbling dependence on foreigners, would rise up and defeat the Viet Cong. From the announcement of the peace talks in March 1968, Buu had made it his special mission to mobilize the population against the VC. In May 1968, he briefly joined with the Vietnamese Revolutionary Farmers' Party and two moderate Buddhist groups to form Vietnam's Workers' and Farmers' Association. Its objective was to inspire the working class to "struggle to protect the country against the Communists." While focusing its energies against the insurgent VC threat, the short-lived organization also warned against "reactionary, irresponsible fake democratic elements," presumably including elements within the Saigon government.[47] In his public addresses, Buu urged peasants to defend their country and warned that under communist rule dissent would not be tolerated. Addressing the Dinh Tuong Province Tenant Farmers convention, Buu exhorted his audience:

> All right, brothers and sisters, the Americans and Government of South Vietnam have spent a lot of time and many lives trying to win your hearts and minds. If you really want peace and freedom and prosperity, then it is time to get off your seats and start supporting your nation with your hearts and minds—and through action—not just sighs and words.[48]

Buu had always viewed South Vietnam's (and his own) heavy dependence on outsiders as a distinct liability. With Americans everywhere, the U.S. embassy virtually a shadow government, and even the AFL-CIO now a permanent presence, the South Vietnamese appeared to others, and often to themselves, as little more than postcolonial pawns of the West. At times, Buu himself seemed resentful of Americans. On at least one occasion, he frankly admitted his admiration for the Viet Cong's persistence against its more potent foe. "You can reach the moon, but little Vietnam has stopped you," he told an American in 1969.[49] Vietnamization offered the opportunity, Buu believed, to finally break his country's awkward reliance on the Americans and realize a true victory. Yet Buu also understood the other side of the coin: painful as it might be, his country's survival depended on the West. In order to maintain the vital flow of aid, South Vietnam must assume the trappings of democracy and order; it must appear to be a country in which everyone worked together.

In the past—while always trying to protect the CVT's autonomy—Buu had forged working alliances with the French and later the Diem regimes. The CVT pursued a similar course of coexistence and cooperation with the Thieu government, in part to improve South Vietnam's image in the eyes of the world. Buu viewed Thieu as corrupt, mercurial, and indifferent to the plight of the poor; nevertheless he sought channels of influence within the government, first to ensure his organization's survival, then to help erect a facade of national unity from which to lobby for social reform and continuing foreign aid.[50] Thieu, in turn, needed Buu, whose organization had the support of influential Americans and provided South Vietnam with at least the veneer of a pluralistic democracy. Buu and the CVT always supported Thieu's hard line on peace negotiations but always with the demand that "free labor" and "the right to strike" be granted workers in North Vietnam as preconditions for the talks.[51] In early 1969, Thieu dispatched Buu along with a team of South Vietnamese politicians on a three-week tour of the United States. The group was to defend the government's "position at the Paris Peace Talks" and lobby for aid. In Washington, the AFL-CIO helped arrange appointments for the CVT chief with prominent American legislators and officials.[52]

In July 1968, President Thieu came to Buu with a proposition. Encouraged by the U.S. embassy eager to see the president expand his political base, Thieu proposed to create a new alliance called the Lien Minh (National Alliance for Social Revolution), which would be composed of nationalist groups, including the CVT, the military-based National Salvation Front under Senator Tran Van Don, and other religious and ethnic parties. No doubt, the South Vietnamese president hoped such an organization would lend order to the country's chaotically fragmented political scene, which was plagued with well over one hundred political parties.[53]

Officials in Washington, bogged down with bad news about Vietnam, seized on the new development as rare good news. Johnson aide and eternal optimist W. W. Rostow saw Lien Minh as "the most hopeful nationalist political organization to appear thus far." But there was cause for concern as well. Officially, Lien Minh professed political neutrality, but Thieu confided to Ambassador Ellsworth Bunker that he planned to direct it from "behind the scenes." While Thieu insisted that the alliance would have no likeness to Diem's repressive Can Lao, a certain resemblance could not be denied.[54]

In August 1968, Thieu ventured to the CVT headquarters at 14 Le Van Duyet Street for a long morning meeting with Buu. The two discussed the political risks each faced in forming the alliance. Thieu assured Buu that the new organization would help him pursue much needed social reforms. That afternoon, Buu, Thieu, Senator Don, and other participants launched Lien

Minh.[55] Soon after the inauguration, supporters established chapters across the country.[56]

Despite the fanfare surrounding the inauguration of the new alliance, Lien Minh crumbled almost immediately. Thieu devoted little attention to cultivating the coalition, it lacked a clear mandate, and infighting plagued the organization. From the start, the political alliance seemed more indicative of the U.S. embassy's approach to the problem of political fragmentation than a genuine South Vietnamese response. While Lien Minh did manage to establish a corps of organizers and several regional chapters, after only a few weeks it collapsed.[57]

Buu, always preoccupied with protecting the CVT's autonomy, had fretted all along that Lien Minh, which required collaboration with opportunists such as Senator Don, a slick and ambitious figure who had engineered the coup against Diem in 1963, was too confining and reminiscent of Diem's Can Lao Party.[58] Furthermore, Lien Minh, with its ties to Thieu, appeared ill-positioned to champion urgently needed social reforms. Increasingly, the CVT became convinced that only a radical program of land reform truly would inspire the peasantry to challenge the Viet Cong. Thieu, while promising land redistribution, seemed reluctant to move on the issue.[59] Frustrated, Buu began to look in new directions.

In frequent discussions with U.S. trade unionists, Buu expressed interest in building a base for political operations similar to the AFL-CIO's Committee for Political Education (COPE), possibly even a CVT-sponsored political party. In October 1968, Buu asked Irving Brown to supply him with a representative from COPE to prepare his organization for expanded political activity.[60] Buu clearly understood the risks involved and had always personally shied away from direct political activity for fear of compromising the CVT. But he desperately wanted to expand the confederation's influence, and like many in his organization, especially younger members, he felt the pull of American-style democracy. Having already entered the electoral fray in 1967, he moved to expand and formalize the CVT's political work.[61]

Weighing his options, Buu chose the risky course of launching his own political party. Following the Tet Offensive, he told the British embassy that he had "concluded that a political party must be formed with the real roots amongst the people."[62] His American and British allies, who believed organized labor must take an active lead in building democracy, had long urged him to directly enter politics. Labor-friendly deputy U.S. ambassador to Saigon, Samuel Berger, a former labor attaché with strong ties to American labor, in particular, argued that the CVT had "definite political potential."[63] Traditionally, the organization avoided politics, although behind the scenes it contributed to campaigns and endorsed slates of candidates. Buu deeply feared tarnishing or even destroying the confederation by openly subjecting it to the clamor and intense rivalries of South Vietnamese politics. But with the U.S. military and civilian presence diminishing and few other parties or political personalities focused on "awakening the conscience of the masses," Buu cautiously decided to take the risk. The Cong Nong Party (Worker-Farmer Party), which Buu tentatively introduced in November 1969, purported to be an entity independent of the CVT. Yet its connection to the labor movement was obvious.[64] Borrowing the CVT's pluralistic aims of uniting farmers, laborers, urban workers, minority groups, and various religious sects, Buu proposed to include a diverse conglomeration of largely underrepresented groups, possibly including his old allies in the Cao Dai, in his new political party.[65]

Eschewing the "flashy Saigon inauguration ceremony" typically associated with new political parties, Buu announced the official launching of the Cong Nong Party during the festivities accompanying the CVT's twentieth anniversary in 1970.[66] Addressing the change in policy, Buu painstakingly justified the launch.

> During twenty years of operation we have seen that many of our problems stemmed from the political setup. At the present moment we feel that it is time for the CVT to have more direct political activity. We have always supported parties with a platform in favor of workers, but now we want to assure a continuous and strong representation for workers in the legislature.[67]

Rather than modeling his organization on the AFL-CIO's COPE, Buu seemed to have in mind something approximating Britain's Labour Party, an independent organization with strong ties to the Trade Union Congress (TUC).[68] He specifically asked the British embassy for copies of the Labour Party's constitution and "any documents covering its relationship with the TUC."[69] Yet Buu remained impressed with the AFL-CIO's close working relationship with the U.S. government. As he finalized plans for the Cong Nong, he traveled to Washington seeking expert political advice from the AFL-CIO.[70]

Buu desperately sought to avoid any impression that the Cong Nong represented a challenge to Thieu's leadership. Rather, he presented the CVT's political debut as part of his mission to politicize and mobilize the masses. Although he personally disliked and distrusted Thieu, Buu kept the South Vietnamese president informed as he organized the party, and Thieu apparently encouraged his work.[71] But Buu also clearly aimed to provide the CVT with sufficient political leverage to force an agenda of social reform on a reluctant government.

The CVT's political venture did enjoy considerable success. Using CVT unions and social centers as a base, the party, which aimed to train a cadre of some three thousand organizers, quickly spread to forty provinces and many cities. In the Senate elections in 1970, the Cong Nong won sixteen of sixty seats. It also performed reasonably well in provincial elections.[72]

Most importantly, even before the establishment of the Cong Nong, the growing presence of the CVT in national and provincial politics enabled it to press for programs long on its agenda, including civilian military training. Not only did Buu regard arming civilians against the Viet Cong as essential to the war effort, but he hoped it would deflect the ever present threat of compulsory service for men of draft age. Historically, Saigon's ruling regimes had balked at sponsoring civilian militias. However, the Tet Offensive persuaded some officials that the masses could be effectively mobilized. With the express support of the CVT, the South Vietnamese government inaugurated a program of civilian military training. In May of 1968, eighteen thousand Saigon workers participated in short training courses in weapons handling and military tactics jointly administered by the Labor and Defense Ministries. The CVT pushed for the implementation of similar programs around the country.[73] Buu enthusiastically told General Lansdale that "everyone must defend the country." He vowed to work toward a "moral mobilization" of the population modeled on Viet Cong tactics.[74]

Civil self-defense training remained controversial, however. Employers were reluctant to grant workers leave for training, and there was also the potential for Viet Cong infiltration. But both Buu and his American supporters anticipated benefits. Workers and peasants presumably would feel more connected to the struggle against communism, and self-defense units would relieve the South Vietnamese army of guard duty at factories and other strategic places.[75] However problematic, the establishment of self-defense units seemed to be the fulfillment of Irving Brown's plan, first presented in 1961, to develop the CVT's paramilitary capacity.

Land reform, however, was the foremost goal of the CVT's venture into politics. Buu recognized the VC campaign against exploitative landlords long had been its most effective propaganda tool. The CVT had actually petitioned the Saigon government not to distribute land back to landlords in villages reclaimed from the Viet Cong. Rather than the halfhearted land reform initiatives previously undertaken in South Vietnam—efforts Buu dismissed as "too vertical . . . by decree from above"—the CVT advocated a policy that would involve the peasantry more actively in the process.[76] A massive land redistribution program granting free land to tillers, Buu hoped, would co-opt the land issue and provide a vital step toward the democratization that had been so elusive for South Vietnam.[77] The U.S. government, desperate for anything that might mobilize the population at large, also embraced the cause of land reform.[78] The South Vietnamese National

Assembly, however, balked at drafting legislation that might alienate the powerful landowning class.[79]

Nonetheless, Buu embarked on an aggressive campaign to transform his country's tenant class into landowners, a goal of "greatest importance" and an utmost priority for the CVT, he told an audience of peasants in An Giang.[80] Working together, the CVT (through the Cong Nong) and the American embassy pushed a reluctant General Assembly and President Thieu to embrace "the most sweeping land reform programs carried out in the twentieth century in a noncommunist country."[81] Senator Trinh Quang Quy, a former high-ranking CVT officer and Cong Nong member, opened the Senate debate, telling the assembly that land reform would rally peasants to fight for their country, "leaving the Communists no place to stand."[82] Finally, on March 26, 1970, Thieu capitulated and signed the "land to the tiller" program into law. It proposed to transfer three million acres of prime farmland in the delta and central lowlands from landlords to tenant families. In contrast to the forced redistribution of land practiced by Hanoi, the land to the tiller program compensated landlords with a 20 percent immediate cash payment and the balance in eight-year bonds.[83] Acceptance of the plan signaled a major breakthrough, though one that was perhaps too long delayed.

Determined next to help transform South Vietnam's peasants into landowners, the CVT established an extensive chain of cooperatives, providing low-cost seed and farm equipment. By the summer of 1970, rice cultivation had risen and thousands of Vietnamese peasants had become landowners.[84] "We would be perfectly content to have to change our name from Tenant Farmers' Federation to Farmers' Federation," declared Tenant Farmers' Federation President Vo Van Giao, voicing his hopes for the land redistribution program.[85]

As the CVT moved in new directions, it also remained an active urban force. In 1969, it launched a campaign to organize thirty-eight textile factories. This quickly led to the affiliation of a new union, the Federation of Textile Workers.[86] Despite the raging war, the CVT was not reluctant to call for work stoppages. As the 1969 Tet celebration approached (and workers grew apprehensive about forthcoming holiday expenses), CVT affiliates, undaunted by the costly strikes the previous year leading up to the Tet holiday, initiated strikes against Air Vietnam, the Grall Hospital in Saigon, and a paper factory in Bien Hoa.[87] Meanwhile, the CVT expanded its social work and was soon operating eighteen "social centers" in Saigon and outlying provinces.[88]

Its American supporters celebrated the CVT's post-Tet gains and burgeoning involvement in politics. The AFL-CIO long had hoped that the CVT and Buu would expand their political operations and ultimately evolve into a "third force," charting a democratic alternative between communism and the oppressive Saigon government. Irving Brown was particularly optimistic. The Cong Nong Party, he predicted, "may become the one last hope for a political alternative" in South Vietnam.[89]

Conclusion

The difficult several months following the Tet Offensive may have ended on a bright note with the CVT increasingly stable and long overdue social, political, and economic reforms coming to South Vietnam. Yet these developments were largely fleeting, and the larger picture remained grim. Flaws in the foundations of free trade unionism, once unnoticeable, now were obvious to all. At home, facing an open revolt against the war among many liberals and severely challenged by Reuther's ALA, the AFL-CIO appeared permanently on the defensive. In Vietnam, its joint sponsorship with USAID of a labor institute in Saigon seemed an egregious violation of trade union autonomy. Worst of all, the CVT, the organization in which free trade unionists had staked so much, appeared ambivalent at best to AFL-CIO support. Throughout 1968 into 1969, the world was changing at a dizzying pace as the spirit of détente swept through Western Europe, anticommunist liberalism disappeared from the White House, Americans searched desperately for an exit strategy from Vietnam, and the CVT seemed increasingly determined to chart its own course. None of these developments provided much comfort for free trade unionists.

George Meany and Tran Quoc Buu in conversation with President Lyndon Johnson, May 20, 1964. (Photograph courtesy of the National Archives.)

Eager to counter the growing antiwar movement, Meany pressed AFL-CIO affiliates to launch projects supporting the war. Here members of Transport Workers' Union Local 500 of Pan American Airways in Miami, Florida, load Christmas gifts for U.S. soldiers stationed in Vietnam. (Photograph courtesy of the George Meany Memorial Archives.)

Both the AFL-CIO and the CVT struggled against corruption and resistance to free trade unionism in the ports of Saigon. Here an AFL-CIO delegation poses with CVT trade unionists outside the newly constructed Newport Hiring Hall. (Photograph courtesy of the George Meany Memorial Archives.)

In the fall of 1967, an AFL-CIO delegation, including Joseph Keenan *(far left)* and Irving Brown *(far right)*, visited Vietnam to set in motion a permanent AFL-CIO labor institution dedicated to promoting free trade unionism in Southeast Asia. The next year the AFL-CIO and the Agency for International Development launched the Asian American Free Labor Institute (AAFLI). (Photograph courtesy of the George Meany Memorial Archives.)

Seeking to counterbalance negative perceptions of the South Vietnamese state, in 1968 the AFL-CIO sponsored a lecture tour by Dr. Phan Quang Dan, an anticommunist who had been jailed by the Ngo Dinh Diem regime but served in subsequent Saigon governments. Here Dan poses with Meany *(left)*, Ambassador Henry Cabot Lodge *(far left)*, and George Delaney *(right)*. (Photograph courtesy of the George Meany Memorial Archives.)

Vietnamese peasants received titles to land as part of the Land to the Tiller progam, 1970. True land reform was a long-held goal of the CVT. (Photograph courtesy of the National Archives.)

An odd pairing: Buu and antiwar congresswoman Bella Abzug during Buu's lobbying trip to Washington in March 1975. (Photograph courtesy of the George Meany Memorial Archives.)

The highlight of Buu's lobbying trip to Washington in 1975 was a meeting with President Gerald R. Ford. (Photograph courtesy of the Gerald R. Ford Presidential Library.)

As Saigon tottered, the *AFL-CIO News* promised a reign of terror should South Vietnam fall. (Courtesy of the George Meany Memorial Archives.)

7 Entangling Alliances and Mounting Costs, 1970–71

The parade of reversals afflicting the AFL-CIO in the late 1960s continued into the 1970s. Critics gleefully exposed the questionable arrangements made by the supposedly independent U.S. trade unionists to the glare of daylight, and growing numbers of trade unionists, especially at the rank and file level, defied Meany and joined the peace movement. In Saigon, the CVT also faced mounting challenges, including an expanded campaign of terrorism by the VC and charges of corruption within its own ranks.

Reeling from the setbacks of 1968 and 1969, free trade unionists struggled to adapt to new circumstances both at home and abroad. Desperate to preserve free trade unionism in Vietnam, the acrobatics required of both the AFL-CIO and the CVT grew more complicated. For survival, the CVT made limited common cause with President Thieu. Meanwhile, the AFL-CIO, defiantly clinging to its Vietnam agenda, forged an awkward, symbiotic relationship with President Richard Nixon, a bond made entirely possible by the divisive, painful war in Vietnam.

"The Price We Paid for Mr. Meany's Support on Vietnam"

As President Richard Nixon took the oath of office in January 1969, uppermost in the minds of free trade unionists was anxiety over the future of foreign aid spending. By the end of the 1960s, the AFL-CIO was, through its international programs such as AAFLI, a leading recipient of expenditures. In its endeavors to promote free and independent trade unions worldwide, the federation had become ever more dependent on foreign aid subsidies. Even its allies in South Vietnamese labor seemed confused as to the exact boundaries separating the U.S. government and the AFL-CIO.

As with virtually everything else, the unpopular war in Vietnam complicated the foreign aid picture for organized labor. Aid had always been controversial in a country where many voters leaned toward isolationism and tended to view foreign aid as a wasteful diversion from pressing problems at home. As passions deepened over the war in Southeast Asia, attitudes hardened, and the debate surrounding aid grew ever more contentious.[1] By the late 1960s, the Far Left had developed a biting critique of foreign aid. Radicals argued that aid appropriations were hardly selfless acts of humanitarianism but rather were part and parcel of an imperialistic drive to expand American influence and "open-door" market values.[2] Meanwhile President Nixon—borrowing a critical approach from the Right—proposed to economize and streamline foreign aid by redirecting it through multilateral channels such as the World Bank and the International Monetary Fund, thereby avoiding politically loaded, waste-laden, nation to nation aid.[3] In his drive to expand and preserve his international programs, Meany increasingly faced harsh criticism from both ends of the political spectrum.[4]

Over the years, the AFL-CIO fashioned its defense of foreign aid around ideals of charity and anticommunism. Pointing to the large proportion of AID dollars spent domestically, labor also argued that aid provided valuable jobs at home, contributing to full employment. Yet as the Vietnam War grew more controversial labor found it more and more difficult to make the case for aid. William S. Gaud, the AID administrator, described the bitter yearly congressional battle over foreign aid appropriations as an annual "cliff hanger."[5] On one occasion Senator Wayne Morse of Oregon threatened Gaud that, short of serious negotiations in Vietnam, he planned to vote against all aid appropriations.[6] By mid-1968, both liberals and conservatives were clamoring for reductions in foreign aid, imperiling AAFLI and the AFL-CIO's other overseas projects. To appease critics, President Johnson promised to tighten procedures and address balance of payments issues by ordering more aid dollars be spent domestically.[7] Nonetheless Congress slashed AID's appropriation for 1968 to the lowest amount in the agency's history.[8]

It was thus with trepidation that the AFL-CIO faced the presidency of Richard Nixon. A Republican who had been fiercely opposed by the AFL-CIO, Nixon promised to be no friend to free trade unionism. The new president, within several months of taking office, launched plans to reform foreign aid by creating the Overseas Private Investment Corporation, a semipublic organization designed to shift aid administration into private hands.[9] The Nixon administration, AFL-CIO vice president Joseph Bierne warned Meany, risked "losing sight of the social development aspect" of foreign aid, adding that "there can be very little possibility for American labor playing a distinct positive role in international banking mechanisms."[10]

Although Nixon stopped short of directly threatening the AFL-CIO's AID-financed labor institutes, federation leaders remained nervous.[11] Meany's top priority in his first meeting with the new president, on March 13, 1969, was shielding AAFLI and his other aid-financed programs. Despite their many differences, Meany and Nixon shared an abiding anticommunism and a fixation with foreign affairs. The pair devoted two-thirds of their meeting to a wide-ranging discussion of the state of the world. Meany "talked at length about the AFL-CIO program of training union leaders." Apparently impressed, Nixon "expressed interest and support for continuation of the [labor] program."[12]

Nixon's endorsement undoubtedly came with expectations and strings attached; nevertheless, it was gratifying. Challenges remained, however, especially from the AFL-CIO's onetime liberal supporters. Throughout 1969, sensational revelations about the federation's foreign operations and dealings with the CIA continued to surface. On April 28, 1969, the *Washington Post* published a story detailing AFL-CIO and AID cooperation in Vietnam. Labor and state "cohabitate in a murky, twilight world," concluded the article.[13] In May 1969, the *New Republic* ran a long piece by Richard Dudman entitled "Agent Meany." Noting the AFL-CIO president's insistent distinction between free and unfree unions, Dudman charged the federation with rank hypocrisy; it had "slavishly followed U.S. policy" and thus "blurred the sharp distinctions between government and free trade unions." Turning to Vietnam, though presenting no specific evidence, Dudman alleged that AAFLI had undercut strikes and betrayed the CVT.[14]

The AFL-CIO quickly denounced the Dudman piece and proclaimed itself "proud" of its overseas activities, which were "based upon our unalterable devotion to freedom." The financial records of its international missions, the AFL-CIO claimed, somewhat disingenuously, were regularly audited, and AID reported all expenses to Congress.[15]

However, Secretary of State William Rogers, distressed by the negative publicity, issued a circular advising all U.S. embassies to disavow any connection between the "educational" work of the AFL-CIO's foreign institutes and "covert" operations.[16] Assistant Secretary of Labor George Weaver then prepared an internal memo refuting Dudman's allegations that "the AFL-CIO is the CIA's handmaiden for dark deeds." Charges that the AFL-CIO "slavishly" followed the U.S. government were "patently false," Weaver asserted. Anyone familiar with the AFL-CIO's international work, he claimed, knew that the federation, while generally supporting American policy, "differed substantially in specific instances with U.S. foreign policy over time and continues to do so." In addition, he noted that "many of our ambassadors abroad have been terribly inconvenienced" by representatives of the AFL-CIO's international labor institutes. But, Weaver privately acknowledged, the Dudman piece would "further damage" the "already tarnished image the AID program has among the American people."[17] Catching wind of the official effort to shield AFL-CIO overseas operations, Victor Reuther drafted a letter to Nixon demanding that the president "terminate the use of public funds to sustain the frequently secret operation of a private organization, the AFL-CIO."[18]

The charges against the AFL-CIO soon found themselves on the desk of one of the severest critics not only of foreign aid but also of American foreign policy in general, Senator J. William Fulbright.[19] The AFL-CIO long regarded Fulbright as a bitter foe of free trade unionism. A segregationist from a right to work state, the senator had a decidedly antilabor record. His characterization of U.S. foreign policy as "arrogant" and driven by knee-jerk anticommunism deeply offended free trade unionists. His reputation as an intellectual particularly irked federation staffers, who dubbed the senator "half-bright."[20] Fulbright and the AFL-CIO clashed perennially over issues from civil rights to fiscal policy to foreign affairs. In the summer of 1969, as the Senate weighed foreign aid appropriations, he pointed to the several million dollars earmarked for the AFL-CIO's labor institutes and "wondered" aloud, with a United Press International reporter hovering nearby, "if this represented the price we paid for Mr. Meany's support in Vietnam." Fulbright's comments, which immediately appeared in print, struck at the essence of free trade unionism, insinuating that American organized labor had sold out and become a tool of the state.

An outraged Meany demanded an immediate hearing before Fulbright's Senate Foreign Relations Committee. The August 1, 1969, confrontation recalled for veteran observers the bitterness and rancor of the McCarthy era.[21] Meany opened by branding Fulbright's comments a "gratuitous insult to the American labor movement." Frequently interrupting Meany's testimony, Fulbright charged the federation with doing "subcontracting work" for the CIA. Meany returned fire, violently hurling accusations back at the senator. After three and a half hours of invective, the two bloodied combatants shook hands, signaling an end to the showdown. Yet Fulbright could not resist sneering, "I hope you don't treat all your associates with the rudeness with which you treat me." Meany growled back: "I'm here because of your rude remarks about me."[22]

Meany's animated and angry defense of free trade unionism rang hollow to many. By 1969, much of the press had come to view the AFL-CIO president as an anachronism. Meany, liberal columnist Mary McGory wrote, "was fighting history, not Fulbright. The country has changed about Vietnam."[23] The country also had changed about the cold war. No longer did anticommunism carry the resonance it had in the immediate postwar years.

By 1969, Fulbright's neoisolationism, fueled by mounting questions about the cost of the Vietnam War, mirrored more closely the national mood.[24]

Nor could Fulbright's questions about labor's autonomy be easily dismissed. If not precisely correct about foreign aid as a "payoff," labor's AID arrangement appeared unseemly, at the very least a painful contortion of free trade union ideals. While AFL-CIO officials satisfied themselves by resolutely refusing to provide any accounting for government subsidies, their controversial alliances armed critics with much ammunition. And, even within the house of labor those critics grew in number.

"A Time to Speak Out"

Before 1970, openly antiwar labor leaders were few in number. The Paris peace talks, which began in 1968, relieved some of the immediacy of the war issue, as did the steady withdrawal of U.S. troops from Vietnam. Reflecting this trend, peace activists in the labor movement sponsored no follow-up to the November 1967 Chicago Labor Assembly for Peace. Coordination between antiwar trade unionists remained limited. "The lack of communication between the various peace centers or actions in terms of the labor movement is lousy," lamented one peace-minded trade unionist.[25] Those speaking out publicly against the war often walked a fine line, struggling to express their dissent without further damaging the precarious liberal-labor alliance. Several dovish members of the UAW Executive Board worked actively on Robert F. Kennedy's 1968 presidential campaign, but virtually all returned dutifully to support Vice President Humphrey in the general election in 1968. Likewise, while Reuther's ALA clearly was against the U.S. policy on Vietnam, the organization avoided making the war a litmus test and shunned alliances with the mainstream antiwar movement. Those with antiwar leanings remaining within the AFL-CIO, such as Jerry Wurf of ACFSME and Jacob Potofsky of the ACWA, expediently sidestepped the Vietnam issue out of fear of angering Meany and alienating their membership.

Nixon's April 30, 1970, decision to send U.S. troops into Cambodia changed everything. The president's objective was to destroy Viet Cong sanctuaries nestled in Cambodian territory. In a nationally televised address, he defended his action as also necessary to fend off challenges to U.S. global credibility; his nation would not act "like a helpless, pitiful giant," he defiantly asserted. Nixon's words and actions provoked the peace movement as never before. Violent antiwar demonstrations exploded across the country. During a protest at Kent State University, National Guard troops shot and killed four students. Scores of universities, overwhelmed by protests, temporarily shut down.

The Cambodian invasion and the domestic tumult that followed jolted awake labor's once dormant doves.[26] Walter Reuther, in a statement made the day before his death, warned Nixon that the invasion represented "a repudiation of your oft-repeated pledge to bring this tragic war to an end and not to escalate it."[27] Indignant at the invasion, other labor leaders joined Reuther's protest. Jerry Wurf, the youthful activist president of AFSCME, had long harbored reservations about the war but feared open opposition would cost him a leadership role on the AFL-CIO Executive Council. To remain in Meany's good graces, Wurf had squelched an antiwar resolution proposed at the 1966 AFSCME convention. But following the Cambodian invasion Wurf acted on his convictions. When the Executive Council met to consider a proposed statement of support for Nixon on Cambodia, Wurf defied Meany and voted against the measure. For Wurf, it was a symbolic moment. "George realized he didn't have a bunch of yes men anymore," he explained. Herman Kenin, president of the American Federation of Musicians; William Pollack of the Textile Workers; and Patrick Gorman of the Amalgamated Meat Cutters joined Wurf in opposition. Gorman issued a particularly sharp dissent: "We have never followed blindly and never will, every edict that emanates from the official headquarters in Washington, especially where war is the issue. The AFL-CIO is not infallible."[28]

Elsewhere, AFL-CIO vice president Jacob Potofsky, long resentful of Meany's dictatorial style and all-consuming anticommunism, also openly broke with the AFL-CIO's pro-war position. In his keynote address to the 1970 ACWA convention, appropriately entitled "A Time to Speak Out," he lamented a country "beset by a host of problems." The war in Vietnam, he concluded, "underlies practically all our troubles."[29] Frank Rosenblum, ACWA secretary treasurer, then followed Potofsky with a personal attack on Meany, whom he blamed for alienating America's youth with his hawkish stand on the war. Meany, scheduled to speak later at the clothing workers' convention, abruptly canceled his appearance.[30] Fifty-two years earlier, Rosenblum and Potofsky had muted their opposition to World War I. But in the face of mounting antiwar sentiment everywhere, neither could keep silent.[31]

Despite growing outspokenness, antiwar labor leaders refrained from organizing a national coalition of unionists opposed to the war. Meany's grip remained tight, as did fears of damaging the Democratic Party and pushing more rank and file members into the Wallace or Nixon camps. Nevertheless, especially among the secondary tier of labor leaders, antiwar sentiment swelled. The San Francisco Bay Area Labor Assembly for Peace smoothly integrated its activities with those of the mainstream and student peace movements.[32] Elsewhere, Michigan AFL-CIO Federation president Gus Scholle passionately attacked the war and built an effective coalition of local antiwar unionists.[33]

Even in areas long considered safe ground, Meany and the labor hawks encountered opposition. Cleveland, Ohio, a heavily unionized city, home to large numbers of ethnic Eastern Europeans, seemed like an unlikely place to find a trade-union-based antiwar movement. In fact, in the 1950s the city's workers formed the Cleveland Council on World Affairs, which sponsored anticommunist workshops, films, and educational activities.[34] During the early years of the war, few among Cleveland's labor leaders dared speak out. In 1967, when Auda Romine, secretary treasurer of Local 500 of the Amalgamated Meat Cutters and Butcher Workmen of America, criticized the war at a union gathering, her audience responded with boos and taunts. Shaken but undaunted, Romine sought out other antiwar unionists in the Cleveland area. In July 1969, she and fellow trade union activists cosponsored a national convention of antiwar groups held in Cleveland. Leo Fenster, a radical UAW activist, gave the keynote address.[35]

The Cambodian incursion provided the turning point. Outrage over the invasion drove Cleveland's antiwar labor activists to join forces with striking students at Case Western Reserve University. Together they took out a full-page ad in the *Cleveland Plain Dealer,* protesting Nixon's invasion. Signers of the ad later proposed an antiwar resolution at the July meeting of the Ohio AFL-CIO convention. The resolution failed, but the close vote energized peace advocates.[36] Before long, the growing group of dovish laborites allied itself with the mainstream antiwar movement, joining demonstrations against the Cambodian invasion. The following year, the Cleveland AFL-CIO Federation of Labor adopted an antiwar resolution. In January 1973, the once reticent Cleveland federation issued a pointed denunciation of Nixon's Christmas bombing of North Vietnam and called for an immediate end to the "senseless and idiotic warfare in southeast Asia."[37]

Yet even as they grew in number the trade union doves generally made it a point to distance themselves from the mainstream peace movement, especially as protests grew violent and radicalism proliferated. In 1971, Michigan AFL-CIO chief Gus Scholle consented to be named one of the sponsors of an antiwar rally, but he "strongly urge[d] that every precaution be taken to prevent any attempt to create violence of any kind."[38] Patrick Gorman, the antiwar president of the Amalgamated Meat Cutters, and other antiwar trade unionists went further, warning that should "acts of terrorism continue, repression will come down heavier not only on the youth but on the labor movement and other progressive forces."[39] Even in antiwar "unions such as the United Automobile Workers and the Amalgamated Clothing Workers," reported the *New York Times,* "many workers who support their union's stand against the war are disturbed by the student protests."[40] Expanding numbers hardly shrank the cultural gaps separating antiwar trade unionists and the mainstream peace movement, gaps that remained and in many ways grew.

Nonetheless, by the early 1970s the antiwar movement within organized labor undeniably was expanding, soon resembling a broad crusade with growing strength on the grassroots level. No longer could Meany dismiss such sentiment as inconsequential or "planned in Hanoi." Hardly the result of alien subversion, opposition to foreign entanglements such as the Vietnam War reflected deep-seated American ambivalence to involvement in world affairs, inclinations felt as deeply by workers as any other group. The internationalism so central to free trade unionism, in fact, never fully resonated with the rank and file, which was often more oriented toward parochial, populist concerns. Patriotism and attacks on antiwar protesters continued to sell well in certain corridors, but calls for allegiance to nebulous ideals of international solidarity and third-world development increasingly fell flat. The appeal of the peace movement for some and the Wallace candidacy for others suggests the limits of free trade unionism and the growing gulf between Meany and his constituency.

The Blue-Collar Strategy

In many ways antiwar sentiment among trade unionists bespoke a larger sense of discontent—the "blue-collar blues," as it quickly became popularly known—a phenomenon that only recently has received serious treatment from historians.[41] Economic challenges clearly fed the sense of alienation felt by many in the lower-middle and working classes. Workers had achieved unprecedented security in the years after World War II, but their advances usually lagged behind those of the increasingly prosperous middle class.[42] A host of cultural, social, and racial issues also left many workers resentful, angry, and alienated.[43] The painful war in Southeast Asia heightened this sense of frustration. In the late 1960s, rank and file union members were as divided as the rest of the country by the Vietnam War. Those opposing the war often encountered the less than subtle wrath of pro-war trade unionists, while those following Meany's line faced the antipathy of growing numbers of liberals and the antiwar media. For all, there lingered considerable indignation over the fact that the working classes provided the majority of draftees for the war.[44]

Newly elected president Richard Nixon was quick to sense political opportunity in the blue-collar blues epidemic and the fissures created by the Vietnam War. In 1968, he had not fared particularly well with union voters, but, ever the opportunist, he saw potential political gain in the growing gulf between labor and the Democratic Party, a chasm that was largely the product of the Vietnam War. As Johnson had done in the early 1960s, Nixon set out to transform his relationship with organized labor. Having implemented a "Southern Strategy" to lure southerners to the Republican Party, he now hoped to pull in blue-collar voters. Nixon assigned this task to his aide Charles (Chuck) Colson, a self-proclaimed "partisan for the 'hardhats.'" The "blue-collar strategy" aimed to play off the resentment of antiwar protesters and social change to attract both working voters and union leaders to a new coalition.[45] Nixon's odd psychological makeup no doubt contributed to his interest in cultivating labor. Self-consciously an outsider who had risen from humble origins, Nixon instinctively identified with union leaders, whom he noted in his diary had "character and guts . . . and patriotism."[46]

Colson made little headway during the first year of the Nixon presidency. Both the rank and file and union leaders remained distrustful. But the Cambodian invasion revitalized his mission and provided him with a valuable ally—Jay Lovestone. The septuagenarian ex-communist, who continued to head the AFL-CIO's foreign policy operations, watched the Democratic Party's abandonment of the cold war with undisguised contempt. Calls to pull back from international commitments seemed to Lovestone a dangerous return to the isolationism and appeasement of the pre–World War II era. Initially, he feared Nixon would hasten these trends. He saw Nixon's Vietnamization policy as evidence that the "administration would be inclined to flee from the Asian theater" and complained bitterly of the president's "bookkeeping attitude on foreign assistance."[47]

The Cambodia invasion, however, brought an instantaneous change of heart.[48] Suddenly the ex-communist saw a tough, uncompromising side to the president. Unbeknownst to Meany, Lovestone arranged a private tête-à-tête with Colson on May 5, 1970. He told Colson that Nixon was the "first president since Harry Truman to have real guts." Lovestone vowed "to activate all the international resources of the AFL-CIO" in support of the president, and the pair drafted a pro-Nixon statement for the AFL-CIO Executive Council, praising the Cambodian incursion.[49] Several days later, Nixon personally briefed the federation's Executive Council on the Cambodian situation. The president received a warm welcome.[50] Lovestone and Colson continued their clandestine rendezvous every two weeks, discussing foreign policy and planning strategies to garner labor support for Nixon.[51]

As the pair connived, a series of spontaneous pro-war rallies in New York City by "hard-hat" construction workers excited their interest. The counterdemonstrations began on May 8, when construction workers attacked peace protesters in Manhattan, allegedly in retaliation for an act of desecration against the American flag; related protests quickly flared in other cities.[52] Basking in the media attention, the New York hard hats began holding daily demonstrations in the financial district. Union leaders—in particular Peter Brennan, president of the Building and Construction Trades Council of Greater New York—seized control of the previously spontaneous protests.[53]

To Colson and Lovestone, the hard-hat rallies presented an inviting opportunity to counterbalance the growing antiwar movement. Through Lovestone, Colson urged Brennan and others to organize a major, highly publicized, pro-war rally to be held simultaneously on May 20 in several cities. Hard-hat leaders needed little prompting. Brennan and construction union officials eagerly organized the massive demonstration.[54] The May 20 march in New York City drew between 100,000 to 150,000 protesters; smaller rallies took place in San Diego, Pittsburgh, Buffalo, and other cities.[55]

In an overt effort to align himself with the hard-hat demonstrations, Nixon invited its organizers to the White House for a "serious, in-depth briefing on the situation in Cambodia." As cameras snapped, Brennan presented Nixon with a hard hat, a "symbol of our support for our fighting men and for your efforts in trying to bring the war to a proper conclusion." Emotions swelled when Michael Donovan, a member of the Executive Committee of Brennan's Building and Construction Trades Council whose son had died in Vietnam, approached Nixon. "Mr. President," he said, "if someone would have had the courage to go into Cambodia sooner, they might have captured the bullet that took my son's life." The president appeared "visibly moved."[56]

Expedited by the deep, painful divisions over the Vietnam War, Colson appeared on the verge of achieving his mission. Following the visit to the White House by the hard-hat leadership, the Nixon administration's "political cultivation of labor" shot into high gear. Nixon invited seventy labor leaders and their wives, including the Meanys, to an elegant Labor Day dinner on September 7, 1970.[57] The Nixonites specifically targeted the Meany family for "cultivation." White House chief of staff H. R. Haldeman suggested that Meany's "daughters be given a certain amount of play" and be included "in Mrs. Nixon's tea for the wives of labor leaders."[58] In October, Nixon summoned Meany, Brown, and Lovestone to the White House for a "national security briefing."[59] In December, he met personally with AFL-CIO vice president Joseph Keenan, who, White House staffers noted opportunistically, "is a devoted Catholic and important labor leader, and is moving away from the Democrats."[60]

Aside from political wooing, the blue-collar strategy had a more serious, policy-oriented side. The White House assigned Assistant Secretary of Labor

Jerome Rosow the job of devising specific policy initiatives aimed at blue-collar voters. Rosow issued his recommendations in March 1970 in a report entitled "The Problem of the Blue-Collar Worker." He prescribed tax relief, subsidized housing, expanded public transportation, and educational grants for the lower-middle class.[61] Lukewarm about the specifics, Nixon nevertheless ordered "some initial implementation of the Rosow blue collar report even if it is only symbolic."[62] By the fall of 1970, Colson was positively gleeful. "The ground is plowed to bring them [organized labor] into the fold," he announced.[63]

But more than Colson's machinations or Rosow's initiatives, the president's hard line on Vietnam remained the primary force driving the blue-collar strategy. Nixon craved the AFL-CIO's political support on the war; the federation, in turn, needed the president's support to keep AAFLI and its international operations afloat. Vietnam made possible a remarkably awkward but still symbiotic political marriage. As opposition to the war intensified, the administration and the AFL-CIO provided each other with mutual comfort and support. On April 7, 1971, in advance of a presidential speech on Vietnam to be delivered that evening, Henry Kissinger privately briefed Meany at the AFL-CIO headquarters. "We would appreciate any support which you might be able to give us," probed Nixon's national security adviser. "It involves the fabric of our country and maybe, if we do not succeed, the country won't be worth being President of." Meany readily concurred and complained of the damage done by recent revelations regarding the My Lai massacre, "the result of this peacenik-sort of pounding of the press," according to the labor chief. Meany and Kissinger then swapped stories about facing down antiwar demonstrators on college campuses, Kissinger at the Massachusetts Institute of Technology and Meany at Randolph-Macon College. "I think the professors are worse than the students," opined Meany to the former professor. "I know you've got your problems on the economy but we appreciate your support in this area," offered Kissinger as the meeting closed.[64]

It was, in fact, Meany's antipathy for Nixon's economic policies that proved the undoing of the president's blue-collar strategy. By 1970, Vietnam-related economic growth, which had generated near record levels of employment, began to slow. Unemployment shot up almost two percentage points to approach 6 percent. Meanwhile, with the first signs of stagflation—stagnant wages and rising prices—the cost of living inched upward. The hard hats were hardest hit. By mid-1971, unemployment among construction workers stood at twice the national average, with some trades edging toward 50 percent.[65]

Dusting off Keyserling's decades-old prescriptions, the AFL-CIO blamed budget cutbacks resulting from the gradual withdrawal from Vietnam for the softening economy. As a recourse, it prescribed federal spending increases. "The only game plan for America is full employment," argued Meany in 1971.[66] Leon Keyserling himself proposed a full-employment plan he dubbed the "Freedom Budget," counseling massive government investment in the economy.[67] But Keyserling found little support from liberals. Rachelle Horowitz, who worked with Keyserling, recalled that the Freedom Budget "was opposed by two groups: fiscal conservatives and, sadly, peaceniks in the anti-Vietnam War movement who argued that you couldn't have both guns and butter."[68] In particular, antiwar liberals viewed with swelling disdain the AFL-CIO's calls for increased defense spending, insisting that ending the war would bring a "peace dividend," which would allow the country to address its pressing social needs. Once passionate advocates of full-employment economics, liberals increasingly abandoned ship.[69]

Meanwhile, fiscal conservatives, in particular Milton Friedman and his "monetarist" associates, broadened and amplified their attacks on government spending and Keynesian economics.[70] During his first two years in office, Nixon embraced a cautious monetarist approach, while preserving and even expanding key liberal policies.[71] Yet his initial efforts failed to curb inflation. By 1971, frustration set in among Nixon's advisers. Wage pressure, from unions in particular, became the convenient target of blame. "Our problems come because of the high wages demanded by the workers of this country," complained White House economic adviser Arthur Burns.[72] Likewise, CEA chairman Paul McCracken worried that "the construction industry continues to cause us extremely serious problems in our attempts to reduce inflation. Wage increases appear to be accelerating instead of subsiding."[73] Far from cultivating labor, some in the Nixon administration increasingly moved to scapegoat blue-collar workers.

Bowing to those who tied inflation to rising wages, Nixon took desperate measures. On August 15, 1971, he instituted price and wage controls.[74] The announcement—a blatant negation of the AFL-CIO's growth panacea for all economic problems—bewildered many in the federation. "They have substituted the damaging philosophy of scarcity for the rewarding philosophy of abundance," lamented Keyserling.[75] But Nixon's economic proposal placed Meany back on familiar turf. As he had a quarter of a century before, during World War II, he promptly positioned himself as the leading critic of price and wage controls. He pounded the Nixon plan as "an assertion of dictatorial power completely foreign to the American concept of freedom."[76] Inevitably under the controls, Meany insisted, the authorities would expend more effort controlling wages than prices.[77] To ensure that prices remained within the established controls, Meany deputized "watchdog" groups to carefully monitor and report on prices.[78] After years of painfully contorting his free trade union ideals to accommodate an expanding relationship with government agencies, especially to further his foreign policy objectives, Meany briefly revived his dormant antistatism with a vengeance—and to much acclaim.

Meany's barrage against Nixon drew rare praise from the media. The septuagenarian graced the cover of *Life*. "At 77," waxed the magazine's Hugh Sidey, "George Meany has been reborn."[79] Even his enemies in the labor movement marveled at his new lease on life. "George is acting the great trade union leader he is capable of being. . . . If this fine man could reconcile himself to the idea that the war is one of the blackest pages in America's history, he would soon develop into one of the best loved labor leaders in the world," privately noted Patrick Gorman, the adamantly antiwar president of the Amalgamated Meat Cutters.[80]

With his cultivation campaign on the rocks, Colson urged Nixon to invite Meany for an "off the record" breakfast to discuss events in "Laos and Southeast Asia" and to let the plumber know that "the door remains open."[81] Elsewhere, however, White House officials scrambled to slam the door shut. Nixon aid Desmond Baker circulated an angry memo assailing Meany as "so interested in seeing the Democratic Party recapture the White House in 1972 that he will oppose President Nixon whatever he does."[82] White House staffers convened a special meeting to coordinate a response to Meany's attacks. The ad hoc committee, which included Colson (now apparently determined to take a harder stand), George Shultz, H. R. Haldeman, Treasury Secretary John Connally, and Donald Rumsfeld, resolved to freeze Meany out; the president "should not at this time engage in any further dialogue with Meany privately or publicly." In public, the administration would seek to "deliberately isolate Meany. . . . This effort if properly done could separate Meany from his membership."[83]

Despite the rift with the Nixon White House and Meany's energetic campaign against price and wage controls, organized labor found few friends on the liberal side of the aisle. Increasingly, the Democratic Party was becoming the party of peace and neoisolationism. As chasms widened between liberals and labor, especially on issues of foreign policy, the camps exchanged bitter fire. Liberal senator Harold Hughes (D-Iowa) cautioned that the Democrats had "better disengage from that segment [labor]." Reuther's successor as president of the UAW, Leonard Woodcock, complained that "labor has been the victim of social snobbery by the Democrats and by liberals and intellectuals generally."[84]

Growing divisions between liberals and labor soon infected the debate over foreign aid funding. With the Democrats in control, Congress began radically rethinking foreign aid. In early November 1971, labor's archvillain, Senator Fulbright (D-Ark.), led the U.S. Senate in rejecting Nixon's proposed foreign aid budget for fiscal year 1972. Liberal senators such as Frank

Church (D-Idaho) and Majority Leader Mike Mansfield (D-Mont.) joined forces with conservatives, including Robert Dole (R-Kans.), to squelch aid appropriations. Both the White House and the AFL-CIO were stunned. Nixon bitterly ruminated that Fulbright and Mansfield "are unashamedly eager to see the U.S. defeated in war.[85]

The foreign aid crisis led to renewed cooperation between the AFL-CIO and the Nixon administration. An aid cutoff, even if temporary, imperiled the federation's overseas operations, including AAFLI, which depended on AID funding. Meany pleaded for a continuing resolution and fumed angrily that the Senate had created an "intolerable crisis."[86] His advisers warned him that absent foreign aid funding Southeast Asia "would within weeks crumble since one half of all the economies of Laos and South Vietnam . . . depend on AID."[87]

The Senate finally reached a compromise in which economic and military aid were to be separately funded and administered, but its final aid appropriation was nearly a billion dollars less than the administration's request.[88] The bitter legislative clash again revealed an isolated labor movement with few reliable allies. Although federation leaders remained close to particular members of the Democratic Party, the prospect of an unfriendly Democrat winning the White House in 1972 increasingly presented a greater threat than four more years of Nixon.

From every standpoint—political, economic, social, and cultural—organized labor, both its leadership and its membership, struggled during the early years of the Nixon administration. The president, seeking to derive political advantage from labor's weakness, fashioned a largely transparent effort, his blue-collar strategy, to win the allegiance of labor leaders. Differences on economic policy, however, laid bare the crassly political nature of Nixon's plan. By the end of 1971, little trust remained between the Nixon administration and the AFL-CIO. Nonetheless, the war in Vietnam supplied the adhesive that preserved the awkward marriage of convenience between Nixon and free trade unionists.

"But a Drop of Fresh Water"

By the early 1970s, free trade unionists had tired of the havoc wreaked on their political landscape by Vietnam. Meany, like the rest of the country, looked forward to the day when U.S. troops could pull out of Vietnam. "Frankly, we don't think there is any disagreement about getting out—getting our people out of Southeast Asia," he told reporters in 1970. Yet the AFL-CIO consistently praised Nixon's efforts to find "peace with honor," and Meany insisted that the federation remained, as he put it, "completely opposed to the idea of bugging out" before South Vietnam appeared securely able to defend itself.[89] Seeking support, Meany joined with other embattled cold warriors in founding the liberal Citizens Committee for Peace with Freedom in Vietnam, which was financed in part by a yearly AFL-CIO contribution.[90] Younger federation staffers joined "Negotiations Now!" which, despite its name, advocated an uncompromising line in the peace talks and preservation of a noncommunist government in South Vietnam.[91] Yet these initiatives did little to repair a damaged liberal coalition or revitalize the cold war, in which the AFL-CIO had invested so much.

In Vietnam, the CVT had made significant gains in the aftermath of the Tet Offensive, but by 1971 its progress seemed to stall. The ever present challenges burdening the CVT—corruption, internal rivalries, hostile Saigon authorities, and determined VC opposition—all seemed to worsen.

Its American supporters had heartily endorsed the formation of the Cong Nong, the CVT's political party, a development Vietnamese trade unionists hoped might energize millions of previously apathetic South Vietnamese. The Nixon administration and the AFL-CIO hoped that the Cong Nong would play an active role in the upcoming presidential election set for October 3, 1971. Rumors circulated that Buu would run as a candidate for president or vice president.[92] The balloting, Americans hoped, would be an opportunity to showcase nation-building and democracy in South Vietnam before a skeptical world.

The election, however, proved disappointing for both the CVT and South Vietnam. In the shadow of the recent collapse of the Lien Minh and in the absence of a tradition of direct political participation, Buu confided to the American labor attaché that he was finding it difficult to "elicit interest in the CVT's political ambitions."[93] Fearing rather than embracing democracy, President Thieu, described by one observer as "self-controlled and suspicious," pressured opposition candidates, including former vice president Ky, forcing them one by one out of the race.[94] Embarrassed at the prospect of a one-candidate election, Ambassador Ellsworth Bunker urged Buu and other potential candidates to enter the race.[95] But rather than entering the fray Thieu's opponents, particularly Ky, railed against the president's disregard for the democratic process and called for an election boycott.[96] Buu, fearing Thieu's wrath, also resisted Bunker's entreaties. In the United States, the specter of the uncontested election caused embarrassment and consternation.[97] With no alternative short of supporting Ky's boycott, the CVT endorsed Thieu. The polls opened in October with Thieu as the sole presidential candidate. The largest electoral turnout in South Vietnamese history relieved, to some degree, the embarrassment of the undemocratic election.[98] Yet genuine democracy, most observers, including the CVT, recognized, remained a distant goal for South Vietnam.

Likewise, the promise of genuine land reform floundered. Under the auspices of the land to the tiller law, hundreds of thousands of acres passed into peasant hands. But the program still fell far short of expectations. Landlords resisted forfeiting property, and "village authorities" in charge of the redistribution frequently accepted bribes to pass land along to "nontillers." While millions of U.S. aid dollars helped compensate landowners, the program remained perpetually in debt, no doubt the result of the corruption so ubiquitous in South Vietnamese society.[99] Even after peasants received land, substantial needs remained. New owners required training, seed, tractors, and other equipment. Buu talked of an "educational revolution" to complement the land revolution. Yet the CVT lacked the resources to meet the tremendous need. Meanwhile, as a result of budget cutbacks AID did not have the resources to intervene as it had in the past.[100] Ironically, just as substantial change began to come to the Vietnamese countryside, U.S. support, once nearly infinite, began to wither.

Intensifying Viet Cong terrorism compounded the CVT's struggles. Such tactics long had hampered trade union organizing. In the "lull" after Tet in 1968, American and South Vietnamese forces took control of large tracts of land formerly held by the Viet Cong, providing the CVT with a temporary reprieve from violence. But as the U.S. military presence receded the Viet Cong, supplemented heavily by North Vietnamese army regulars, reasserted itself in the countryside. In the early 1970s, the guerrillas took direct aim at the CVT's rural affiliates.[101] The VC also expanded its campaign of urban terrorism, again focusing on the CVT. In early 1970, VC agents dynamited the CVT headquarters in the city of Dalat. By July of 1970, according to AFL-CIO estimates, some sixty CVT officials had lost their lives to VC violence in the most recent wave of incidents.[102]

In the fall of 1971, as the one-candidate presidential elections approached, VC-inspired demonstrations and terrorism increased in Saigon. Buu presented a particularly tempting target. He constantly heard of threats against him and always traveled accompanied by bodyguards. On September 21, 1971, two kilos of VC-planted dynamite rocked the CVT headquarters, where Buu had a small apartment. Alarmed, residents of the surrounding neighborhood poured into the streets. Despite a six-foot hole in an exterior war and the collapse of an interior wall in the building, the dust cleared to reveal no casualties. Having retired to his bedroom just before the blast, Buu escaped unscathed. Trade unionists well knew that they were lucky, as just days before a similar bombing at a nightclub had killed fifteen and left fifty-seven injured.[103] Two weeks after the attack on their union headquarters, CVT-affiliated lambretta (motorcycle cabs) drivers jammed Saigon roads to protest the VC bombing.[104] Amid the terrorism, life in general grew more difficult for Buu and the CVT. Undermined by the piecemeal

U.S. withdrawal, the South Vietnamese economy imploded. Unemployment and inflation ravaged Saigon, and labor conflicts grew in the wake of the economic downturn.[105]

Concurrently, the CVT faced opposition from rival trade unionists. Vo Van Tai, who had left the CVT following the tumult of early 1968, established the National Confederation of Labor (NCL) to challenge what he saw as lethargy in the CVT. In the summer of 1971, with the Federation of Railroad Workers, Tai attempted to launch a general strike to protest rising income taxes. While the two-day strike had little impact short of closing some banks, and the NCL remained minuscule, for some Tai's militancy served as a reminder of the CVT's shortcomings.[106]

Meanwhile, serious "internal dissension" also ravaged the CVT. The source of trouble was Buu's politically ambitious wife, Mrs. Huynh Ngoc Nu, who operated a confederation-owned business and had a reputation for corruption. Resentment of Madame Nu ran highest in her native province of Bien Hoa. Before her marriage to Buu in 1961, she had served as general secretary of the CVT. In 1956, she held a seat in the National Assembly. Once the CVT developed a political party, Madame Nu, much to the consternation of local CVT officers, schemed to return to her old post in the Bien Hoa CVT, possibly as a launching pad for national office. Perhaps seeking to protect his own position, the sitting Bien Hoa CVT secretary treasurer publicly accused her of corruption.[107] At the same time, critics leveled charges of malfeasance against Buu's brother, Tran Quoc Khanh, who worked for the Farmer-Labor Party and had involved himself in CVT business affairs. The "young turks" of the CVT, who idealized "democracy" and direct action, seethed at the corruption seeping into their organization. They pressed Buu to clean house and rein in his relatives. Buu, while acknowledging problems with his family, declined to act.[108]

The CVT, of course, had no monopoly on corruption in South Vietnam, and wives of high-ranking Saigon officials frequently involved themselves in questionable business dealings. Resisting ubiquitous corruption required a purity of character rarely found in political or labor leaders. While corruption certainly existed within the CVT, political and personal rivalries contributed significantly to the distribution and exaggeration of the charges.[109]

The allegations had particularly unfortunate ramifications outside South Vietnam. When embassy reports of accusations against Buu's family reached the State Department in Washington, Robert Walkinshaw, the department's Asian labor adviser and a close Reuther ally, passed them along to Meany's rivals. Officials in the UAW then heralded the CVT's troubles as further evidence of misbegotten AFL-CIO overseas initiatives.[110]

By the early 1970s, struggles against corruption, the actions of the Saigon authorities, and intensifying VC terrorism had left CVT officers with a sense of stagnation and frustration. The CVT's perennial struggle to organize Saigon's dockworkers was perhaps most emblematic of the organization's intractable challenges. In the mid-1950s, the confederation, in cooperation with President Diem, had launched an attack on the exploitative *cai*, manipulative labor subcontractors who held a stranglehold on Saigon's ports. Yet, despite Diem's supposed victory over corruption, organized labor still proved little match for organized crime on the docks. Mimicking the Viet Cong, the *cai* simply retreated, maintained local cadres, and then returned at a more opportune time.

In 1965, President Teddy Gleason of the International Longshoremen's Association designed an American-style hiring hall to reform retrograde labor practices on the docks. Hopes for change ran high, but again the underworld resurfaced. "The same 'cai system' exists as before, with lion's shares of the worker's wages going to the cai, and the genuine workers having little to show as profits," lamented CVT general secretary Quyen in 1968.[111] In 1970, Buu renewed the attack on the *cai* system, but according to the U.S. Embassy he accomplished little and made "enemies of entrenched, wealthy and highly connected officials, including those recruiting the stevedores, the employers, the police and officials of the Ministry of Interior."[112] Seeking to jump-start the process, AAFLI, in conjunction with the CVT, conducted a "feasibility study" for a hiring hall at Newport, Saigon's major military port; such a project, it concluded, was "definitely feasible." But the study warned of potential retaliatory violence from "labor-brokers."[113] By the following year, AAFLI had made some progress, hiring a staff and establishing by-laws and operating procedures for the hiring hall, but by the end of 1972 nothing had been built. And soon economic chaos enveloped South Vietnam, as the U.S. presence dramatically declined.[114]

Compounding matters, Buu, always under tremendous strain, began exhibiting signs of age and weakness. By 1970, at fifty-eight, he was already known as a "conscientious hypochondriac," who was "recurrently ill and under frequent medical treatment for hypertension and high blood pressure."[115] When he visited Paris in December 1970, an American observer worried that he appeared "not in the best form" and "was showing his age."[116] Both Americans and South Vietnamese began to fear losing the politically astute leader of the CVT, who, despite his liabilities, remained of singular importance. Yet stability and progress for the CVT and AAFLI remained elusive. As stresses mounted, many in the CVT despaired of ever making a difference in their troubled country. Surveying the vast array of obstacles facing his organization, General Secretary Tran Huu Quyen lamented that the CVT "was but a drop of fresh water—we cannot dilute the salt ocean."[117]

A World of Woes

In the years following the Tet Offensive, both the AFL-CIO and the CVT entered controversial, compromising relationships with questionable, self-interested politicians: Nixon in the United States and Thieu in South Vietnam. Both arrangements brought immediate dividends. Nixon protected the AFL-CIO's shadowy network of overseas operations, and the South Vietnamese general helped preserve the CVT in the intense environment following the Viet Cong attacks of early 1968. Yet costs accompanied the dividends. Both organizations struggled with charges of having compromised their integrity. Sensationalized revelations regarding corruption in South Vietnam and American labor's alliances with the CIA only fueled allegations and suspicions.

Labor's mounting problems in the early 1970s mirrored larger national and international developments. Anticommunism as a political force sputtered and stalled, as did the once strong, postwar political coalition. These developments and a rapidly changing social, cultural, and political scene left the leadership of American labor at loose ends and its membership plagued by a disconnect observers described as the blue-collar blues. All the while, the AFL-CIO and the CVT remained defiantly optimistic about the course of the war and the potential for genuine social change in South Vietnam, but the hour was growing late.

8 "The Last of the Cold War Mohicans," 1972–75

In 1956, *Pravda* mockingly dismissed George Meany as the "last of the cold war Mohicans."[1] A meaningless slur at the time, by the 1970s the epithet carried more than a ring of truth. In the wake of the painful war in Vietnam, even the old cold warrior Richard Nixon embraced détente and accommodation with the East. Large segments of a hopelessly splintered liberal coalition, meanwhile, jettisoned anticommunism, foreign policy activism, and military preparedness altogether. A sharp economic collapse, in which millions of Americans lost their jobs, added to the AFL-CIO's sense of deepening woe. With few options, Meany maintained his on-again, off-again relationship with Nixon—a relationship his critics decried as an unholy alliance.

In Vietnam, desperation marked the CVT's last years. The U.S. withdrawal in early 1973 left South Vietnamese trade unionism vulnerable to both mounting Viet Cong terrorism and the reactionary Thieu regime. Rapid reduction of American aid destroyed the South Vietnamese economy and further complicated the plight of the CVT. In the end, the AFL-CIO stood virtually alone in lobbying for continuing aid to Saigon.

In 1975, George Meany celebrated his eighty-first year, his harsh, unyielding rhetoric virtually unchanged since the 1930s. Well suited to the expansive economy and cold war politics of the postwar era, by the 1970s free trade unionism was at best an anachronism and at worst a cover for unsavory covert dealings. The once proud labor movement was now severely compromised.

"The Odor of Johns about Them"

Nixon's blue-collar strategy stalled in 1971, the victim of the president's ill-conceived price and wage control program. That year the AFL-CIO and the Nixon administration joined ranks briefly in a political battle to preserve foreign aid funding, but all told their relations remained frosty.[2] A nadir came in March 1972, when a truculent Meany made a public show of angrily quitting Nixon's Pay Board, the agency that oversaw the administration's economic controls program. Meany's resignation came with more than its share of Vietnam-related irony, a war whose shadow seemed increasingly inescapable. Meany quit "to avoid any inference of complicity" in the board's decision to nullify a pay raise for West Coast longshoremen, a union ironically headed by Meany's nemesis, the antiwar activist and suspected communist Harry Bridges. To protest the board's injunction, Bridges called on his East Coast counterpart, the International Longshoremen's Association, to join a national strike, which would halt shipping on both coasts smack in the middle of an election year. But to add another odd twist the East Coast ILA determined, in view of Nixon's recent mining of Haiphong Harbor, that the hour was wrong for such a potentially costly strike. "Can you imagine us blockading U.S. ports at the very moment the president is blockading North Vietnam?" asked an ILA official.[3]

While Nixon may have taken some solace in averting a major strike, his relationship with Meany continued to unravel. The president's flirtation with détente further soured the relationship. The blue-collar strategy appeared to be moribund.[4] Sensing that his carrots had failed, Charles Colson—who had been assigned the "responsibility for squeezing, cajoling, and jawboning Meany," as one White House aide put it—reached for the stick.[5] In April 1972, he asked White House aide General Alexander Haig to conduct an "exhaustive" review of federal funds "squirreled away in various accounts" designated for AFL-CIO international programs. "I have no problem if the AFL-CIO finds out what the White House is asking," added Colson. "In fact, that might be very salutary under the circumstances of Mr. Meany's present silence on international issues and the vicious attacks on the President on domestic issues."[6] The message, of course, was pure blackmail: future outspokenness would imperil labor's overseas initiatives, including AAFLI. Haig's investigation turned up roughly $6 million earmarked for the AFL-CIO's 1972 foreign operations, with $1.6 million designated for AAFLI.[7] Meany's continuing attacks on Nixon now jeopardized the federation's generous government subsidies, affirmation of the sagacity of the now long discarded mandate to preserve free trade union autonomy.

However, it proved to be the continuing war in Vietnam, rather than Colson's machinations, that repaired fractured fences between the AFL-CIO and Nixon. A North Vietnamese offensive in early 1972 lent new immediacy to the federation's fears for the fate of South Vietnam and the CVT. At its February meeting, the AFL-CIO Executive Council warned, "Recent months have seen a series of developments in Asia which will affect profoundly the destiny of our country." Steadfastness in Vietnam remained a federation imperative.[8] As the country moved into an election year in 1972, Vietnam emerged as *the* litmus test for the AFL-CIO president. Asked by an interviewer if he wanted to see Nixon beaten, Meany responded, "I don't want to see him defeated by somebody who is advocating surrender. I don't believe in surrender in Vietnam."[9]

Determined to preserve its hawkish agenda in Vietnam, the AFL-CIO saw few attractive options among the Democratic presidential contenders. Liberals in the party had forsaken the war in Southeast Asia, some abandoning the cold war perspective altogether. Even the old stalwart Hubert Humphrey, labor's champion in 1968, had turned sharply against the war, as had the 1968 Democratic nominee for vice president, Senator Edmund Muskie, also a contender for the 1972 nomination. Federation hopes rested solely with Washington senator Henry Jackson, an increasingly rare liberal cold warrior who still maintained a hard line on Vietnam.[10] But Senator George McGovern, unapologetically demanding immediate withdrawal from Vietnam, overwhelmed Humphrey, Muskie, and Jackson in the Democratic primaries.

The AFL-CIO leadership recoiled at McGovern's swift march to the Democratic nomination. "My right arm will wither before I vote for McGovern," Lovestone told Colson.[11] McGovern, of course, possessed liberal credentials, but he promised to be no friend to the federation's "guns and butter," full-employment agenda. In fact, he proposed sharp defense cutbacks. Positioning himself as an "antiestablishment" candidate, the senator peppered speeches with derogatory references to "big labor" and "union power brokers."[12] Worse, McGovern not only fervently attacked the war in Vietnam, but he rejected wholesale the anticommunist, cold war agenda. In a 1971 fund-raising letter, he suggested that withdrawal from Vietnam would only mark the beginning of his crusade to "free" the country "from the last vestiges of cold war paranoia." McGovern seemed almost to delight in offending the moral sensibilities governing free trade unionism. "I think communism is another economic system that doesn't happen to fit my view of how society ought to be organized, but I'm willing to live in a world of diversity," he told an interviewer.[13]

Unwilling to exist in such a world and seeking to "rescue" the Democratic Party, Meany held a "secret meeting" with Senator Ted Kennedy in May. He urged the Massachusetts senator, whom Meany considered "the lesser evil," to enter the race.[14] Kennedy demurred, however, and the Democratic convention that year only confirmed to Meany just how much labor had lost. Union leaders found themselves unwanted guests as younger activists swarmed into the convention, treating their elders with barely concealed contempt. Calls for immediate withdrawal from Vietnam echoed throughout the convention hall. The political ground had shifted dramatically, and labor now found itself on hostile terrain. Party insurgents and labor regulars seemed almost unrelated species. Surveying the Miami Beach convention, Meany lamented its seizure by "people who looked like Jacks, acted like Jills, and had the odor of Johns about them."[15]

McGovernites were not Meany's only problem. Also gnawing at his sensibilities was a new activism among trade unionists opposed to the war. In March 1972, the peace-minded Teamster general secretary Harold Gibbons joined a small delegation of antiwar trade unionists in a high-profile trip to Hanoi, where they met with the North Vietnamese premier, Le Duc Tho, and several American prisoners of war.[16] In the summer of 1972, the growing ranks of dovish unionists met in Saint Louis to form Labor for Peace, a new organization espousing immediate withdrawal from Vietnam. Its founding convention drew nearly a thousand delegates and featured a keynote address by Mrs. Martin Luther King Jr. Seeking to reach workers opposed to the war but put off by the extremism of the antiwar movement, several speakers addressed the economic impact of Vietnam, in the process impugning full-employment, guns and butter economics. "This war has undermined the economy of our country, lengthened the rolls of unemployed and placed greater hardships on the backs of the working poor," raged the ACWA official Frank Rosenblum.[17]

Antiwar trade unionists finally established a viable organization. But its reach remained limited. Speaking to the Saint Louis gathering, Emil Mazey acknowledged that Labor for Peace did not "represent the majority of the labor movement." Even in Mazey's audience, serious differences existed. A motion by radicals to organize a one-day general strike to protest the war divided the gathering. Moderates objected vehemently and eventually sidelined the proposal, but the contention reflected the fragility of Labor for Peace and its alienation from the growing radicalism of the mainstream peace movement.[18]

Meany and virtually the entire AFL-CIO leadership remained contemptuous of growing antiwar sentiment within their ranks. Caught between a president whose domestic policies he opposed and a Democratic candidate whose foreign policies he despised (and whose domestic program he mistrusted), Meany chose neutrality. A few days after the Democratic convention, the AFL-CIO Executive Council voted, twenty-seven to three, to abstain from issuing an endorsement. President Nixon greeted the news enthusiastically as carrying the "potential of becoming one of the most important developments of the 1972 campaign."[19] Roughly a week later, Meany joined Nixon, Secretary of the Treasury George Shultz, and Secretary of State William Rogers for a well-publicized round of golf, ending a year and a half of bitter sniping between plumber and president. On the links, Meany assured Nixon of his neutrality.[20] The friendly game combined with Meany's known contempt for McGovern amounted to a Nixon endorsement.

Meany grew increasingly annoyed as McGovern's unfolding campaign showed no signs of moderation (while revealing ample signs of disorganization). Following the well-managed Republican convention, Meany asked George Shultz for a private meeting. Avoiding a direct endorsement, the AFL-CIO president carefully reviewed for Nixon's treasury secretary how the president might appeal to union voters. Despite reservations about détente, Meany thought Nixon was "perfect on foreign policy." Although he was a supporter of civil rights, Meany explained that he had come to appreciate Nixon's reservations about busing. He recommended a Labor Day speech stressing the importance of "free collective bargaining and industrial peace." This, he assured Shultz, would appeal to blue-collar voters. On the controversial topic of defense spending, he commended the president for emphasizing national security without connecting it to the issue of jobs. Workers, Meany explained, understand the importance of defense spending, but to speak openly about its economic impact would "just undermine the national security argument." In the margins of John Ehrlichman's transcript of the meeting, Nixon scribbled "right" alongside Meany's advice.[21] Still, Nixon, eager to make defense spending an issue to attract working Democrats, ordered the Defense Department to prepare a general report on the relationship between military spending and economic growth. The resulting study, *The Economics of Defense,* promised hard times should McGovern get his defense cuts.[22] But in stump speeches Nixon, adopting Meany's counsel, never openly linked defense spending and employment. The Defense Department's report performed that task for the president. The issue hung over the campaign.

Despite the AFL-CIO's avowed neutrality, Meany allowed both individual unions and AFL-CIO staff members to pursue their own political convictions. Ignoring McGovern's shortcomings and differences on Vietnam, many union leaders, including AFL-CIO vice presidents James Bierne and Joseph Keenan, could not bring themselves to desert the Democratic Party. In the fall of 1972, they formed the National Labor Committee for the Election of McGovern-Shriver.[23] But the group, competing against Meany's deafening silence, made little headway in bridging the cultural gap between labor and the McGovern camp. Each side clung stubbornly to the clichés of the other; one saw only reactionary, beer-guzzling hard hats, the other only scurrilous, flag-desecrating hippies.

On election day, Nixon won the bulk of the blue-collar vote. But workers did not favor Republican congressional candidates. Many split their ballots between a Republican president and a Democratic Congress. Meany had pumped AFL-CIO funds into congressional elections rather than the presidential race, and perhaps voters were responding to his implicit instructions. To many liberals, however, Meany's refusal to endorse McGovern lingered as a bitter betrayal by an obdurate, vindictive old man.

In 1968, organized labor had stood virtually alone in heralding the Humphrey candidacy amid a crumbling liberal coalition. In 1972, it found itself outside a reformulated Democratic Party looking in. The ideals of free trade unionism, especially anticommunism and guns and butter economics, no longer ranked as Democratic priorities. The liberal coalition was a casualty of the battlefields of Vietnam, and no replacement appeared on the horizon.

"These Are Hard Times for Americans"

Following his landslide victory, Nixon hoped to resuscitate his blue-collar strategy and press on toward his goal of a major political realignment. He appointed as his second-term secretary of labor Peter Brennan, president of the Building and Construction Trades Council of Greater New York and organizer of the Manhattan hard hat rallies. And the president revived his courtship of labor leaders. When the January 1973 Paris agreement finally ended direct U.S. involvement in Vietnam, Nixon sent Meany an appreciative note: "Now that we have finally achieved peace with honor in Vietnam, I particularly want you to know how much I have appreciated the support you have given during these difficult years to the policies that made that achievement possible. . . . [H]istory will prove you have been right."[24]

Yet repercussions from the unpopular war continued. In late 1972, after Nixon had managed to curb "stagflation" long enough to be reelected, prices again began to rise. By the fourth quarter of 1973, driven by the oil embargo of the Organization of the Petroleum Exporting Countries (OPEC), inflation soared to nearly 10 percent and unemployment rose steadily.[25] The impact of full-fledged stagflation rippled though the economy. Automobile sales fell precipitously, and General Motors laid off or furloughed over one hundred thousand workers.[26] In 1974, the economy slumped to near depression conditions, as unemployment shot to over 7 percent and inflation rose above 12 percent.

Scrambling to respond, the AFL-CIO dusted off its full-employment playbook. Blaming price controls, exports to communist countries, and high interest rates for the ravaging stagflation, the federation prescribed public works projects and government spending, especially on defense.[27] Distracted by Watergate and swayed by conservative economic advisers who blamed freewheeling Vietnam era spending for the downturn, the Nixon administration paid little heed to the recommendations. At least one Nixon adviser concluded that unemployment was the direct result of the end of the Vietnam War, which he described as "a massive public employment program which absorbed 4% of the labor force."[28]

The Nixon-labor dalliance unraveled yet again amid bitter exchanges over the handling of the economy and the brewing Watergate scandal. At the tenth biannual AFL-CIO convention, delegates unanimously demanded Nixon's resignation. Meanwhile, the AFL-CIO's relations with Secretary of Labor Peter Brennan deteriorated to such an extent that Meany insisted on conducting business solely through Secretary of the Treasury George Shultz.[29]

Nor could the AFL-CIO expect comfort from liberal Democrats. Transformed by Vietnam, most liberals prescribed defense cuts not increases and dismissed organized labor as an anachronistic, selfish interest group. Efforts to revive full-employment economics with the Full Employment and Balanced Growth Act (Humphrey-Hawkins Act), for instance, accomplished little.[30]

At the end of 1973, Meany could only lament that these were "hard times for Americans." Looking ahead to 1974, he predicted, "We will most likely find prices going up, and unemployment going up. Going down will be the standard of living of American workers."[31] The repercussions of the Vietnam War left the AFL-CIO a weak and divided organization just as it was facing its greatest economic challenge. At eighty years of age, Meany could do little more than watch events unfold.

"The World Has Stepped up Its Tempo of Going to Pieces"

In January 1973, Tran Quoc Buu was in Washington, DC, attending a dinner at the South Vietnamese embassy. There he watched Nixon on television announce the successful completion of negotiations with North Vietnam. As he listened, Buu could not hide from American friends his cynicism regarding the president's phrase "peace with honor."[32] His suspicions proved well grounded: for the CVT, the American withdrawal brought neither peace nor honor. For the next two years, Buu and his AFL-CIO supporters struggled to persevere in the face of nearly insurmountable odds, including a declining economy, oppression at the hands of President Thieu, internal dissension within the CVT, criticism from abroad, and finally the 1975 North Vietnamese invasion.

Even before the completion of the negotiations in Paris, events painfully conspired against the CVT. On March 30, 1972, the North Vietnamese army launched the Easter Offensive (the Nguyen Hue Campaign), a conventional military invasion of the South designed to capitalize on diminishing U.S. combat strength. For several weeks, the fate of South Vietnam hung in the balance. Finally, Nixon turned the tide by unleashing a massive bombing campaign, code named Linebacker I. During the bitter fighting, the North Vietnamese imprisoned or killed some thirty lower-level CVT officers and left thousands of union families homeless. In the hard-hit border province of Binh Long, about fifty miles north of Saigon, the invaders murdered the entire CVT provincial leadership. Again, South Vietnamese labor geared up for a relief campaign to assist its decimated membership and again called on the AFL-CIO for help. Meany responded immediately with an emergency cash grant.[33]

Alongside the so-called Easter Offensive, South Vietnam wrestled with a severe economic depression, far eclipsing in magnitude the recession in America. With American intervention in 1965 had come massive U.S. aid. Years of abundant jobs and economic growth resulted, furnishing the CVT with significant leverage over employers. Expanding American companies, such as the RMK-BRJ construction firm, which at its peak employed 150,000 Vietnamese, created an economic boom. But the U.S. disengagement removed the American economic scaffolding. With little need for new construction, RMK-BRJ discontinued operations in Vietnam, as did other U.S. firms.[34] Unemployment rose to nearly one-fifth of the workforce, and inflation soared to 65 percent. During the Easter Offensive, vital rubber-producing regions fell into the hands of the North Vietnamese. Refugees from the countryside fled southward, streaming into Saigon, where joblessness, despite the large number of Vietnamese conscripted by the military, soared to near four million. Rather than boiling rice, impoverished fishermen took to cooking the staple into a souplike substance to stretch it over several meals. Officials increasingly feared social unrest and street rioting.[35]

In many ways, the crisis was foreordained. The success of the CVT had been largely synthetic, spurred by a thriving economy and induced by war and an unprecedented American commitment of resources. Eager to promote democracy, the U.S. government and the AFL-CIO had pressured reluctant South Vietnamese authorities and employers to work with organized labor, greatly accelerating the rise of the CVT (though at the same time exposing South Vietnamese labor to charges of overdependence on outsiders). With the backing of the American government, Buu's organization targeted U.S. firms and won substantial victories. American officials hoped to impress skeptical South Vietnamese and the larger world with the spectacle of an independent labor movement achieving concrete gains for its membership. But the international community had paid little attention, and now the Americans were leaving, their money in tote.

Rising unemployment severely burdened South Vietnamese labor. Increasingly, CVT-sponsored strikes led nowhere. A walkout by Vietnamese AID employees failed miserably. The agency, itself having suffered severe cutbacks, was unable to meet union demands.[36] A CVT campaign for national austerity and renewal led to the closing of some bars and theaters, but this only put more Vietnamese out of work. Many unionists, especially younger members, blamed the Thieu regime for failing to help those hurt by the economic collapse.[37] But Buu and others in leadership positions kept largely silent for fear of creating yet more turmoil, which might be exploited by the enemy. Instead, they meekly prescribed the creation of labor-management teams to address the problem of unemployment. Buu also helped organize yet another political alliance, the People's Front against Communist Aggression, quickly dubbed "Buu's front," to unite the country against the economic downturn and pursue the CVT's long-stated goal of mobilizing the public at large against insurgent threats.[38] The new front, however, accomplished little.

In the wake of the Easter Offensive, President Thieu greatly complicated life for the CVT. The South Vietnamese president suddenly declared martial law and banned all strikes. Since its founding, the CVT had regarded the right to strike as an indispensable component of democracy. Nevertheless, Buu, who had resolutely resisted such incursions in the past, chose to acquiesce and supported the ban. His action appeared to many a sad capitulation to a corrupt government. Even during the difficult Diem era, labor had made no such concession. But Buu insisted that the CVT was now on the inside and needed to make sacrifices to maintain stability. "Now the situation—the danger—is different," he explained.[39] Thieu's labor minister, Dam Sy Hien, proudly acclaimed the CVT's no-strike pledge: "Our workers and their leaders realized by themselves that strikes are out of the question when the country is in danger."[40]

Not all trade unionists were as quiescent as Hien suggested. In October 1972, the CVT's Petroleum and Chemical Workers Union defied the government mandate and launched a strike involving eighteen hundred workers. Both management and labor worked hard to quickly resolve the strike, which awkwardly coincided with the peace negotiations and American elections.[41] Younger CVT leaders, idealizing American democracy, particularly chafed at Buu's willingness to work with Thieu, especially after the general moved to curtail the rights of South Vietnam's many political parties.[42] They appealed to CVT general secretary Quyen, who was known for his militancy and antipathy toward Thieu, to intercede with Buu. Quyen sympathized with the "young turks," but he eschewed breaking with his old friend Buu, a close collaborator since the 1940s, when both had been prisoners of the French.[43] Soon the young turks were threatening to resign en masse if they were not given more power in the organization.[44]

The CVT's youth auxiliary showed even less patience. When the U.S. embassy translated an article in the CVT's Cong Nong student magazine, they discovered an angry attack on American "imperialism." "Vietnamization is only the change of color of the dead," proclaimed the CVT-affiliated student group. "[N]ationalist forces and civic organizations should stop their internal disputes to work efficiently for the salvation of the country." For the students, the only answer was for "the authorities of both NVN and SVN to evade courageously from the control of the Great Powers and to settle the war in a compromise."[45] Buu, a vigorous supporter of the war himself, had always tolerated radical elements within the CVT. Yet the increasing tensions within the South Vietnamese labor movement led some American officials to doubt Buu's control of his organization.[46]

Buu shared many of the concerns of the youth group, if not its militant tone. He always had viewed the American presence in his country as a decidedly mixed blessing and looked forward in some ways to a U.S. departure. Despite his anticommunism, he understood that the vast majority of workers and peasants (like the CVT student group) simply wanted peace. Buu privately expressed these concerns to American officials and warned that President Thieu was subverting the peace negotiations.[47] Nevertheless, he remained unwilling to undercut the Saigon regime at a difficult hour. Instead, he continued to publicly suppress his apprehensions and support the president. "Buu has not overnight become an ardent admirer of President Thieu, but he feels that in the current situation it is important to support the president," concluded the American embassy.[48] The CVT's attempts to remain in Thieu's good graces did bring at least one immediate reward. In March 1973, following the signing of the Paris Accords, the South Vietnamese president appointed Buu to a delegation pursuing negotiations with the National Liberation Front. The delegation, however, had only a "vague mandate" and no real power. It amounted to little more than a public relations ploy intended to reassure Americans of South Vietnamese democracy and good faith.[49]

During this time, according to rogue agent Frank Snepp, the CIA "succeeded in turning Buu into a collaborator." The agency, Snepp claimed, had used Buu "quite profitably as an instrument for keeping the union loyal to Thieu." Saigon station chief Thomas Polgar even considered cultivating Buu as a safe candidate to run against Thieu in a future election to avoid a repeat of the 1971 specter of a one-man race (no surprise, since U.S. officials had appealed to the CVT president to enter the 1971 race).[50] Buu's CIA ties, however, almost certainly dated from the 1950s and represented one among a multitude of arrangements the veteran trade union leader made over three decades to insulate himself and his organization. While the CIA viewed Buu as valuable support for Thieu, the CVT chief most likely regarded the CIA as leverage against the mercurial South Vietnamese leader, with whom cooperation was a distasteful but necessary burden. The reputation of having shadowy, ruthless friends also served Buu in his dealings with non-CVT unions and communist infiltrators, and even in his conflicts with AAFLI. But whatever the advantages, Buu's CIA ties, long subject of rumors in Saigon, gnawed at his credibility, further impeding the organization's legitimacy and claims to *doan the*. Such remained the paradoxical choices of life in South Vietnam.

Despite Buu's attempts to support the Saigon government, trouble with Thieu was on the horizon. After accepting the Paris Accords, Thieu moved to cement his control in South Vietnam. Gossip swirled that the president intended to create a national labor union loyal to his administration. Buu discreetly kept Meany appraised of Thieu's rumored plans in case AFL-CIO intercession became necessary.[51]

Fearing diminishing influence as American troops departed, Meany decided to press Thieu personally. In April 1973, the South Vietnamese president arrived in Washington on a state visit. In recognition of American labor's support for his government, Thieu agreed to meet with federation leaders at Blair House.[52] The forty-minute meeting was cordial. Meany politely reviewed the AFL-CIO's long-standing support of the CVT, his high regard for the organization, and what he saw as the singular importance of independent labor unions to democratic countries. The subtext, of course, should have been clear: the federation—increasingly a lone defender of South Vietnam—regarded future support for Thieu's government as contingent on the health of the CVT. The trade union delegation left the meeting feeling that it had gone "very well" and they had a commitment from Thieu.[53]

In the months that followed, however, Thieu tightened his control over South Vietnam. When Buu's Cong Nong Party and other political groups protested, the South Vietnamese leader established his own "Democracy (Dan Chu) Party," blatantly modeled on Diem's oppressive Can Lao. Buu's refusal to join the Democracy Party prompted a spiteful Thieu to launch a labor wing of Dan Chu to compete directly with Cong Nong.[54] Officials of the CVT ominously viewed the Democracy Party's labor wing as a first step toward creating a national labor union under Thieu's direct control.[55]

Thieu also moved to squelch labor protest. When railroad workers initiated a peaceful strike, police arrested four top union officials. The authorities held them for several months without charges, trial, or revealing their whereabouts to families or associates. When pressed, Thieu finally charged the incarcerated unionists as communist agents.[56] Without leverage, the U.S. government could mount only a symbolic protest: Secretary of Labor Peter Brennan declined Thieu's invitation to visit Vietnam.[57]

As the union leaders languished in jail, the AFL-CIO once again readied a high-level mission to Saigon to lobby for their release. With Irving Brown unavailable (perhaps evidence of the AFL-CIO's exasperation with the ongoing struggles in Vietnam), Meany tapped Hunter Wharton, president of the Operating Engineers Union, to lead a delegation that included Benjamin Sharman, the international affairs representative for the International Association of Machinists, and Morris Palladino, the new director of AAFLI. Arriving on July 2, 1973, the group met first with U.S. ambassador Graham Martin (who had replaced Bunker earlier that year). Martin then accompanied the delegation to the presidential palace, where it pressed Thieu to release the prisoners. Martin bluntly recalled Thieu's assurances to Meany. After much prodding, eventually the general indicated that the matter soon would be resolved.[58] Although Thieu insisted on trying the labor leaders for endangering national security, the court quickly released them.[59]

While contending with the volatile Saigon leadership, the CVT also faced mounting foreign criticism. In April 1973, as Thieu campaigned to break the CVT, the German magazine *Der Spiegel* published an incendiary exposé by Heinz Pella, a West German aid administrator. It decried German humanitarian support for a "Confederation of South Vietnamese reactionaries who maintain armed tactical units." Branding Buu a "pasha," Pella blasted the close relationship between the CVT and Thieu, impugned the confederation's many business interests (among other things, claiming that the CVT sold chemical fertilizer on the black market), and assailed the blatant nepotism practiced by Buu.[60] The charges, while hardly novel, had veracity. Insiders at the CVT acknowledged that profiteering plagued its business ventures, and the questionable activities of Buu's brother and wife remained a sore point, especially for young trade unionists.[61] These problems were hardly unique to the CVT. Corruption remained an exasperating, dogged fact of life in South Vietnam, and it often had the tacit approval of American officials. "A little corruption oils the machinery," Ambassador Martin liked to say.[62] But many South Vietnamese found the ubiquitous corruption—known as *than nhung*—increasingly demoralizing. "The house leaks from the roof," was a lament frequently heard on the streets of Saigon.[63] The CVT's internal squabbles, exposed by the *Spiegel* piece, were yet more evidence of the debilitating and divisive curses hobbling South Vietnam (which was no doubt Pella's intent).

Its reputation maligned, the CVT scrambled into damage control mode. To rebut the charges, Buu convened a high-profile news conference on May 21, 1973, at the CVT headquarters. Beside him appeared CVT officers, the

AAFLI Vietnam director, a representative of the West German International Support Institute (ISI), and the South Vietnamese labor minister. Buu opened with a tirade against his accuser, angrily refuting the charges that he had pocketed aid money. The ISI representative then rose to back Buu, offering to make public records he claimed would refute Pella's charges. The AAFLI representative echoed the gainsaying chorus. Tenant Farmers' Federation president Vo Van Giao next disputed Pella's claims of corruption in the CVT's fertilizer distribution program. Explaining how the program aimed to circumvent corrupt merchants by selling fertilizer directly to farmers, Giao insisted that inflation rather than black market speculation had generated the rise in fertilizer prices.[64] Later he prepared a sharp written rejoinder to the West German publication, condemning Pella's charges as "a direct insult to 500,000 workers." Defending the CVT's paramilitary units, Giao pointed to the numerous acts of terror against CVT officials and the assassination attempt on Buu. "Do you really think that people living under these conditions of insecurity must remain passive and not even defend themselves?" he asked.[65]

Despite its exaggerated conclusions and lack of context, the *Spiegel* piece injured the CVT. Pella depicted a corrupt, compromised organization, the antithesis of the independence and virtue (*uy tin*) the CVT strove to embody. It dealt a direct blow to the confederation's claim to legitimacy and leadership. A year later, AAFLI officers found Buu still brooding over the article and threatening to suspend West German subsidies. His lingering bitterness eventually brought the former director of the Adenauer Foundation, a German relief organization that had provided aid to the CVT, to Saigon for a personal visit with Buu to "smooth ruffled feathers."[66] Still, the organization's international reputation was severely wounded at a dangerous hour.

Nor did Buu find much comfort or support from the ranks of international labor. The ICFTU, still bitter over its breach with the AFL-CIO, continued to ignore South Vietnamese labor. Meanwhile, the Christian International (IFCTU), in which Buu remained a vice president, grew increasingly radical and critical of the cold war. In 1968, as a symbol of its shifting orientation, it renamed itself the World Council of Labor (WCL).[67] By 1973, the WCL had grown so opposed to the Vietnam War—"in complicity with our enemy," Buu charged—that the CVT terminated its quarter-century affiliation.[68] Buu encountered similar hostility elsewhere in the world. In August 1973, he traveled to Algiers for a conference of nonaligned nations. There he immediately confronted a proposal to recognize the National Liberation Front as the true government of South Vietnam. Buu protested that the resolution would "bestow honor and decency on a prostitute and do it in the home of a real lady."[69] Even the CVT's parent organization, the

French CFDT (having undergone a painful evolution that involved dropping the appellation *Christian* from its name), came out firmly against the war, going as far as joining with the communist CGT in a "stop the bombing campaign."[70] Watching obstacles pile up for the CVT, Buu wrote Meany despairingly, "Since our last conversation, the world has stepped up its tempo of going to pieces. The disaster in Vietnam and Cambodia is appalling in its potential impacts and consequences."[71]

Ironically, as Lovestone was bemoaning the fate of Southeast Asia, a most unlikely source acknowledged the effectiveness of South Vietnamese organized labor. The National Liberation Front long had sought to infiltrate the workers movement in the South. In the early 1970s, it accelerated the campaign.[72] Yet, while students and intellectuals proved easy targets, South Vietnamese workers—considered the supreme prize—seemed impenetrable, remaining either anticommunist or solidly neutral. In 1974, Tran Bach Dang, a leading Viet Cong agent in charge of infiltrating mass movements in Saigon, made the mistake of openly lamenting the steadfast opposition of South Vietnamese workers to Viet Cong advances. He quickly found that he had committed an unpardonable ideological sin. The VC authorities demoted him for his honesty.[73]

Amid the chaos and setbacks of 1972 and 1973, the CVT continued to operate effectively. Even as vast numbers of South Vietnamese refugees poured into the country's cities, the CVT launched an urban organizing campaign aimed at the banking, electrical, textile, transportation, oil, and chemical industries. The confederation targeted 312 firms employing fifty-seven thousand workers.[74] It also affiliated several new unions, including the Port and Allied Workers Union of Saigon and an organization that represented movie actors and technicians, prompting a union official to quip that "now we have beauty on our side too."[75] Along with organizing, CVT cadres chartered several new cooperatives, which purchased commodities in bulk for redistribution at low cost to union members.[76] The CVT's political party, Cong Nong, also enjoyed growth, eventually controlling 20 of the 159 seats in the lower house of the General Assembly.[77] Buu even launched a campaign to create a South Vietnamese labor attaché program in foreign embassies.[78]

Tensions persisted between AAFLI and the CVT. Buu's relationship with AAFLI director Morris Palladino, whom the CVT chief regarded as undiplomatic and dictatorial, was particularly bad. However, AAFLI did begin to show evidence of utility. In 1972, it sponsored extensive training programs, involving twenty-two hundred Vietnamese trade unionists.[79] Despite strains, the CVT also grew to appreciate AAFLI as a source of political support and a useful lobbying channel to U.S. and South Vietnamese authorities.

Yet the CVT, like South Vietnam as a whole, was living on borrowed time, still dependent on the United States and facing grave uncertainty as the U.S. military pulled out. Particularly painful was the discontinuation of AID's Saigon Labor Bureau in 1973, a victim of funding cuts. The demise of AID/LAB came as yet another blow to the CVT, which long had relied on the bureau for advice, money, and support.[80] Soon the struggling organization would face even greater challenges.

"While the Fighting Might Stop, the Killing Would Not"

South Vietnam's last year, 1974–75, saw its international and domestic prestige plummet to new lows. Paradoxically, however, Buu's importance grew. In August 1974, AAFLI representatives reported "a lot of traffic of politicians, generals and other notables up and down President Buu's stairs of late." Apparently as South Vietnam's military situation worsened Buu's value as a lobbyist in America grew. The mercurial Thieu now moved to make peace with the CVT. The president sought Buu's advice on cabinet appointments and permitted the CVT to revive its Cong Nong Party.[81] In return, Buu made several high-profile trips to Washington to plead for continuing aid.

The CVT president's increased stature, however, hardly compensated for his country's darkening prospects. As the Watergate scandal paralyzed Washington, Congress refused to extend aid to Saigon. Facing a crisis, Buu increasingly came to see Thieu, despite the leader's belated cultivation of the CVT, as a liability, especially as a string of anticorruption protests erupted in Saigon. Shelving his earlier attempt at peaceful coexistence, in October 1974 Buu lashed out at Thieu. The government, he charged, was "inefficient and corrupt." Both Thieu and the North Vietnamese, Buu insisted, needed to dedicate themselves honestly to implementing the Paris Accords.[82]

Yet Buu continued to serve the South Vietnamese cause. When a U.S. congressional delegation that included the outspoken Bella Abzug visited Saigon and clashed sharply with President Thieu over conditions in South Vietnamese prisons, Buu was called in to "calm" the group. He met with four members of the delegation. "We are in need of both continuity and political change," he told them. Explaining that he regretted the recent arrests of journalists, Buu added that he was not convinced the reporters were beaten, as they had claimed.[83]

Despite Buu's best efforts, even as he met with the Americans events were moving with blinding swiftness toward a denouement. In early 1975, the North Vietnamese, as they had in 1972, launched a full-scale conventional invasion of the South. This time no American firepower intervened to halt the advance. As Hanoi's forces swept ahead, disturbing reports reached Buu of CVT officials singled out for reprisals. When Phuoc Binh Province fell, Buu sent an urgent telegram to Meany: "We lost two more CVT province leaders and thousands of members of our rubber plantation workers union, all civilians, slaughtered by communists backed by Russian tanks, artillery and limitless ammunition." Buu urged the AFL-CIO to muster support to stop the North Vietnamese march.

Immediately, Meany forwarded Buu's letter to President Gerald Ford and congressional leaders.[84] Condemning members of Congress who suggested that terminating American funding might save lives by ending the war, Meany warned, "While the fighting might stop, the killing would not."[85]

As prospects in Vietnam worsened, the AFL-CIO Executive Council issued a strongly worded statement urging support for President Ford's proposed $300 million aid package for South Vietnam; only AFSME president Jerry Wurf dissented.[86] In March, the federation also helped to arrange a high-profile lobbying trip for Buu to Washington. With increasingly steeled positions, by 1975 many in Congress refused to meet with official representatives of the South Vietnamese government. The AFL-CIO, however, still had sufficient clout to arrange meetings between Buu (a nongovernmental official) and key members of Congress. Buu arrived in Washington on Saint Patrick's Day for one last desperate round of lobbying, including meetings with Senators Henry Jackson and Edward Kennedy. "Give us sufficient aid to survive. Do not let us die slowly, agonizingly," Buu pleaded.[87]

The highlight came when Buu joined a small delegation of South Vietnamese leaders for a personal meeting with President Ford. Secretary of State Henry Kissinger had recommended the meeting to Ford as an opportunity "to express your concern over developments in Indochina and to demonstrate your support for Vietnam." Buu, Kissinger advised, "is not fully a supporter of Thieu, but he is a staunch anti-communist who clearly prefers Thieu to a Communist regime." He suggested that Ford break the ice with "I understand that you're known as the George Meany of South Vietnam."[88] Ford (eschewing the Meany comparison) greeted Buu and six South Vietnamese officials on March 25. Having visited the White House eleven years before, Buu was clearly the most experienced member of the delegation, and he dominated the meeting. Careful to emphasize his independence, he explained that the CVT did not "agree with President Thieu on everything" but supported him in the war against the North. He recalled for Ford his twenty-year affiliation with the AFL-CIO and U.S. government. "Always before, we could count on the United States. But now, the statements being made are more damaging than the bombs of the North. These announcements have encouraged the Communists," he warned the president.

Obviously, both men aimed their conversation at larger audiences. Ford—appreciating Buu's value in his battle to pressure Congress for aid—explained that he and Meany also had disagreements, "but we agree that we must support people who want to be free if they are willing to fight." As he left, Buu made one last request: "Whatever you can do, do it quickly."[89]

Buu also hoped a change of government in Saigon might hasten aid from the United States or spur negotiations with the northern invaders. On his return from Washington, he joined Bui Diem, the former ambassador to the United States, and Tran Van Do, a former foreign minister, in an effort to persuade Thieu to step aside. For three hours, Buu, Diem, and Do pressed Thieu at the presidential palace. "National unity," they tried to explain, was essential if the Americans were to be persuaded to intervene in the present crisis. Given the crisis, only a new government, they argued, could provide such unity. Thieu listened but remained unmoved. In the days following the meeting, Buu and Diem approached possible candidates to take the mantle of the country's leadership.[90] Thieu did permit, at least, a reshuffling of his government, in which Nguyen Ba Can, formerly the leader of the CVT's Cong Nong Party, became prime minister.[91]

Throughout April more and more territory fell to the invading army. The CVT kept Meany appraised by phone. The news was dire. According to accounts, the North Vietnamese army continued to target the CVT, seizing records, and arresting and killing union leaders. Meany marshaled the information as a part of an eleventh-hour drive to press Congress to take action. But the anticommunist-liberal coalition had imploded. Congress, particularly its liberal membership, was dead set against new appropriations.[92]

On April 21, Thieu finally stepped down in favor of his vice president. The North Vietnamese, now on the outskirts of Saigon, threatened to destroy the city unless an acceptable party took the helm of leadership. Buu became a key player in the scramble to set up a new government. Meanwhile, he urged CVT members to "rise up and push the government to fight. To flee is to die, to fight is to survive."[93]

As the southern regime crumbled, Meany urgently contacted Ambassador Graham Martin to ensure that CVT labor leaders would be included in any evacuation plans. Beginning his career as a National Recovery Administration commissioner before becoming an aide to Averell Harriman, Martin almost personified the old-line liberal coalition, languishing in the moral ambiguity and sheer confusion of Saigon's final days. To cope with events, the ambassador assumed a dreamy air of denial. Recalling how he "started out in government in the labor field," Martin personally assured Meany that there was no cause for concern. "The tide of public opinion is turning on the naked aggression of the North Vietnamese," the ambassador insisted. He thanked the AFL-CIO for its support and assured Meany that in the wholly unlikely event of an evacuation trade unionists would be among those slated for rescue.[94]

Strangely, even as the North Vietnamese army pressed toward Saigon, the city retained an air of normalcy. In mid-April, the CVT negotiated a substantial pay increase for Vietnamese employees of Shell Oil.[95] American companies continued to operate and plan for the future.[96] Few seemed to believe that the United States, after all it had invested in Vietnam, would allow the country to fall.

At the end of the month, however, reality struck home. In the final hours, the gravity of the situation came crashing down on Ambassador Martin, who struggled to initiate his evacuation plan, Operation Frequent Wind, without panicking the population. When Kissinger pressured the ambassador to speed up the evacuation, an overwhelmed Martin angrily retorted, "Do you want us to abandon any interest in orphans? If so, I'll send out the 5 with IRC [International Rescue Committee]. Do you want to tell George Meany we have no interest in labor leaders? If so I'll send the AAFLI guy."[97]

As Saigon teetered, Emil Lindahl, the embassy labor attaché, readied nervous CVT officers and their families for evacuation. They were to meet at an appointed time and board buses destined for the Tan Son Nhut airport. But on April 28, North Vietnamese pilots, in captured U.S. aircraft, bombed the airport, throwing the embassy's plans into chaos. Officials scrambled to implement an alternative arrangement, evacuating refugees from the U.S. embassy by helicopter. On April 29, Buu called roughly two hundred CVT officers and their families to confederation headquarters on 14 Le Van Duyet Street. There the group debated "what to do next." Seeing little option, they chose to flee. But under the revised helicopter plan only Buu could be accommodated. Again the CVT turned to the Americans. As hysteria engulfed the city, Lindahl struggled to make arrangements for the remaining members, including Buu's wife, now without an escape route. Miraculously, he found space on a barge docked at the Port of Saigon. In the midst of chaos, the trade unionists and their families made their way to the port. As Saigon fell, they drifted out into the South China Sea.[98]

The CVT headquarters in Saigon was among the first targets of incoming North Vietnamese and Viet Cong forces. The victors promptly posted guards in front of the building and strung a banner across it, reading "People's Revolutionary Committee." The new regime immediately dissolved the CVT and ordered all future labor activities to be coordinated by the state through a new committee now housed in the CVT compound. Radio broadcasts ordered union members to report to the authorities and took special aim at Buu, who was denounced as a "traitor." Floating toward safety, the CVT refugees listened in grim silence as radio announcers read lists of those wanted by authorities; some heard their own names crackle over the airwaves. In the vanquished city, an observer noted constant activity at 14 Le Van Duyet Street as the new government formed worker organizations. In the midst of the bustle, for several days no one thought to remove a portrait of Buu from the wall.[99]

After three days at sea, the exhausted CVT refugees arrived in the Philippines and eventually made their way to a refugee camp in Guam. There they reunited with Buu. The group later moved on to Fort Chaffee, Arkansas, where AAFLI and the AFL-CIO Department of Community Services worked to find them sponsors.[100] Trade unionists to the end, in Arkansas the evacuees immediately elected committees to delegate duties, represent interests, and air grievances. Questioned about the fall of Saigon, Buu referred to his dashed hopes of mobilizing large-scale popular opposition to the communists. The South Vietnamese government, he complained, "had monopolized all the means to fight so that the people and democratic organizations had nothing to fight with, and therefore, were not really involved in the struggle."[101]

Meanwhile, the depressing parade of reports seeping out of the former Republic of Vietnam continued. According to refugees, the invading North Vietnamese marked CVT cadres for reprisals. Stories of arrests, forced labor, and executions poured into the AFL-CIO headquarters.[102] But there was little Meany or the AFL-CIO could do for the Vietnamese unionists they had protected for more than a decade. Devastated at the loss of a lifetime's work, Buu retreated into a lonely exile. He died in Paris in 1976.

"Last of the Cold War Mohicans"

In the wake of the Vietnam debacle, Meany, while insisting that he had not budged from his ardent anticommunism, seemed to reassess his tactics. In 1974, he arranged for the resignation of Jay Lovestone, whom he may have suspected had not been entirely loyal over the years. Increasingly Meany came to rely on a circle of young socialists, led by Thomas Kahn, with roots in the anticommunist tradition of socialist activists Max Shachtman and Michael Harrington. The group, which began as part of the Young People's Socialist League, harbored deep animosity toward the New Left and counterculture. Bucking their generation, they idolized Meany as a paragon of virtue. When Harrington turned against the Vietnam War and supported George McGovern for president in 1972, Kahn and others broke from the mainstream socialist movement and formed an anticommunist, progressive, political organization, Social Democrats, USA (SDUSA). In the late 1970s, Kahn's ascension to the head of the AFL-CIO International Affairs Department signaled the arrival of a new generation no less committed to anticommunism but wielding a more sophisticated rhetoric, emphasizing human rights. Many in the SDUSA circle later found themselves working in the Reagan administration.[103]

To some degree, Meany also seemed aware that the federation's awkward relationship with the U.S. government, which had strained the ideals of free trade unionism, had backfired. With the fall of South Vietnam imminent, he appeared on the Dick Cavett television show. Referring to his support for Johnson and Nixon on Vietnam, Meany confessed, "If I'd known then what I know now I don't think we would have backed them." At an AFL-CIO Executive Council meeting in early 1975, he again complained of having been "deceived by Nixon and Kissinger on Vietnam."[104] Later, Meany qualified his comments. While maintaining that "self-determination" for South Vietnam was the "basic principle" behind American involvement, he complained that "the American people were not told the truth as to the actual conduct of the war, the prospects for Vietnamization, etc." But he added that his "fundamental belief in the role of the United States as the Chief defender of freedom has not changed one bit."[105] More than anything else, Meany's admissions seemed to be a belated attempt to reclaim a semblance of the independence the federation had sacrificed fighting its cold war.

To his critics, Meany's late-night television confession rang hollow. Longtime Meany antagonist Leon Davis, president of New York City's Hospital Workers Local 1199, dismissed the confession as "too damned late." Union members, he blasted, had "a right to know why the AFL-CIO is now isolated not only from the socialist world but also from its former friends in the movements of Western Europe."[106]

Davis correctly surmised that Meany's second thoughts about American policy in Vietnam hardly meant second thoughts about his anticommunism or his commitment to an independent South Vietnam. He also correctly assessed the damage to and divisions in American organized labor caused by the Vietnam War. Unfortunately for Meany, these repercussions hardly ended with the fall of Saigon.

In the aftermath of the war, President Ford announced plans to open U.S. borders to thousands of Vietnamese refugees. But with the U.S. unemployment rate nearing 10 percent many Americans questioned whether, after bearing the expense for the war, the country could absorb the new immigrants. Meany cavalierly dismissed such reservations. In customary hyperbole, he assailed the "meanness of spirit" of those who would turn away the refugees.[107] He accepted a high-profile position on the seventeen-member presidential advisory committee on the resettlement of Vietnamese refugees. He also committed the AFL-CIO Community Services Department to aiding the resettlement, dedicated federation funds to the cause, and asked all federation locals and affiliates to help find jobs for refugees.[108]

But the immigration issue, historically painful for organized labor, could not be so easily settled. With a faltering economy and a labor movement rife with tension, Meany faced opposition. When the Kansas State Federation of Labor protested the influx of Vietnamese refugees, Meany—assuming his bully mode—blasted the resistance as "deplorable," paramount to "denying our heritage." The Kansas wing of the AFL-CIO had "a perfect right to take that position," Meany offered. "And they have a perfect right to rescind it once they know our position."[109]

While Meany could still intimidate federation affiliates, employers were another matter. With employment opportunities declining, assimilating immigrants proved to be a divisive challenge. "The heart of the problem is jobs—and unless they are forthcoming more readily, many refugees will remain in the camps through Christmas," lamented the head of the AFL-CIO Community Services Department.[110] Moved by the plight of the refugees, an Ohio manufacturer offered to sponsor two immigrant families with housing and jobs in his plant. He then proposed spinning his initiative into a national program involving other small and medium-sized businesses, but, he warned, the plan would require suspending union provisions regarding seniority in layoffs and rehiring. "We have an emergency situation which warrants a generous approach that requires that we bend a little," he pleaded. The National Association of Manufacturers showed some interest in the proposal, but the AFL-CIO, warning that the industrialist was "engaged in a one man crusade to destroy seniority," rejected the plan outright.[111]

Less altruistic employers also seized on the immigrant crisis. Keith Johnson, president of the International Woodworkers of America, appealed directly to Meany when a Portland, Oregon, employer used Vietnamese refugees to break a strike. The "practice of sending refugees who do not speak English or realize that they are being used by unscrupulous persons to work behind a picket line poses a threat to organized labor," Johnson warned.[112] The threat quickly snowballed. The sporting goods manufacturer AMF-Head hired Vietnamese refugees to help break an ACWA-organized strike at its Boulder, Colorado, plant. In Egg City, California, an employer hired fourteen refugees to end another work stoppage. Outraged, Meany leaned heavily on the White House to address the problem, threatening to resign from his position on the presidential advisory commission if he did not see action. Scrambling to keep Meany on board, the "White House went to work" contacting the Red Cross and utilizing other connections to find alternative employment for the strikebreaking refugees. In the case of the Boulder strike, "pressure was brought to bear" on the refugees and they resigned from their jobs.[113]

Even as he continued to experience the fallout from Vietnam, Meany remained an unreconstructed anticommunist. Now in his eighties, he continued to assail détente and human rights violations in the Soviet Union, in the process earning the admiration of Soviet dissident Alexander Solzhenitsyn.[114] Meany resisted President Gerald Ford's initiatives to sell grain to the Soviet Union and continued to push for a stronger national defense. Likewise, the AFL-CIO's response to the growing economic crisis of the 1970s remained a call for higher wages, public works projects, and a return to the principles of full employment first set out in the Employment Act of 1946.

Meany's and the AFL-CIO's effectiveness, however, had diminished considerably. Among liberals, full-employment economics and high defense spending no longer held currency. Meanwhile, conservatives adopted an increasingly strident antilabor rhetoric, blaming high blue-collar wages for inflation and the economic downturn. To many, Meany seemed little more than an anachronism. "When Meany starts talking about Détente, flinging around his Cold War rhetoric of the early 1950s, there is no chance for logical consideration of that delicate issue," complained liberal columnist Carl Rowan in 1975.[115] "Once upon a time, organized labor in this country was in the vanguard of the liberal movement in foreign policy as well as domestic. But not any longer. . . .George Meany, often makes the US Chamber of Commerce sound like a cabal of wild-eyed Bolsheviks," editorialized the *Connecticut Register*.[116] Even within the labor movement many chafed at the "over-the-hill" image of a labor leader in his eighties clinging to power. "We're not organizing 85-year-olds, we're organizing 18-year-olds, and they think his brain is pickled," publicly lamented the president of the International Association of Machinists.[117]

In testimony before the Foreign Affairs Committee in 1975, Meany seemed to acknowledge, though defiantly, the ground he had lost. Assailing the neoisolationism of many liberals, Meany offered, "I cannot help but wonder what has become of the word liberalism. I always thought that liberalism had to do with the defense of freedom—and that the defense of freedom did not stop at the water's edge." Later that year, as if reveling in his reputation as an anachronism, when asked whom he favored for president in the 1976 election, Meany snapped, "Harry Truman."[118]

Conclusion

Why Are We in Vietnam? asked Norman Mailer in his best-selling 1967 novel. Over thirty years later his question still perplexes leading scholars of the war.[119] Other questions about Vietnam persist with equal stubbornness in debates among historians, political scientists, and the public at large. Why did the United States remain in Vietnam long after it was clear that its initial objectives could not be achieved? What accounts for the U.S. failure? And why does this war, which began almost forty years ago, maintain such a hold on the collective consciousness of so many Americans? Despite volumes written treating the causes and consequences of the war, satisfying conclusions to these questions remain elusive, like a nearly complete puzzle with key pieces missing. Shifting our perspective from the elite policymakers to the parallel story of American labor's painful and complex Southeast Asian experience adds to our understanding of these "why" questions and yields valuable pieces of the puzzle; simultaneously, it generates a number of tantalizing "what if" questions.

In answering the why question about U.S. intervention in 1965, scholars have pointed to an amorphous anticommunism that inexorably bound policymakers to the logic of containment and a universalistic foreign policy. Organized labor's free trade union ideology represents a working example of the depth, potency, and sophistication of these perspectives. Hardly a passing fancy, anticommunism had deep roots for free trade unionists, some of whom were former communists. Likewise, anticommunism served in many ways as an outlet, a vehicle through which to criticize state encroachment on the prerogatives of organized labor, even as most trade union leaders embraced greater labor-government cooperation. Although the anticommunism of free trade unionists at times placed its adherents at odds with official U.S. foreign policy and other unionists, by the late 1940s it provided an alluring avenue toward respectability, a way of defining oneself as part of the ruling establishment; as C. Wright Mills suggested, union leaders became "new men of power." Supremely ambitious, free trade unionists eagerly took their anticommunism abroad, in many ways conducting their own foreign policy. While often defined by an unseemly secretiveness and ruthlessness, at heart the idealistic hope of promoting independence and self-determination for the workers of the world drove these operatives.

Vietnam offers a case in point. Free trade union goals in Southeast Asia went far beyond halting the spread of the Red Menace. While Meany and his crowd viewed communism as a monolithic, aggressive, spreading virus, they also recognized the necessity of constructing democratic alternatives, such as the CVT, if the disease was to be overcome. The AFL-CIO's "unstinting" support for the war in Vietnam, however shrill and impetuous, emerged from these deeply felt imperatives. The goal was a democratic South Vietnam.

A secondary but still important component of free trade unionism, and one that also contributed to support for the war in Vietnam, was full-employment economics as interpreted by economic guru Leon Keyserling. Believing aggressive government investment capable of spurring almost limitless growth, labor held that the U.S. economy could thrive on both massive social spending at home and enterprising activism abroad: guns and butter. Increasingly, mainstream organized labor, driven both by anticommunism and full-employment economics, championed higher defense spending. As the crisis in Vietnam deepened, organized labor had no doubt that the economy not only could withstand intervention but actually would grow as a result of the engagement. While it was not a motive for AFL-CIO support for intervention in Vietnam, waging war in Southeast Asia fit comfortably with U.S. labor's economic worldview.

In the case of free trade unionism, the ideological perspectives propelling America toward the Vietnam War appear as real forces, evolving from real experiences, rather than abstractions. On the eve of U.S. intervention, the AFL-CIO was ideologically predisposed to support action. Beyond this, unrecognized by historians, the federation already had devoted more than a decade to supporting a promising labor movement in Vietnam.

The giant personality and equally behemoth political ambitions of Lyndon Johnson and his relationship with organized labor help complete the picture. Isolated and suspicious of Kennedy liberals, the new president desperately craved allies. By the force of his personality, combined with his aggressive approach to foreign and domestic issues, Johnson transformed a chilly relationship with organized labor into a passionate love affair. Historians have made much, with good reason, of LBJ's fears of a right-wing-driven "Who Lost Vietnam?" debate circumscribing his options in Southeast Asia. Determined to shield his liberal Great Society programs from conservative attack, the argument goes, Johnson played it tough in Vietnam. But this analysis underestimates the potency of the anticommunist Left, particularly the labor movement. Weakness in Vietnam not only presented perils from the Right, but it also endangered Johnson's hard-won intimacy with labor. Running for president in 1968, Vice President Hubert Humphrey faced similar dilemmas. To distance himself from the war imperiled AFL-CIO support when labor stood almost alone among liberals in the Democratic candidate's corner.

Like Johnson, Richard Nixon coveted labor's support. He dreamed of incorporating blue-collar Americans into a "new majority" political party. Vietnam served those aims well. While free trade unionists found little to admire in the president's domestic policies, his hawkishness on Vietnam and willingness to fund the AFL-CIO's foreign operations stood in sharp contrast to the growing hostility from labor's former allies on the Left. Nixon deeply believed that retreat in Vietnam would damage U.S. credibility, but the politics of Vietnam, while unnerving to the president in many ways, served him in his dealings with labor and set up his landslide victory in 1972. A retreat from Vietnam, Nixon understood, would have undermined his precious blue-collar/new majority strategy.

Labor's story in Vietnam also adds to our understanding of the painful "whys" relating to the U.S. failure in Southeast Asia. Paralleling the overall U.S. mission, the AFL-CIO entered Vietnam with an ambitious agenda: to transform the struggling South Vietnamese labor movement into a political, economic, and military wellspring of reform and renewal. But such plans trapped the CVT in an inescapable paradox. For success and survival, it depended on U.S. support, but that very dependence compromised the organization's legitimacy (*uy tin*) and its efforts to unify and motivate the Vietnamese people (*doan the*). The AFL-CIO (which, given its own preoccupation with autonomy, proved remarkably insensitive) struggled to come to terms with a client who both needed and resented its patronage. South Vietnamese trade unionists chafed at the dictatorial style and presumptions of some U.S. laborites, who were eager to impose an American-style solution to all problems. These tensions reflected, in microcosm, the frequently strained official U.S.–South Vietnamese relationship and portended an overall mission destined for failure. In short, the Americans, by their very saving presence, fatally tainted their South Vietnamese hosts. A stalemate might be achieved and defeat might be delayed indefinitely, but the U.S. government, despite its hegemonic power, could never legitimize South Vietnam; indeed, it accomplished quite the opposite.

If the AFL-CIO's "unstinting" support for the war provides clues, pieces of a larger puzzle, to understanding the U.S. intervention, persistence, and ultimate failure in Vietnam, labor's experience also helps explain the painful resonance of the war. The AFL-CIO's intolerance of dissent, dogmatic adherence to the logic of anticommunism, and sheer hawkishness alienated many in its own ranks. It also opened up a grave divide between labor and liberals, significantly contributing to the collapse of the New Deal coalition. Alliances required by the war belied the federation's claim to absolute autonomy, the essence of free trade unionism. In its association with the CIA and AID, the AFL-CIO appeared to many to be a junior partner in a corrupt corporate mechanism.

The federation limped out of the Vietnam War a divided and weakened organization, just as seismic economic shifts overtook the nation. Whether or not Vietnam caused the economic turmoil and other challenges of the 1970s, it severely weakened organized labor's ability to react to these challenges. To belabor the puzzle image: if one were to put together a jigsaw puzzle, with each piece representing contributions to the decline of organized labor, the final image would be unrecognizable without the Vietnam War.

Provocative "what if" questions hang over this study as well. With regard to the fate of organized labor: what if there had been a change of leadership at the AFL-CIO before the Vietnam War? Under a Walter Reuther, for instance, the federation might have taken a direction more along the lines of the ill-fated Alliance for Labor Action, cautiously critical of the war and open to alliances with the Left. Those who bemoan Meany's regime and support for the Vietnam War lament a "missed opportunity" for labor to move to the center of the 1960s and 1970s protest movements, providing direction to the disparate, unfocused groups that demanded economic, political, and social change. A more holistic movement that married the energy of left-wing radicalism to the untapped militancy of the working class would have brought permanent change, many on the Left seem convinced today, and averted the disturbing right turn the country took in the late 1970s.

But, as trade unionists who joined the peace movement discovered, while political common ground might be found, cultural divisions were not so easily transcended. The chaos so eagerly embraced by young radicals represented a threat to the hard-won stability and tenuous prosperity of American workers. As labor historians such as Robert Zieger, Michael Kazin, and others have begun to explore, an essential conservatism, offset by occasional militancy in defense of material objectives and workplace dignity, best defines the mind-set of most workers. Neither the ambitious free trade unionism of Meany, with its internationalism and "bear any burden" moral imperatives, nor the social progressiveness of Walter Reuther neatly matched the aspirations of the American rank and file. In the end, while the calamitous divisions and deep wounds of the Vietnam War might have been mitigated, the alienation of the "blue-collar blues" seems to have been unavoidable.

"What if" questions also surround the other labor movement considered by this study, the Vietnamese Confederation of Labor. From the early 1950s to 1975, the CVT, despite its shortcomings, offered a real, democratic vision for South Vietnam. But it faced a number of nearly debilitating obstacles. In particular, its American sponsors never provided adequate support, and a host of autocratic South Vietnamese leaders never fully recognized the legitimacy of the CVT. After 1965, U.S. officials grew somewhat more supportive, though perhaps more out of deference to the political influence of the AFL-CIO than the potential seen in the CVT. South Vietnamese labor, however, never played a major role in U.S. pacification plans.

For American policymakers, one of the great frustrations of the war was the inability of Saigon's leaders to mobilize its citizenry, to win the "hearts and minds" battle. The CVT, with its roots in the revolutionary movement, its appreciation of both modernity and Vietnamese tradition, and its broad urban and rural base, appeared precisely the sort of "third force" sought by

Americans. If at an early stage American officials had cultivated the CVT and other democratic forces in Vietnam, events might have unfolded differently. However, it is hard to imagine a scenario in which U.S. officials, from a country beset with deeply ambivalent attitudes toward organized labor, could have embraced trade unionism as the essential bulwark against communism. Likewise, as suggested earlier, American intrusion and cultivation were just as likely to damage and taint as to nourish and support. Still, there can be little doubt that unexplored alternatives did exist in Vietnam.

Putting aside speculation, we are left with a sense of two labor organizations, one centered in Washington and the other in Saigon, both driven by far-reaching ambitions—those of staving off communism and humanizing the emerging liberal capitalist system—all the while striving to remain independent, uncompromised forces. Briefly, these interlocking agendas appeared obtainable. In the end, however, the alluring promise of a world system in which independently operating labor movements might play a shaping role proved ephemeral. The Vietnam War more than any other factor laid bare the contradictions and paradoxes in which labor operated in the second half of the twentieth century. Despite expectations otherwise, the place of organized labor in both the national and international systems remains insecure and fragile, pinched, as it were, between a river and a mountain.

Notes

Introduction

1. Val Lorwin, *The French Labor Movement* (Boston, 1954), 136; Alain Ruscio, *Les Communistes français et la guerre d'Indochine, 1944–1954* (Paris, 1985), 251–65.

2. This study primarily examines the leadership of the organized labor movement rather than its diverse membership. For convenience's sake, I frequently refer generically to "labor" or "organized labor." While it would be a grave mistake to portray organized labor as a monolith, at times a general consensus did exist among labor leaders on particular issues. I have striven to limit my generic use of the word *labor* to instances in which such a consensus arguably existed. In discussing anticommunism in the 1950s, for instance, a relative unanimity existed among the leaders of mainstream American organized labor. For events that occurred later, when this consensus broke down during the Vietnam War, I have been careful to refer to particular elements of the labor movement.

3. Richard Trumka, "On Becoming a Movement," *Dissent* 39 (winter 1992): 58.

4. Nelson Lichtenstein, *Labor's War at Home: The CIO in World War II* (New York, 1982), ix. Peter Levy, in *The New Left and Labor in the 1960s* (Urbana, IL, 1994), also begins his study with a recounting of the clash between the hard hats and the peace protesters (1–2).

5. Historians today have virtually ignored the existence of a South Vietnamese labor movement. "In one of the least well studied activities of the second Indochina war," noted Alexander Woodside, "representatives of world Catholic labor unions and the largest American labor unions (which strongly supported the American war machine in Vietnam) visited Saigon frequently and sponsored training classes for southern labor union cadres, after 1956." Alexander Woodside, *Community and Revolution in Modern Vietnam* (Boston, 1976), 287. Also see James L. Tyson, *Target America: The Influence of Communist Propaganda on U.S. Media* (Chicago, 1981), 145–54. Tyson charged the Western media of the time with deliberately dismissing the significance of the South Vietnamese labor movement as part of a "continuing world-wide Communist effort to destroy free labor unions by propaganda."

6. Philip Foner, *U.S. Labor and the Vietnam War* (New York, 1989), 86–87.

7. Trinh quang Quy Phong, *Trào lâo-dong Việt-Nam* (Saigon, 1970), 118.

8. Kevin Boyle, *The UAW and the Heyday of American Liberalism, 1945–1968* (Ithaca, NY, 1995).

9. Christopher L. Tomlins, *The State and the Unions: Labor Relations, Law, and the Organized Labor Movement in America, 1880–1960* (New York, 1986), 147. For other works offering generally negative evaluations of American labor-state relations in the postwar period, though with very different emphases, see Patrick Renshaw, *American Labor and Consensus Capitalism, 1935–1990* (Jackson, MS, 1991); Michael Davis, *Prisoners of the American Dream: Politics and Economics in the History of the U.S. Working Class* (London, 1986); David Brody, "The Breakdown of Labor's Social Contract," *Dissent* 39 (winter 1992): 32–41; and David Brody, *Workers in Industrial America: Essays on the Twentieth-Century Struggle* (New York, 1980); as well as works by legal scholars Karl Klare, Katherine Stone, and James Atleson. Melvyn Dubofsky, *The State and Labor in Modern America* (Chapel Hill, NC, 1994) offers a more sanguine view of labor's relationship with the state. For a sense of the general corporate environment in which organized labor operated, see Michael Hogan, *The Marshall Plan: America, Britain, and the Reconstruction of Western Europe, 1947–1952* (New York, 1987).

10. Ronald Radosh, *American Labor and United States Foreign Policy* (New York, 1969), 4. Works taking a similarly dim view of organized labor's foreign policy include Beth Sims, *Workers of the World Undermined* (Boston, 1992); and Elizabeth McKillen, *Chicago Labor and the Quest for a Democratic Diplomacy, 1914–1924* (Ithaca, 1995). One nation where the activities of American labor have received some notice is Italy. Both Federico Romero, *The United States and the European Trade Union Movement, 1944–1951* (Chapel Hill, NC, 1992), and Ronald Filippelli, *American Labor and Postwar Italy, 1943–1953* (Stanford, 1989) have impugned the AFL's efforts in that nation. A limited work (commissioned by the AFL-CIO) that provides a more positive appraisal is Philip Taft, *Defending Freedom: American Labor and Foreign Affairs* (Los Angeles, 1973). In this regard, also see Archie Robinson, *George Meany and His Times* (New York, 1981), 123–39.

11. See Robert McMahon, "U.S.-Vietnamese Relations: A Historiographical Survey," in *Pacific Passages: The Study of American-East Asian Relations on the Eve of the Twenty-First Century*, edited by Warren I. Cohen (New York, 1996), 329. McMahon argues that the majority of historians treat the Vietnam War "as if policy elites operated in some kind of curious isolation from the rest of American society. We need to know much more about the conjunction between state and society—one of the crucial insights of the corporatists—if we are to fully comprehend the meaning of the Vietnam War in its widest context."

12. George C. Herring, "'Peoples Quite Apart': Americans, South Vietnamese, and the War in Vietnam," *Diplomatic History* 14 (winter 1990): 1–23. Works that have included thoughtful considerations of the South Vietnamese include Frances FitzGerald, *Fire in the Lake: The Vietnamese and the Americans in Vietnam* (New York, 1972); and Allan E. Goodman, *Politics in War: The Bases of Political Community in South Vietnam* (Cambridge, MA, 1973).

Chapter 1

1. See for instance George Lipsitz, *Rainbow at Midnight: Labor and Culture in the 1940s* (Champaign and Chicago, 1994), 179. Lipsitz argues that "anticommunism

enabled them [U.S. labor leaders] to gain admission to the corporate-liberal elite. In return, they provided a firm commitment to labor peace at home and economic expansion overseas. If this bargain had not actually been consummated in real-life events, only the most paranoid conspiratorial mind could have thought it up." While a sense of shaping important events in league with important people no doubt appealed to most labor leaders, the driving force behind their interest in foreign policy, I conclude, was ideology, particularly the ideals of free trade unionism.

2. Samuel Gompers, *Seventy Years of Life and Labor: An Autobiography* (New York, 1984), 134.

3. Stuart B. Kaufman, *Samuel Gompers and the Origins of the AFL, 1848–1896* (Westport, CT, 1973), 200–202; Nick Savatore, "Introduction," in Gompers, *Seventy Years of Life and Labor,* xviii.

4. On Gompers and the AFL in politics, see Dubofsky, *State and Labor,* 51–60; Gus Tyler, *The Labor Revolution: Trade Unions in a New America* (New York, 1967), 200; and especially Julie Greene, *Pure and Simple Politics, the AFL and Political Action, 1887–1917* (New York, 1998). Greene depicts the early AFL as heavily involved in politics, a harbinger of what later became interest group liberalism.

5. Dubofsky, *State and Labor,* 69–74.

6. Florence Thorne, *Samuel Gompers, American Statesman* (New York, 1957), 145; Gompers, *Seventy Years of Life and Labor,* 135; Simeon Larson, *Labor and Foreign Policy: Gompers, the AFL, and the First World War, 1914–1918* (Cranbury, NJ, 1975), 20. By the time of the world war, Gompers had moved sharply from Marxist notions of international working-class unity and recognized patriotism and nationalism as a basic and natural "force—a primal instinct." He hoped that the overriding instinct of patriotism might triumph over class interests and unify the country. Indeed, patriotism continued to be a strong, reliable, rhetorical theme for labor throughout the twentieth century, profoundly shaping blue-collar views of the Vietnam War. On labor and the powerful ideological influence of patriotism, see Gary Gerstle, "The Politics of Patriotism: Americanization and the Formation of the CIO," *Dissent* 33 (1986): 84–94.

7. Samuel Gompers, *American Labor and the War* (New York, 1919), 41; Larson, *Labor and Foreign Policy,* 102. Desirable permanent gains included a breakthrough on the seminal labor issue of the time—union recognition. Also see Gary Clifford, "Leonard Wood, Samuel Gompers, and the Plattsburg Training Camps," *New York History* 52 (1971): 169–89. While stridently supporting the war, Gompers remained concerned for the fate of democracy as the country mobilized. He advocated a small standing army with widespread military training and pressed General Leonard Wood to democratize the preparedness program and military training.

8. Larson, *Labor and Foreign Policy,* 117–18. Worker gains, critics complained, often fell short of business profits.

9. Radosh, *American Labor and United States Foreign Policy,* 17–18.

10. Gerald Stearn, *Gompers* (Englewood Cliffs, NJ, 1971), 81. Interviews with refugees convinced Gompers that the Bolsheviks forcibly conscripted Russian workers into the army and industry while banning collective bargaining and free unions.

11. Samuel Gompers and William English Walling, *Out of Their Mouths: A Revelation and Indictment of Sovietism* (New York, 1921).

12. Samuel Gompers, "Our Shield against Bolshevism," *McClure's,* May 1919, 17.

13. Steven Fraser, "Dress Rehearsal for the New Deal: Shop-Floor Insurgents, Political Elites, and Industrial Democracy in the ACW," in *Working-Class America,* edited by Daniel Walkowitz and Michael Frish (Urbana, IL, 1983), 213–33; David Dubinsky and A. H. Raskin, *A Life with Labor* (New York, 1977), 118–44. Developments in the needle trades mirror a national neocapitalist movement that promoted cooperative corporate arrangements between business, labor, and government. In this regard, see Hogan, *Marshall Plan,* 4–10; Ellis Hawley, *The Great War and the Search for Modern Order* (New York, 1970); and Robert H. Zieger, *Republicans and Labor, 1919–1929* (Lexington, KY, 1969).

14. Nelson Lichtenstein, "American Trade Unions and the 'Labor Question': Past and Present," in *What's Next for Organized Labor? The Report of the Century Foundation Task Force on the Future of Unions* (New York, 1999).

15. Alan Brinkley, *The End of Reform: New Deal Liberalism in Recession and War* (New York, 1995), 220.

16. Steven Fraser, *Labor Will Rule: Sidney Hillman and the Rise of American Labor* (New York, 1991), 62–65; Gus Tyler, *Look for the Union Label: A History of the International Ladies' Garment Workers' Union* (Armonk, NY, 1995), 209–25.

17. On labor and the New Deal coalition, see J. David Greenstone, *Labor in American Politics* (New York, 1969), 39–80; David Plotke, *Building a Democratic Political Order: Reshaping American Liberalism in the 1930s and 1940s* (New York, 1996); and Sidney Milkis, *The President and the Parties: The Transformation of the American Party System since the New Deal* (New York, 1993), 66–67.

18. Victor Silverman, *Imagining Internationalism in American and British Labor, 1939–1949* (Urbana, IL, 1999), 5; Fraser, *Labor Will Rule,* 183–97; Steven Fraser, "Sidney Hillman," in *Labor Leaders in America,* edited by Melvyn Dubofsky and Warren Van Tine (Urbana, IL, 1987), 213. On the creation of the WFTU, see Peter Weiler, *British Labour and the Cold War* (Stanford, 1988), 55–69.

19. On Catholic corporatism, see Douglas Seaton, *Catholics and Radicals* (New York, 1981), 14–31. The 1931 Papal encyclical *Quadragesimo Anno* proposed the creation of mediating "industrial councils" made up of members of the business and labor communities.

20. On the CIO corporate vision, see Brinkley, *The End of Reform,* 203–9; David Brody, "The New Deal and World War II," in *The New Deal,* edited by John Braeman, Robert Bremner, and David Brody (Columbus, 1975), 281–85; Filippelli, "The History Is Missing Almost," 26–29; Nelson Lichtenstein, *The Most Dangerous Man in Detroit: Walter Reuther and the Fate of American Labor* (New York, 1995), 164–65.

21. On corporatism and its international implications, see Michael Hogan, "Corporatism: A Positive Appraisal," *Diplomatic History* 10 (fall 1986): 363–67.

22. Neither of Meany's biographers, Archie Robinson or Joseph Goulden, emphasizes his early interest in socialism. Nor does historian Robert Zieger in "George Meany: Labor's Organization Man," in *Labor Leaders in America,* edited by Melvyn Dubofsky and Warren Van Tine (Urbana, IL, 1987), 324–40. Zieger acknowledges in passing the influence of Irish nationalism on his subject's intellectual development. Theodore C. Liazos, in "Big Labor, George Meany, and the Making of the AFL-CIO, 1894–1955," Ph.D. diss., Yale University, 1998, 141, notes Meany's later ties to New York socialists. In *George Meany: The Making of a Freedom Fighter* (New York, 1979), Gus Tyler, who extensively interviewed Meany, most

fully develops his early interest in socialism. Tyler published his short biography of Meany through the Eighty-fifth Birthday Tribute to George Meany Committee. The author found the booklet at Cornell University's Catherwood Library.

23. Liazos, "Big Labor, George Meany, and the Making of the AFL-CIO," 26.

24. Jack Barbash Oral History, 9, GMMA; Joseph Goulden, *Meany* (New York, 1972), 18–20.

25. Tyler, *George Meany,* 3.

26. Secretary's Minute Book, New York Building Trades Council, Robert F. Wagner Labor Archives, New York University (NYU), New York. The author consulted the minute book while it was still in the possession of the AFL-CIO before its transfer to the Wagner Archives at NYU. On the conservative, supposedly parochial nature of the building trades in Meany's day, see Melvyn Dubofsky, "George Meany: The Perfect Bureaucrat," *New Politics* 10 (winter 1973): 31–34.

27. Tyler, *George Meany,* 3.

28. Secretary's Minute Book, New York Building Trades Council, NYU; Tyler, *George Meany,* 3. At the conference, Meany first encountered Charles Zimmerman, the aggressive communist leader of an ILGWU local, who later (after disavowing his communist past) headed the AFL-CIO's Civil Rights Committee.

29. Philip Zausner, *Unvarnished: The Autobiography of a Union Leader* (New York, 1941), 79–86.

30. Robinson, *George Meany and His Times,* 124–25; Liazos, "Big Labor, George Meany, and the Making of the AFL-CIO," 114. The Comintern inaugurated its boring from within strategy in 1921. In the United States, the Trade Union Educational League, under William Z. Foster, took the initiative.

31. Secretary's Minute Book, New York Building Trades Council, NYU.

32. Robinson, *George Meany and His Times,* 44, 90–92.

33. On Meany's close relationship with Dubofsky, see Evelyn Dubrow Oral History, 1/11, Merger Oral History Collection, GMMA.

34. Dubinsky and Raskin, *A Life with Labor,* 57–58. On the battle to control the ILGWU, see Nadel Stanley, "Reds versus Pinks: A Civil War in the International Ladies' Garment Workers' Union," *New York History* 66 (1985): 48–72.

35. Dubinsky and Raskin, 240–41; Theodore Draper, *American Communism and Soviet Russia* (New York, 1960), 422; Ted Morgan, *A Covert Life: Jay Lovestone—Communist, Anti-communist, and Spymaster* (New York, 1999), 91–104.

36. Robinson, *George Meany and His Times,* 57; Jacob Clayman Oral History, 8, GMMA.

37. Robinson, *George Meany and His Times,* 57–62, 89. Meany even allowed his name to appear on ballots as an elector on behalf of Dubinsky's ALP.

38. Ibid., 84; Liazos, "Big Labor, George Meany, and the Making of the AFL-CIO," 156, 253. Heading the state labor federation, Meany sought to shield New York workers from the bitter labor divisions brewing on the national level.

39. Robinson, *George Meany and His Times,* 83.

40. Tyler, *Look for the Union Label,* 218. On communism in the CIO, see Harvey Klehr and John E. Haynes, "Communists and the CIO: From the Soviet Archives," *Labor History* 35 (1994): 442–46. For a positive appraisal of communist activities in the CIO, see Harvey Levenstein, *Communism, Anti-communism, and the CIO* (Westport, CT, 1981).

41. Robinson, *George Meany and His Times,* 283; Dubinsky and Raskin, 273. Later, when communists began infiltrating the ALP, Dubinsky pulled out of the party and helped found New York's Liberal Party.

42. Robinson, *George Meany and His Times,* 64–67; Goulden, *Meany,* 52–57; Liazos, "Big Labor, George Meany, and the Making of the AFL-CIO," 148–53. During the prevailing wage controversy, General Johnson contributed to the acrimony by suggesting that the strike was the work of communists, an accusation sure to infuriate Meany (Goulden, 67). Four years later Meany again clashed with the WPA when it attempted to cut wages. The second clash resulted in a personal meeting between Meany and Roosevelt.

43. Dubinsky and Raskin, 205–6.

44. Tyler, *George Meany,* 5; Dubinsky, 247.

45. *New York Times,* December 13, 1940; Woll to William Green, December 12, 1945, box 78, Dubinsky Papers, Kheel.

46. Meany speech to Syracuse Federation of Labor, September 2, 1940, 7/1, Meany Secretary Treasurer Papers, GMMA. On Red Fascism, see Thomas G. Paterson and Les Adler, "The Merger of Nazi Germany and Soviet Russia in the American Image of Totalitarianism, 1930s–1950s," *American Historical Review* 7 (April 1970): 146–64.

47. Craig Phelan, *William Green: Biography of a Labor Leader* (Albany, 1989), 159. Key national labor leaders of the time, including AFL president William Green and United Mine Workers president John L. Lewis, remained avowed isolationists. For an appreciation of the successes of the AFL during the difficult Depression years, see Christopher L. Tomlins, "The AFL Unions in the 1930s: Their Performance in Historical Perspective," *Journal of American History* 65 (summer 1979): 1021–42.

48. Nelson Cruikshank Oral History, 8–9, GMMA; Dubinsky and Raskin, 225–26. Like Meany, Woll was a Roman Catholic and shared little of the hostility of others in the AFL toward organizing industrial workers.

49. Dubinsky and Raskin, 243. Alongside Woll, Meany, Dubinsky, and Lovestone, AFL vice president George Harrison and AFL International representative Robert Watt should be included among the influential group of AFL internationalists. They not only contributed their global concerns to the federation, but they also introduced a new ethnic diversity and tolerance. On the white, Anglo Saxon majority on the AFL Executive Council, Woll made a special effort to welcome Dubinsky as a member. "Woll had made me kosher in the AFL leadership, which had no great love for Jews," Dubinsky later remembered.

50. Robert Alexander, *The Right Opposition: The Lovestonites and the International Communist Opposition of the 1930s* (Westport, CT, 1981), 120–31; Paul Buhle, "Lovestonites," in *Encyclopedia of the American Left,* edited by Mari Joe Buhle, Paul Buhle, and Dan Georgakas (New York, 1990). While comprised of only four hundred to one thousand members, the Lovestonites included in their ranks future noted theologian Will Herberg and Bertram Wolfe, later a prominent historian of the Bolshevik revolution. See "Draft Resolution on the Situation in the Trade Union Movement," 115/3, Dubinsky Papers, Kheel. Noting Stalin's oppression of trade unions in the Soviet Union and the CIO's "toleration and even support of Stalinism," the Lovestonites declared, circa 1939, that their "fundamental attitude to Stalinism can, therefore, be nothing but uncompromising opposition." See "Declaration by

Independent Labor League," December 29, 1940, 276/4b, Dubinsky Papers, Kheel; *New York Post,* January 10, 1940; Henry Allen More to Dubinsky, October 4, 1940, 276/4b, Dubinsky Papers, Kheel; and Morgan, *A Covert Life,* 124. The 1940 Nazi conquest of Europe particularly devastated Lovestone and hastened his political reorientation away from radicalism. The Nazi-Soviet alliance, Lovestone lamented, eliminated "virtually the entire European labor movement, a growth of decades." Radicalism seemed only to have paved the road to fascism. With this epiphany, Lovestone jettisoned his lifelong commitment to revolution. Instead he concluded that the only hope for "genuine American socialism" lay with the pragmatic and independent American labor movement. Increasingly, he came to see himself, as his biographer explained, in the role of an indispensable "crusader," called upon to oust "communists from the American labor movement."

51. I. Minkoff to Dubinsky, September 3, 1940, 78/3d, Dubinsky Papers, Kheel.

52. Dubinsky and Raskin, 243.

53. Robinson, *George Meany and His Times,* 131; Matthew Woll, "Now It Can Be Told," *American Federationist,* June 1945.

54. Arthur Goldberg to General William J. (Wild Bill) Donovan, August 15, 1946, box 3, Goldberg Papers, Library of Congress (LC); Dubinsky and Raskin, 245; Goulden, 118; David Stebenne, *Arthur Goldberg, New Deal Liberal* (New York, 1996), 33; Denis MacShane, *International Labour and the Origins of the Cold War* (New York, 1992), 79. The OSS was the precursor to the Central Intelligence Agency. Lovestone's contact with the OSS no doubt provided him with an early entry into the intelligence community, which evolved later into a relationship with the CIA.

55. Dubinsky and Raskin, 243–45.

56. "Minutes of the Executive Committee," December 10, 1940, 78/3d, Dubinsky Papers, Kheel. Tensions between the State Department and AFL began even before Hitler's 1941 invasion of the Soviet Union. In late 1940, for instance, when the AFL considered sponsoring an international conference of refugee unionists from totalitarian countries, Matthew Woll insisted on inviting Russian refugees to publicize Stalin's repression of labor. Yet he anticipated stiff resistance from the State Department, which wished to avoid pushing the Soviets into actively entering the war on the side of the Axis.

57. Dubinsky and Raskin, 244.

58. Arthur Goldberg to Bowden, September 29, 1942, box 1, Goldberg Papers, LC. The CIO joined the Anglo-Soviet Union Committee. Tensions between the AFL internationalists and the State Department surfaced again in 1943 when David Dubinsky insisted, in defiance of the State Department, on organizing a memorial service for Henryk Ehrlich and Victor Alter, two Polish socialists executed by Stalin during the war. Dubinsky, 249–50; Fraser, *Labor Will Rule,* 519. Hillman and Murray were conspicuously absent from the memorial. Walter Reuther, a UAW official and future president, did attend.

59. Robinson, *George Meany and His Times,* 121; Liazos, "Big Labor, George Meany, and the Making of the AFL-CIO," 240. Meany was careful not to spread word of his 1944 vote for Dewey.

60. *American Federationist,* December 1944.

61. Anthony Carew, *Labour under the Marshall Plan: The Politics of Productivity*

and the Marketing of Management Science (Detroit, 1987), 63. The federation launched the FTUC with an appeal for a million dollars from affiliated unions.

62. Regarding labor tensions during the war, see Lichtenstein, *Labor's War at Home,* esp. 110–35, his chapter "The Social Ecology of Shop-Floor Conflict," and Dubofsky, *State and Labor,* 188–91. Labor relations during World War II, Dubofsky explains, "led workers to rebel simultaneously against their employers, the state, and even their own union leaders." Meg Jacobs, in "'How about Some Meat': The OPA, Consumption Politics, and the Building from the Bottom Up, 1941–1946," *Journal of American History* 84 (December 1997): 910–41, argues that organized labor was part of a radical liberal coalition that sought to use the OPA as a "means to control profits." While this was true, perhaps, of certain members of the CIO, Meany and the AFL obviously had little faith in wartime price and wage controls.

63. Lipsitz, *Rainbow at Midnight,* 69–95; Paul Koistinen, *The Hammer and the Sword: Labor, the Military, and Industrial Mobilization, 1920–1945* (New York, 1979), 1, 4, 128–239, 336. Koistinen, describing the military as "rife with virulent labor-haters," argues that "unions simply did not have the power to win for themselves a partnership in the war production program."

64. Meany CBS address, June 17, 1943, 7/3, Meany Secretary Treasurer Papers, GMMA. Robinson, *George Meany and His Times,* 115; Koistinen, *The Hammer and the Sword,* 265, 274. Also see Meany radio address, May 29, 1943, 7/3, Meany Secretary Treasurer Papers, GMMA; and Bureau of Labor Statistics, "The Cost of Living Index of the Bureau of Labor Statistics: A Review and Appraisal of the 'Cost of Living' by George Meany and R. J. Thomas," Washington, DC, February 25, 1944. Nelson Lichtenstein, in "From Corporatism to Collective Bargaining: Organized Labor and the Eclipse of Social Democracy in the Post-war Era," in *The Rise and Fall of the New Deal Order, 1930–1980,* edited by Gary Gerstle and Steven Fraser (Princeton, 1989), 125, argues that while the wages of higher-paid, skilled workers may have suffered under the War Labor Board, those of "low-paid workers in labor-short industries" did somewhat better. For Meany's sharp critique of labor-state relations during the Korean War, see George Meany, "Labor's Role in the Defense Mobilization Program," *Proceedings of the Academy of Political Science* 30 (1971): 118–27.

65. Melvyn Dubofsky and Warren Van Tine, *John L. Lewis: A Biography* (New York, 1978), 456–57.

66. Brinkley, *The End of Reform,* 205; Koistinen, *The Hammer and the Sword,* 752.

67. Meany address to Bricklayers Convention, circa 1946, 7/22, Meany Secretary Treasurer Papers, GMMA; George Meany, "Let's Get Back to Collective Bargaining," *American Federationist,* October 1946. In a 1946 *American Federationist* editorial, Meany complained that while wartime "control was often highly objectionable and unfair, the unions of the AFL did not balk." But with peace, he went on, "the principle of free and untrammeled collective bargaining . . . should again become fully operative." On the revival of collective bargaining in the immediate postwar years, see Lichtenstein, "From Corporatism to Collective Bargaining," 122–52; and Lichtenstein, *Labor's War at Home,* 16.

68. Meany speech to Commonwealth Club, June 28, 1946, 7/6, Meany Secretary Treasurer Papers, GMMA; Fraser, *Labor Will Rule,* 213–14. Meany's comments also may have been prompted by the stated interest of communists such as Joseph Curran and Harry Bridges in extending the no-strike pledge into peacetime.

69. Phelan, *William Green,* 166; Brody, *Workers in Industrial America,* 173–214; Hogan, *Marshall Plan,* 15–16; Robert M. Collins, *More: The Politics of Economic Growth in Postwar America* (New York, 2000), 23. Brody suggests that a backlash on the part of "corporate officials" led to the curtailment of labor's expansive vision in the immediate postwar years. While no doubt such a backlash occurred, organized labor's tense relationship with the state during the war years proved equally disillusioning for those trade unionists who earlier had flirted with corporatism and economic planning. On the business counteroffensive, see Elizabeth Fones-Wolf, *Selling Free Enterprise: The Business Assault on Labor and Liberalism, 1945–1960* (Urbana, IL, 1994).

70. George Meany, "Labor Day Guest Editorial," *Camden Union Reporter,* August 14, 1946.

71. Meany speech to Catholic Labor Alliance, Chicago, March 13, 1951, 7/12, Meany Papers, GMMA.

72. Undated speech, circa 1947, box 61, Meany Papers, GMMA. No doubt a sense that the New Deal state favored the CIO fed Meany's mounting antistatism.

73. Matthew Woll, "Woll Talks Plainly to NAM," *American Federationist* (December 1948), 28.

74. As quoted in Lichtenstein, "The Eclipse of Social Democracy," 140.

75. William Green, "Free Trade Unions," *American Federationist,* November 1944.

76. "Free Trade Unions," *American Federationist,* June 1945.

77. Meany to "Voice of the Union Cement, Lime, Gypsum and Allied Workers," circa 1946, 7/15, Meany Secretary Treasurer Papers, GMMA.

78. "Free Labor versus Slave Labor: The Irrepressible Conflict," *Free Trade Union News,* January 1947; Matthew Woll, "The Main Issue before Mankind: Human Rights versus State Power," *American Federationist,* October 1947; Matthew Woll, "Slavery Old and New," *American Federationist,* December 1948.

79. On the republican language adopted by early American artisans and laborers, see Eric Foner, *Tom Paine and Revolution* (New York, 1976), 103–6; and Alan Dawley, *Class and Community: The Industrial Revolution in Lynn* (Boston, 1976), 59–72. On the "free soil" ideology that contributed to the Civil War, see Eric Foner, *Free Soil, Free Labor, Free Men* (New York, 1970).

80. Meany to New York State Federation of Labor, July 31, 1950, box 7, Secretary Treasurer Papers, GMMA.

81. George Meany, "Free Trade Unionism: Its Aims in the Struggle against the Totalitarian Menace," *Free Trade Union News,* August 1951.

82. Phelan, *William Green,* 172; Alan Derickson, "Health Security for All? Social Unionism and Universal Health Insurance, 1935–1958," *Journal of American History* 80 (March 1994); Edmund F. Wehrle, "For a Healthy America: Labor's Struggle for National Health Insurance, 1943–1949," *Labor's Heritage* 5 (summer 1993): 28–45; Lichtenstein, *The Most Dangerous Man in Detroit,* 220–21. While emphasizing public planning more than the AFL, the CIO leadership in the postwar period backtracked on what Lichtenstein described as "their prewar lexicon of power, justice, and industrial democracy." Also see Walter Reuther, "Our Fear of Abundance," *New York Times Magazine,* September 16, 1945.

83. Tomlins, *The State and the Unions.* Legal scholar Christopher Tomlins argues

that the AFL's relationship with the state became so awkward and constraining that the federation ultimately sacrificed its ideological claim as a genuine labor movement through its participation in the National Labor Relations Board apparatus. Tomlins describes the result as a "counterfeit liberty" that relegated the AFL to the status of a mere agent for union member interests. Free trade unionists at the AFL certainly feared such a capitulation, as should be evident from the above discussion.

84. On the evolution and triumph of the full employment approach during the war years, see Brinkley, *The End of Reform;* Collins, *More,* 6–21; and Lipsitz, *Rainbow at Midnight,* 165–69. Also see Dubofsky, *State and Labor,* 127; and Fraser, *Labor Will Rule,* 274.

85. Lynn Turgeon, *Bastard Keynesianism: The Evolution of Policy Making since World War II* (Westport, CT, 1996), 126; David C. Colander and Harry Landreth, eds., *The Coming of Keynesianism to America: Conversations with the Founders of Keynesian Economics* (Brookfield, VT, 1996), 218–23; Collins, 18. Leon Keyserling described the early economic outlook of the New Deal as a "raw Keynesianism" but one that "didn't come from Keynes." Keyserling was a student of Rexford Tugwell and Richard T. Ely at Columbia University in the 1920s. He later attended Harvard Law School and began but never finished work on a Ph.D. in economics at Columbia. In 1933, he came to Washington with Tugwell to work in the New Deal, eventually finding his way to Wagner's office. Keyserling insisted that Keynes's influence had been overstated and that general efforts to address economic problems through government spending were well under way before Keynes gained prominence.

86. John H. G. Pierson, "A Full Employment Program," *American Federationist,* August 1945. Also see Paul Hoffman, "For More and More Jobs," *American Federationist,* May 1945; and Leon Keyserling, "Housing and Full Employment," *American Federationist,* June 1946.

87. The Employment Act of 1946 clearly was a weaker version than would have been preferred by labor. See Brinkley, *The End of Reform,* 260–63; and Karen Orren, "Union Politics and Postwar Liberalism in the U.S., 1946–1979," *Studies in American Political Development* 1 (1986): 244.

88. Lichtenstein, "From Corporatism to Collective Bargaining," 131–33. Lichtenstein laments the CIO's decision to sacrifice far-reaching goals in favor of "maintenance of economic growth and expansion of the welfare state."

89. John Lewis Gaddis, *Strategies of Containment: A Critical Appraisal of Postwar American National Security Policy* (New York, 1982), 197; Ernest May, ed., *American Cold War Strategy: Interpreting NSC-68* (Boston, 1993), 106, 154; Collins, 23.

90. Edmund F. Wehrle, "Welfare and Warfare: Organized Labor Approaches the Military Industrial Complex, 1949–1964," *Armed Forces and Society* 4 (summer 2003), 525–46.

91. Historian Elizabeth McKillen has emerged the prime advocate of this view of labor's leadership as intoxicated by reveries of corporatism and "liberal internationalism." See Elizabeth McKillen, "The Corporatist Model, World War I, and the Public Debate over the League of Nations," *Diplomatic History* 15 (spring 1991): 181, 196.

92. Robinson, *George Meany and His Times,* 132; Liazos, "Big Labor, George Meany, and the Making of the AFL-CIO," 283–84.

93. *New York Herald,* September 13, 1945; *Daily Express of London,* September

13, 1945; Liazos, "Big Labor, George Meany, and the Making of the AFL-CIO," 283–84.

94. William Doherty Oral History, 3, 1/10, Merger Oral History Project, GMMA; *Daily Express of London,* September 13, 1945.

95. Fraser, "Sidney Hillman," 213. On the creation of the WFTU, also see Weiler, *British Labour and the Cold War,* 55–69.

96. Fraser, *Labor Will Rule,* 547; Weiler, 69–70.

97. Fraser, *Labor Will Rule,* 544–46. The creation of the WFTU deeply divided the State Department. George Kennan, warning of Soviet intentions to commandeer the new organization as a base from which to infiltrate the trade union movements of Western Europe, led the opposition forces. William Doherty Oral History, 16, GMMA. The AFL internationalists felt particularly betrayed by the British TUC, an organization that the AFL had supported both morally and financially since the outbreak of World War II. As TUC moved toward a permanent alliance with the Soviets, AFL international representative Robert J. Watt angrily reminded the British of how communists had picketed AFL meetings in 1940 in protest of its support for TUC during the period of the Stalin-Hitler pact. Tensions between TUC and the AFL nearly boiled over when TUC president Walter Citrine asked AFL president William Green for money owed by the AFL to the old IFTU in order to help launch the WFTU. The normally staid Green grew "flush" and in uncharacteristic language bluntly told Citrine that there would be no AFL funds going to the WFTU.

98. "Memorandum of Meeting held in Mr. Matthew Woll's Office," December 5, 1945, 78/4a, Dubinsky Papers, Kheel. On December 5, 1945, Woll, Lovestone, and Stefano Romaldi met with "free trade union" leaders from Chile, Peru, and Spain to establish closer cooperation between the AFL and unions in Latin America.

99. Ben Rathburn, *The Point Man: Irving Brown and the Deadly Post-1945 Struggle for Europe and Africa* (London, 1996), 28, 43–46, 89–93.

100. Irving Brown, interview with Archie Robinson, September 29, 1976, 37/14, Brown Papers, GMMA.

101. Lovestone to Brown, June 24, 1947, 29/2, Brown Papers, GMMA. On the financial problems of the FTUC, see Carew, *Labour under the Marshall Plan,* 65–69. See also Woll to Green, January 15, 1948, 6/20, Lovestone Papers, GMMA. Facing enormous challenges with only meager support from the AFL, Woll and Lovestone sought funding sources outside of the federation, including the American Overseas Aid Campaign, a conglomeration of American private relief agencies.

102. Liazos, "Big Labor, George Meany, and the Making of the AFL-CIO," 302. The AFL strategy in Western Europe might be described best as "covert activity to separate socialists from communists."

Chapter 2

1. Mark McLoad and Nguyen Thi Deiu, *Culture and Customs of Vietnam* (Westport, CT, 2001), 1.

2. Woodside, *Community and Revolution,* 204.

3. David Marr, *Vietnamese Tradition on Trial, 1920–1945* (Berkeley, 1981), 1–13; Douglas Dacy, *Foreign Aid, War, and Economic Development: South Vietnam, 1955–1975* (New York, 1986), 1; Jacques Despuech, *Le Trafic des Piastres* (Paris, 1974), 28–29; Françoise Direr, "L'Économie," in *Vietnam, L'histoire, la terre, les*

hommes, edited by Alain Ruscio (Paris, 1993), 167. Direr estimates that industry made up around 10 percent of the Indochinese economy in 1939. Most produced goods were exported.

4. William Duiker, *Vietnam: Nation in Revolution* (Boulder, 1983), 28–29. Other scholars, however, stressing the importance of security and national prestige, argue that Duiker overstated his economic interpretation. Stein Tonnesson, in *The Vietnamese Revolution of 1945: Roosevelt, Ho Chi Minh, and De Gaulle in a World at War* (London, 1991), 40, argues that naval officers, not capitalists, served as the driving force behind the initial conquest. Also see Anthony Short, *The Origins of the Vietnam War* (London, 1989), 12. Regardless of the initial motivations, cupidity seems to have been the strongest single force driving French colonialism in Indochina.

5. Bernard Fall, *The Two Vietnams: A Political and Military Analysis* (New York, 1963), 36; Virginia Thompson, *French Indochina* (London, 1937), 49.

6. Firsthand accounts of conditions on Vietnam's rubber plantations can be found in Tran Tu Binh, *The Red Earth, A Vietnamese Memoir of Life on a Colonial Rubber Plantation* (Athens, OH, 1985); and Paul Monet, *Les Jauniers* (Paris, 1930). Also see Stanley Karnow, *Vietnam: A History* (New York, 1983), 118; Joseph Buttinger, *Vietnam: A Dragon Embattled* (New York, 1967), 49; Duiker, *Vietnam,* 31, 36; and Woodside, *Community and Revolution,* 210–12.

7. Tonnesson, *The Vietnamese Revolution of 1945,* 43.

8. Thompson, *French Indochina,* 249, 55.

9. Ibid., 49.

10. Buttinger, *Vietnam: A Dragon Embattled,* 56.

11. Duiker, 36; Fall, *Two Vietnams,* 37.

12. Hue-Tam Ho Tai, *Radicalism and the Origins of the Vietnam Revolution* (Cambridge, MA, 1992); 218–19; Karnow, *Vietnam,* 117–18. The radical workers' section of the Vietnamese Nationalist Party, the VNQDD, carried out the assassination despite the disapproval of the mainstream party, which feared French retaliation for the murder. See Foster Rhea Dulles, "French Problems in Indo-China," *Current History* 26 (May 1927), 197–202. Dulles reported in 1927 on a nationalist strike at a school in Saigon that spread "to some industrial groups." She also recorded the existence of "Soviet cells" operating against French rule but dismissed the nationalists as amounting to roughly "500 malcontents."

13. Woodside, *Community and Revolution,* 5, 27; Neil Jamieson, *Understanding Vietnam* (Berkeley, 1993), 100–176. Also see Trinh Van Thao, *Vietnam du Confucianism au Communism: Un essai ininéraire intellectuel* (Paris, 1990) for an intellectual history of the issue of modernity in Vietnam.

14. Duiker, 37; George McT. Kahin and John W. Lewis, *The United States in Vietnam* (New York, 1967), 11; Joseph Buttinger, *Vietnam: A Political History* (New York, 1968), 179–81; Hue-Tam Ho Tai, *Radicalism and the Origins of the Vietnam Revolution,* 222–23. A mutiny of Vietnamese soldiers garrisoned at Yen Bay in north-central Tonkin added to the tensions of 1930. On peasant upheavals in Southeast Asia during the 1930s, also see James Scott, *The Moral Economy of the Peasant* (New Haven, 1976).

15. Buttinger, *Vietnam: A Dragon Embattled,* 109; Short, *The Origins of the Vietnam War,* 30.

16. Bernard Fall, *The Vietminh Regime* (New York, 1956), 139.

17. Woodside, *Community and Revolution,* 287. Woodside also details a 1936 strike by Saigon's autobus drivers.

18. D. R. SarDesai, *Vietnam: The Struggle for National Identity* (Boulder, 1992), 49. Duiker, 36; Hue-Tam Ho Tai, *Radicalism and the Origins of the Vietnam Revolution,* 226. The "idiom of class-based social analysis," Hue-Tam Ho Tai explains, "produced a drastic intellectual reorientation" toward recruitment of the working classes.

19. MacShane, *International Labour and the Origins of the Cold War,* 248; Fall, 27; John Loss, "The Rise of the Labor Movement in South Vietnam," M.A. thesis, University of Texas, 1975, 3–10.

20. William Henry Chamberlin, "A New Deal for French Indo-China?" *Asia* 37 (July 1937): 476.

21. Loss, "The Rise of the Labor Movement in South Vietnam," 10; Mark Philip Bradley, *Imagining Vietnam and America: The Making of Postcolonial Vietnam, 1919–1950* (Chapel Hill, 1999), 68.

22. Fall, *Two Vietnams,* 37.

23. Arnold Beichman, "Report on Vietnam," July 26, 1964, 5/27, Lovestone Papers, Kheel.

24. "Inaugural Speech of Tran Quoc Buu at 20th Anniversary of CVT in Saigon," October 30, 1969, 31/9, Department of International Affairs, Country Files, GMMA. In his speech, Buu recalled his own and the CVT's early history. On the nationalist protests of 1940, see David G. Marr, *Vietnam, 1945: The Quest for Power* (Berkeley, 1995), 159–62; Donald Lancaster, *The Emancipation of French Indo-China* (New York, 1961), 85; and Ngo Van, *Vietnam, 1920–1945: Révolution et contre-révolution sous la domination coloniale* (Paris, 1995), 279–83.

25. Bradley, *Imagining Vietnam and America,* 39.

26. Marr, *Vietnamese Tradition on Trial,* 314–15.

27. Trinh Quang Quy, *Phong Trào lao-dông Viêt-Nam* (Saigon, 1970), 90. Quy described Quyen, Buu, and Giao as "inseparable" from their days in prison onward, equating their friendship to that between the characters Luu, Quan, and Truong in the Chinese novel *The Three Realms.*

28. *Washington Evening Star,* February 23, 1969. Buu made his comments to *Star* reporter Richard Critchfield. The Belgian newspaper *La Cité,* on February 1, 1973, reported that Buu also knew Pham Van Dong, later the communist premier of the Democratic Republic of Vietnam, while at Paulo Condore, but the dates of Dong's incarceration do not appear to match those of Buu. On Le Duan's single-minded drive, see Robert Brigham, "Why the South Lost the American War in Vietnam," in *Why the North Won the Vietnam War,* edited by Marc Jason Gilbert (New York, 2002), 101–12.

29. See Buttinger, *Vietnam: A Dragon Embattled,* 250–53; Buttinger, *Vietnam: A Political History,* 196–98; Marr, *Vietnam, 1945,* 84–85; Douglas Pike, *History of Vietnamese Communism, 1925–1976* (Stanford, 1978), 30–31; and Pierre-Bernard Lafont, "Les sects Religieuses," in *Vietnam, L'histoire, la terre, les hommes,* edited by Alain Ruscio (Paris, 1993), 95. From its foundations, the Cao Dai actively supported the nationalist cause. In 1945, Cao Dai leader Trang Quang Vinh cooperated with the Japanese against the French. Later the Cao Dai joined ranks with the Viet Minh, but it broke away in 1947.

30. "Memorandum from Lansdale for Special Distribution," November 15,

1965, box 1, Lansdale Collection, National Security Archives (NSA), Washington, DC; Edward Lansdale, *In the Midst of Wars: An American's Mission to Southeast Asia* (New York, 1972), 152–53; *Herald-Tribune,* May 10, 1964. Buu described his work with the Cao Dai in a "long reminiscence" to his friend and confidant, General Edward Lansdale, who later retold the story in *In the Midst of Wars: An American's Mission to Southeast Asia* (New York, 1972). Lansdale identifies Buu and the Cao Dai as serving in Viet Minh regiments 7 and 8; in a memorandum of a 1965 conversation with Buu, the Cao Dai regiment is identified as regiment 25. Charles Finch to State Department, August 15, 1969, box 1226, Central Foreign Policy Files, Economic, Labor and Manpower, Records of Department of State, RG 59, National Archives (NA), College Park, MD. In 1965, Cao Dai adherents enthusiastically greeted Buu in their Holy See in Tay Nihn. Buu recalled for those assembled his early work with the Cao Dai. On the Cao Dai and Viet Minh, see Marr, *Vietnam, 1945,* 266–467; Karnow, *Vietnam,* 143; and Buttinger, *Vietnam: A Political History,* 259–60.

31. Duiker, *Vietnam,* 43; William Duiker, *The Communist Road to Power in Vietnam* (Boulder, 1981), 131–32.

32. Kahin and Lewis, 28; Duiker, *The Communist Road to Power in Vietnam,* 133.

33. "Bio Data, Tran Quoc Buu," 31/3 International Affairs Department, Country Files, GMMA; William Duiker, *Ho Chi Minh* (New York, 2000), 408.

34. Woodside, *Community and Revolution,* 187.

35. "Memorandum of Conversation, Buu, Leonard Unger, Condon," July 22, 1965, box 1339, Central Foreign Policy Files, Economic, Labor and Manpower, Records of Department of State, RG 59, NA.

36. Trinh Quang Quy, *Phong Trào lao-dông Việt-Nam,* 9–11. Quy, after 1947, sought to distance himself from the Viet Minh. In 1954, after the division of Vietnam, he fled south and later joined the CVT. Ultimately, he became a leading CVT official and a senator in the South Vietnam Assembly, where he eventually chaired the Senate's Labor and Social Affairs Committee. In 1970, Quy published a twentieth-anniversary history of the South Vietnamese labor movement, which offers the best history of the CVT's and Buu's early years. Also on this early history see "Syndicalism au Vietnam," box 12, Mission to Vietnam, Office of the Director, Classified Subject Files, Records of U.S. Assistance Agencies, RG 469, NA. While this document designates neither the author nor the date produced, it appears to have been written by someone at the CVTC in the early 1950s. Gilbert Jouan also outlined the early history of the CVTC in a 1956 letter, Jouan to French Minister of Overseas Affairs, February 2, 1956, 5H 37, CFDT Archives.

37. Neil Sheehan, *A Bright Shining Lie* (New York, 1988), 155–58; Woodside, *Community and Revolution,* 305.

38. Maurice Lariviere, L'Inspector du Travail to Conseiller aux Affaires Sociales, September 22, 1950, "Consideration des Syndicat Libre" folder, HCI CS/109, CAOM. For instance, French officials, concerned that colonial Vietnam had not been admitted to the International Labor Organization in Geneva, planned a campaign to gain admittance.

39. Fall, *The Viet Minh Regime,* 140; Alice Shurcliff, "The Trade Union Movement in Vietnam," *Monthly Labor Review* 72 (January 1951): 31.

40. P. Maeght to M. le Conseiller au Affaires Sociale, March 15, 1949, "Force Ouvrière" folder, HCI CS/109, CAOM.

41. LaFond to Lovestone, September 19, 1950, 46/27, Lovestone Papers, GMMA; R. Faurillou, "Rapport Du Secrétaire du Syndicat des Employés de Commerce de la Confédération Générale du Travail, Force Ouvrière, en Indochine," 46/27, Lovestone Papers at GMMA; Shurcliff, "The Trade Union Movement in Vietnam," 30; lA, Bouzanquet to M. Bollarent, High Commissionaire en Indochine, May 28, 1948, "Force Ouvrière" folder, HCI CS/109, CAOM; "Confédération Générale des Travailleurs Chrétiens," 22 January 1951, HCI CS/109, CAOM. By 1947, the CGT-FO had organized roughly forty-eight hundred French civil servants in Vietnam. Jack Kantrowitz, in "L'Influence Américaine sur Force Ouvrière: Myth ou Réalité?" *Revue Française de Science Politique* 28 (1978): 717–49, notes the efforts of both the AFL and CIO in pushing the FO to adopt a more favorable approach to nationalist movements in the third world.

42. MacShane, *International Labour and the Origins of the Cold War,* 239. The European labor movement long had been divided between Christian and socialist labor factions. In France, CFTC membership numbered over five million. The organization was affiliated with the International Federation of Christian Trade Unions.

43. "Confédération Géneralé des Travailleurs Chrétiens," January 22, 1951, HCI CS/109, CAOM.

44. "Jouan to M. Scherer, le Conseiller aux Affaires Sociales," September 25, 1948, "Travailleur Chrétiens" folder, HCI, CS/109, CAOM.

45. "Confederation Géneralé des Travailleurs Chrétiens," January 22, 1951, HCI CS/109, CAOM.

46. Joseph Zisman, "Labor in Indochina," October 1952, box 4, Office of Labor Affairs, Far East Country Files, 1948–61, Records of the U.S. Foreign Assistance Agencies, RG 469, NA; Su Tri Nguyen, interview with the author, Houston, TX, February 7, 2003. Su Tri Nguyen, CVT commissioner of information, research, and propaganda in the late 1960s, also recalled the contribution of Father Alexis Parrel of the Foreign Missionaries of France to shaping the early CVT. Parrel remained in Indochina into the 1960s. On Catholic corporatist teaching regarding labor relations during this era, see Gary Gerstle, "Catholic Corporatism, French Canadian Workers, and Industrial Unions in Rhode Island," in *Labor Divided: Race and Ethnicity in United States Labor Struggles, 1835–1960,* edited by Robert Asher and Charles Stephenson (Albany, 1990), 213–15; and Woodside, *Community and Revolution,* 286–87. Buu, according to Woodside, later advocated policies based on a "triangular principle" in which business, labor, and government representatives would gather to resolve problems. The triangular principle clearly evolved from Jouan's advocacy of *chambres mixtes de métiers.*

47. These observations are based on discussions with Su Tri Nguyen and Robert Senser.

48. H. Guiriec to Haut Commissioner, February 5, 1948, HCI, CS/109, "Confederation des Syndicat Libre" folder, CAOM.

49. "Confédération Généralé des Travailleurs Chrétiens," January 22, 1951, HCI CS/109, CAOM.

50. Jouan to French Minister of Overseas Affairs, February 2, 1956, 5H 37, CFDT Archives; Trinh Quang Quy, *Phong Trào lao-dông Viêt-Nam,* 131.

51. Le Chef du Service Central d'Action Sociale to M. le Gouverneur Général, January 23, 1951, "Travailleurs Chrétiens" folder, HCI CS/109, CAOM.

52. John G. Dean, "Memorandum for Files: Discussion with Nguyen Van Huyen, Minister of Social Action," January 19, 1954, box 3, Mission to Vietnam, Office of the Director, Subject Files, 1950–54, Records of the U.S. Foreign Assistance Agencies, RG 469, NA.

53. Donald Heath to Department of State, October 22, 1953, box 4, Office of Labor Affairs, Labor Programs Division, Far East Country Files, 1948–61, Records of the U.S. Foreign Assistance Agencies, RG 469, NA. Perrier began his career in Vietnam before World War II as a colonial administrator and rose to head the Sûreté Générale after the war. I am indebted to Christopher Goscha for the information on Perrier.

54. Su Tri Nguyen, interview; Nguyen Ngoc Huy, "The Possible Role of Elections in a Political Settlement," in *Electoral Politics in South Vietnam,* edited by John C. Donnell and Charles Joiner (Lexington, MA, 1974), 105; Stephen B. Young, "The Mandate and Politics in Vietnam," in *Electoral Politics in South Vietnam,* edited by John C. Donnell and Charles A. Joiner (Lexington, MA, 1974), 22–23.

55. David Halberstam, *Ho* (New York, 1987), 92–98; Duiker, *Communist Road to Power,* 172–73.

56. Trinh Quang Quy, *Phong Trào lao-dông Viêt-Nam,* 32–33; Donald Heath to State Department, December 15, 1950, box 3, Office of Labor Affairs, Far East Country Files, 1948–61, Records of the U.S. Foreign Assistance Agencies, RG 469, NA; "Confederation Géneralé des Travailleurs Chrétiens," 22 January 1951, HCI CS/109, CAOM.

57. Trinh Quang Quy, *Phong Trào lao-dông Viêt-Nam,* 37.

58. Ibid., 158; Dacy, *Foreign Aid, War, and Economic Development,* 1, 10, 111. Alongside labor reforms, Bao Dai also initiated "a soft approach to agrarian reform based on land tenure." Economist Douglas Dacy describes the Vietnamese economy in the early 1950s as "top-heavy" with roughly 80 percent of the population involved in agricultural production, and circa 150,000 Vietnamese civilians either serving in the French army or involved in military-type service. Industry was limited to a few factories, producing beer, soft drinks, and light textiles. In addition to recruiting urban workers such as pedicab drivers and dockworkers, the CVTC focused considerable attention on organizing rural workers.

59. Buttinger, *Vietnam: A Dragon Embattled,* 780–81.

60. Trinh Quang Quy, *Phong Trào lao-dông Viêt-Nam,* 30–38. The CVTC's Vietnamese name was Tông Liên Doan Lao Công Vietnam.

61. "Tableau d'effectifs du Syndicats affiliés à la CVTC," February 22, 1954, SPCE/77, CAOM; Buttinger, *Vietnam: A Dragon Embattled,* 1066. Buttinger estimated the number as forty-five thousand.

62. Jouan to French Minister of Overseas Affairs, February 2,1956, 5H 37, CFDT Archives.

63. ICFTU Regional Fund Committee, "Summary of Report of the Mission to Vietnam (20 June–24 July 1953)," 51/5, George Meany Papers, GMMA; Robert Senser, interview with the author, Reston, VA, April 16, 1997; Su Tri Nguyen, interview. Like the majority of Vietnamese, Buu was a nonpracticing Buddhist (Nguyen Duc Dat, interview by author, Falls Church, VA, 29 April 1997). On his deathbed in 1976, according to an aide, Buu called for a Roman Catholic priest.

64. "Note de Renseignements concernant la CVTC," July 1954, SPEC-77, CAOM.

65. Trinh Quang Quy, *Phong Trào lao-dông Viêt-Nam,* 36.

66. Alexis Parrel, "Le Syndialism Chrétien au Vietnam," December 1954, 5H 37, CFDT Archives.

67. Buttinger, *A Dragon Embattled,* 780–81.

68. Robinson, *George Meany and His Times,* 151.

69. Ibid.

70. Brown to Lovestone, May 17, 1947, 11/17, Lovestone Papers, GMMA.

71. Meany, "The Marshall Plan and American Labor," December 5, 1947, 7/7, Meany Secretary Treasurer Papers, GMMA; MacShane, *International Labour and the Origins of the Cold War,* 139.

72. Hogan, *Marshall Plan,* 22, 88, 334–35, argues that the Marshall Plan should be seen as part of the "New Deal synthesis," and "a neo-capitalist formulation that also included Keynesian economic strategies."

73. Carew, 80–83.

74. Stephen Burwood, "American Labor and Industrial Unrest in France, 1947–1952," Ph.D. diss., State University of New York, Binghamton, 1991, 205–6; Annie LaCroix-Riz, "Autour d'Irving Brown: L'AFL et la Sicission Syndicale Française, 1944–1947," *Mouvement Sociale* (1990): 79–118; Kantrowitz, 717–49; Frances Stonor Sauders, *The Cultural Cold War: The CIA and the World of Arts and Letters* (New York, 1999), 67, 87. In contrast to the above studies, MacShane, in *International Labour and the Origins of the Cold War,* 273, downplays the role of Brown and the AFL in creating the FO: "At best, the AFL acted as an occasional nursemaid once the Force Ouvriere was born but did not beget the new organization." Grose claims that CIA funds allowed the AFL to break a 1947 communist-inspired general strike in France. See Peter Grose, *Gentleman Spy: The Life of Alan Dulles* (New York, 1994), 280–81.

75. Carew, 101–2; Sauders, *The Cultural Cold War,* 155–56.

76. Irving Brown Oral History, 8, 37/14, Brown Papers, GMMA; Irving Brown, "Democracy Wins a Battle," *American Federationist,* May 1948. For instance, regarding American labor's support of the Italian Confederation of Workers' Trade Unions (CISL), see Filippelli, *American Labor and Postwar Italy, 1943–1953;* and Romero, *The United States and the European Trade Union Movement.*

77. Anthony Carew, "The American Labor Movement in Fizzland: The Free Trade Union Committee and the CIA," *Labor History* 39 (February 1998): 25. Liazos, in "Big Labor, George Meany, and the Making of the AFL-CIO," 292, similarly concludes that it was "not the case that the AFL simply agreed to do the CIA's bidding" and that the CIA and AFL "fought continuously."

78. Carew, "The American Labor Movement in Fizzland," 26–42; Thomas Braden, "I'm Glad the CIA Is Immoral," *Saturday Evening Post,* May 20, 1967. While the CIA funding of the FTUC apparently ended in 1958, Carew concludes that "it is reasonable to suppose that a working relationship between Lovestone and more especially Brown and the CIA continued in subsequent years" (Carew, 40). David Dubinsky described a meeting in 1951 between Woll, Lovestone, himself, and General Walter Bedell Smith, head of the CIA. At the meeting, Dubinsky told Smith to keep the CIA out of labor affairs in Italy (Dubinsky, 259). See also Thomas Mongold, *Cold Warrior: James Jesus Angleton, the CIA's Master Spy Hunter* (New York, 1991), 314–15, 428–29. Lovestone, however, according to Thomas Mongold, appears to have continued working with the CIA.

79. Graenum Berger, *Not So Silent an Envoy: A Biography of Ambassador Samuel Berger* (New York, 1992), 82–90, 216.

80. MacShane, *International Labour and the Origins of the Cold War,* 136; Jon V. Kofas, "U.S. Foreign Policy and the World Federation of Trade Unions, 1944–1948," *Diplomatic History* 26 (winter 2002): 23, 52–57. Kofas argues that together the State Department and the AFL waged an unrelenting war against the WFTU. The CIA also invested heavily in this "divisionist campaign." The extent to which the Marshall Plan and the AFL contributed to the weakening of the WFTU and communist labor movements in Western Europe is a matter of some debate among historians. Tony Carew, *Labour under the Marshall Plan,* and Peter Weiler, *British Labour and the Cold War* (90–128), see the Marshall Plan and the work of the AFL as pivotal to alienating the communists and dividing the WFTU. MacShane, in *International Labour and the Origins of the Cold War,* 2, by contrast, argues that the cold war in European labor "was not external to the trade union movement but grew from existing political divisions, resurfacing as soon as the fighting stopped in 1945." While the role of the Marshall Plan should not be overemphasized, this study concludes that it did play a key role in tipping the scales in favor of anticommunists in both Europe and the United States.

81. Silverman, *Imagining Internationalism in American and British Labor,* 54–55, 174.

82. "Report on the Help of the WFTU to the Trade Unions in Colonial Countries or Mandated Territories," June 1946, box 119, CIO Secretary-Treasurer's Office, Walter Reuther Library, Wayne State University, Detroit, MI (henceforth Reuther Library). The WFTU did intervene to some extent in October 1945 when the French de Gaulle government arrested several Indochinese workers in France. The group apparently had been protesting reported clashes between the French army and native workers in Vietnam. Intervention by the WFTU and CGT appears to have led to their release. The opening of negotiations between the DRV and French government, according to the report, quelled tensions among the nearly twenty-five thousand Vietnamese expatriated workers in France. Shurcliff, "The Trade Union Movement in Vietnam," 32. The WFTU finally affiliated with the Viet Minh's General Confederation of Trade Unions in 1949. Representatives of the TCD attended the 1949 WFTU conference in Milan, Italy.

83. "WFTU Session of the Executive Bureau, 19–24 November 1947," CIO Secretary-Treasurer's Office, Reuther Library.

84. William Doherty Oral History, 14, GMMA; David McDonald Oral History, 12, GMMA.

85. Peter Weiler, "The U.S., International Labor, and the Cold War: The Breakup of the World Federation of Trade Unions," *Diplomatic History* 5 (winter 1981): 1–22; Hogan, 140–42, 202–4.

86. Irving Brown Oral History, 37/15, Brown Papers, GMMA; Weiler, 114; Carew, 268n. Carew notes that in "its early days the ICFTU was very much an appendage of the Marshall Plan."

87. Harry Martin to Ambassador Harriman, December 15, 1949, 33/34, Lovestone Papers, GMMA. The atmosphere was so positive at the conference that both David Dubinsky and Walter Reuther talked openly of merging the AFL and CIO.

88. Meany speech to Geneva Conference, 26 June 1949, 7/10, Meany Secretary-Treasurer Papers, GMMA.

89. Carew, *Marshall Plan,* 119.

90. Harry Martin to Ambassador Martin, December 15, 1949, 33/34, Lovestone Papers, GMMA. Tensions over the TUC and colonialism surfaced at the ICFTU founding convention in London, when trade unions from British colonies "turned savagely on Britain's colonial policy." On the awkward relationship between the TUC and British colonialism see Weiler, 126, 211–13, 329n; and Anthony Carew, "Conflict within the ICFTU: Anticommunism and Anticolonialism in the 1950s," *International Review of Social History* 41 (1996): 147–81.

91. While the Marshall Plan proved a great boon for organized labor in Western Europe, neither the AFL nor the CIO entirely approved of its administration. While maligned by some historians for complacency in allowing business interests to control the administration of the ERP, Meany complained frequently and bitterly of business's domination of Marshall Plan administration. See for instance, *AFL News Reporter,* December 19, 1951, where Meany angrily decried mounting inflationary pressure on European workers made worse by "taxes which workers pay but businesses don't."

92. Carew, 63.

93. Ibid., 63–65.

94. Sheehan, *A Bright Shining Lie,* 165–66; Frank Giles, *The Locust Years: The Story of the Fourth French Republic, 1946–1958* (New York, 1994), 57. In 1946, French communists, although they refused to advocate liquidating Indochina as a French holding, did favor negotiations with Ho Chi Minh to end the war. But Maurice Thorez, head of the French Communist Party and vice premier in the coalition government, blocked his deputies in the General Assembly from threatening appropriations for the Indochinese War. Also on this issue see Edward Mortimer, *The Rise of the French Communist Party, 1920–1947* (Boston, 1984), 349; Ruscio, *Les Communistes français et la guerre d'Indochine,* 8–15; George McT. Kahin, *Intervention: How America Became Involved in Vietnam* (New York, 1986), 22–23; and Bradley, *Imagining Vietnam and America,* 148.

95. Lorwin, *The French Labor Movement,* 117; Mortimer, *The Rise of the French Communist Party,* 356; Philip Williams, *Politics in Post-war France: Parties and the Constitution in the Fourth Republic* (London, 1953), 19; Giles, *The Locust Years,* 57.

96. Irving Brown, "speech," May 1947, 10/8, Brown Papers, GMMA.

97. Ruscio, *Les Communistes français,* 264.

98. Williams, *Politics in Post-war France,* 56, 174; Giles, *The Locust Years,* 138, 196; François Fejto, *The French Communist Party and the Crisis of International Communism* (Boston, 1967), 34.

99. George Ross, *Workers and Communists in France: From Popular Front to Eurocommunism* (Berkeley, 1982), 60–63. Ross argues that the communist tactics of sabotaging the Indochinese War backfired and alienated the party from the economic interests of the French working class: "[T]he CGT leadership had a great deal of trouble persuading rank-and-file militants to subordinate the economic struggle to the peace questions." Ironically, the AFL-CIO later would experience a similar struggle with its membership over the federation's unpopular support for the Vietnam War.

100. Lorwin, *The French Labor Movement,* 136.

101. Burwood, "American Labor and Industrial Unrest in France," 347–48; Ruscio, 251–65.

102. Pierre Ferri-Pisani to Meany, January 10, 1955, 49/2, Lovestone Papers, GMMA; Lorwin, *The French Labor Movement,* 135; Arnold Beichman, interview with the author, Philadelphia, PA, March 27, 1997.

103. Victor Reuther, *The Brothers Reuther and the Story of the UAW: A Memoir* (Boston, 1976), 412; Weiler, 113; Ruscio, 261–62. While no direct proof appears to exist that either CIA money or AFL funds aided Ferri-Pisani in his efforts, according to Carew (69), the AFL had access to CIA money to aid its overseas efforts beginning in early 1948. Correspondence between Brown and Lovestone during these years is filled with cryptic references to "fizz kids" and "spaghetti deals." George Meany always vehemently denied direct or indirect receipt of CIA funds. It would seem, however, that the semiautonomous nature of the FTUC allowed for ties to the CIA, all the while providing the AFL leadership with a certain plausible deniability.

104. As quoted in Burwood, "American Labor and Industrial Unrest in France," 232.

105. Hogan, 236, 314. Hogan notes that the 1949 "fall" of China to the communists lent urgency for Americans to the situation in Indochina. No doubt this was also the case for the AFL.

106. *Free Trade Union News,* September 1950.

107. FTUC, *Soviet Imperialism Plunders Asia,* March 1951, 59/19, International Affairs Department, GMMA.

108. "Minutes of the Meeting of the Executive Council of the AFL," January 22–February 5, 1952, GMMA; *AFL New Reporter,* February 6, 1952. Also see addresses by James B. Carey at the thirteenth annual National Farm Institute meeting, Des Moines, Iowa, February 17, 1951, CIO press releases. The CIO, through Vice President James Carey echoed AFL calls for Indochinese independence. Noting the communist threat and important raw materials located in the region, Carey also called for the "immediate creation of an ECA [Economic Cooperation Administration] for the nations of Southeast Asia."

109. Brown to Oldenbroek, December 30, 1949, 10/5, Brown Papers, GMMA.

110. FTUC, *Soviet Imperialism Plunders Asia,* March 1951.

111. S. R. Mohan Das, "Ho Chi Minh: Vietnamese Nationalist or Soviet Agent?" *Free Trade Union News,* January 1951.

112. "Report on Emergency Committee Meeting," March 16 and 18, 1950, 50/19, Meany Papers, GMMA.

113. Le Conseiller aux Affaires Sociales to M. le Haute Commissionaire, August 24, 1950, "Mission d'information de la CISL" folder, HCI, CS/109, CAOM.

114. J. H. Oldenbroek to Leon Pignon, June 26, 1950, "Mission d'information de la CISL" folder, HCI, CS/109, CAOM.

115. "Emploi du Temps," n.d., "Mission d'information de la CISL" folder, HCI, CS/109, CAOM.

116. *Free Trade Union News,* December 1950; John Brophy, *A Miner's Life* (Madison, 1964), 298; Irving Brown, "The Role of Labor in International Relations," September 29, 1950, 10/5, Brown Papers, GMMA. In a speech in 1950, Brown commented enthusiastically on the recent ICFTU mission to Asia.

117. John Getz to M. Robert Rebouillet, October 4, 1950, "Mission d'information de la CISL" folder, CS/109, CAOM; Joseph Zisman, "Labor in Indochina," October 1952, box 4, Far East Country Files, Office of Labor Affairs, 1948–61, Records of the U.S. Foreign Assistance Agencies, RG 469, NA.

118. Cruikshank to S. D. Berger, April 16, 1952, box 3; Joseph Zisman, "Labor in Indochina" October 1952, box 4, Office of Labor Affairs, Far East Country Files, 1948–61, Records of the U.S. Foreign Assistance Agencies, RG 469, NA.

119. Kenneth Grenville, *The Saving of South Vietnam* (Sydney, 1972), 131, 133.

Chapter 3

1. "Memorandum," October 19, 1951, box 2, Mission to Vietnam, Office of the Director, 1948–61, Subject Files, 1950–54, Records of the U.S. Foreign Assistance Agencies, RG 469, NA. The earliest American aid to Vietnam was administered through the "Comité National De L'Aide Économique Américaine," which did take an interest in labor-related issues. Typically, it funded an artisan center at the Cité Nguyen-tri-Phuong that promoted light industry and helped support a state school for welfare workers. The committee, however, did not directly aid the nascent CVTC. By 1952, the Americans had also established the Special Technological and Economic Mission to Vietnam, Cambodia, and Laos (STEM), another possible conduit of support to the CVTC. Perhaps cautious about the anemic state of industry in Vietnam, STEM focused its assistance in areas other than organized labor. Concerns among those in the U.S. AID mission about limited industrial development in Vietnam did have legitimacy. Woodside, in *Community and Revolution*, 204–5, describes industry as "concentrated in a few places such as Tonkinese mines, or cities of Saigon, Hanoi, Haiphong, and Nam Dinh." However, these nascent industries saw numerous labor disturbances, which were often tied to the nationalist and communist causes.

2. Malcolm Gaar, Acting Education Officer, to John Tobler, March 28, 1952, box 1, Mission to Vietnam, Agriculture and Natural Resources Divisions, Classified Files, 1948–61, Records of U.S. Foreign Assistance Agencies, RG 469, NA.

3. ICFTU Regional Fund Committee, Seventh Meeting, "Summary of Report of the Mission to Vietnam (20 June–24 July 1953)," 51/4, Meany Papers, GMMA.

4. Although the issue never reverberated in the United States like it did in Europe, the conflict between European socialist and Christian unions did divide some American trade unionists. With the founding of the ICFTU, some U.S. labor leaders sought to incorporate Christian unions into the new organization. But while George Meany and AFL Asian representative Richard Deverall, a devout Catholic, worked for unification of the ICFTU and IFCTU, Lovestone and Brown, rooted in the socialist perspective, viewed the IFCTU as soft on communism and an unworthy addition to the ICFTU. Tensions over the issue also surfaced within the CIO. During the ICFTU founding conventions, Walter Reuther argued against any accommodation with European Christian unions. During an argument over the issue, longtime Reuther antagonist Allan Haywood called the UAW president a "no-good, bigoted, anti-Catholic, son-of-a-bitch." See Irving Brown to Meany, December 28, 1949, 30/13, Brown Papers, GMMA; and David McDonald Oral History, 13, GMMA. On Meany's sympathies toward the IFCTU, see "Minutes of the International Committee Meeting," January 7, 1954, 7/25, Michael Ross Papers, GMMA.

5. Donald Heath to Secretary of State, September 3, 1953, box 4, Office of Labor Affairs, 1948–61, labor programs division, Far East Country Files, Records of the U.S. Foreign Assistance Agencies, RG 469, NA.

6. James T. Shotwell to Meany, October 4, 1955, 24/2, Meany Papers, GMMA.

7. "ICFTU Emergency Committee Meeting," February 1–2, 1955, 51/10, Meany Papers, GMMA.

8. Lovestone to Meany, November 29, 1954, 56/4, Meany Papers, GMMA.

9. Carew, 183; David Anderson, *Trapped by Success: The Eisenhower Administration and Vietnam, 1953–1961* (New York, 1991), 70–75, 133–34. Debate raged within the Eisenhower administration regarding aid projects in Vietnam. Secretary of Defense Charles Wilson led the battle to limit aid to South Vietnam. Michael Abramson, in "Delusions of Development: The Eisenhower Administration and the Foreign Aid Program in Vietnam, 1955–1960," *Journal of American-East Asian Relations* 5 (summer 1996): 157–82, argues that in Vietnam the Eisenhower administration eventually adopted W. W. Rostow's notion that foreign aid could breed "development." Abramson refers to "liberal amounts of capital and technical assistance to the Diem government." Indeed, after the initial years of his presidency, Eisenhower did warm up to foreign aid, though not enough in Southeast Asia to suit free trade unionists. In particular, the Eisenhower administration eschewed funding projects that directly aided organized labor, in sharp contrast to the later Kennedy, Johnson, and Nixon administrations. For a brief general treatment of foreign aid under Eisenhower, see Katherine Sibley, "American Foreign Aid," in *The Encyclopedia of American Foreign Policy*, edited by Alexander DeConde, Richard Dean Burns, and Fredrik Logevall (New York, 2002), 96–97.

10. *Le Figaro*, January 7, 1954. For similar CIO complaints about foreign aid under Eisenhower, see "Report of International Affairs Committee," November 12, 1953, 7/24, Michael Ross Papers, GMMA.

11. Emmet J. McCarthy to Leland Barrows, Director of USOM, "Activities of CVTC," December 13, 1954, box 12, Mission to Vietnam, Office of the Director, Classified Subject Files, Records of U.S. Foreign Assistance Agencies, RG 469, NA.

12. "Dr. W. R. Russell, Deputy Director for Technical Services; Subject: Proposed Revisions in FOA FY 1955 Labor Program for Underdeveloped Areas," box 16, Mission to Vietnam Program and Requirements Divisions, Subject Files, 1950–57, Records of U.S. Foreign Assistance Agencies, RG 469, NA.

13. *American Federationist*, February 1953, January 1953.

14. Collins, 42–51.

15. John W. Sloan, *Eisenhower and the Management of Prosperity* (Lawrence, KS, 1991), 69–70.

16. "Summary of Conversations with Dr. Burns," November 17, 1954, 2/10, Ruttenberg Papers, GMMA; Ruttenberg, "Memoranda to Mr. Walter Reuther," November 17, 1954, 1/10, Ruttenberg Papers, GMMA.

17. On Eisenhower's New Look diplomacy, see Gaddis, *Strategies of Containment*, 131–50. On foreign aid cuts, see Stephen Ambrose, *Eisenhower*, vol. 2: *The President* (New York, 1984), 86; and Burton Kaufman, *Trade and Aid: Eisenhower's Foreign Economic Policy, 1953–1961* (Baltimore, 1982). While Eisenhower resisted the calls of conservative Republicans such as Robert Taft to massively slash foreign aid, he cut appropriations from previous levels under Truman, thus earning the enmity of labor's internationalists.

18. Irving Brown Oral History, 42, GMMA; Lovestone to André LaFond, November 30, 1953, 47/1, Lovestone Papers, GMMA.

19. Michael Ross to Jacob Potofsky, April 29, 1954, 214/8, ACWA Papers, Kheel.

20. *AFL News Reporter*, 28 May 1954.

21. Brown, "The Geneva Conference Opens," April 27, 1954, 11/5, Irving Brown Papers, GMMA.

22. Ibid.

23. Goldberg to Lovestone, April 28, 1954, 37/11, Lovestone Papers, GMMA.

24. Goldberg to Lovestone, May 8, 1954, 37/11, Lovestone Papers, GMMA. For Dr. Dan's statements regarding the conference, see Dr. Phan Quan Dan, "The Vietnamese Stance regarding the Big Five Conference at Geneva," n.d., 63/10, Lovestone Papers, GMMA; and "The Colonial People and Geneva," *Free Trade Union News*, May 1954.

25. Goldberg to Lovestone, May 17, 1954, 37/11, Lovestone Papers, GMMA.

26. Goldberg to Lovestone, May 5, 1954, 37/11, Lovestone Papers, GMMA.

27. Goldberg to Lovestone, May 17, 1954, 37/11, Lovestone Papers, GMMA. See James Cable, *The Geneva Conference of 1954 on Indochina* (New York, 1986), 67–69, for a description of the general atmosphere at the conference.

28. *AFL News Reporter,* 14 May 1954. The AFL newspaper complained that while Eisenhower used the domino analogy in reference to Indochina, Dulles had indicated that a loss of Indochina was "not fatal." For a study of Eisenhower's 1954 approach to the Vietnam question, see Richard Immerman, "Between the Unattainable and the Unacceptable: Eisenhower and Dienbienphu," in *Reevaluating Eisenhower: American Foreign Policy in the 1950s,* edited by Richard A. Melanson and David Mayers (Urbana, IL, 1987), 120–54.

29. Harry Goldberg, "Report on the Geneva Conference," June 1954, 37/11, Lovestone Papers, GMMA.

30. *American Federationist,* June 1954.

31. *AFL News Reporter,* July 13, 1954.

32. Meany speech to American Legion Convention, September 1, 1954, 59/44, Meany Papers, GMMA.

33. Robert Zieger, *The CIO, 1935–1955* (Chapel Hill, 1995), 330–31.

34. J. R. Deborde to M. Commissaire General, May 4, 1954, HCI SPEC/77, CAOM.

35. Meany speech to the National Press Club, June 29, 1955, 59/66, Meany Papers, GMMA.

36. *Pravda,* 16 June 1956.

37. Collins, 18–39; Alvin Cohen, "Leon Keyserling," in *Biographical Directory of the Council of Economic Advisers,* edited by Robert Sobel and Bernard S. Katz (New York, 1988), 126–30; Keyserling vita, January 15, 1954, 62/17, Meany Papers, GMMA. In the vita he sent to George Meany, Keyserling refers to pressing Edwin Nourse, the first chairman of Truman's Council of Economic Advisers, to "support and popularize full employment policies before congressional committees and in public forums." Keyserling managed to alienate many in Congress with his partisan approach as chairman of the CEA. See Sloan, *Eisenhower and the Management of Prosperity,* 42.

38. Leon Keyserling, "Memorandum re. Project to Encourage Economic Expansion," January 15, 1954, 62/17, Meany Papers, GMMA. Keyserling sent an identical proposal to CIO president Walter Reuther.

39. On Keyserling's continuing influence after leaving government service, see Collins, 44–45.

40. Conference on Economic Progress, "Toward Full Employment and Full Production," Washington, DC, 1954.

41. "AFL Economic Committee Report, National Defense, 1954," 62/17, Meany Papers, GMMA.

42. "Testimony on Defense Production Act to Be Presented by the CIO Committee on Economic Policy," March 10, 1953, 6/20, Goldfinger Papers, GMMA. On Defense Manpower Policy No. 4, see Wehrle, "Welfare and Warfare."

43. Kim Moody, *An Injury to All: The Decline of American Unionism* (London, 1988), 61. According to Moody, the AFL-CIO merger was made possible because the "CIO leaders had abandoned their social welfare legislative agenda as impractical."

44. Jack Barbash Oral History, 5, GMMA.

45. Kevin Boyle, *The UAW and the Heyday of American Liberalism, 1945–1968* (Ithaca, NY, 1995), 103.

46. *New York Times Magazine,* December 4, 1955.

47. I. W. Abel Oral History, 5, GMMA. Meany had a particular distaste for former communist Michael Quill, head of the New York City transportation workers union.

48. Arthur J. Goldberg, *AFL-CIO: Labor United* (New York, 1956), 226. Although the soon to merge organizations had substantive differences with regard to foreign policy, the AFL and CIO jointly lobbied the ICFTU's world congress at Vienna in 1955 for an international organizing campaign aimed at the developing world.

49. On the AFL and CIO's differences regarding contact with the Soviets, see Joseph Curran, interview, 61, Merger Oral Interviews, GMMA; and Lichtenstein, *The Most Dangerous Man in Detroit,* 344. When Nikita Khrushchev arrived for a state visit in 1960, both Reuther and fellow AFL-CIO vice president James Carey met the Soviet leader at San Francisco. Meany not only refused to attend the meeting, but he sought to block other members of the AFL-CIO executive branch from doing so.

50. "Notes on Career of Jay Lovestone," box 317, Presidential Papers of Walter Reuther, Reuther Library.

51. Goulden, 275–78.

52. Meany to Charles J. MacGowan, 9 March 1955, 31/8, Meany Papers, GMMA.

53. Matthew Woll, "An Historic Declaration," *Free Trade Union News,* July 1953.

54. Meany speech to National Religion and Labor Foundation, December 13, 1955, 59/12, Meany Papers, GMMA.

55. In his otherwise excellent study of the UAW during this period, Kevin Boyle (*The UAW and the Heyday of American Liberalism,* 104) misinterprets Meany's December 1955 speech as having "endorsed the White House's [foreign policy] views." Meany was unquestionably a sharp critic of Eisenhower's foreign and domestic policies, which he attacked as weak, needlessly frugal, and lacking in activism. While Meany aimed his famous speech at liberals, he was also clearly reacting to the recent summit in Geneva, as well as Eisenhower's tolerance for neutralism and growing interest in easing cold war tensions. While Eisenhower has traditionally been seen as a conventional cold warrior, recent studies suggest that the president took a more nuanced approach, especially on the neutralism question. H. W. Brands, in *The Specter of Neutralism: The United States and the Emergence of the Third World, 1947–1960* (New York, 1989), for instance, argues that, contrary to their rhetoric, Eisenhower and Dulles generally tolerated neutralism in the third world. Like these

later revisionists, Meany saw a more moderate, facilitative Eisenhower. Unlike Eisenhower revisionists, Meany found these traits unappealing.

56. Meany speech to National Religion and Labor Foundation, December 13, 1955, 59/12, George Meany Papers, GMMA.

57. Goulden, 272.

58. *New York Times,* April 3, 1956. Also see Lichtenstein, *The Most Dangerous Man in Detroit,* 340–41, for reaction to the Meany address; and Edmundo Nolasco to Meany, 21 February 1956, 55/7, Meany Papers, GMMA. Meany was not without his following among budding third-world anticommunist trade unionists. An additional motive for his controversial speech may have been to reassure international supporters of U.S. labor's continuing anticommunism, despite the merger and the tone of the new administration. At least it had that effect on some. An anticommunist labor organizer in the Philippines wrote Meany that "Just as a Carpenter saved the world 2,000 years ago from pagan Rome, a plumber today with the help of other men of goodwill may still save Asia and the rest of the world."

59. *Free Trade Union News,* April 1956.

60. Mohau to Lovestone, March 17, 1956, 54/32, Meany Papers, GMMA; Herbert Hill, "The Importance of Race in American Labor History," *International Journal of Politics, Culture, and Society* 9 (winter 1995): 317–26. Hill has sharply disputed sanguine views of race relations in the UAW such as that offered by Walter Reuther in India.

61. On continuing racial discrimination within the UAW, see Boyle, *The UAW and the Heyday of American Liberalism,* 120, 163–64; and Herbert Hill, "Racism within Organized Labor: A Report of Five Years of the AFL-CIO, 1955–1960," *Journal of Negro Education* 30 (spring 1961): 109–18.

62. "Bulletins de Renseignments," February 25, 1954, HCI, SPEC/77, CAOM.

63. "Bulletins de Renseignments," February 19, 1954, HCI, SPEC/77, CAOM.

64. "Notes pour M. le General D'Armee Commissaire General de France," December 6, 1954, HCI SPEC/77, CAOM; Alexis Parrel, "Le Syndicalism Chrétien au Vietnam," 5H 37, CFDT Archives.

65. Trinh Quang Quy, *Phong Trào lao-dông Viêt-Nam,* 41.

66. "Labor Report," February 5, 1955, box 15, Office of Labor Affairs, Labor Programs Division, Far East, Country Files, 1948–61, Records of the U.S. Foreign Assistance Agencies, RG 469, NA; Dacy, *Foreign Aid, War, and Economic Development,* 2. A rough total of some nine hundred thousand refugees fled from the north to the south.

67. Buu to Lucien Tronchet, July 22, 1954, 31/3, Country Files, International Affairs Department Papers, GMMA.

68. Buu to "Travailleurs du Monde," July 8, 1954, HCCI SPEC/77, CAOM.

69. "Memorandum of contacts with Mr. Gilbert Jouan and ICFTU concerning Vietnam," July 27, 1954, 31/3, Country Files, International Affairs Department Papers, GMMA.

70. Oldenbroek to Mungat, August 7, 1954; Oldenbroek to Jodoin, August 7, 1954, 31/3, Country Files, International Affairs Department Papers, GMMA; Jouan to Tessier, August 5, 1954, 5H 37, CFDT Archives. Working through Jay Krane of the ICFTU, Jouan did manage to arrange some joint actions between ICFTU and Christian trade unionists.

71. Trinh Quang Quy, *Phong Trào lao-dông Viêt-Nam,* 41; Emmet J. McCarthy to

Leland Barrows, Director of USOM, "Activities of CVTC," December 13, 1954, box 12, Mission to Vietnam, Office of the Director, Classified Subject Files, Records of U.S. Foreign Assistance Agencies, RG 469, NA. The CVTC perennially exaggerated its membership rolls, so exact numbers are difficult to ascertain. Emmet McCarthy, an assistant to the American ambassador, estimated the CVTC membership at sixty thousand in 1954, while the CVTC claimed to have over three hundred thousand members. Likewise, there was some confusion over the issue of the actual dues-paying membership. The CVTC at times affiliated members for only a token dues payment, thus inflating its membership numbers but also opening its ranks to many who otherwise would not have been able to afford union membership in this very poor country.

72. Jodie Eggers to Leland Barrows, June 13, 1955, box 12, Mission to Vietnam, Office of the Director, Classified Subject Files, Records of U.S. Foreign Assistance Agencies, RG 469, NA.

73. Jouan to Tessier, September 16, 1954, 5H 37, CFDT Archives.

74. Buu to Tessier, October 17, 1954, 5H 37, CFDT Archives.

75. Trinh Quang Quy, *Phong Trào lao-dông Việt-Nam,* 52.

76. McCarthy to Barrows, Director of USOM, "Activities of CVTC," December 13, 1954, box 12, Mission to Vietnam, Office of the Director, Classified Subject Files, Records of U.S. Foreign Assistance Agencies, RG 469, NA.

77. Cecil Currey, *Edward Lansdale: The Unquiet American* (Boston, 1988), 135.

78. Ibid., 153.

79. "Briefing for the Ambassador and Chargé d'Affaires," folder C2768, "Top Secret," Summer, 1954, box 1, Viet Nam, Saigon Embassy, Top Secret Subject Files, Records of the Foreign Service Posts, Department of State, RG 84, NA. The two CIA agents in question were Paul V. Harwood and Roger Pierre. Also see Elbridge Durbrow Oral History, 36, Lyndon B. Johnson Presidential Library, Austin, TX (henceforth LBJ Library). According to American ambassador Elbridge Durbrow, the CIA had thoroughly infiltrated the Can Lao, of which Buu was a founding member. Ellen Hammer, in *A Death in November: America in Vietnam, 1963* (New York, 1987), 250, identifies Buu, without citing evidence, as being in the employ of the CIA. Journalist Arnold Beichman interviewed a Saigon-based CIA agent, in either 1964 or 1965, who complained of Buu's failure to follow the CIA line and claimed to have threatened Buu (Beichman, interview).

80. "La Confédération Viêtmienne du travail chrétin et le Mouvement d'Union Nationale pour la Paix," January 13, 1953, HCI, SPEC/77, CAOM.

81. "Note," June 1954, 5H 37, CFDT Archives; "Bulletin de Renseignement," July 4, 1954, HCI, SPEC/77, CAOM.

82. Gaston Tessier to Nhu, March 26, 1954, 5H 37, CFDT Archives.

83. Heath to State Department, January 5, 1954, and March 19, 1954, box 3, Office of Labor Affairs, Labor Programs Division, Far East, Country Files, 1948–61, Records of the U.S. Foreign Assistance Agencies, RG 469, NA; Buttinger, *Vietnam: A Dragon Embattled,* 785. Buttinger incorrectly identified Nhu as having "achieved some prominence as an organizer of a Catholic trade union movement modeled on France's Force Ouviere, the Christian oriented trade union movement." As detailed in chapter 2, the roots of the CVTC date to 1948, and Nhu played no role in its founding. Likewise, the FO, a secular French labor federation, was distinctly not

affiliated with France's Christian trade union movement. Also see Sheehan (*A Bright Shining Lie,* 179), who repeats Buttinger's incorrect assertions about Nhu and the CVTC. Sheehan adds assertions that the CIA "financed Nhu's agitation to have Diem named prime minister by channeling money to him through the French union." The CIA did have ties to both the CVTC and the FO in France. While it is possible that the agency channeled funds to Nhu through its trade union connections, I have found no corroborating evidence.

84. CIA, Current Intelligence Memorandum, Subject: "Cast of Characters South Vietnam," August 28, 1963, box 128a, President's Office Files, Vietnam General, JFK Library; Durbrow to State Department, March 2, 1959, in Department of State, *Foreign Relations of the United States, 1958–1960* (Washington, DC, 1990), 1:145–48 (Hereafter *FRUS,* with year and volume number). The full name of the Can Lao was Can Lao Nhan Vi Cach Mang Dang (Personalist Labor Revolutionary Party). According to Durbrow, Buu joined Nhu's organization as early as 1952. See Ton Vy, "The U.S.-Diem Regime," *Vietnam Studies* 18–19 (1968): 35. The National Liberation Front later excoriated the CVT for its ties to Diem: "Through yellow trade-unions, it [the Can Lao Party] took over the General Federation of Trade Unions, which had a Christian leadership, whose prestige it tried to raise by various means (giving trade-union cadres American-style training, providing relief for workers)."

85. "Bulletin de Renseignments" July 2, 1954, "CVTC" folder, HCI, SPEC/77, CAOM.

86. David Lan Pham, *Two Hamlets in Nam Bo: Memoirs of Life in Vietnam through Japanese Occupation, the French and American Wars, and Communist Rule, 1940–1986* (London, 2000), 85.

87. On the Binh Xuyen, see Young, *The Vietnam Wars,* 48–49; George Herring, *America's Longest War* (New York, 1986), 52–54; and Robert Shaplen, *The Lost Revolution: The U.S. in Vietnam, 1946–1966* (New York, 1966), 103, 119–20.

88. Eggers to Barrows, June 13, 1955, box 12, Office of the Director, Classified Subject Files, Records of U.S. Foreign Assistance Agencies, RG 469, NA.

89. Eggers to Barrows, June 29, 1955, box 28, Mission to Vietnam, Office of the Director, Subject Files, Records of U.S. Foreign Assistance Agencies, RG 469, NA.

90. Shaplen, *Lost Revolutions,* 146–47.

91. Durbrow to State Department, March 2, 1959, *FRUS, 1958–1960,* 1:145–48; Jodie Eggers to State Department, December 12, 1955, box 14, Office of Labor Affairs, Labor Programs Division, Far East, Country Files, 1948–61, Records of the U.S. Foreign Assistance Agencies, RG 469, NA; "Rapport Moral Pronounce le 7 Mars 1954 par Tran Quoc Buu," SPEC/77, CAOM. Roughly two years before, French authorities had estimated the CVTC membership at forty thousand. The CVTC's insistence on including non-dues-paying "members" (or members who paid nominal dues) in its estimates no doubt contributed to the confusion over actual numbers.

92. Eggers to Barrows, July 5, 1956, "Monthly Report," box 18, 1948–61, Mission to Vietnam, Office of the Director, Subject Files, 1954–57, Records of U.S. Foreign Assistance Agencies, RG 469, NA.

93. Eggers to Barrows, November 3, 1955, "Monthly Report," box 18, Mission to Vietnam, Office of the Director, Subject Files, 1954–57, Records of U.S. Foreign Assistance Agencies, RG 469, NA.

94. Reinhardt to State Department, May 26, 1956, box 15, Reinhardt to State Department, 31 March 1956, box 14, Office of Labor Affairs, Labor Programs Division, Far East, Country Files, 1948–61, Records of the U.S. Foreign Assistance Agencies, RG 469, NA; Dacy, *Foreign Aid, War, and Economic Development,* 4. Diem also promoted a series of agrarian reforms in January and February 1955, which limited rents, interest payments, and redistributed idle land.

95. Eggers to Golda Stander, June 29, 1956, box 14, Office of Labor Affairs, Labor Programs Division, Far East, Country Files, 1948–61, Records of the U.S. Foreign Assistance Agencies, RG 469, NA; "Record of Conversation: Present Situation of the CVTC," July 11, 1956, box 15, Jay Krane Papers, Reuther Library.

96. Eggers to Barrows, May 8, 1956, box 12, Office of the Director, Classified Subject Files, Office of the Director, Subject Files, RG 469, NA; McCarthy to Barrows, Director of USOM, "Activities of CVTC," December 13, 1954, box 12, Mission to Vietnam, Office of the Director, Classified Subject Files, Records of U.S. Foreign Assistance Agencies, RG 469, NA.

97. Eggers to Barrows, July 5, 1956, "Monthly Report," box 18, Mission to Vietnam, Office of the Director, Subject Files, 1954–57, Records of U.S. Foreign Assistance Agencies, RG 469, NA.

98. Woodside, *Community and Revolution,* 286.

99. "President Diem's May Day Message to Vietnamese Workers," May 1, 1956, box 15, Office of Labor Affairs, Labor Programs Division, Far East, Country Files, 1948–61, Records of the U.S. Foreign Assistance Agencies, RG 469, NA.

100. Eggers to Barrows, November 3, 1955, "Monthly Report," box 18, Mission to Vietnam, Office of the Director, Subject Files, 1954–57, Records of U.S. Foreign Assistance Agencies, RG 469, NA.

101. *AFL News-Reporter,* May 27, 1955.

102. Eggers to Barrows, June 5, 1956, "Monthly Report for May 1956," box 18, Mission to Vietnam, Office of the Director, Subject Files, 1954–57, Records of U.S. Foreign Assistance Agencies, RG 469, NA.

103. Eggers to Barrows, September 13, 1955; Eggers to Barrows, July 5, 1956, box 18, Mission to Vietnam, Office of the Director, Subject Files, 1954–57, Records of U.S. Foreign Assistance Agencies, RG 469, NA; "Record of Conversation: Present Situation of the CVTC," July 11, 1956, box 15, Jay Krane Papers, Reuther Library.

104. Eggers to Barrows, June 5, 1956, "Monthly Report for May 1956," box 18, Mission to Vietnam, Office of the Director, Subject Files, 1954–57, Records of U.S. Foreign Assistance Agencies, RG 469, NA.

105. Eggers to State Department, December 12, 1955, box 14, Office of Labor Affairs, Labor Programs Division, Far East, Country Files, 1948–61, Records of the U.S. Foreign Assistance Agencies, RG 469, NA.

106. Eggers to Barrows, "Monthly Report for February 1956," March 8, 1956, box 12, Mission to Vietnam, Office of the Director, Subject Files, Records of U.S. Foreign Assistance Agencies, RG 469, NA.

107. Eggers to Barrows, February 14, 1956, box 14, Office of Labor Affairs, Labor Programs Division, Far East, Country Files, 1948–61, Records of the U.S. Foreign Assistance Agencies, RG 469, NA.

108. Eggers to Barrows, October 15, 1956, box 15, Office of Labor Affairs, Labor Programs Division, Far East, Country Files, 1948–61, Records of the U.S. Foreign Assistance Agencies, RG 469, NA.

109. Ibid.

110. Shaplen, *Lost Revolution*, 146–47. Durbrow to State Department, September 5, 1960, *FRUS, 1958–1960*, 1:560–61. Some American reports out of Vietnam indicated a break in the Can Lao Party between a Nhu faction and Le Van Dong, the minister of agriculture, with whom Buu was thought to be allied.

111. Richard Deverall, "Uprising the Viet Minh," January 30, 1957, 57/10, Meany Papers, GMMA. On the uprisings, see Edwin E. Moise, *Land Reform in China and North Vietnam* (Chapel Hill, NC, 1983), 178–240; and Edwin E. Moise, "Land Reform and Land Reform Errors in North Vietnam," *Pacific Affairs* 49 (spring 1976): 70–92. Moise estimates that the North Vietnamese authorities executed around five thousand peasants who participated in the uprisings.

112. Speech of Carlos P. Romulo to John Carroll Society, Washington, DC, Chapter, April 25, 1954, 24/19, Meany Papers, GMMA.

113. Angier Biddle Duke to Meany, November 18, 1955, 22/11, Meany Papers, GMMA; Meany to John W. O'Daniel, July 26, 1956, 31/3, Department of International Affairs, Country Files, GMMA. Paul Buhle, in *Taking Care of Business: Samuel Gompers, George Meany, Lane Kirkland and the Tragedy of American Labor* (New York, 1999), 182, incorrectly suggests a link between the AFVN and the AFL-CIO.

114. Deverall to Meany, March 7, 1960, 57/15, Meany Papers, GMMA.

115. Deverall to Meany, September 14, 1960, 57/12, Meany Papers, GMMA; "Activities of Mr. Van in Vietnam," n.d., Jay Krane Papers, Reuther Library. Headed by Nguyen Khan Van, a bitter enemy of Buu and the CVTC, the Workers' Union of Vietnam, which evidently drew its strength from Chinese workers in Cholon, never impressed outsiders. The ICFTU disaffiliated the organization in the early 1960s.

116. Deverall to Meany, March 13, 1959, 57/11, Meany Papers, GMMA.

117. Lovestone to Meany, June 9, 1952, box 8, Meany Papers, GMMA.

118. Deverall to Meany, January 13, 1959, 57/11, Meany Papers, GMMA.

119. ICFTU Executive Board Meeting, Vienna, May 1–18, 1955, 51/11, Meany Papers, GMMA.

120. CIP Press Clipping, "The IFCTU and the ICFTU should Cooperate in Asia," March 18, 1959, 57/4, Meany Papers, GMMA.

121. Buu to Tessier, November 22, 1955, 5H 37, CFDT Archives.

122. Jouan to Tessier, April 26, 1956, 5H 37, CFDT Archives.

123. On liberal developmentalism, see Akira Iriye, "Culture," *Journal of American History* 77 (1990): 99–107; and Thomas Zeiler, "Development Do It! Globalization for Diplomatic Historians," *Diplomatic History* 25 (2001): 529–51. On the AFL-CIO's early interest in what historians later termed liberal developmentalism, see Stanley Ruttenberg memo to Meany, "Background Information on Foreign Aid," May 13, 1958, 4/49, Ruttenberg Papers, GMMA; and Meany, "Foreign Aid for Peace and Freedom," May 23, 1963, 60/20, Meany Papers, GMMA.

124. Eggers to Barrows, June 13, 1955, box 12, Office of the Director, Classified Subject Files, Records of U.S. Foreign Assistance Agencies, RG 469, NA.

125. Eggers to Golda Stander, June 9, 1955, box 14, Office of Labor Affairs, Labor Programs Division, Far East, Country Files, 1948–61, Records of the U.S. Foreign Assistance Agencies, RG 469, NA.

126. Eggers to Stander, June 29, 1956, box 14, Office of Labor Affairs, Labor Programs Division, Far East, Country Files, 1948–61, Records of the U.S. Foreign Assis-

tance Agencies, RG 469, NA. On overall plans for foreign aid in South Vietnam in 1957, see Dacy, *Foreign Aid, War, and Economic Development,* 2.

127. Rudolph Marginot to George Brown, August 29, 1957, 31/3, International Affairs Department, Country Files, GMMA.

128. "FY 1957 Operational Program Vietnam," p. 43, box 15, Office of Labor Affairs, Labor Programs Division, Far East, Country Files, 1948–61, Records of the U.S. Foreign Assistance Agencies, RG 469, NA.

129. Eggers to Barrows, October 15, 1956, box 15, Office of Labor Affairs, Labor Programs Division, Far East, Country Files, 1948–61, Records of the U.S. Foreign Assistance Agencies, RG 469, NA.

130. Buu to Tessier, October 4, 1958, 6H 235, CFDT Archives.

131. Morel to Tessier, April 29, 1958, 6H 235, CFDT Archives.

132. Irving Brown memo, June 26, 1959, 11/15, Irving Brown Papers, GMMA.

133. Eggers to Leland Barrows, April 9, 1957, "Monthly Report," box 18, Mission to Vietnam, Office of the Director, Subject Files, 1954–57, Records of U.S. Foreign Assistance Agencies, RG 469, NA.

134. Morel to Tessier, April 10, 1958, 6H 235, CFDT Archives.

135. Bowers to Krane, February 13, 1958; "Confidential-BR, Singapore," box 15, Jay Krane Papers, Reuther Library.

Chapter 4

1. On the shifting orientation of New Frontier diplomacy, see Gaddis, *Strategies of Containment,* 201–5. Gaddis describes foreign policy under Kennedy and Johnson as undergirded by the assumption that the United States possessed both the means and the moral imperative to challenge the potential expansion of communism anywhere in the world. The AFL-CIO, in its aggressive, ideologically driven foreign policy, clearly pursued such a universalistic approach.

2. *AFL-CIO News,* October 1, 1960.

3. Nat Goldfinger to Keyserling, October 26, 1960, 1/50, Goldfinger Papers, GMMA.

4. Robinson, *George Meany and His Times,* 218–21; John Herling Oral History, 23–25, JFK Library.

5. George Meany to Sam Rayburn, January 9, 1961, Office of the President, Copy Books, Micro 7, GMMA. Also see "Report of the AFL-CIO Economic Policy Committee Submitted to the Executive Council," February 23, 1961, in *AFL-CIO Executive Council Statements and Reports, 1956–75,* edited by Gary Fink (Westport, CT, 1977), 759. The high rate of unemployment and the second recession in three years gravely concerned the AFL-CIO. Meany warned Sam Rayburn in early 1961 that "the country stands today on the threshold of the gravest economic crisis since the Great Depression of the thirties. The current statistics are alarming. . . . the long-range outlook is even grimmer."

6. Walter Heller to George Meany, October 6, 1961, 1/45, Goldfinger Papers, GMMA; *AFL-CIO News,* December 31, 1960; Walter Heller, *New Dimensions of Political Economy* (New York, 1967), 27–34. Heller notes that Kennedy had initial doubts about Keynesian economics. The president frequently received phone calls from Galbraith in India urging more public spending and no tax cuts. See David Calleo, *The Imperious Economy* (Boston, 1982), 11–12. According to Calleo, to the Kennedy

administration economic growth "seemed the first and best answer to the country's problems."

7. Collins (*More,* 50–53) sees Kennedy as immediately adopting a growth-focused, full-employment agenda. However, some Keynesians were disappointed by Kennedy's timidity. James Tobin of the CEA recalled that "those of us at the council were disappointed by his caution at the beginning of the administration. We were trying to persuade the president to be more audacious in economic policy." Likewise, Leon Keyserling occasionally worried that Kennedy was not aggressive enough in employing the full powers of the government to address the recession. For this viewpoint, see Seymour Harris, "Economics of the Kennedy Years" in *John F. Kennedy and the New Frontier* (New York, 1966), 61–87; Gerald Strober and Deborah Strober, eds., *Let Us Begin Anew: An Oral History of the Kennedy Presidency* (New York, 1993), 243; Allen Matusow, *The Unraveling of America: A History of Liberalism in the 1960s* (New York, 1984), 49–51; and Boyle, *The UAW and the Heyday of American Liberalism,* 150. But, while Keyserling and Tobin felt that early Kennedy economics fell short of their ideals, his aggressive expansion of defense and other spending greatly impressed the full-employment-minded AFL-CIO in 1961.

8. Collins, *More,* 56; Theodore Sorensen, *Kennedy* (New York, 1965), 608; Kennedy to Secretary of Defense, Secretary of Labor, Administrator General Services Administration, February 2, 1961, Procurement Policy Branch, General Correspondence, 1961, Office of the Quartermaster General, RG 92, NA; Memorandum from Major General and Quarter Master General A. T. McNamara, May 2, 1961, box 3, Procurement Policy Branch, General Correspondence, 1961, Office of Quartermaster General, RG 92, NA; R. V. Lee, Major General, USA, "Subject: Procurement in Labor Surplus Areas," January 19, 1961, box 3, Procurement Policy Branch, General Correspondence, 1961, Office of Quartermaster General, RG 92, NA. The deputy assistant secretary of defense for supply and logistics ordered that "active steps" be taken to place contracts in labor surplus areas. Kennedy and McNamara applied pressure to their subordinates to ensure that every effort would be made to enforce the revived policies. The army's quartermaster general, in turn, issued a memo to procurement officers, explaining that it was the "duty of the Department of Army to respond to this request by exerting every possible effort to alleviate this most pressing economic problem."

9. *AFL-CIO News,* July 29, 1961.

10. W. W. Rostow to Arthur Goldberg, February 1, 1961, box 81, President's Office Files, JFK Library.

11. Executive Council Minutes, February 23, 1961; Solomon Barkin to William Pollock, February 19, 1962, 4/54, Ruttenberg Papers, GMMA. Textile Workers economist Solomon Barkin was particularly celebratory over the administration's first year in office: "I believe that we are witnessing the recreation of an atmosphere in Washington which resembles the one we experienced in the days of the Roosevelt Administration. Our advice and counsel are being sought on many matters of direct interest to trade unions."

12. Sibley, "American Foreign Aid," 98–100. U.S. foreign aid was first administered by the Economic Cooperation Administration (1948–51). The AFL and CIO worked closely with the agency in Europe. In 1951, it was renamed the Mutual Security Agency. In 1953, it became the Foreign Operations Administration, only to be

renamed the International Cooperation Administration in 1955. Shifting organization names and revamping underscores the incertitude and ambivalence of many policymakers and the general public regarding foreign aid. Organized labor shared none of this ambivalence and remained a forceful supporter of aid.

13. Dean Rusk to William Schnitzler, April 14, 1961, Meany Papers, 1940–80, 76/6, GMMA.

14. Meany, "Foreign Aid for Peace and Freedom," 1963 [a pamphlet reprint of Meany's May 23, 1963, congressional testimony on foreign aid], 60/20, Meany Papers, 1940–80, GMMA; Stanley Ruttenberg, "Background Information on Foreign Aid," May 13, 1958, 4/49, Ruttenberg Papers, GMMA. In 1958, while plotting strategy for foreign aid lobbying, AFL-CIO research director Ruttenberg explained to Meany, "we should not ignore the fact that foreign aid helps our domestic economy . . . 80 cents of every dollar of mutual security funds is spent here in the U.S. An estimated 600,000 jobs in 45,000 American firms is provided by the aid program."

15. *Washington Post,* January 10, 1961; Meany to Omer Becu, March 9, 1961, 3/13, Lovestone Papers, Kheel.

16. *Washington Post,* January 10, 1961.

17. Meany to Becu, September 5, 1963, Office of the President, Micro 81, GMMA.

18. Meany to Kenneth Kelly, April 2, 1962, Office of the President, Micro 81, GMMA.

19. "Members of the Advisory Committee on Cooperatives to the Administrator of AID," December 16, 1963, box 140, White House Central Files, Ex FG 105–4, LBJ Library.

20. "A Program for Labor Action in Latin America," May 25, 1961, Goldberg to Kennedy, May 26, 1961, box 81, President's Office Files, JFK Library; Stanley Ruttenberg, "For a Free World: Alliance for Progress," *Free Trade Union News,* June 1962.

21. George Meany Oral History, 26, JFK Library.

22. *AFL-CIO News,* August 11, 1962; *Public Papers of Presidents of the United States: John F. Kennedy, 1962* (Washington, DC, 1963), 607–8.

23. Meany to Potofsky, January 2, 1964, 27/313, ACWA Papers, Kheel.

24. On public opinion and foreign aid, see Hogan, 190.

25. Sibley, "American Foreign Aid," 100; Jean Edward Smith, *Lucius D. Clay: An American Life* (New York, 1990), 673.

26. *Free Trade Union News,* April 1963.

27. Kenneth J. Kelley to Meany, April 8, 1963, 76/9, George Meany Papers, 1940–80, GMMA.

28. "Memorandum of the Vice President for Irving Brown," n.d., 18/8, Irving Brown Papers, GMMA. Touring Africa, Humphrey, to the delight of labor leaders, frequently stressed the necessary relationship between democracy and free trade unions.

29. These general conclusions regarding Brown emerged from research in the Brown Papers and conversations with historian Tony Carew.

30. Michael Ross to Lew Johnson, November 8, 1961, 31/3, International Affairs Department, Country Files, GMMA.

31. C. M. James, "Conversation with Dr. Phan Quang Dan," March 10, 1970, FCO15/1331, PRO.

32. Trinh Quang Quy, *Phong Trào lao-dông Việt-Nam,* 118.

33. Shaplen, *The Lost Revolution,* 146–47, 158–59; Z, "The War in Vietnam: We Have Not Been Told the Whole Truth," *New Republic,* March 12, 1962. The 1960 formation of the National Liberation Front in South Vietnam no doubt added to the AFL-CIO's sense of urgency.

34. Irving Brown, "Report on Vietnam Trip," November 17–21, 1961, 31/3, International Affairs Department, Country Files, GMMA.

35. Ibid. By early 1961, communist advances in Laos had forced Kennedy into a position of negotiating a neutral coalition government.

36. Ibid.

37. Ibid.

38. Ernest Lee to Meany, May 15, 1964, 31/3, International Affairs Department, Country Files, GMMA; Irving Brown, "The Role of Labor in International Relations," September 29, 1950, 10/5, Brown Papers, GMMA. Brown's interest in molding the CVTC into a "paramilitary" force was inspired by his suspicions that the Cominform (the Communist Information Bureau, coordinating the communist parties of the USSR with those of Europe) was developing, as Brown put it in 1950, "what I call para-military forces which could sabotage the shipment and delivery of arms to the Atlantic Pact." On the halfhearted efforts of Bao Dai and later Diem to develop their country's paramilitary potential see Nguyen Duy Hinh and Tran Dinh Tho, *The South Vietnamese Society* (Washington, DC, 1980), 53.

39. Ho-Thong-Minh to Brown, April 4, 1962, 8/17, Brown Papers, GMMA; "Free Democratic Party of Vietnam Overseas Organization: Background Features Information and Analysis," n.d., 8/4, Brown Papers, GMMA; Pham-Huy-Co to Lovestone, April 2, 1962, 14/5, Lovestone Papers, GMMA. Both Brown and Lovestone were in contact with exiled nationalist leader Dr. Pham Huy Co, who urged Lovestone to lobby Governor Averell Harriman, the assistant secretary of state for Far East Affairs, against the oppressive Diem regime. See "CIA Current Intelligence Memorandum, Subject: Cast of Characters in SVN," August 28, 1963, box 128a, President's Office Files, JFK Library. A CIA profile described Co as an exile in Paris since 1954, with ties to Dr. Dan's democratization movement. Co apparently had contacts in South Vietnam and was responsible for several leaflet campaigns in Saigon. The CIA described him as "relatively capable but not forceful and somewhat arrogant."

40. "Minutes of Labor Advisory Committee on Foreign Assistance," January 7, 1969, 11/11, Joseph Keenan Papers at Catholic University. At a 1969 meeting, Meany explained that Buu had traveled to Washington in 1962 or 1963 and the two met for the first time later. I found no other evidence of this trip.

41. *John Herling's Labor Letter,* April 16, 1960.

42. ICFTU "International Solidarity Fund Committee," June 1964, box 482, Lovestone Papers, Hoover.

43. "ICFTU International Solidarity Fund Committee, Brussels, September 1961," 61/19, Meany Papers, GMMA. According to the report, in 1961 membership in the Fédération des Travailleurs des Plantation du Vietnam numbered about 21,556.

44. Becu to ICFTU members, July 25, 1963, box 353, Lovestone Papers, Hoover.

45. Meany to Omar Becu, September 5, 1963, Office of the President, micro 81, GMMA. Also see Peter Mass, *Manhunt: The Incredible Pursuit of a CIA Agent Turned Terrorist* (New York, 1986), 23–24. Wilson was actually a CIA agent using the Sea-

farers International Union as cover. The CIA did go to great lengths to establish Wilson's cover, including putting him through Cornell's Industrial Relations School. Therefore, it is plausible that neither Meany nor Seafarer's president Paul Hall knew of Wilson's agency affiliation. Wilson later claimed to have interceded with Ambassador Henry Cabot Lodge to free Buu from incarceration following the assassination of Diem in 1963. Later he gained infamy (and a lengthy prison sentence in 1982) as an arms dealer and terrorist agent for Libya.

46. Harry Goldberg, "Memo on Vietnam," August 9, 1963, 31/3, International Affairs Department, Country Files, GMMA.

47. Harry Goldberg, "Meeting with Vietnam Exile Leaders," September 16, 1963, 31/3, International Affairs Department, Country Files, GMMA; *Herald-Tribune,* May 10, 1964. Huyeh Sanh Thong, a representative of the Democratic League of Vietnam and a lecturer at Yale, attended the meeting with Brown. Thong later joined with seventy other exiles signing a general appeal to Kennedy not to stand in the way of efforts to remove Diem. The *New York Times* published the appeal. See Kahin, 204; and Karnow, *Vietnam,* 340. Following the early 1964 coup that brought General Khanh to power, Hoan became prime minister of South Vietnam.

48. "Memorandum for the Record, Subject: Conversation with Mr. Ho Thuong Minh," October 15, 1963, box 1, Vietnam Documents, Joint Chiefs of Staff Central Files, 1963, Records of John F. Kennedy Collection, RG 218, NA. Brown arranged the meeting with Krulak through General Maxwell Taylor, with whom Brown had been friendly since their days together in postwar Europe.

49. Roger Hilsman, "U.S. Objective in South Vietnam," n.d., box 128a, President's Office Files, JFK Library; "Checklist of Actions for GVN to Ensure Popular Support," September 14, 1963, box 1, Vietnam Documents, Joint Chiefs of Staff Central Files, 1963, Records of John F. Kennedy Collection, RG 218, NA. Administration officials, including Hilsman, urged the removal of Nhu and that his influence be replaced with that of Buu and other popular leaders.

50. Hammer, *A Death in November,* 190, 250; Forrestal to President, August 27, 1963, *FRUS, January–August 1963, Vietnam, 1961–1963,* 3:658; Director of Bureau of Intelligence and Research to Secretary of State, September 15, 1963, *FRUS, August–December 1963, Vietnam, 1961–1963,* 4:212. Buu was loudly calling for Nhu's removal by the fall of 1963 and apparently supporting General (Big) Minh as the next leader of South Vietnam.

51. Jose Maria Aguirre to Ernest Lee, December 13, 1963, 31/3, International Affairs Department, Country Files, GMMA.

52. *Central Intelligence Bulletin,* October 15, 1963, CIA–RDP79T009–75A00730014001–S (accessed through CIA Records Search Tool, Declassification Database).

53. Rusk to Saigon Embassy, November 3, 1963; Saigon Embassy to State Department, November 4, 1963, *FRUS, January–August 1963, Vietnam, 1961–1963,* 4:550–51, 560–61; Tran Van Don, *Our Endless War: Inside Vietnam* (San Rafael, CA, 1978), 110. In this autobiography, coup leader General Tran Van Don seems to admit that the new government had arrested Buu and then released him at the request of Ambassador Lodge.

54. *Free Trade Union News,* December 1963.

55. David Dubinsky Oral History, May 7, 1969, LBJ Library, 15. "I was a great

admirer of Roosevelt, I was a great admirer of Kennedy, an admirer of Truman, but I think what he [Johnson] has done in the field of social welfare, of civil rights, and domestic problems, that is no match for anyone else," recounted Dubinsky in 1969.

56. Jack Conway Oral History, 16, Merger Oral Interviews, GMMA; Boyle, *The UAW and the Heyday of American Liberalism,* 92, 98–100; Robert Caro, *Years of Lyndon Johnson: Master of the Senate* (New York, 2002), 817–18.

57. Lyndon Johnson to George Meany, September 26, 1960, 31/13, Meany Papers, GMMA.

58. Boyle, *The UAW and the Heyday of American Liberalism,* 181–82.

59. Horace Busby to Johnson, May 5, 1961, box 1, Vice Presidential Security Files, LBJ Library; *AFL-CIO News,* May 13, 1961.

60. James A. Suffridge, "Comments and Observations Relative to the May 9–29, 1961, Round the World Trip with Vice President Johnson," 67/22, Meany Papers, 1940–80, GMMA. Also see James Suffridge, "The Urgent Needs of Asian Workers," *American Federationist,* July 1961.

61. Johnson to Kennedy, "Observations on Labor and Working Conditions in Southeast Asia," May 21, 1961, box 57, Office of Secretary, Arthur Goldberg, General Records of the Department of Labor, RG 174, NA. For Johnson's general report from Vietnam, see "Paper Prepared by the Vice President," n.d., *FRUS, Vietnam, 1961–1963,* 1:149–51.

62. Walter Heller, "Memorandum for the President," December 17, 1963, box 31, White House Central Files, EX LA 7, LBJ Library.

63. George Meany Oral History, 4–6, LBJ Library.

64. Walt Whitman Rostow, interview with the author, Austin, TX, June 2, 1997.

65. Potofsky Oral History (June 6, 1964), 735, box 188, ACWA Papers (5619), Kheel; Lichtenstein, *The Most Dangerous Man in Detroit,* 388–89; Boyle, *The UAW and the Heyday of American Liberalism,* 183–86. Johnson also forged a close friendship with Walter Reuther, who, like Meany, described the Johnson-labor relationship as one of unprecedented intimacy.

66. Joseph Keenan Oral History, 14, LBJ Library; Goldberg to Johnson, August 26, 1964, box 31, White House Central Files, Ex LA 7, LBJ Library. Johnson's success in courting labor was such that he even considered asking union leaders to privately commit to a strike moratorium during the 1964 campaign. However, Supreme Court Justice Arthur Goldberg, a former AFL-CIO counsel, persuaded the president that such an arrangement would compromise organized labor's hallowed sense of autonomy.

67. "News Conference of the Honorable Robert S. McNamara," July 11, 1963, 13/41, AFL-CIO Department of Legislation, GMMA; H. L. Nieburg, *In the Name of Science* (Chicago, 1966), 343. Contemporary praise for McNamara's reorganization efforts can be found in William Kaufman, *The McNamara Strategy* (New York, 1964); and Jules Duscha, "Arms and the Big Money Men: Congressmen, Contractors, and the 'Defense' Pork Barrel," *Harper's,* March 1964, 39–47.

68. For examples of labor complaints of lack of representation see "Summary of the Labor Advisory Committee to the Office of Emergency Planning," September 20, 1961, RG 1, Micro 7, U.S. Government Departments, 1960–61, GMMA. Also see the comments of Machinists' president P. L. Siemiller in "The Advanced Planning Briefing for the Department of Defense," *AFL-CIO News,* 16 April 1966.

69. Nate Weinberg to Walter Reuther, August 5, 1963, 3/43, Goldfinger Papers, GMMA.

70. Statement by the AFL-CIO Executive Council, "The National Economy," August 15, 1963, Executive Council, AFL-CIO Executive Council Minutes, GMMA. For Walter Reuther's concerns about Kennedy's timidity, see Lichtenstein, *The Most Dangerous Man in Detroit,* 363.

71. *AFL-CIO News,* May 13, 1963. Also see Herbert Parmet, *JFK: The Presidency of John F. Kennedy* (New York, 1983), 246. Some in the Kennedy administration were aware that the president's moderation on economic issues had displeased organized labor. Walter Heller alerted the president in the fall of 1962 that labor leaders were watching "the spectacle of the Administration's economic troops marching off to fight the problems of balance of payments, inflation, and economic growth with undisguised dismay." Trade union leaders, he cautioned, feared getting "the dirty end of the stick—big cuts for the fat cats, some crumbs for the little folk and no reform." In response to sluggish economic growth, Kennedy did propose tax cuts, but to organized labor such cuts were a sorry substitute for fiscal spending aimed at full employment.

72. U.S. Department of Labor, *International Labor* (November–December 1963), 9.

73. Meany to Johnson, March 3, 1964, box 124, White House Central Files, Name Files, LBJ Library.

74. Leon Keyserling, *Progress or Poverty: The U.S. at a Cross-Roads* (Washington, DC, 1964); James T. Patterson, *America's Struggle against Poverty, 1900–1985* (Cambridge, MA, 1986), 113–14; Lichtenstein, *The Most Dangerous Man in Detroit,* 391. Keyserling criticized the War on Poverty for focusing too closely on the downtrodden rather than stressing overall economic growth. Still, historian Arthur Schlesinger Jr. credits Keyserling's studies of poverty in the 1950s as an early inspiration for Johnson's poverty program. See his *A Thousand Days* (New York, 1965), 1010.

75. Fredrik Logevall, *Choosing War: The Lost Chance for Peace and the Escalation of War in Vietnam* (Berkeley, 1999), xvii–xxii.

76. Lodge to State Department, January 9, 1964, box 1340, Central Foreign Policy Files, 1964–66, Labor and Manpower, General Records of the Department of State, RG 59, NA. On the chaos following Diem's assassination, see Herring, *America's Longest War,* 110–11.

77. Telegram from Department of State to Embassy Vietnam, February 1, 1964, *FRUS, Vietnam, 1964,* 1:53. Also see Kahin, 203–5; and Tran Van Don, *Our Endless War,* 121–27.

78. Lodge to State Department, February 6, 1964, box 1340, Central Foreign Policy Files, 1964–66, Labor and Manpower, General Records of the Department of State, RG 59, NA. Khanh's charges against Buu appear to have had no merit. Most likely Khanh saw Buu and the CVTC as a political threat.

79. Victor Riesel, "Hungry Viet Workers," *New York Journal American,* September 25, 1964.

80. Meany to Buu, March 9, 1964, 31/3, Department of International Affairs, Country Files, GMMA.

81. James Forrestal memo, April 16, 1964, box 12, Confidential Files, CO 301, LBJ Library.

82. Dean Rusk to Johnson, "Subject: Your Meeting with Tran Quoc Buu," May 19, 1964, box 12, Confidential Files, CO 301, LBJ Library.

83. Buu to President Johnson, May 20, 1964, 39/7, Irving Brown Papers, GMMA.

84. "Memorandum for President," May 19, 1964, box 1340, Central Foreign Policy Files, 1964–66, Labor and Manpower, General Records of the Department of State, RG 59, NA.

85. Irving Brown to Meany, June 1, 1964, 1/27, Lovestone Papers, Kheel; Herring, "A People Quite Apart," 2–3; Truong Nhu Tang, *A Vietcong Memoir* (New York, 1985), 137. An outgrowth of its painful colonial past, strong antiwhite, anti-Western currents ran through Vietnamese society. The South Vietnamese leadership walked a near impossibly fine line, requiring at least a facade of autonomy and yet close cooperation with and dependence on outsiders. U.S. officials, at least to some degree, were aware of the predicament facing South Vietnam. See Theodore White to Kennedy, October 11, 1961, box 128, President's Office Files, JFK. Journalist White warned Kennedy of "the gross fact of race-hatred, hatred of the white man in general, originally of the French, now converted by clever Communist tactics into a hatred of Americans." Diem, according to White, already was tainted by his close association with the Americans; to his critics, the president was known as "Mei Diem," translated as "America's Diem." While Buu desperately needed American help, he could ill afford to be seen as too closely associated with the United States (Kahin, 206). General Khanh shared similar fears concerning his relations with Americans.

86. Saigon Embassy to State Department, May 5, 1964, box 1340, Central Foreign Policy Files, Labor and Manpower, General Records of the Department of State, RG 59, NA; Jay Lovestone to AFL-CIO Executive Council, May 13, 1964, box 429, Lovestone Papers, Hoover. Reforms instituted by General Khanh included the ratification of International Labor Organization provisions against discrimination in employment, inspection of industry and commerce, and the abolition of the labor-contracting system on the waterfront. In addition, Khanh appointed Nguyen Le Giang, a former vice president of the CVTC, as his labor minister.

87. *Le Croix,* January 4, 1964. IFCTC president August Vandistendael pronounced in early 1964 that the qualifier *Christian* in the CVTC name was not of "primordial importance." The Christian International itself was undergoing a liberalization in response to the reforms of Vatican II. By the early 1970s, the Christian International had also moved to deemphasize its affiliation with the Catholic Church by changing its name to the World Labor Council.

88. Tö-Thanh-Tuyên, "Speech Delivered on the Occasion of the Seminar of the PSI Secretariats, Hel din Singapore, 1964, Subject: Vietnamese Workers Movement," Singapore, 1964.

89. Arnold Beichman, "Report on Vietnam," July 26, 1964, 5/27, Lovestone Papers, Kheel; Beichman, interview. During one of Buu's trips to the United States, journalist Arnold Beichman, recalling their earlier visit to the slums of Saigon, took the CVT leader on a tour of Harlem. When asked to compare an American slum to Saigon's poverty-stricken neighborhoods, Buu responded, "Ici, c'est un paradis" (Here, this is a paradise).

90. Arnold Beichman, "Report on Vietnam," July 26, 1964, 5/27, Lovestone Papers, Kheel.

91. Ibid.

92. Arnold Beichman to George Meany, July 1, 1964, 31/3, International Affairs, Country Files, GMMA.

93. Rand Corporation, "U.S. Economic Assistance in Vietnam: A Proposed Reorientation," Washington, DC, July 1964, 64. An evaluation prepared by the Rand Corporation already had recommended substantial aid to the CVT's Tenant Farmers' Union to counterbalance the power of South Vietnam's landlords. Rand's reference to South Vietnamese labor was one of the rare occasions when the CVT merited recognition by U.S. planners.

94. Labor News Conference, Program 22, Series 4 [transcript of a Mutual Radio Program], September 20, 1964.

95. Taylor to State Department, November 14, 1964, box 1340, Central Foreign Policy Files, Labor and Manpower, General Records of the Department of State, RG 59, NA.

96. Irving Brown to Lovestone, August 4, 1964, 1/28, Lovestone Papers, Kheel.

97. Condon to State Department, August 21, 1965, 39/9, Brown Papers, GMMA; Kahin, 228–29. The Buddhist Institute for Secular Affairs was the secular and political arm of the Unified Vietnam Buddhist Church, which was founded on January 4, 1964, by South Vietnam's eleven main Buddhist sects.

98. Riesel, "Hungry Viet Workers," *New York Journal American*, September 25, 1964. Taylor's working relationship with organized labor dated from the German occupation, when he worked with Irving Brown. From that time, Taylor was considered a friend of organized labor.

99. Buu and Quyen to "comrades militants et adherents," August 28, 1964, 7H 6 97, CFDT Archives.

100. Lovestone to Dr. Dan, October 8, 1964, box 707, Lovestone Papers, Hoover; John Condon to State Department, October 10, 1964, box 1340, Central Foreign Policy Files, Labor and Manpower, General Records of the Department of State, RG 59, NA; *Saigon Post*, September 23, 1964.

101. Jean Lacouture, *Vietnam between Two Truces* (New York, 1966), 196; *New York Times*, September 21, 1964; Lovestone to Phang Quang Dan, October 8, 1964, box 707, Lovestone Papers, Hoover; Kahin, 227.

102. Truong Nhu Tang, *A Vietcong Memoir*, 91. The Viet Cong, like the CVT, was mobilizing to take advantage of the weakness of the Khanh government.

103. Lacouture, *Vietnam between Two Truces*, 196–98.

104. *New York Times*, September 16, 1964.

105. John Condon to State Department, September 30, 1964, box 1340, Central Foreign Policy Files, Labor and Manpower, General Records of the Department of State, RG 59, NA; *Le Monde*, September 17, 1964. Although he was committed to democratic reform, Buu was obviously frustrated by the failure of Khanh to control both the chaos of Saigon in 1964 and VC infiltration in the countryside. Labor attaché John Condon believed Buu and other labor leaders wanted a "benevolent dictatorship which would thwart if not reverse completely the recent expansion of Buddhist political influence and which would enforce order and discipline in the name of the war effort."

106. *Le Monde,* September 22, 1964.

107. Lacouture, *Vietnam between Two Truces,* 196.

108. Max Clos, "La Capitale Paralysée Hier Matin Par Grève," *Le Figaro,* September 22, 1964.

109. Buu to Lovestone, September 22, 1964; Meany to Buu, September 23, 1964, both in 31/3, International Affairs Department, Country Files, GMMA. In his telegram, Meany also vowed to "continue our efforts to persuade American and Vietnamese governments to support this democratic policy in interest of victory, Vietnamese national freedom and social and economic progress."

110. Telegram from Embassy in Vietnam to Department of State, September 24, 1964, *FRUS, 1964–1966, Vietnam 1964,* 1:787.

111. *New York Times,* September 21, 1964; *New York Times,* September 22, 1964.

112. *Saigon Post,* September 23, 1964. According to the newspaper account, the workers themselves "arrested" the alleged spy for trying to "stir up" the crowd.

113. Lacouture, *Vietnam between Two Truces,* 196; *Saigon Post,* October 9, 1964. The Vimytex strike ended roughly two weeks after the general strike. For the NLF version of the 1964 general strike see Ton Vy, "The Workers' Struggle," in *Vietnamese Studies, No. 8: South Vietnam, 1954–1965* (Hanoi, 1966), 104–6. Throughout its existence, NLF propaganda pointed to South Vietnamese labor strife as evidence of widespread discontent with the ruling regime and the U.S. presence. The NLF, however, largely ignored the organizing role of the CVT and dismissed its president as "the reactionary Tran Quoc Buu . . . camouflaged as a 'trade union militant.'"

114. *Saigon Post,* October 10, 1964.

115. Chester Bain, *Vietnam: The Roots of Conflict* (Englewood Cliffs, NJ, 1967), 133. General Khanh aggressively purged Diem's Can Lao Party from South Vietnam in 1964. The perception of Buu's continuing association with the Can Lao Party, however unfair, hardly helped him in Khanh's eyes.

116. John Condon to State Department, October 1, 1964, box 1340, Central Foreign Policy Files, Labor and Manpower, General Records of the Department of State, RG 59, NA. On the intense rumor culture of Saigon, see Sheehan, *A Bright Shining Lie,* 353.

117. Condon to State Department, October 3, 1964, box 1340, Central Foreign Policy Files, Labor and Manpower, General Records of the Department of State, RG 59, NA.

118. *Saigon Post,* October 5, 1964.

119. *New York Times,* October 10, 1964.

120. On the September 13, 1964, coup, see Kahin, 231.

121. Department of Labor Memorandum on the Buu arrest, 1964, box 734, Lovestone Papers, Hoover.

122. Rusk to Saigon Embassy, October 13, 1964, box 1340, Central Foreign Policy Files, Labor and Manpower, General Records of the Department of State, RG 59, NA; "Statement by George Meany, President of the AFL-CIO on Vietnam," October 13, 1964, 31/3, International Affairs Department, Country Files, GMMA.

123. *Saigon Post,* October 15, 1964; *Le Monde,* October 14, 1964.

124. Maxwell Taylor to Lovestone, October 19, 1964, 31/3, International Affairs, Country Files, GMMA; *Saigon Post,* October 19, 1964.

125. Gérard Esperet to IFCTU, October 12, 1964, 7H 697, CFDT Archives; Dom.

Ilito, Secretary General of the Union of Congolese Workers to Saigon, October 29, 1964, 7H 697, CFDT Archives.

126. Adlai Stevenson to Ambassador Volio, October 14, 1964; Rusk to Stevenson, October 16, 1964, both in box 1340, Central Foreign Policy Files, Labor and Manpower, General Records of the Department of State, RG 59, NA.

127. *New York Times,* October 23, 1964; *Saigon Post,* October 24, 1964.

128. Buu to George Meany, October 26, 1964, 31/3, International Affairs Department, Country Files, GMMA; Meany to Buu, October 28, 1964, Micro 81, Office of the President, GMMA. Meany responded to Buu's acquittal with elation. He cabled Buu, proclaiming that the decision of the court "can be considered a triumph for justice in your country. While we do not view this verdict as the end of the problems you face we do feel that it should serve as an inspiration for greater efforts to build a strong, free trade union movement which will be the best guarantee to social and economic progress for the worker of Vietnam, as well as of eventual victory against the aggressive forces of international communism."

129. Meany to Rusk, November 16, 1964, Micro 81, Office of the President, GMMA.

130. Altaffer to author, June 23, 1998.

131. Altaffer to author, June 30, 1998. Altaffer recalled of Baldanzi: "He was ready to listen and more important he held Buu as the head of the CVT in esteem. He respected any true union leader, especially one who had acquired leadership on the picket line."

132. Baldanzi to Meany, December 23, 1964, Baldanzi "Vietnam Diary," November 27–December 12, 1964, box 514, Lovestone Papers, Hoover; Morgan, *A Covert Life,* 337.

133. Condon to State Department, December 8, 1964; Condon to State Department, December 10, 1964, box 1340, Central Foreign Policy Files, Labor and Manpower, General Records of the Department of State, RG 59, NA.

134. Baldanzi to Meany, December 23, 1964, box 514, Lovestone Papers, Hoover.

Chapter 5

1. *U.S. News and World Report,* January 25, 1965.

2. *New York Times,* February 12, 1965; Robert Topmiller, "The Lotus Unleashed: The Buddhist Struggle Movement in South Vietnam, 1964–66," Ph.D. diss., University of Kentucky, 1998, 40–45.

3. *Free Trade Union News,* August 1966.

4. Kahin, 298–300.

5. Minutes of the Labor Advisory Committee on Foreign Assistance, February 20, 1965, box 249, Papers of Secretary of Labor Willard Wirtz, General Records of the Department of Labor, RG 174, NA.

6. Thomas Altaffer, interview with the author, Alameda, CA, July 6, 2001.

7. Ibid.

8. George Ball to Saigon Embassy, February 5, 1965, box 1340, Central Foreign Policy Files, General Records of the State Department, RG 59, NA.

9. The triumvirate of generals did not replace Khanh until June 1965. In the interim, Phan Huy Quat led a civilian government.

10. J. O. Moreton, "The Leaders of South Vietnam: A Few Pen Pictures," August

10, 1970, FCO 15/1331, PRO; Director of Police Hoa Van Mui to Buu, August 10, 1965, 39/9, Irving Brown Papers, GMMA.

11. John Condon to State Department, September 30, 1965, box 1340, Central Foreign Policy Files, General Records of the State Department, RG 59, NA; Su Tri Nguyen, interview.

12. John Condon to State Department, August 21, 1965, 39/9, Irving Brown Papers, GMMA.

13. Kahin, 206.

14. *Saigon Post,* July 16, 1965. Kirsch's arrival warranted mention in Saigon's newspapers.

15. Henry Kirsch to George Meany, n.d., 63/12, Lovestone Papers, GMMA. Also see Morgan, *A Covert Life,* 336. Apparently relying on Kirsch's claim, author Ted Morgan confidently identifies Altaffer as "a CIA agent working under labor cover." I could find no evidence that Altaffer was a CIA operative, although the vast majority of CIA sources remain closed. In correspondence with me, Mr. Altaffer would neither confirm nor deny an affiliation with the CIA.

16. John Condon to State Department, August 11, 1965, box 1339, Central Foreign Policy Files, 1963–66, General Records of the Department of State, RG 59, NA.

17. Kirsch to Meany, n.d., 63/12; Lee to Meany, July 26, 1965, 6/9, Lovestone Papers, GMMA.

18. Kirsch to Meany, "Report on Mission to Vietnam," July 30, 1965, box 582, Lovestone Papers, Hoover.

19. Altaffer to Meany, August 3, 1965, 31/4, Country Files, International Affairs Department, GMMA.

20. Taylor to State Department, March 16, 1965; Taylor to State Department, June 1, 1965, both in box 1340, Central Foreign Policy Files, 1963–66, General Records of the Department of State, RG 59, NA.

21. *New York Times,* July 3, 1965.

22. Lodge to State Department, September 10, 1965, box 1339, Central Foreign Policy Files, 1963–66, General Records of the Department of State, RG 59, NA. For instance, the leader of the railway workers union, having recently split from the CVT, accused Buu of intercepting five million piastres promised him by Irving Brown. Such accusations, though probably exaggerated and usually the product of complex, internal rivalries, forever swirled around Buu and took a toll.

23. Ibid.

24. Condon to State Department, August 9, 1965, box 1340, Central Foreign Policy Files, 1963–66, General Records of the Department of State, RG 59, NA; "Bulletin No. 7/1965," 63/12, Lovestone Papers, GMMA. Throughout the year, the Federation of Railroad Workers in South Vietnam sharply attacked Buu. In an editorial in a union publication, the railway workers urged the Americans not to "desert the Free World and the people by taking Mr. Buu as their savior."

25. Lee to Lovestone, August 5, 1965, 6/9, Lovestone Papers, GMMA; Sheehan, *A Bright Shining Lie,* 526–27; Herring, "A People Quite Apart," 10. An AID province pacification officer, John Paul Vann, made a similar proposal in 1965 to place the Saigon government under American receivership.

26. AFL-CIO Press Release, October 4, 1965; George Meany, "Turn for the Better in Vietnam," *American Federationist* (October 1965), 2.

27. Lindahl to Lovestone, October 3, 1965, 31/4, Lovestone Papers, GMMA.

28. "Report No. 22A from Harry Goldberg," November 22, 1965; "Report No. 22B from Harry Goldberg," November 30, 1965, both in 39/5, Lovestone Papers, GMMA.

29. Memorandum, November 30, 1965, box 1, Lansdale Materials, NSA.

30. Saigon Embassy to State Department, November 2, 1965, box 1340, Central Foreign Policy Files, 1963–66, General Records of the Department of State, RG 59, NA.

31. Lodge to State Department, November 5, 1965, box 1340, Central Foreign Policy Files, 1963–66, General Records of the Department of State, RG 59, NA.

32. Ernest Lee to Lovestone, January 17, 1966, 68/17, Meany Papers, GMMA.

33. Porter to State Department, May 6, 1966, box 31, Vietnam Country Files, Vol. 52, LBJ Library.

34. Porter to State Department, May 17, 1966, box 1340, Central Foreign Policy Files, 1963–66, General Records of the Department of State, RG 59, NA; *New York Times*, May 18, 1966. Also see Marily Young, *The Vietnam Wars, 1945–1990* (New York, 1991), 166–68; and Karnow, *Vietnam*, 445–50, for details of Ky's crackdown on the Buddhists.

35. *Free Trade Union News*, August 1966. From personal experience, Buu recognized how easily the Buddhists could be infiltrated. He vividly recalled having disguised himself as a Buddhist monk—which required only that he shave his head and don a saffron robe—to avoid detection by the French authorities during the 1940s.

36. Lodge to State Department, August 5, 1966, box 1339, Central Foreign Policy Files, 1963–66, General Records of the Department of State, RG 59, NA; Young, 166–68; Kahin, 421. The CVT's improving relationship with Ky seems to contradict historian George McT. Kahin's view that never "had any South Vietnamese government stood more naked of indigenous backing" as the Ky government.

37. Nam Pham, interview with the author, Baltimore, April 23, 1998.

38. C. E. Pestill, November 9, 1965, FO 371/180600, PRO.

39. Lodge to State Department, June 11, 1966, box 1339, Central Foreign Policy Files, 1963–66, General Records of the Department of State, RG 59, NA. Vo Van Giao, the president of the Tenant Farmers' Union explained its recent success: "In previous years the peasants were very much against the government. As a result a good number, especially under the Diem regime, joined the Viet Cong principally because they had no choice. It was very good for them to have the opportunity to know the Viet Cong, and it is natural that they are becoming sick and tired of the Viet Cong as well. . . . The union is neither the Viet Cong nor the government, so the union appeals to them."

40. "Statement by the Vietnamese Plantation Workers," box 1300, Central Foreign Policy Files, 1967–69, RG 59, NA; E. H. Peck, "The Economic Situation," November 10, 1965, FO 371/180600, PRO. The CVT's Federation of Plantation Workers issued a statement in the summer of 1967 detailing the problems of rural workers: "The cost of living has been increasing without respite, giving much trouble to the working class in general and to the plantation workers in particular. Workers in other fields of production have been granted wage increases or some form of allowances. Only the plantation workers have been forgotten." Also see Directorate of Intelligence Memorandum, "The Situation in Vietnam," April 26,

1967, CIA-RDP79T00826A001900010017-7 (accessed through CIA Records Search Tool, Declassification Database).

41. Lodge to State Department, October 30, 1966, box 1339, Central Foreign Policy Files, 1963–66, General Records of the Department of State, RG 59, NA; Lansdale to Lodge, July 29, 1966, box 2, Lansdale Materials, NSA. Buu, hoping the Americans might intercede, also expressed fears of Loan to a Lansdale aide, the infamous CIA operative Lucien Conein.

42. Lutz Baehr, interview with the author, New London, CT, October 4, 1999.

43. "Memorandum for the Record," George H. Melvin to Lansdale, January 9, 1967, box 2, Lansdale Materials, NSA; Vy Pham, interview; Bunker to LBJ, May 31, 1967, in *The Bunker Papers, Reports to the President from Vietnam, 1967–1973,* edited by Douglas Pike (Berkeley, 1990), 32. Facing elections later that year, Ky apparently felt compelled to mend fences with the CVT. In late May, Buu was among Ky's guests at a banquet designed to promote the airman's campaign for the presidency.

44. Trinh Quang Quy, *Phong Trào lao-dông Viêt-Nam,* 56–57.

45. Saigon Embassy to State Department, March 9, 1967, box 1300, Central Foreign Policy Files, 1967–69, General Records of the Department of State, RG 59, NA. The break between Bui Luong, formerly a CVTC official of some prominence, and Buu came in the late 1950s. It was related to issues of power and standing within the CVTC. Luong focused much of his attacks on the CVTC's alleged misuse of foreign aid. Acquiring aid for his own rival organization, the Vietnamese Labor Force for United Action, appears to have been his motive.

46. Porter to State Department, 4 January 1967, box 1300, Central Foreign Policy Files, 1967–69, RG 59, NA; Vy Pham, interview.

47. Sheehan, *A Bright Shining Lie,* 623–24. RMK-BRJ was a joint venture in Vietnam between two large American construction firms, Raymond International and Morrison-Knudsen, and Brown and Root and J. A. Jones. Brown and Root and J. A. Jones, a Texas-based firm, had close, long-standing connections to LBJ.

48. White House Conference on International Cooperation to Ernest Lee, n.d., 68/16, Meany Papers, GMMA.

49. Lee to Meany, "Conversation with Tran Quoc Buu," July 14, 1966, 68/17, Meany Papers, GMMA; Lodge to State Department, February 23, 1967, box 1301, Central Foreign Policy Files, 1967–69, RG 59, NA. In February 1967, three thousand CVT members struck an RMK-BRJ construction site at Long Binh. They managed to win substantial concessions.

50. Minutes of Labor Advisory Committee on Foreign Assistance, August 17, 1966, box 357, Papers of Secretary of Labor Willard Wirtz, General Records of the Department of Labor, RG 174, NA; Lee to Lovestone, August 16, 1966, 64/14, GMMA. AFL-CIO staffer Ernest Lee proposed an AFL-CIO-Asian Institute as a counterpart to AIFLD and ALC.

51. David E. Bell to Meany, December 29, 1965, 61/11, Lovestone Papers, GMMA. Beginning in late 1965, partly through the efforts of Jay Lovestone, AID inaugurated an initiative "for financing small projects" undertaken by ALC and AIFLD "without the detailed advanced review and approval we have normally required."

52. Jacob Potofsky, interview with Nate Gold, July 6, 1964, box 188, ACWA Papers, Kheel.

53. *AFL-CIO News*, August 21, 1965.

54. Lovestone to Buu, December 17, 1965, 9/7, Lovestone Papers, GMMA.

55. *Proceedings of the Sixth Constitutional Convention of the AFL-CIO, San Francisco, CA, December 9–12, 1965* (Washington DC, 1966), 67–71.

56. Ibid., 152.

57. Ibid., 76–86.

58. Ibid., 95.

59. Ibid., 567.

60. *New York Times*, December 11, 1965; Levy, *The New Left and Labor in the 1960s*, 47–48. Reports of the incident emphasized the age gap between those heckling from the gallery and those responding from the floor.

61. *John Herling's Labor Letter*, December 25, 1965.

62. *Proceedings of the Sixth Constitutional Convention of the AFL-CIO*, 562.

63. Ibid., 560–67.

64. *New York Times*, December 16, 1965.

65. ACWA Executive Board, "Statement on Vietnam," February 18, 1966, box 181, ACWA Papers, Kheel.

66. *National Guardian*, May 5, 1966.

67. *The Dispatcher*, October 14, 1966.

68. Lovestone to Meany, October 25, 1965, 1/43, Lovestone Papers, Kheel.

69. "For the President," December 13, 1965, box 125, White House Central Files, Name Files, LBJ. In many ways, Johnson's Great Society programs answered Reuther's longtime calls for community empowerment, full employment, and social spending. In fact, rumors circulated that Reuther was in line for a cabinet appointment under LBJ. Johnson briefly had considered Reuther for secretary of the Department of Housing and Urban Development (HUD) under a plan that would have transferred many of the functions of the Office of Economic Opportunity to HUD. The White House, however, anticipated resistance from "builders and mortgage people," and the offer was never made.

70. Lichtenstein, *The Most Dangerous Man in Detroit*, 420.

71. Boyle, *The UAW and the Heyday of American Liberalism*, 227.

72. Douglas Fraser Oral History, 11, GMMA.

73. "Victor Reuther's Request for Governor Harriman's Help in Facilitating Unofficial Contact with Soviet Trade Unionists," March 15, 1966, box 429, Averell Harriman Papers, LC. In March 1966, Victor Reuther asked Undersecretary of State Averell Harriman to help establish a program to facilitate "unofficial ties" between American and Soviet trade unionists. Harriman turned the request over to officials in the Johnson administration, who were "sure that George Meany would be strongly opposed to such contact on any basis whatsoever." Fearing Reuther's plan would upset the relationship between Meany and Johnson at a time when Meany's help was needed for the Vietnam issue, the Johnson administration turned down Victor Reuther's request.

74. Paul Schrade Oral History, 484, UCLA Library Oral History Program, Los Angeles.

75. *Los Angeles Times*, May 22, 1966; *Washington Post*, May 23, 1966.

76. Reuther to Meany, June 9, 1966, box 207, Dubinsky Papers, Kheel. In June 1966, an AFL-CIO delegation walked out of a meeting of the International Labor

Organization, a branch of the United Nations. The ILO's recognition of a labor leader from the Soviet bloc triggered the American protest. Meany and Walter Reuther spent the next day together, but the issue never came up. Yet soon after Reuther complained vehemently to the *Washington Post* that the walkout was a violation of President Johnson's "effort of bridge-building and broadening the understanding between people in order to improve relations with East Europe."

77. Jack Conway, Oral History, 21, GMMA.

78. AFL-CIO Executive Council Minutes, August 22–24, 1966; *Washington Post*, August 23, 1966. By a vote of twenty-one to two, the council rebuked Victor Reuther for his comments regarding the CIA. Walter Reuther voted against the motion.

79. *New York Times*, August 23, 1966.

80. *New York Times*, August 27, 1966.

81. Wirtz to Johnson, November 14, 1966, box 125, White House Central Files, Name Files, LBJ.

82. "UAW Administrative Letter," December 28, 1966, box 516, Records of Secretary Willard Wirtz, General Records of Department of Labor, RG 174, NA.

83. Boyle, *The UAW and the Heyday of American Liberalism*, 227–28, explains Reuther's erratic behavior during this period as related to his growing frustration with the Johnson administration. In Meany, Boyle argues, Reuther found a "proxy" for the president, "someone he could attack with all the scorn that the doves were now heaping on Johnson."

84. Braden, "I'm Glad the CIA Is Immoral"; William J. Donovan to Lovestone, July 29, 1949, 33/2, GMMA. In 1949, former OSS chief and Lovestone friend General Donovan introduced Braden to Lovestone as "a man of initiative and judgement," who had agreed to become the executive director of the American Committee on United Europe, a CIA front. See Morgan, *A Covert Life*, 338–40, for a discussion of the Braden revelations.

85. *Washington Evening Star*, May 9, 1967.

86. *Washington Post*, May 8, 1967; *New York Times*, May 8, 1967.

87. Saigon Embassy to State Department, April 15, 1967, box 1300, Central Foreign Policy Files, 1967–69, General Records of the Department of State, RG 59, NA.

88. Thomas Gleason, Paul Hall, and Joseph Curran to President Johnson, February 15, 1966, box 374, Papers of Secretary of Labor Willard Wirtz, General Records of the Department of Labor, RG 174, NA.

89. *New York Times*, February 26, 1966; *New York Times*, February 21, 1966. The *New York Times*, which later would complain that labor's CIA connections had eroded its autonomy, protested "union-made foreign policy." The maritime unions, the newspaper argued, had "no superior wisdom in the conduct of the total war effort."

90. Anthony Solomon to Gerald O'Brien, March 4, 1966, box 23, White House Central Files, Ex LA 7, LBJ.

91. Some laborites did argue that military spending was detracting from domestic spending and social gains at home. See Raymond Dickow, "Vietnam: Dissent within Labor," *Butcher Workman*, February 1967. Across the country, Dickow wrote, "one hears union workers expressing grave concerns over cutbacks of war on poverty programs." Workers, he claimed, "are convinced that the nation cannot afford both guns and butter." See also Charles D. Davis to Meany, December 12,

1966, 31/5, International Affairs Department, Country files, GMMA. Davis, a retired member of the Railway Clerks and UAW, wrote Meany complaining: "Some of your people may trade their sons for a fat defense job now, but tomorrow they will trade everything to the military dictatorship now being nourished in the capital."

92. Collins, *More,* 53.

93. As quoted in Mark Linder, *Wars of Attrition: Vietnam, the Business Roundtable, and the Decline of Construction Unions* (Iowa City, 1999), 17.

94. Califano to Johnson, December 23, 1965, box 125, White House Central Files, Name Files, LBJ. Califano did advise the administration to submit a "tight" budget so as to prevent any efforts by "right wingers in the Congress . . . to gut the Great Society programs using the Vietnam war as an excuse." Larry Berman, in *Planning a Tragedy: The Americanization of the War in Vietnam* (New York, 1982), argues that American intervention resulted from Johnson's fears that abandoning Vietnam would leave him politically vulnerable and endanger War on Poverty programs. Yet—as the Califano memo suggests—the Johnson administration clearly saw the war as threatening, not saving, its domestic programs.

95. Keyserling to Johnson, November 25, 1966, box 119, White House Central Files, Name Files, LBJ.

96. E. Ernest Goldstein to Johnson, September 7, 1967, box 125, White House Central Files, Name Files, LBJ.

97. Meany to Johnson, July 29, 1967, 34/16, Department of Legislation, GMMA.

98. Gardner Ackerly to Johnson, November 27, 1967, box 125, White House Central Files, Name Files, LBJ.

99. *Public Papers of the Presidents of the United States: Lyndon Baines Johnson, 1966* (Washington, DC, 1967), 96–109.

100. Califano to Nicholas Katzenbach, July 28, 1966, box 31, White House Central Files, Ex LA 7, LBJ. The primary advocate for a tax hike was CEA chairman Gardner Ackley. On the tax hike and Ackley, see Jeffrey Helsing, *Johnson's War/Johnson's Great Society: The Guns and Butter Trap* (Westport, CT, 2000), 225–28.

101. Collins, 30, 94–95; "1967 AFL-CIO Legislative Fact Sheet, no. 2," Pamphlet Collection, GMMA. The AFL-CIO actually offered its support for a wartime surtax but strongly opposed "LBJ's way of applying it." On inflation, taxes, and the Johnson administration see Irving Bernstein, *Guns or Butter: The Presidency of Lyndon B. Johnson* (New York, 1996), 358–78; and Robert Warren Stevens, *Vain Hopes, Grim Realities: The Economic Consequences of the Vietnam War* (New York, 1976), 74–81. See also *Proceedings of the Seventh Constitutional Convention of the AFL-CIO* (Washington, DC, 1968), 672–75. Addressing the AFL-CIO convention in late 1967, President Johnson continued to insist on the viability of a guns and butter economy, but he also called on labor to "restrain its demands for excessive wage increases," indicating concern about emerging inflation and foreshadowing the coming era in which organized labor would be blamed for rapidly rising prices.

102. Donald F. Kettl, "The Economic Education of Lyndon Johnson: Guns, Butter, and Taxes," in *The Johnson Years,* vol. 2, edited by Robert Divine (Lawrence, KS, 1987), 54. Also see David Halberstam, *The Best and the Brightest* (New York, 1972), 733. Halberstam, arguing that the president obscured the real costs of the Vietnam War in order to preserve his War on Poverty programs, labeled Johnson's economic

program "a living lie." Kettl, however, argues against any deliberate distortions, suggesting that the choices were less clear than Halberstam contended.

103. Wirtz to Johnson, May 25, 1966, box 61, Confidential Files, LBJ.

104. "Confidential Report to CWA Executive Board: CWA Opinion Poll, no. 25–66," CWA Presidential Archives, Wagner Archives, NYU. The CWA poll was conducted by mail, with questionnaires mailed randomly to union members "in numbers proportionate to the voting population density of each geographical area." Twenty-five percent of the questionnaires were completed and returned. Also see Levy, *The New Left and Labor in the 1960s,* 48, 231; and Boyle, *The UAW and the Heyday of American Liberalism,* 221. The CWA polling results reflect the findings of contemporary polls showing that a majority of workers disapproved of the war. A poll of Michigan unionists conducted by the UAW showed 51 percent favoring negotiations and 19 percent favoring immediate withdrawal. Subsequent polls showed that increasing numbers of trade unionists were opposed to the war—in numbers always above those of the general population. In 1967, UAW pollsters concluded that "On the whole, UAW members are considerably more dove-like today than is the electorate as a whole" (Boyle, 221). Martin Seymour Lipset, "The President, the Polls, and Vietnam," in *America and the Asian Revolutions,* edited by Robert Jay Lifton (Chicago, 1970), 101–16. Lipset, however, cautions that such polling belies many complexities and concludes that "most Americans are, in fact, both hawks and doves."

105. P. Foner, *U.S. Labor and the Viet-Nam War,* 48–67.

106. *ADA World Magazine,* July 1967. Tyler made a similar argument in "The Liberal Crisis," *The New Leader,* October 23, 1967; and "ADA's Option," *New Republic,* December 23, 1967. Also see Steven M. Gillon, *Politics and Vision: The ADA and American Liberalism, 1947–1985* (New York, 1987), 177–93. Gillon presents the ADA battle over Vietnam as a three-way clash between labor-liberal traditionalists led by Tyler, moderates led by Skull, and reformers prodded by Allard Lowenstein. A coalition of moderates and reformers eventually won the ADA over to the antiwar, anti-Johnson position.

107. Joseph Bierne to George Meany, January 26, 1966, 4/28, CWA Presidential Papers, Wagner Archives, NYU.

108. Lee White to Victor Riesel, November 20, 1965, 4/8, CWA Presidential Papers, Wagner Archives, NYU.

109. *AFL-CIO News,* June 4, 1966; Al Loewenthal to Jay Lovestone, March 13, 1967, 31/6, International Affairs Department, Country Files, GMMA. The IUE contributed heavily to the building of Dong Lac, a resettlement village located near Cam Ranh Bay in Khanh Hoa Province. See Chester Cooper to Paul Jenning, December 27, 1966, box 125, White House Central Files, Name Files, LBJ. A White House aide informed the IUE that it could "count on the cooperation of Federal agencies, particularly AID, in carrying out your program in Vietnam."

110. Reuther to Meany, January 31, 1966, box 302, UAW President's Office, Walter Reuther Papers, Reuther Library.

111. Karl F. Feller to Meany, January 20, 1966, 68/17, Meany Papers, GMMA. Leo Chern to Meany, October 10, 1967, 40/15, Meany Papers, GMMA. In addition to help from American unions, the German Labor Federation (DGB) also lent aid to the CVT, including money for the construction of a nursery for refugee children.

The nursery was to be named for Hans Boeckler, the late chairman of Germany's trade union movement. The International Rescue Committee also provided support to the CVT.

112. *AFL-CIO News,* January 15, 1966; Lodge to State Department, April 21, 1967, box 1300, Central Foreign Policy Files, 1967–69, General Records of the Department of State, RG 59, NA.

113. Saigon to State Department, January 12, 1967, box 1300, Central Foreign Policy Files, 1967–69, General Records of the Department of State, RG 59, NA.

114. Charles J. Cervello to Bierne, May 24, 1966; Glenn Watts to Cervello, n.d., CWA Presidential Papers, Wagner Archives, NYU.

115. *New York Times,* November 13, 1966.

116. Alan Burch to George Meany, "Preliminary Report on Mission to Investigate AFL-CIO Direct Aid to CVT," October 25, 1967, 31/7, International Affairs Department, Country Files, GMMA; Leonhart to Johnson, September 21, 1967, box 228, White House Central Files, LBJ; William S. Gaud Oral History, 28–30, LBJ; *Saigon Post,* March 28, 1968. Administrators at AID argued that by 1967 the waste and inflation associated with the initial influx of foreign aid into Vietnam had subsided. Nevertheless, a negative public impression lingered, and as late as 1968, AID administrator James Grant identified substantial corruption problems in the administration of American aid.

117. J. Thomas, "Call by Mr. Tran Quoc Buu, May 24, 1967," FCO 15/573, PRO.

118. "Six Main Points of the [Robert] Comer Report," October 5, 1966, box 13, Confidential Files, CO 301, LBJ. Elections in October 1966, in which 80 percent of registered voters participated, paved the way for the more comprehensive elections of 1967.

119. D. G. S. Waterstone, "The Fifth National Congress of the CVT," May 10, 1967, FCO 15/573, PRO.

120. Robert Shaplen, *The Road from War: Vietnam, 1965–1971* (New York, 1971), 161.

121. Goodman, *Politics in War,* 145–46; Roger Martin, "The Political Groups of South Vietnam," October 8, 1969, FCO 15/1012, PRO.

122. Saigon to State Department, November 29, 1967, box 1300, Central Foreign Policy Files, 1967–69, RG 59, NA.

123. "Report to the President on the Vietnam Trip (August 28, 1967–September 6, 1967)," box 81, White House Central Files, Country Files, LBJ; *AFL-CIO News,* September 23, 1967; *Saigon Post,* August 27, 1967; David Sullivan, "Report on Vietnam," *American Federationist* (October 1967), 9; U.S. Embassy to State Department, September 5, 1967, box 65, NSC Files, Country Files, Vietnam, LBJ. Historians continue to debate the fairness of the September 1967 elections. Herring, in *America's Longest War,* 160, argues that the elections were "neither as corrupt as critics charged nor as pure as Johnson claimed." M. Young (*Vietnam Wars,* 184), however, contends that with the encouragement of the American embassy the elections were "heavily stage-managed." Also see Ngo Vinh Long, "South Vietnam," in *The Vietnam War,* edited by Peter Lowe (New York, 1998), 78. Long labels the election "a cruel farce." The disqualification of the CVT's slate clearly suggests a ruling government eager to limit opposition. Yet the Sullivan report and the CVT's subsequent decision to join Don's slate suggest that the election had some legitimacy, especially for a nation at war.

124. "Statement of Mr. David Sullivan, Vice President of the AFL-CIO and President of the Building Service Employees International Union," n.d., box 81, White House Central Files, Country Files, LBJ; "Analysis of Election Returns in South Vietnam," September 1967, 14/3, Joseph Keenan Papers, Catholic University. Also see *CVT News*, August 1967. The CVT urged members to vote in 1967 "with intelligence, with prudence, with integrity but above all vote." It established a "Committee for Civic Activities" to oversee the election. On the success of the Don slate, see Theresa Tull, "Broadening the Base: South Vietnamese Elections, 1967–1971," in *Electoral Politics in South Vietnam*, edited by John Donnell and Charles Joiner (Lexington, MA, 1974), 42. The Worker-Farmer-Soldier slate won almost a million votes "from a wide spectrum of the Vietnamese population."

125. "Report by the Civic Action Committee of the Office of the CVT on the Results of the Elections to the House of Representatives of the Republic of Vietnam," October 22, 1967, 63/14, Jay Lovestone Papers, GMMA; Dacy, *Foreign Aid, War, and Economic Development*, 12. In addition to the successful election, the South Vietnamese gross national product began to expand in 1967 after a sluggish 1966. While the economy remained top-heavy in the service sector and dependent on foreign aid, some stability had been achieved.

126. William Connell to Rostow, October 19, 1967, box 13, Confidential Files, CO 301, LBJ. Meany proved unable to attend the inauguration, and David Sullivan returned as the official representative of the AFL-CIO.

127. Ernie Lee to Meany, July 14, 1966, "Conversation with Tran Quoc Buu," 31/5, International Affairs Department, Country Files, GMMA. In conversations with AFL-CIO officials in July 1966, Buu estimated that within a year military operations would be successfully completed.

128. George P. Delaney and the AFL-CIO Team Members, October 25, 1967, 14/3, Joseph Keenan Papers, Catholic University; Bunker to LBJ, October 18, 1967, in Pike, *The Bunker Papers*, 209. Ambassador Bunker notified the president of Keenan's arrival and how the mission might be of use to the White House: "The purpose of the visit is to discuss union-to-union aid programs with officers of the CVT. However, we feel sure we will get some strong statements of support for our whole Vietnamese policy position, which should be of real benefit."

129. George P. Delaney and the AFL-CIO Team Members, October 25, 1967, 14/3, Joseph Keenan Papers, Catholic University. Also see J. Thomas, "Call by Mr. Tran Quoc Buu," May 24, 1967, FCO 15/573, PRO. As recorded in "Trade Union Organisations in South Vietnam Summary," February 16, 1967, FCO 15/573, PRO, British officials also came to appreciate the awkward position of the CVT with regard to foreign aid. "[T]here is indeed a danger that the CVT's authority may be undermined because of the favour it enjoys with both the Americans and the government," wrote one British foreign service officer in 1967.

130. P. Foner, 48–67; James P. Gannon, "Wobble in Labor's Pro-Vietnam Stance," *Wall Street Journal*, November 9, 1967.

131. On Victor Reuther's trip to South Vietnam and his positive impressions of the CVT, see "Program of Visit, Victor C. Reuther, January 17–19, 1965"; and Victor Reuther to To Thanh Tuyen, February 24, 1965, both in box 47, UAW International Affairs Department, Reuther Library. Victor Reuther traveled to Saigon several months before the full-scale U.S. invasion.

132. *Chicago Daily News*, November 13, 1967; Labor Leadership Assembly for Peace, *Labor Voice for Peace*, Chicago, January 1968.

133. Martin Luther King, Jr., "Domestic Impact of the War in America," November 11, 1968, 51/30, Lovestone Papers, GMMA.

134. *AFL-CIO News*, December 16, 1967.

135. *Proceedings of the Seventh Constitutional Convention of the AFL-CIO*, 270–82.

136. On Operation Chaos, see Thomas Powers, *The Man Who Kept the Secrets: Richard Helms and the CIA* (New York, 1979), 315–20; and Bruce Shulman, *Lyndon Johnson and American Liberalism* (Boston, 1995), 146. The CIA operation turned up nothing and quickly evolved into a program to harass and disrupt the antiwar movement. See also Michael Beschloss, *Reaching for Glory: Lyndon Johnson's Secret White House Tapes, 1964–1965* (New York, 2001), 357. In telephone conversations, Meany and Johnson complained bitterly to each other about communist gains both internationally and nationally. In a June 15, 1965, conversation, Johnson complained about communists in the Dominican Republic and "what they're doing all over the world." Meany countered, denouncing what "they're doing right here in our country," particularly "in the colleges." Johnson ended with an emphatic "God bless you! I'm awful grateful I've got a man like you."

137. *New York Times*, January 5, 1968.

138. *New York Post*, December 13, 1967.

139. Foner, 62.

140. Mazey to Meany, January 15, 1968, box 515, Lovestone Papers, Hoover.

141. Foner, 141.

142. *AFL-CIO News*, December 16, 1967.

143. Paul Schrade Oral History, 484, UCLA Library Oral History Program, Los Angeles, 378.

144. See, for instance, Directorate of Intelligence Memorandum, "The Situation in Vietnam," April 26, 1967, CIA–RDP79T00826A0019000 10017–7 (accessed through CIA Records Search Tool, Declassification Database). "Possibly to avoid a confrontation with the GNV [Government of South Vietnam]," the CIA reported in 1967, the CVT appeared to be making no demands for pay raises for government workers. However, Vo Van Tai, president of the CVT's Saigon Labor Council and a rival to Buu within the confederation, was pressing for increases, "possibly to embarrass Buu."

145. Despuech, *Le Trafic des Piastres*, 28–29. The CEE, founded by the French in 1900, actually encompassed three plants in the Saigon vicinity: in Cho Quan, Cau Kho, and Cholon. The Saigon government purchased the plants from the French in 1967 for close to one billion piastres. See also "Round-Up Letter," November 29, 1967, FCO 15/1012, PRO. British observers described the CEE sale as marking "a further stage in declining French economic influence in South Vietnam."

146. Bunker to LBJ, July 5, 1967, Pike, *The Bunker Papers*, 76. U.S. ambassador Ellsworth Bunker predicted that the AID grant would "establish a modern independent and self-supporting public power company to operate both the new plant and the facilities now operated by the CEE whose franchise expires Dec. 31."

147. Bunker to State Department, December 14, 1967, box 1300, Central Foreign Policy Files, 1967–69, General Records of the Department of State, RG 59, NA; "Activities Syndicales: Creation du syndicat de la Compagnie des Eaux et de l'Elec-

tricité installée à Saigon," March 2, 1954, SPEC/77, CAOM. Founded in March 1954, the CVT's Water and Electrical Workers Union dated from the waning days of French colonialism.

148. Goldberg, "The Electrical Workers Strike in Vietnam," January 18, 1968; Goldberg, "The Electrical Workers Strike in Vietnam," January 29, 1968; Goldberg, "Latest Report from Saigon Situation," January 23, 1968, all in 31/8, International Affairs Department, Country Files, GMMA. See also *Saigon Daily News*, August 23, 1967.

149. See note 148.

150. Bunker to State Department, December 28, 1967, box 1301, Central Foreign Policy Files, 1967–69, General Records of the Department of State, RG 59, NA.

151. "Communiqué Issued by National Police," 30 December 1967, box 1301, Central Foreign Policy Files, 1967–69, RG 59, NA.

152. Bunker to State Department, January 9, 1968, box 1300, Central Foreign Policy Files, 1967–69, General Records of the Department of State, RG 59, NA.

153. Nam Pham, interview with the author, Baltimore, April 23, 1998.

154. Bunker to State Department, January 11, 1968, box 1300, Central Foreign Policy Files, 1967–69, General Records of the Department of State, RG 59, NA; *Saigon Post*, January 10, 1968; "Round-Up Letter," January 24, 1968, FCO 15/482, PRO. The negotiations between the CVT and electrical company were complicated by a debate between South Vietnamese officials and the French former owners of the CEE as to who would pay the severance packages and raises.

155. Saigon to State Department, January 11, 1968, box 1300, Central Foreign Policy Files, 1967–69, General Records of the Department of State, RG 59, NA; Trinh Quang Quy, *Phong Trào lao-dông Viêt-Nam*, 102; "Round-Up Letter," January 24, 1968, FCO 15/482, PRO.

156. Saigon Embassy to State Department, January 11, 1968, box 1226; Bunker to State Department, January 12, 1968, box 1227, Central Foreign Policy Files, Viet S, General Records of Department of State, RG 59, NA; *Saigon Post*, January 15, 1968; *Saigon Daily News*, January 13, 1968. FitzGerald, *Fire in the Lake*, 451. FitzGerald incorrectly writes that Tai was imprisoned for voicing doubts about the continuation of the war during the recent elections.

157. *Saigon Post*, January 12, 1968.

158. Bunker to State Department, January 12, 1968, box 1227, Central Foreign Policy Files, Viet S, General Records of Department of State, RG 59, NA.

159. *Saigon Post*, January 15, 1968; *Saigon Daily News*, January 14, 1968; *Le Monde*, January 15, 1968; Bunker to State Department, January 15, 1968, box 1227, Central Foreign Policy Files, Viet S, General Records of Department of State, RG 59, NA; Saigon to State Department, January 19, 1968, box 1300, Central Foreign Policy Files, Viet S, General Records of Department of State, RG 59, NA. Prime Minister Nguyen Van Loc issued the back to work order.

160. Vy Pham, interview; Su Tri Nguyen, interview. The CVT's "young turks" viewed Quyen as an ally within the ranks of the older confederation leadership but understood that if pushed he would always side with his old friend Buu.

161. *Saigon Post*, January 16, 1968; *Saigon Daily News*, January 16, 1968. When questioned about Buu's absence, Quyen explained that Buu was in charge of "outside relations," while he handled internal issues. In all probability, Buu was trying to

keep the lines of communication with the government open and to present himself as a conciliatory figure.

162. Phuong Ahn, "Saigon Diary," *Saigon Daily News,* January 20, 1968.

163. *Saigon Post,* January 15, 1968; Trinh Quang Quy, *Phong Trào lao-dông Viêt-Nam,* 107.

164. Goldberg, "The Electrical Workers Strike in Vietnam," January 18, 1968; Goldberg, "The Electrical Workers Strike in Vietnam," January 29, 1968; Goldberg, "Latest Report from Saigon Situation," January 23, 1968, all in 31/8, International Affairs Department, Country Files, GMMA. See also *Le Monde,* January 17, 1968. The events of the strike are also detailed in Trinh Quang Quy, *Phong Trào lao-dông Viêt-Nam,* 101–22.

165. Bunker to State Department, January 20, 1968, box 1300, Central Foreign Policy Files, 1967–69, General Records of Department of State, RG 59, NA.

166. *Washington Daily News,* February 29, 1968.

167. *The Machinist,* January 25, 1968. Individual AFL-CIO affiliates did denounce the handling of the strike. The machinists labeled it "a black eye," and wondered "whether or not Saigon's police chief is really working for the VC."

168. *Business Week,* February 3, 1968.

169. Bunker to Secretary of State, January 25, 1968, box 1, Saigon Embassy, Files of Ellsworth Bunker, Records of Foreign Service Posts of Department of State, RG 84, NA. For Rusk's warning to Bunker that the AFL-CIO was threatening to take a stronger, more public position on the Saigon labor situation, see Rusk to Saigon Embassy, January 17, 1968, box 1227, Central Foreign Policy Files, Viet S, General Records of Department of State, RG 59, NA.

170. Bunker to State Department, January 24, 1968, box 1301, Central Foreign Policy Files, 1967–69, General Records of Department of State, RG 59, NA.

171. Bunker to State Department, January 20, 1968, box 1300, Central Foreign Policy Files, 1967–69, General Records of Department of State, RG 59, NA.

172. Bunker to State Department, February 5, 1968, box 1226, Central Foreign Policy Files, Viet S, General Records of Department of State, RG 59, NA; Bunker to State Department, February 5, 1968, box 1300, Central Foreign Policy Files, 1967–69, General Records of Department of State, RG 59, NA; AFL-CIO Executive Council Statement, "The Sharpened Crisis in Vietnam," February 20, 1968; Vy Pham, interview. According to CVT vice president Vy Pham, trade unionists, noticing that the Viet Cong was abandoning its traditional black garb, had suspected that an attack was afoot for several months. Union cadres, he claims, informed the U.S. embassy, but their warnings were ignored. On South Vietnamese foreknowledge of the coming Tet Offensive, see John Prados, "Impatience, Illusion, and Asymmetry: Intelligence in Vietnam," in *Why the North Won the Vietnam War,* edited by Marc Jason Gilbert (New York, 2002), 144.

173. Bunker to Johnson, February 29, 1968, box 105, NSC Files, Vietnam, LBJ.

174. Bunker to State Department, February 19, 1968, box 1300, Central Foreign Policy Files, 1967–69, General Records of Department of State, RG 59, NA.

175. Irving Brown, "Memo: CVT and Present Vietnam Situation and Proposals for AFL-CIO," February 6, 1968, box 582, Lovestone Papers, Hoover.

176. Howard T. Robinson to Goldberg, February 6, 1968, 6/11, Lovestone Papers, GMMA.

177. Rusk to Bunker, January 28, 1968, box 1301, Central Foreign Policy Files, 1967–69, General Records of Department of State, RG 59, NA.

178. Bunker to Rusk, January 29, 1968, box 1301, Central Foreign Policy Files, 1967–69, General Records of Department of State, RG 59, NA.

179. AFL-CIO Executive Council Statement, "The Sharpened Crisis in Vietnam," February 20, 1968.

180. Buu to Meany, February 16, 1968, 31/8, International Affairs Department, Country Files, GMMA.

181. Lovestone to Meany, February 7, 1968, box 379, Lovestone Papers, Hoover. Lovestone's reference to the coalition government of Russian socialist Alexander Kerensky, a government that lasted from April to November 1917, when it was overthrown by the Bolsheviks, reflected Lovestone's continuing preoccupation with the Russian revolution as the defining event of his time.

182. Brown to Lovestone, March 4, 1968, 1/31, Lovestone Papers, Kheel.

183. On the political fallout from the Tet Offensive in the United States, see Herring, *America's Longest War,* 186–87; Young, 225–27; and Bernstein, *Guns or Butter,* 476–77.

184. Lansdale to Bunker, February 15, 1968, box 2, Lansdale Materials, NSA. Lansdale asked the South Vietnamese minister of labor to thank the CVT personally for its loyalty and support during the Tet Offensive.

185. Calvin Mehlert to Lansdale, February 28, 1968, box 106, NSC Files, Vietnam Files, LBJ. The arrests of Tai and Quyen were part of a larger post-Tet police roundup, which included the arrest of Truong Dinh Dzu, runner-up to Thieu in the recent presidential campaign, who advocated recognition of the NLF.

186. "Protest concerning the Arrest of Mr. Tran Huu Quyen, General Secretary of the CVT, and Mr. Vo Van Tai, General Secretary of the CVT Saigon-Gia Dinh Council of Unions; and Request for their Release," February 23, 1968, box 1300, Central Foreign Policy Files, 1967–69, General Records of Department of State, RG 59, NA.

187. "What the CVT Has Done for the Country during 1968," *Cong Nhan,* February 8, 1969.

188. Lansdale to Bunker, February 27, 1968, box 106, NSC Files, Vietnam Files, LBJ.

189. State Department to Saigon, January 18, 1968, box 1301, Central Foreign Policy Files, 1967–69, General Records of Department of State, RG 59, NA.

190. Bundy to Saigon, February 24, 1968, box 1226, Central Foreign Policy Files, 1967–69, General Records of Department of State, RG 59, NA.

191. Bunker to Johnson, February 29, 1968, box 105, NSC Files, LBJ; Bunker to State Department, February 27, 1968, box 1, Saigon Embassy, Files of Ellsworth Bunker, Records of Foreign Service Posts of Department of State, RG 84, NA.

192. Mehlert to Lansdale, February 28, 1968, box 106, NSC Files, Vietnam Files, LBJ.

193. Lansdale Memo, February 28, 1968, box 2, Lansdale Materials, NSA. Thieu told General Lansdale that Loan never informed him of the second round of arrests of trade union leaders. The South Vietnamese president apparently wanted to fire the police chief but feared the American reaction. While many U.S. officials viewed Loan as a hindrance, especially after the well-publicized Tet photograph of the summary execution, he may have had supporters in the CIA and elsewhere. On May 5, 1968,

Loan was injured in a raid and subsequently stepped down from his various security posts.

194. Minutes of the Labor Advisory Committee on Foreign Assistance, March 11, 1968, box 594, Papers of Secretary of Labor Willard Wirtz, General Records of the Department of Labor, RG 174, NA.

195. Fernand Audie to Lovestone, March 16, 1968, 31/8, International Affairs Department, Country Files, GMMA; *Saigon Post,* March 14, 1968.

196. Fernand Audie to Lovestone, March 16, 1968, 31/8, International Affairs Department, Country Files, GMMA; Bunker to State Department, March 18, 1968, box 1300, Central Foreign Policy Files, 1967–69, General Records of Department of State, RG 59, NA.

Chapter 6

1. John L. Moore, "Washington Pressures/Weakened ADA Seeks 'Silent Majority' Support," *National Journal,* September 5, 1970; Boyle, *The UAW and the Heyday of American Liberalism,* 236. Reuther refused to join the walkout, "explaining that while he shared their anger with the ADA, he could not sever 'the liberal-labor coalition'" (Gillon, *Politics and Vision,* 210–13, 271). The ADA fueled the resentment of laborites when the editors of *ADA World* refused to print a spirited defense of President Johnson written by Keyserling. The rejected piece included an angry attack on the ADA chairman John Kenneth Galbraith, whom Keyserling blamed for betraying the principles of full-employment economics. Keyserling printed one hundred copies of his critique of the ADA at his own expense and distributed them to the ADA's national board. The AFL-CIO later published his article in *Free Trade Union News* (March 1968). Both the Vietnam issue and that of full-employment economics were intertwined deeply in the Keyserling-Galbraith debate, which actually began in the 1950s. Keyserling angrily rejected Galbraith's contention that the private sector was "affluent" and wasteful. To Keyserling, aggressive consumption, high wages, and full employment remained the key to an expanding economy.

2. Lovestone to Meany, April 1, 1968, 3/46, Lovestone Papers, Kheel.

3. Lichtenstein, *Most Dangerous Man,* 423, 426. Reuther lined up behind Humphrey following the vice president's declaration of candidacy. Boyle, in *The UAW and the Heyday of American Liberalism,* 238–39, recounts a virtual "rebellion" within the UAW staff in favor of the Kennedy candidacy and against the Johnson and Humphrey ticket.

4. *New York Times,* May 1, 1968. McCarthy consistently attacked guns and butter economics. Noting the stock market jump with Johnson's announcement that he would not run for reelection, McCarthy argued that the war had shaken the country's confidence in investment and delayed important social spending. Earlier the AFL-CIO had supported McCarthy in his campaigns for Congress.

5. Albert Eisele, *Almost to the Presidency* (San Francisco, 1972), 200, 246. Throughout the 1960s, Meany had been a great admirer of Humphrey. When asked by President Johnson in 1964 to offer the names of three possible vice presidents, Meany replied, "I have only one choice—Hubert Humphrey."

6. Stephen C. Shadegg, *Winning's a Lot More Fun* (New York, 1969), 162.

7. Meany to Clifton Caldwell, International VP, Amalgamated Meat Cutters and Butcher Workmen of North America, June 25, 1968, 32/25, Meany Papers, GMMA.

8. While labor historians often have chided union leaders for failing to take an aggressive lead on issues of race, in truth racism always has flourished among American workers. Arguably, labor leaders such as Meany, though hardly in the vanguard of the civil rights movement, took far more progressive positions than those of the often reactionary rank and file. The Wallace candidacy lay bare those painful fissures between racial liberals such as George Meany and a more problematic rank and file. On Wallace and working voters, see Kenneth Durr, *Behind the Backlash: White Working-Class Politics in Baltimore, 1940–1980* (Chapel Hill, NC, 2003), 120–47.

9. I. W. Abel Oral History, 36, LBJ Library; Griffing Brancroft, "Racism, Reaction and George Wallace," *American Federationist* (September 1968). Also see "An Open Letter from Alabama Unionists, Warning: Wallace No Friend of Working People or Their Unions," 39/15, Meany Papers, GMMA. The AFL-CIO distributed an open letter from the Alabama AFL-CIO noting their governor's antilabor record. "Don't make the mistake we made in Alabama. Don't be so taken in by Wallace's appeals to prejudice that you forget your own pocketbook. We did, and we've been paying for it ever since," the letter warned.

10. Victor Riesel, "Inside Labor," November 6, 1968; Theodore H. White, *The Making of the President, 1968* (New York, 1969), 364–66. For an effective analysis of Wallace's appeal to working people, see Kazin, 221–42.

11. Hubert Humphrey to Lyndon Johnson, 16 February 1968, box 111, WHCF, Name file, LBJ Library. Victor Reuther visited Vice President Humphrey in early February to offer the UAW's "full and unqualified support" to Johnson's reelection. In his discussions with Humphrey, Victor Reuther severely criticized both the ADA and the McCarthy candidacy. "Memo," 25 March 1968, 39/14, Meany Papers, GMMA. Although Reuther and the UAW eventually endorsed Humphrey, according to one report, the UAW nearly endorsed RFK at an Executive Board meeting on March 19, 1968. A telephone call from the White House concerning ongoing negotiations in the areospace industry, however, dissuaded the UAW.

12. *New York Times,* 10 March 1968.

13. *New York Times,* 13 March 1968; AFL-CIO, *To Clear the Record: The AFL-CIO Report on the Disaffiliation of the UAW* (Washington, DC, 1969), 33. Meany's assistant Lane Kirkland prepared a summary and defense of AFL-CIO actions regarding the UAW disaffiliation.

14. Victor Riesel, "Inside Labor," 4 March 1968, box 19, Victor Riesel Papers, Wagner.

15. Lichtenstein, *Most Dangerous Man,* 431–32; Boyle, *UAW and the Heyday of American Liberalism,* 247. By 1969, Reuther had enthusiastically joined the antiwar movement and was frequently calling for a U.S. withdrawal from Vietnam.

16. A. H. Raskin, "Labor Morality," *New York Times,* May 11, 1970.

17. Douglas Fraser Oral History, 10, GMMA; "We Take Our Stand for Peace and an End to the War in Vietnam," *Washington Post,* October 14, 1969.

18. Lee to Meany, December 20, 1968, 58/8, Meany Papers, GMMA.

19. *New York Times,* August 31, 1969.

20. *Business Week,* October 31, 1970; *AFL-CIO News,* May 15, 1971.

21. Press and Radio Service of the ICFTU, "Decisions of the ICFTU Executive Board," October 12, 1967, 61/17, Meany Papers, GMMA.

22. "Americans Out of Vietnam! Vietnam for the Vietnamese!" *World Federation of Trade Unions and Vietnam* (June 1968): 3–6.

23. Ernest Conin, "Meany's Folly May Help Reds," *Los Angeles Times*, March 2, 1969.

24. Ernest Lee to Lovestone, November 22, 1968, Lovestone Papers, GMMA; "Stockholm, 24 October 1969—Reuther," 57/16, Lovestone Papers, GMMA. The Swedish trade union federation, in November 1969, particularly incensed Meany by supporting its government's $44 million grant to North Vietnam. On the other hand, the announcement of the Swedish grant led the ALA to send a telegram to the Swedish Metal Workers Union offering congratulations on its government's charity.

25. "Report Number 2942/68, Brussels, November 26, 1968: Re: Meeting of the Executive Board of the International Confederation of Free Trade Unions, November 20–22, 1968," 5/14a, Lovestone Papers, Kheel; Lichtenstein, *Most Dangerous Man*, 343–44. In 1958, Reuther and several other CIO leaders defied Meany and met with visiting Soviet premier Khrushchev.

26. "Report 2942/68, Brussels, November 26, 1968: Re: Meeting of the Executive Board of the ICFTU," 5/14a, Lovestone Papers, Kheel.

27. Meany Press Conference, February 20, 1969, box 734, Lovestone Papers, Hoover.

28. Ibid.

29. *UAW Washington Report*, April 17, 1969.

30. State Department to Saigon, March 4, 1969, box 1300, Central Foreign Policy Files, 1967–69, Records of the Department of State, RG 59, NA.

31. *Saigon Post*, June 4, 1968; Minutes of Labor Advisory Committee on Foreign Assistance, June 17, 1968, and November 12, 1968, box 594, Secretary of Labor, Papers of Willard Wirtz, General Records of the Department of Labor, RG 174, NA; Bunker to Johnson, May 29, 1968, box 105, NSC, Country Files, Vietnam, LBJ. Thieu's appointment of Dam Sy Hien, a CVT official, as labor minister also helped ease tensions between the CVT and Saigon government.

32. "What the CVT Has Done for the Country during 1968," *Cong Nhan*, February 8, 1968; Dacy, *Foreign Aid, War, and Economic Development*, 12. Improved security allowed the South Vietnamese economy briefly to enter the most productive period in its history. Between 1969 and 1971, rice production rapidly rose and the net domestic product increased by 28 percent.

33. Ernie Lee to Rutherford Poats, May 15, 1968, 38/18, Lovestone Papers, GMMA. An AFL-CIO staffer, Ernie Lee, negotiated an arrangement with AID whereby the agency would cover roughly 90 percent of AAFLI expenses. See "Letter of Intent," January 8, 1968, 31/10, International Affairs Department, Country Files, GMMA.

34. "Post Vietnam Report, February 29, 1968, to May 29, 1970," 31/10, International Affairs Department, Country Files, GMMA.

35. *AFL-CIO News*, November 23, 1968; "Director's Report to Board of Trustees Submitted at Special Meeting," February 2, 1969, 58/14, Meany Papers, GMMA.

36. Nguyen Duc Dat, interview. On the cultural sensitivities of the Vietnamese, see Nguyen Duy Hinh and Tran Dinh Tho, *South Vietnamese Society*, 56, 70.

37. "Political Round-Up," December 17, 1968, FCO 15/1001, PRO.

38. *AFL-CIO News*, November 23, 1968; "Director's Report to Board of Trustees Submitted at Special Meeting," February 2, 1969, 58/14, Meany Papers, GMMA.

39. Audie to Gerald O'Keefe, October 2, 1969, 31/9, International Affairs Department, Country Files, GMMA; Nguyen Duc Dat, interview.

40. Bunker to State Department, December 16, 1968, box 1301, Central Foreign Policy Files, 1967–69, Records of the State Department, RG 59, NA; "Post Vietnam Report, February 29, 1968 to May 29, 1970," Fernand Audie, 31/10, International Affairs Department, Country Files, GMMA; *AFL-CIO News,* November 23, 1968.

41. Ernie Lee to Meany, October 22, 1969, 31/9, International Affairs Department, Country Files, GMMA.

42. Berger to State Department, March 24, 1969, box 1300, Central Foreign Policy Files, 1967–69, Records of the State Department, RG 59, NA.

43. "Confidential Report, Assessment USAID/LAB Activities with CVT and Contract Representative Gerald Graf," November 12, 1969, 31/9, International Affairs Department, Country Files, GMMA.

44. Ibid.

45. Audie to Gerald O'Keefe, October 2, 1969, 31/9, International Affairs Department, Country Files, GMMA.

46. "Press Conference," November 19, 1969, box 429, Lovestone Papers, Hoover.

47. Vietnam's Workers' and Farmers' Association to the President of the Republic of Vietnam, May 23, 1968, box 1301, Central Foreign Policy Files, 1967–69, Records of the State Department, RG 59, NA. The Buddhist elements joining the new group were the Theravada Buddhist Sect and the Central Management Board of the Hoa Hao Buddhist Church.

48. Roger Burgess to Gerald Graf, September 4, 1969, box 18, Allan Goodman Papers, Hoover.

49. Saigon to State Department, August 2, 1969, box 1301, Central Foreign Policy Files, 1967–69, Records of the State Department, RG 59, NA.

50. Nguyen Duc Dat, interview; Su Tri Nuyen, interview. One CVT officer described relations between the CVT and Thieu as "friend-enemy."

51. "Vision D'Avenir: Extrait du discours prononcé à l'occasion du 20e anniversaire de la CVT," October 30, 1969, 7H 700, CFDT Archives; "Declaration de La CVT," July 17, 1968, 7H 700, CFDT Archives.

52. Audie to Lovestone, December 20, 1968, 68/10, Meany Papers, GMMA; Lee to Meany, January 2, 1968, 68/16, Meany Papers, GMMA.

53. Berger to State Department, August 13, 1968, box 1300, Central Foreign Policy Files, 1967–69, Records of the State Department, RG 59, NA.

54. Bunker to Rusk, July 17, 1968, box 2, Saigon Embassy, Files of Ambassador, Records of Foreign Service Posts of Department of State, RG 84, NA; Rostow to Johnson, July 12, 1968, box 105, NSC, Country Files, Vietnam, LBJ.

55. Bunker to Rusk, August 7, 1968, box 2, Saigon Embassy, Files of Ambassador, Records of the Foreign Service Posts of Department of State, RG 84, NA.

56. Berger to State Department, September 24, 1969, box 1301, Central Foreign Policy Files, 1967–69, Records of the State Department, RG 59, NA.

57. Bunker to Secretary of State, January 16, 1969, box 6, Saigon Embassy, Files of Ambassador, Records of the Foreign Service Posts of Department of State, RG 84, NA; "Round-Up Letter," July 10, 1968, FCO 15/483, PRO; CIA Directorate of Intel-

ligence, "The Situation in South Vietnam," September 30, 1968, box 68, NSC, Country Files, Vietnam, LBJ; Shaplen, *The Road from War,* 295.

58. Nguyen Duc Dat, interview.

59. Bunker to Rogers, February 26, 1970, box 3, Saigon Embassy, Files of Ambassador, Records of the Foreign Service Posts of Department of State, RG 84, NA. The American ambassador to Saigon, Ellsworth Bunker, frequently lobbied Thieu to implement a serious program of land reform.

60. Brown to Lovestone, October 14, 1968, 1/36, Lovestone Papers, Kheel. While attending the Christian International Congress in Luxembourg in the fall of 1968, Buu met with Irving Brown to discuss his plan to expand the CVT's political activities.

61. Harry Goldberg Report, "Vietnam," July 1, 1969, box 581, Lovestone Papers, Hoover. Buu reiterated to Goldberg in 1969 that personally he "couldn't and wasn't interested in direct political activity." Yet rumors persisted that Buu would seek political office.

62. C. M. MacLehose, "Call on Mr. Tran Quoc Buu, President of the CVT," April 17, 1969, FCO 15/1012, PRO.

63. Berger to State Department, September 24, 1969, box 1301, Central Foreign Policy Files, 1967–69, Records of the State Department, RG 59, NA.

64. Bunker to State Department, November 7, 1969, box 1301, Central Foreign Policy Files, 1967–69, Records of the State Department, RG 59, NA; Shaplen, *The Road from War,* 314, 346. Journalist Robert Shaplen noted that Buu might "finally be ready to come out in the open and lead the party personally. If he does, it could be an important development, he controls several hundred thousand workers and peasants."

65. "Press Conference," November 19, 1969, box 429, Lovestone Papers, Hoover; C. M. MacLehose, "Call on Mr. Tran Quoc Buu, President of the CVT," April 17, 1969, FCO 15/1012, PRO. Buu remained committed to a very American-style notion of pluralism. Despite the CVT's association with the Christian International, Buu, pointing to his own Buddhism and the Catholicism of several key CVT officers, constantly trumpeted the nonsectarian nature of his organization. Following this example, the Cong Nong political party incorporated Hoa Hao peasants, Cao Dai peasants, and workers from the Chan Muslim minority groups, as well as other religious and ethnic minority groups.

66. Bunker to State Department, September 19, 1970, box 1435, Central Foreign Policy Files, 1970–73, Records of the Department of State, RG 59, NA.

67. "A Louder Voice for the Working Man," *Vietnam Features Service,* June 1970, box 1, Robert F. Turner Papers, Hoover.

68. Trinh Quang Quy, *Phong Trào lao-dông Việt-Nam,* 130; Nguyen Ngoc Huy, "The Possible Role of Elections in a Political Settlement," 107. Nguyen Ngoc Huy, founder of Saigon's National Progressive Movement, also modeled his organization on the British Labour Party.

69. MacLehose to Foreign and Commonwealth Office, August 1, 1969, FCO 15/1012, PRO.

70. Buu to Lovestone, January 14, 1969, 31/9, International Affairs, Country Files, GMMA; *AFL-CIO News,* November 22, 1969.

71. Bunker to Rodgers, April 10, 1970, box 3, Saigon Embassy, Files of Ambas-

sador, Records of the Foreign Service Posts of Department of State, RG 84, NA; Senser, interview.

72. Tran Quoc Buu, "Memorandum on the Political Party Situation in South Vietnam and the Position of the CVT," n.d., 31/10, International Affairs Department, Country Files, GMMA; Gordon Cole, "Vietnam Labor's Unifying Role," *American Federationist,* September 1971. On the Cong Nong and other political parties in South Vietnam, see Tull, "Broadening the Base," 35–52.

73. Gwenn R. Boardman, "Strength for the Future: Labor in Vietnam," July 1968, 31/8, International Affairs Department, Country Files, GMMA; James Grant to Ernest Lindley, September 21, 1968, box 101, NSC, Country Files, Vietnam, LBJ. By September 1968, South Vietnam had undergone a "civil self-defense" revolution. Since the Tet Offensive, 420,000 civilians had enrolled in self-defense units, 134,000 had been trained, and 39,000 had been armed.

74. Lansdale to Bunker, April 11, 1968, box 106, NSC, Country Files, Vietnam, LBJ.

75. Bunker to State Department, May 18, 1968, box 1300, Central Foreign Policy Files, 1967–69, Records of the Department of State, RG 59, NA.

76. J. Thomas, "Call by Mr. Tran Quoc Buu," May 24, 1967, FCO 15/573, PRO; British Embassy, "Land Reform in South Vietnam: Background Note," June 24, 1968, FCO 15/1097, PRO; "Communique de la CVTC," December 16, 1954, 5H 37, CFDT Archives. As early as 1954, the CVTC made land reform a principal goal.

77. Nguyen Duc Dat, interview; Nguyen Ngoc Linh, *The Working Man in Vietnam* (Saigon, 1970), 21.

78. Roy Prosterman, "Briefing Paper on Land Reform in South Vietnam"; Rostow to Johnson, October 18, 1968, box 61, NSC, Country Files, Vietnam, LBJ. In October 1968, Johnson sent Ambassador Bunker a "watershed cable," informing him that "[y]our recent reports have encouraged us to believe that the time may be right for a broad new initiative on land reform."

79. "Memo," May 9, 1969, box 18, Allan Goodman Papers, Hoover; Ed Townsend, "Western-Style Labor Movement," *Christian Science Monitor,* December 8, 1969.

80. Saigon to State Department, September 25, 1969, box 1300, Central Foreign Policy Files, 1967–69, Records of the Department of State, RG 59, NA.

81. AID Asia Bureau, "Land Reform, United States Economic Assistance to Vietnam, 1954–1975: Vietnam Terminal Report," December 31, 1975, 79.

82. C. Stuart Callison, *The Land-to-the-Tiller Program and Rural Resource Mobilization in the Mekong Delta of South Vietnam* (Athens, OH, 1974), 87.

83. Ibid., 327–44; *Christian Science Monitor,* March 31, 1970; Dacy, *Foreign Aid, War, and Economic Development,* 15, 113; Stephen B. Young, "Power to the People: Local Development in Vietnam, 1968–1971," in *Electoral Politics in South Vietnam,* edited by John C. Donnell and Charles A. Joiner (Lexington, MA, 1974), 89–91; Grenville, *The Saving of South Vietnam,* 131–32; Nguyen Duc Dat, interview. South Vietnam relied heavily on USAID promises of money to fund the land to the tiller program.

84. Report of Ablin Magail and Antoine Laval, June 19–27, 1970, box 582, Lovestone Papers, Hoover.

85. Linh, *The Working Man in Vietnam,* 21.

86. Bunker to State Department, May 29, 1969, box 1301, Central Foreign Policy Files, 1967–69, Records of the Department of State, RG 59, NA.

87. Saigon to State Department, December 21, 1968, box 1300, Central Foreign Policy Files, 1967–69, Records of the Department of State, RG 59, NA.

88. "What the CVT Has Done for the Country during 1968," *Cong Nhan,* February 8, 1968.

89. Brown to Lovestone, November 18, 1970, and December 1, 1970, box 357, Lovestone Papers, Hoover. Brown also urged his superiors to provide the Cong Nong not only with "material support but organization advisors."

Chapter 7

1. Hogan, 190; Burton Kaufman, "Foreign Aid and the Balance of Payments Problem in Vietnam: Vietnam and Johnson's Foreign Economic Policy," in *The Johnson Years,* vol. 2, edited by Robert Divine (Lawrence, KS, 1987), 79.

2. For an example of New Left criticism of foreign aid, see Lucien M. Hanks, "American Aid is Damaging Thai Society," in *America and the Asian Revolutions,* edited by Robert Jay Lifton (Chicago, 1970), 117–32.

3. Harold Malmgrem, "Willing to Help," *New Republic,* November 1, 1969. The shift toward multilateral aid actually began during the Johnson administration. As one of his earliest acts as head of the World Bank, Robert S. McNamara commissioned a study of foreign aid under the supervision of Lester Pearson. Pearson's study, entitled, "Partners in Development," recommended that aid be administered through multilateral channels and not tied to "political support." The Johnson administration issued a report echoing the basic sentiments of the Pearson report. George Meany and AFL-CIO vice president Joseph Bierne both served on Johnson's commission but refused to sign the body's final report. See "Development Assistance in the New Administration: Report of the President's General Advisory Committee on Foreign Assistance," October 25, 1968, White House Staff Member and Office Files, Hendrick S. Houthakker, Nixon White House Materials, NA. See also James Schlesinger to Henrick Houthakker, August 28, 1970, White House Staff Member and Office Files, Hendrick S. Houthakker, Nixon White House Materials, NA. Nixon commissioned his own study of the foreign aid problem, "Foreign Assistance for the Seventies," which accepted many of the conclusions of the Johnson and earlier Pearson reports and proposed to end the practice of linking aid to the domestic economy.

4. See B. Kaufman, "Foreign Aid and the Balance of Payments," 100.

5. *New York Times,* March 15, 1968.

6. William S. Gaud Oral History, 25, 38, LBJ; B. Kaufman, 96–97.

7. Minutes of Labor Advisory Committee on Foreign Assistance, March 11, 1968, 46/11, Lovestone Papers, GMMA; B. Kaufman, 88–97.

8. Minutes of Labor Advisory Committee on Foreign Assistance, November 12, 1968, box 594, Secretary of Labor, Williard Wirtz, General Records of the Department of Labor, RG 174, NA. See B. Kaufman, 97–103, for details of Johnson's struggles over aid appropriations.

9. "Special Message to Congress on Foreign Aid," May 28, 1969; *Public Papers of the Presidents of the United States, Richard Nixon, 1969* (Washington, DC, 1974), 411–12.

10. Beirne to Meany, October 5, 1970, 2/17, Lovestone Papers, GMMA.

11. Minutes of Labor Advisory Committee on Foreign Aid, March 10, 1969, 207/2, Dubinsky Papers, Kheel. AAFLI staffers feared, at the very least, that Nixon's interest in Africa and Latin America would leave AAFLI, the Asian labor institute, in the position of the least favored of the AFL-CIO's operations.

12. George Shultz, "Memorandum for the Files, Re. Meeting of the President with George Meany and Secretary Shultz, March 13, 1969," box 16, Office of Secretary, George Shultz, General Records of the Department of Labor, RG 174, NA.

13. Bernard Nossiter, "Labor and Government Cooperate on Foreign Policy," *Washington Post,* April 28, 1969. Nossiter, a frequent critic of American labor, also authored "The Hidden Affair between Big Business and Big Labor," *Harper's,* July 1959.

14. Richard Dudman, "Agent Meany," *New Republic,* May 3, 1969. Dudman was the Washington correspondent for the *Saint Louis Post-Dispatch,* in which he published similar pieces exposing the AFL-CIO's close work with the government.

15. Walkinshaw to Saigon, April 28, 1969, box 1301, Central Foreign Policy Files, 1967–69, Records of the Department of State, RG 59, NA.

16. William Rogers circular, n.d., box 18, UAW International Affairs Records, 1968–72, Reuther.

17. Weaver memo, May 20, 1969, box 76, Office of Secretary, George Shultz, General Records of the Department of Labor, RG 174, NA.

18. Draft, Victor Reuther to Nixon, n.d., box 18, UAW International Affairs Records, 1968–72, Reuther.

19. While a critic of the administration of foreign aid, Fulbright, of course, supported many forms of aid, especially those directed at education.

20. For early Fulbright criticism of foreign aid, see *New York Times Magazine,* March 21, 1965.

21. *Newsweek,* August 18, 1969.

22. "Statement by George Meany before the Senate Foreign Relations Committee," August 1, 1969; *AFL-CIO News,* September 6, 1969. Fulbright later added to the acrimony by charging the AFL-CIO with racism, heavy involvement with the CIA, and responsibility for the recent murder of Kenyan labor leader turned politician Tom Mboya.

23. *Washington Evening Star,* August 4, 1969.

24. For instance see Michael Parenti, *The Anti-Communist Impulse* (New York, 1969), 8–11. In his 1969 book "former anti-communist liberal" Michael Parenti, explaining that "Vietnam was for me a crucible for my anti-communist beliefs," depicted anticommunism as akin to a "phobia" and "self-delusion." Also on shifting attitudes of liberals away from anticommunism in the late 1960s see R. Powers, *Not Without Honor,* 324–43.

25. Albert Lannon, Washington Representative of ILWU, to Labor Committee, Detroit Coalition to End the War Now! April 2, 1970, box 1, Detroit Coalition to End the War Now! Papers, Reuther.

26. Foner, 99. Foner writes: "Cambodia produced a reaction from trade unionists that was both greater and qualitatively different from those which had followed previous crises of the Vietnam war."

27. "Telegram," *UAW Solidarity,* June 1970. See Foner, 97–126, for the general

details of labor's reaction to the Cambodian invasion. He notes the "rising opposition in labor's ranks to war" after the invasion.

28. Joseph C. Goulden, *Jerry Wurf, Labor's Last Angry Man* (New York, 1982), 192. According to Wurf's biographer, Meany's refusal to grant the AFSCME president an open AFL-CIO vice presidency slot the year before may have inspired Wurf's defiance. See John Herling, "Labor and Cambodia," July 26, 1970, 134/2, ACWA Papers, Kheel. Ninety percent of the AFL-CIO Executive Council, however, supported Meany's resolution in favor of the Cambodian invasion.

29. "Keynote Address of Jacob S. Potofsky: A Time to Speak Out, ACWA Convention, May 25, 1970," box 184, ACWA Papers, Kheel. Potofsky was absent, perhaps intentionally, from the AFL-CIO Executive Council meeting that endorsed Meany's resolution of support for Nixon's Cambodian invasion.

30. *New York Times,* May 27, 1970.

31. Radosh, *American Labor and United States Foreign Policy,* 17.

32. Labor Assembly for Peace, San Francisco Bay Area to Meany, September 13, 1968, box 581, Lovestone Papers, Hoover.

33. *Detroit Free Press,* May 26, 1970.

34. Paul Klien, Executive Secretary of Cleveland Labor Council for Human Rights to Meany, May 24, 1954, 8/30, Meany Papers, GMMA. Also see the Encyclopedia Britannica film *World Affairs Are Your Affairs,* which details the activities of the Cleveland Council on World Affairs.

35. Jerry Gordon, *Cleveland Labor and the Vietnam War* (Cleveland, 1990), 4.

36. Ibid., 8–11.

37. Ibid.

38. August Scholle to Patricia Gorgan, National Peace Action Coalition, March 10, 1971, box 1, Detroit Coalition to End the War Now! Papers, Reuther.

39. National Peace Action Coalition to Antiwar Trade Unionists, November 14, 1970, box 1, Detroit Coalition to End the War Now! Papers, Reuther.

40. *New York Times,* May 17, 1970; *Detroit News,* August 11, 1975. UAW Executive board member and early peace advocate Emil Mazey, while enormously critical of Meany and the AFL-CIO, could be equally critical of the peace movement, communism, and the New Left. By 1975, for instance, Mazey was vowing to combat what he saw as communist infiltration of the UAW, warning that communists were "becoming active again in our union and they're working in the open."

41. In particular, see Durr, *Behind the Backlash;* Thomas Sugrue, *The Origins of the Urban Crisis: Race and Inequality in Postwar Detroit* (Princeton, 1996) and Heather Thompson, *Whose Detroit? Politics, Labor, and Race in a Modern American City* (Ithaca, NY, 2001).

42. Brendan Sexton, "Middle-Class Workers and the New Politics," in *Twenty-five Years of Dissent,* edited by Irving Howe (New York, 1979), 106–18. Sexton statistically chronicled the failure of the "average production worker" to keep pace economically with the middle class. He found that blue-collar incomes remained significantly below the median family income, thus revealing the "myth" of the middle-class worker.

43. On issues of race, liberalism, and working people see Jonathan Rieder, *Canarsie: The Jews and Italians of Brooklyn against Liberalism* (Cambridge, MA, 1985); J. Anthony Lukas, *Common Ground: A Turbulent Decade in the Lives of Three*

American Families (New York, 1986); and Thomas Edsall and Mary Edsall, *Chain Reaction: The Impact of Race, Rights, and Taxes on American Politics* (New York, 1991). Also see Basil Whiting, "The Suddenly Remembered America," Ford Foundation Report no. 2098, September 1970. For other studies of working-class culture and politics, see William Kornblum, *Blue Collar Community* (Chicago, 1974); Sar Levitan, *Blue-Collar Workers: A Symposium on Middle America* (New York, 1971); Brendan Sexton and Patricia Sexton, *Blue Collar and Hard Hats: The Working Class and the Future of American Politics* (New York, 1971); and Department of Health, Education and Welfare, *Work in America: Report of a Special Task Force to the Secretary of Health, Education, and Welfare* (Cambridge, MA, 1973).

44. Michael Sherry, *In the Shadow of War: The U.S. since the 1930s* (New Haven, 1995), 295–96; Christian Appy, *Working-Class War: American Combat Soldiers and Vietnam* (Chapel Hill, NC, 1993), 41–42.

45. Colson to George Shultz, February 17, 1971, box 77, White House Special Files, Staff Member and Office Files, Charles Colson, Nixon White House Materials, NA.

46. As quoted in Rhodri Jeffreys-Jones, *Peace Now! American Society and the Ending of the Vietnam War* (New Haven, 1999), 217.

47. "Minutes of the Annual Meeting of the Board of Trustees of the AAFLI held on Monday, February 23, 1970," 67/24, Meany Papers, GMMA; Jeffrey Kimball, *Nixon's Vietnam War* (Lawrence, KS, 1998), 104; "Memorandum of Conversation," April 8, 1969, NSC—Name Files, box 828, Nixon White House Materials, NA. Meany shared Lovestone's early reservations about the new president. In 1969, he wrote to Nixon, warning of "disarray" in the administration's Vietnam policies. In a meeting with national security adviser Henry Kissinger on April 8, 1969, Meany complained of "the lack of discipline in the new administration as evidenced by conflicting statements." He offered to make a "strong combined statement" in favor of Nixon's Vietnam policy, if the president felt it necessary.

48. Herring, *America's Longest War,* 236. Historian George Herring termed Nixon's Cambodia address on April 30, 1970, "belligerent" and "provocative." The speech seemed tailored to free trade union sensibilities. Nixon warned that, unless the United States was willing to stand up, "the forces of totalitarianism and anarchy will threaten free nations and free institutions throughout the world."

49. Colson, "Memorandum for H. R. Haldeman," May 5, 1970, box 78, White House Special Files, Staff Member and Office Files, Charles Colson, Nixon White House Materials, NA; "Minutes of Annual Meeting of Board of Trustees of AAFLI," February 13, 1970, 9/11, Keenan Papers, Catholic University. Only several weeks before the Cambodian invasion, Lovestone lambasted the Nixon administration at a meeting of the AAFLI Board of Trustees.

50. Colson, "Memo for the President, Subject: Meeting with Executive Council of AFL-CIO," May 12, 1970, box 20, Office of Secretary, James D. Hodgson, 1970–71, General Records of Department of Labor, RG 174, NA; Colson, "Memorandum for President's Files," March 15, 1970, box 20, Office of Secretary, James D. Hodgson, 1970–71, General Records of Department of Labor, RG 174, NA. Nixon met earlier that spring with the presidents of the AFL-CIO building trades unions. Discussion topics included Laos and Vietnam.

51. Colson to Haldeman, September 14, 1970, box 77, White House Special

Files, Staff Member and Office Files, Charles Colson, Nixon White House Materials, NA; Colson, "Memorandum for Bill Timmons," May 27, 1970, box 78, White House Special Files, Charles Colson, Nixon White House Materials, NA. Among his other plans, Lovestone suggested that Senator Robert Dole or a sympathetic Democrat circulate through the Senate a petition demanding the release of all prisoners of war. Antiwar senators, Lovestone hoped, would refuse to sign such a petition and thus damage themselves in the eyes of voters. Colson saw it as "a great technique to put the Doves on the spot." See Colson to Haldeman, September 14, 1970, box 77, White House Special Files, Staff Member and Office Files, Charles Colson, Nixon White House Materials, NA. At one point, Colson marveled, "The remarkable thing about Lovestone is that every time he has told me what Meany was going to do, Meany subsequently did it."

52. *New York Times,* May 13, 1970; Linder, *Wars of Attrition,* 277. Meany issued an ambiguous statement with regard to hard-hat violence, explaining, "I don't like anybody beating anybody up . . . in my book violence begets violence."

53. *New York Times,* May 21, 1970. A University of Michigan student watching the hard-hat demonstrations commented, "if this is what the class struggle is all about there's something wrong somewhere." Brennan did seek to control some of the violence that marked the early hard-hat protests, urging his ranks, for instance, not to act like "rednecks." For a cultural analysis of the hard-hat demonstrations, see Joshua Freeman, "Hardhats: Construction Workers, Manliness, and the 1970 Pro-War Demonstrations," *Journal of Social History* 26 (1993): 725–44. Freeman interprets the hard-hat demonstrations as "built on earlier struggles against employers and integration." But the Vietnam War also served to trigger deeper, long-term resentments. "Here were these kids, rich kids, who could go to college, who didn't have to fight, they are telling you your son died in vain. It makes you feel your whole life is shit, just nothing," explained one trade unionist quoted by Freeman. Linder, in *Wars of Attrition,* 287, argues that the demonstrations must be seen in the "context of the joint state-employer efforts to control construction wages." Depicting a Nixon-administration-led conspiracy as behind the hard-hat protests, Linder portrays the demonstrations as part of a successful campaign against construction trade workers.

54. Flyer for Building Trades Rally, May 20, 1970, box 20, Office of Secretary, James D. Hodgson, 1970–71, General Records of Department of Labor, RG 174, NA. Brennan, in flyers prepared for the demonstrations, portrayed the rallies as aimed at a broad spectrum: "All Americans are invited to join us, students and workers—long hair or short—bald or bearded. Just bring your love for the only flag we have." The elevation of the flag as a potent political and cultural symbol, a process begun during the hard-hat rallies, culminated during the 1988 presidential campaign, when Vice President George H. W. Bush used the issue to appeal to so-called Reagan Democrats.

55. "Memorandum for the President, Subject: Meeting with Representatives of the Building and Construction Trades Council of Greater New York," n.d., box 20, Office of Secretary, James D. Hodgson, 1970–71, General Records of Department of Labor, RG 174, NA.

56. "Memorandum for the President's Files, Subject: Building and Construction Trades Meeting with the President," May 26, 1970, box 20, Office of Secretary, James

D. Hodgson, 1970–71, General Records of Department of Labor, RG 174, NA; John Dean, *Blind Ambition: The White House Years* (New York, 1976), 36. The hard-hat White House visit drew controversy when *Scanlon's Monthly* published charges that "racketeers" had been among those invited. Subsequent investigations by the FBI revealed that some "shady characters" indeed had been invited with the group.

57. "Dinner Date on Labor Day," *National Journal,* January 30, 1971; H. R. Haldeman, *The Haldeman Diaries: Inside the Nixon White House* (New York, 1994), 191–92. Haldeman called the dinner "a real coup," but few in labor saw it as a genuine gesture. The AFL-CIO's public relations director, Albert Zack, for instance, described it as "politically motivated. It was all a part of the blue collar strategy."

58. Haldeman memorandum for Colson, September 14, 1970, box 38, White House Central Files, Confidential Files, Nixon White House Materials, NA. Haldeman further targeted Meany's secretary, Virginia Tehas, as also "very important" to the "cultivation" campaign.

59. Colson, "Memorandum for the President, Subject: Meeting with George Meany et al.," October 13, 1970, Colson handwritten notes of October 13, 1970, meeting, box 22, Office of Secretary, James D. Hodgson, 1970–71, General Records of Department of Labor, RG 174, NA. Meany used the occasion to lobby for more and better State Department labor attachés. In response, Nixon ordered his secretary of state to conduct an immediate review of the attaché program.

60. "Open Hour at the White House," December 21, 1970, box 22, Office of Secretary, James D. Hodgson, 1970–71, General Records of Department of Labor, RG 174, NA; Robinson, *George Meany and His Times,* 279. The Nixon administration obviously sought to utilize the Roman Catholic backgrounds of many of the labor leaders as a part of its identity politics strategy. Yet the execution of this strategy was often sloppy. On their first meeting after Nixon's election, the president elect introduced Meany to his secretary, Rose Mary Woods, adding, "She's a Catholic too." Meany later furiously commented on the incident: "What the hell was that? As if that was important to me! What did I care what she was?"

61. Jerome M. Rosow, "Memorandum for the Secretary, Subject: The Problem of the Blue-Collar Worker," April 16, 1970, Office of Secretary, James D. Hodgson, 1970–71, General Records of Department of Labor, RG 174, NA; Charles Culhane, "White House Report," *National Journal,* January 30, 1971; Pete Hamil, "The Revolt of the White Lower-Middle Class," *New Yorker,* March 14, 1969. The Rosow report was inspired by Nixon's reading of Pete Hamil's 1969 *New Yorker* article outlining the growing problems of working Americans.

62. John R. Brown, II, to George Shultz, September 26, 1970, box 39, Office of Secretary, James D. Hodgson, 1970–72, General Records of Department of Labor, RG 174, NA; Hodgson to Nixon, August 25, 1970, box 28, Office of Secretary, James D. Hodgson, 1970–71, General Records of Department of Labor, RG 174, NA; "Action Memo and Rosow Blue Collar Report," Attachment B, n.d., box 39, Office of Secretary, James D. Hodgson, 1970–72, General Records of the Department of Labor, RG 174, NA. The president assigned George Shultz, John Ehrlichman, and Attorney General John Mitchell to a working group formed to consider enacting aspects of the plan. Among the measures taken in line with the Rosow report were HUD's Operation Breakthrough, which was designed to "construct attractive homes at lower prices"; new safety and health standards for workers; the Higher Education

Opportunity Act; the Urban Mass Transportation Assistance Act; and the Occupational Safety and Health Act.

63. Colson Memorandum, September 14, 1970, box 22, Staff Review Board Review of Contested Materials, White House Special Files, Colson, Nixon White House Materials, NA.

64. Memorandum of Conversation, April 7, 1971, box 828, NSC Files, Name Files, Nixon White House Materials, NA.

65. *AFL-CIO News,* June 19, 1971; *AFL-CIO News,* January 9, 1971; George Meany, "The Economic Disaster," *American Federationist* (August 1971).

66. *AFL-CIO News,* January 9, 1971.

67. Keyserling to ADA Board Members, January 29, 1968, 45/17, Lovestone Papers, GMMA.

68. Jervis Anderson, *Bayard Rustin: Troubles I've Seen, a Biography* (New York, 1997), 290.

69. On the liberal abandonment of full-employment, growth-oriented economics, see Collins, *More,* 99.

70. Calleo, *The Imperious Economy,* 37; Stevens, *Vain Hopes, Grim Realities,* 135.

71. Anthony Campagna, *The Economic Consequences of the Vietnam War* (New York, 1991), 84–85; Stevens, *Vain Hopes, Grim Realities,* 125–27; Paul McCracken, "Economic Policy in the Nixon Years," *Presidential Studies Quarterly* 26 (winter 1996): 168–69. Linder, in *Wars of Attrition,* 58–264, details the rise of the Business Roundtable, an organization with strong ties to the Nixon administration that was dedicated to limiting the wages and power of construction trade unions, in the early 1970s.

72. *Proceedings of the Ninth Constitutional Convention of the AFL-CIO,* Bal Harbor, FL, 1971, 13. Burns's comments, made in a speech given in January 1971 at Pepperdine University, were quoted by Meany at the AFL-CIO convention later that year. In reviewing Burns's record, Meany added that "if he was working in the USSR, he would have been sent to Siberia. But no, he was promoted."

73. Paul McCracken to Hodgson, November 13, 1970, box 36, White House Central Files, Staff Member and Office Files, Herbert Stein, Nixon White House Materials, NA; *New York Times,* February 24, 1971. Nixon followed McCracken's advice and suspended the Davis-Bacon Act in February 1971. Meany blasted the action as "an open invitation to unscrupulous employers to exploit workers by competitive undermining of fair wage and labor standards."

74. Campagna, *The Economic Consequences of the Vietnam War,* 89–90. The decision to impose the controls—largely a political calculation aimed at improving the economy for the upcoming presidential elections—suggested a strange repudiation of both full-employment economics and the monetarist approach.

75. Leon Keyserling, "The Scarcity School of Economics," Washington, DC, 1974, 84; Haldeman, *The Haldeman Diaries,* 326. Price and wage guidelines actually were introduced under Democrats Kennedy and Johnson. While Keyserling always remained a critic of controls, Keynesian John Kenneth Galbraith, representing in some senses the middle-class component of the Democratic Party, advocated permanent controls on the economy.

76. *AFL-CIO News,* August 4, 1971; *New York Times,* August 20, 1971.

77. *AFL-CIO News,* October 16, 1971; Colson to Shultz, "Subject: George

Meany," October 28, 1970, box 11, Office of Secretary, James D. Hodgson, 1970–71, General Records of Department of Labor, RG 174, NA.

78. Meany to Max Greenberg, October 15, 1971, boxes 25–26, National Union of Hospital and Health Care Employees, Local 1199, Kheel.

79. *Life,* November 19, 1971; *Time,* September 6, 1971. Also see *Newsweek,* September 6, 1971; and Richard Nixon, *RN: The Memoirs of Richard Nixon* (New York, 1978), 521. Meany was vindicated for his harsh stance against price and wage controls by none other than Nixon himself. In his memoirs, Nixon regretted imposing the controls, writing that "the piper must always be paid, and there was an unquestionably high price for tampering with the orthodox economic mechanisms."

80. Gorman to Potofsky, May 6, 1971, box 3, Frank Rosenblum Papers, ACWA Archives, Kheel.

81. Colson to Dwight Chapin, March 12, 1971, box 828, NSC—Name Files, Nixon White House Materials, NA.

82. "George Meany: Economic Chameleon," n.d., box 3, White House Special Files/ Staff Member and Office Files, Desmond J. Baker, Nixon White House Materials, NA.

83. "Memorandum for the Files, Subject: Meeting with Messrs. Connally, Haldeman, Rumsfeld, Shultz, and Colson, 11/18 and 11/27 [1971]," box 28, Office of Secretary, James D. Hodgson, 1970–71, General Records of Department of Labor, RG 174, NA.

84. Stewart Alsop, "Labor and the Liberals," *Newsweek,* January 22, 1971.

85. Randall Woods, *Fulbright: A Biography* (New York, 1995), 237–38, 610.

86. *AFL-CIO News,* November 6, 1971; Dacy, *Foreign Aid, War, and Economic Development,* 21. Not only was the future of AAFLI threatened by the aid holdup, but the entire South Vietnamese economy—heavily dependent on foreign aid—was endangered. As economist Douglas Dacy explained, "When that aid started to dry up, the structure [of South Vietnam's economy] began to crumble."

87. Ernie Lee to Meany, November 3, 1971, box 518, Lovestone Papers, Hoover.

88. *Newsweek,* November 8, 1971; *Newsweek,* November 15, 1971; Woods, *Fulbright,* 610.

89. *AFL-CIO News,* September 5, 1970.

90. Meany to Charles Tyroler, March 18, 1970, 68/10, Meany Papers, GMMA. The Citizens Committee for Peace with Freedom in Vietnam later reconstituted itself as the influential Committee on the Present Danger.

91. "Statement by Clark Kerr, chairman, National Committee for a Political Settlement in Vietnam/Negotiations Now!" 64/5, Meany Papers, GMMA. Prominent among the Negotiations Now! leadership was Thomas Kahn, future head of the AFL-CIO's International Affairs Committee. Also see Buhle, *Taking Care of Business,* 293.

92. Bunker to State Department, September 19, 1970, box 1435, Central Foreign Policy Files, 1970–73, Records of the Department of State, RG 59, NA; Ngoc to Charles Clifford Finch, January 11, 1971, private papers of Robert Senser.

93. Bunker to State Department, August 21, 1969, box 1300, Central Foreign Policy Files, 1967–69, Records of the Department of State, RG 59, NA.

94. J. O. Moreton, "The Leaders of South Vietnam: A Few Pen Pictures," August 10, 1970, FCO 15/1331, PRO; Moreton to Whitehall, August 31, 1971, FCO 15/1475, PRO. British observers concluded that Ky and General Duong Van Minh

had dropped out of the presidential race because "neither thought they could win" rather than as a result of pressure from Thieu.

95. *New York Times,* June 11, 1971; *New York Times,* September 4, 1971; Arthur Dommen, *The Indochinese Experience of the French and Americans: Nationalism and Communism in Cambodia, Laos, and Vietnam* (Bloomington, IL, 2001), 892. Fearing a repeat of the controversial 1971 elections, Saigon CIA chief Thomas Polgar sought Buu as a potential opposition candidate for the October 1975 presidential elections, which, of course, never took place.

96. *New York Times,* September 26, 1971.

97. *New York Times,* September 11, 1971; Haldeman, *The Haldeman Diaries,* 349. Even the veteran hawk Senator Henry Jackson questioned the wisdom of future U.S. involvement in South Vietnam given the "one-man referendum." For a sharply critical perspective on the 1971 presidential elections, see Donald Kirk, "Presidential Campaign Politics: The Uncontested 1971 Election," in *Electoral Politics in South Vietnam,* edited by John C. Donnell and Charles A. Joiner (Lexington, MA, 1974). More sanguine assessments are offered in Herring, *America's Longest War,* 245; and Tull, "Broadening the Base," 50. "No sweeping generalization regarding the honesty of the elections, positive or negative, can be supported," concluded State Department official Teresa Tull.

98. *New York Times,* October 4, 1971. For a sharply critical perspective on the 1971 presidential elections, see Kirk, "Presidential Campaign Politics."

99. Ngoc to Charles Clifford Finch, January 11, 1971, private papers of Robert Senser; Nguyen Duc Dat, interview. These problems aside, many U.S. observers still credit the land to the tiller program with paying substantial dividends. Also see Dacy, *Foreign Aid, War, and Economic Development,* 113; and Callison, *The Land-to-the-Tiller Program and Rural Resource Mobilization in the Mekong Delta of South Vietnam,* 327, 336. Stuart Callison, who studied the implementation of the program for thirteen months in the field between 1971 and 1972, credited "the LTT Program with significantly favorable effects, in both the economic and political spheres." Among "the ironies of the tragic conflict in Vietnam," he concluded, "is that by 1975 the RVN [Republic of Vietnam or South Vietnam] had apparently won the war of insurgency, considered the more intractable threat by their American ally, and then lost the conflict to a conventional invading army." See also Gabriel Kolko, *Anatomy of a War: Vietnam, the United States, and Modern Historical Experience* (New York, 1985), 391–94. Kolko emphasizes the limitations of the land to the tiller program, which was focused primarily on the Mekong Delta and hardly touched central Vietnam. In addition, he claims that landlords learned to manipulate the system and that rising fertilizer prices undermined the entire program. In actuality, he writes, the program "helped . . . hasten the demise of Washington's dependency."

100. R. L. Prosterman, "Vietnam's Land Reform Begins to Pay," *Wall Street Journal,* February 5, 1971; Dacy, *Foreign Aid, War, and Economic Development,* 113.

101. Vy Pham, interview.

102. *Free Trade Union News,* February 1970, July 1970.

103. *Saigon Post,* September 21, 1971; *New York Times,* September 22, 1971; *Chicago Tribune,* September 22, 1971; Tiziano Terzani, *Giai Phong! The Fall and Liberation of Saigon* (New York, 1976), 165. VC agent Nguyen Huu Thai confessed to journalist Tiziano Terzani that his cell had been responsible for the attempt on Buu's life.

104. *Saigon Post,* October 6, 1971.

105. Ngoc to Charles Clifford Finch, January 11, 1971, private papers of Robert Senser; Dacy, *Foreign Aid, War, and Economic Development,* 16. The gradual withdrawal of American troops resulted in the loss of an estimated 150,000 Vietnamese jobs. Meanwhile the advent of worldwide inflation reduced the real value of American dollar support to South Vietnam. By 1972, unemployment was a devastating problem in South Vietnam.

106. Bunker to State Department, August 3, 1971, box 1436, Subject Numeric Files, Records of Department of State, RG 59, NA.

107. Bunker to State Department, December 5, 1969, box 1301, Central Foreign Policy Files, 1967–69, Records of the Department of State, RG 59, NA.

108. Vy Pham, interview.

109. Bunker to State Department, September 19, 1970, box 1435, Central Foreign Policy Files, 1970–73, Records of Department of State, RG 59, NA. Cadres of the CVT vehemently denied all the charges of corruption leveled at Buu and the union, but Saigon labor attaché Charles Finch advised Washington that he suspected some of the charges against Buu had validity. At the same time, Buu had a reputation for living frugally in his quarters in the CVT headquarters. One might conclude cautiously that while corruption was something of a problem, it did not significantly impede the CVT's operations or its political influence. See Nguyen Duy Hinh and Tran Dinh Tho, *The South Vietnamese Society,* 113, on the corrupting role of wives of important South Vietnamese officials: "[T]hese high-placed ladies . . . assumed the additional role of business dealer in the name of their husbands. The high officials saw this arrangement with favor and conveniently pretended knowing nothing about their wives' wheelings and dealings."

110. Senser, interview.

111. "What the CVT Has Done for the Country during 1968," *Cong Nhan,* February 8, 1968.

112. Bunker to State Department, September 19, 1970, box 1435, Central Foreign Policy Files, 1970–73, Records of Department of State, RG 59, NA.

113. "Minutes of the Annual Meeting of the Board of Trustees of the AAFLI held on Friday, April 2, 1971," 67/25, Meany Papers, GMMA.

114. "Board of Trustees Report, AAFLI, 1972," 67/26, Meany Papers, GMMA.

115. Bunker to State Department, September 19, 1970, box 1435, Central Foreign Policy Files, Records of Department of State, RG 59, NA.

116. Watson to State Department, December 15, 1970, box 1435, Subject Numeric Files, 1970–73, Records of Department of State, RG 59, NA.

117. "What the CVT Has Done for the Country during 1968," *Cong Nhan,* February 8, 1968.

Chapter 8

1. *Pravda,* 15 June 1956.

2. Allen J. Matusow, *Nixon's Economy: Booms, Busts, Dollars, and Votes* (Lawrence, KS, 1998), 211; Powers, 339–40.

3. Matusow, *Nixon's Economy,* 196–97.

4. Dean, *Blind Ambition,* 111. While most trade unionists recoiled from the blue-collar strategy, Colson continued to cultivate those outside the mainstream. In this regard, he pressed Attorney General John Mitchell, for instance, to limit or delay prosecutions of labor officials suspected of corruption.

5. J. R. Lehman to General Haig, May 12, 1972, box 828, NSC Files, Name Files, Nixon White House Materials, NA.

6. Colson to Haig, April 21, 1972, box 828, NSC Files, Name Files, Nixon White House Materials, NA.

7. Haig to Colson, July 20, 1972, box 828, Nixon White House Materials, NSC Files, Name Files, NA.

8. AFL-CIO Executive Council Statement, "Storm Clouds Over Asia," February 18, 1972, Bal Harbour, FL, February 14–21, 1972, p. 79, AFL-CIO Executive Council Minutes, GMMA. In addition to Vietnam, the statement lamented a "complete change of U.S. policy toward Communist China, stepped up withdrawal of American forces from Vietnam, the Indo-Pakistan war," and the expansion of Soviet military operations in the region.

9. Robinson, *George Meany and His Times,* 321; *New York Times,* January 26, 1972. The AFL-CIO already had gone on record as promising to support any Democrat running against Nixon.

10. Throughout the 1970s, Meany and the AFL-CIO grew increasingly close to Senator Henry Jackson. In 1970, Thomas Kahn, a young activist associated with socialist leader Michael Harrington and civil rights advocate Bayard Rustin, went to work for Jackson. Kahn later joined the AFL-CIO, eventually heading its International Affairs Department. Jackson's staff—which included Richard Perle and Jean Kirkpatrick—became a refuge for Democrats and socialists disillusioned with the Democratic Party's abandonment of the cold war.

11. "Conversation with Jay Lovestone," June 1, 1972, box 78, Colson Contested Materials, Nixon White House Materials, NA.

12. *AFL-CIO News,* August 12, 1972. Although he had always been a liberal favoring social spending and generally voting pro-labor, in Congress McGovern had repeatedly clashed with the AFL-CIO. He supported the Landrum-Griffith Act in 1959 and voted against the repeal of Section 14b of the Taft-Hartley Act in 1965.

13. "Notes on McGovern," n.d., 77/29, Department of Legislation, GMMA.

14. "Conversation with Jay Lovestone," June 1, 1972, box 78, Colson Contested Materials, Nixon White House Materials, NA.

15. *The Economist,* October 14, 1972.

16. *Today Show* transcript, March 30, 1972, "Teamster VP Gibbons Tells of Trip to North Vietnam," 64/13, Meany Papers, GMMA. Accompanying Gibbons to Hanoi was David Livingston, president of Distributive Workers District 65 in New York, and Clifton Caldwell, vice president of the Amalgamated Meat Cutters and Butchermen of North America. Gibbons admitted that Teamster president Frank Fitzsimmons generally supported the war, but he insisted that there was growing "antiwar sentiment, both among the rank-and-file members of unions and among an awful lot of the secondary leadership."

17. "Labor for Peace," Vertical Files, Tamiment Library, NYU; Michael Pesce, "Notes toward a Blue Collar Reform Movement," in *Pieces of a Dream: The Ethnic Worker's Crisis in America,* edited by Michael Wenk, S. M. Tomasi, and Geno Baroni (New York, 1972), 170. The strategy of emphasizing the economic impact of the war to appeal to blue-collar workers put off by the mainstream antiwar movement was set out by Pesce: "For ten years the opposition from the reform wing of the Democratic Party has been based on questions of morality, legality, political theories and

broad economic impacts. To the working class, this sounds unpatriotic . . . But talk to them about how much money comes out of their pockets to support the war. . . . The latter approach has much better results."

18. Foner, 133–43.

19. Nixon, *RN*, 626; Haldeman, *The Haldeman Diaries*, 471, 487.

20. Nixon, *RN*, 673.

21. Ehrlichman to Nixon, August 25, 1972, box 18, President's Office Files, President's Handwriting, Nixon White House Materials, NA.

22. Assistant Secretary of Defense (Comptroller), *The Economics of Defense Spending: A Look at the Realities* (Washington, 1972), 188. The Defense Department's politically inspired report argued that those "who suggest that we can solve our spending problems by peeling some easy billions off of the defense budget are arguing not only with the Pentagon but with reality." See also *New York Times*, September 4, 1972, in which columnist James Reston found workers deeply concerned about McGovern's proposed defense cut of ten billion dollars over three years. Many workers, Reston wrote, "seem to think of the defense budget more in terms of job security than in terms of military security."

23. National Labor Committee for the Election of McGovern-Shriver, "Work to Win," October 20, 1972. Perhaps the most difficult task facing pro-McGovern trade unionists was convincing working people that defense cuts would not cripple the economy. "Today we can find more jobs in peace than in war," the pamphlet declared. "We do not have to send our sons off to fight in order to keep their parents at work." In place of defense spending, McGovern promised ten billion dollars in spending on pollution control, public transportation, and housing.

24. Nixon to Meany, February 1, 1973, 76/21, Meany Papers, GMMA.

25. Calleo, *The Imperious Economy*, 106.

26. *New York Times*, March 24, 1974. Wallace Peterson, *Silent Depression: The Fate of the American Dream* (New York, 1994), 17. Peterson argues that the economic slide began in 1973, the year that marked the "end of the American dream," and continued to be felt into the 1990s.

27. Philip Buchen to Ford, "Meeting with George Meany," box 51, White House Central Files, Subject Files, PR 7–1, Ford Library. The AFL-CIO also began calling for import quotas and protection for American products, policies it previously had largely eschewed.

28. Edwin Harper, "Memorandum for Secretary Shultz, Don Roger, Paul O'Neill: Possible Hodgson Statement," box 51, White House Central Files, Staff Member and Office Files, Edwin Harper, Nixon White House Materials, NA. On the relationship between the Vietnam War and the economic collapse, see, in particular, Louis Galambos, "Paying the Price of the Vietnam War," *Journal of Policy History* 8 (fall 1996), 166–79. Galambos argues that the war put severe "inflationary pressure" on the U.S. economy, leaving it "unprepared for global competition." The United States, comments Galambos, "lost a vital decade between 1965 and 1975."

29. Ken Cole to Ford, n.d., box 51, White House Central Files, Subject Files, PR 7–1, Ford Library. Meany never fully trusted Brennan, whom he suspected of grandstanding during the hard-hat protests. Resentful of Brennan's continuing support for Nixon as the economy crumbled, and possibly considering him a rival, by 1973 Meany refused to meet with the secretary.

30. Collins, *More,* 167. The Humphrey-Hawkins Act actually became law in 1978 but not without significant modifications, to such an extent that its original intent was lost.

31. *AFL-CIO News,* January 5, 1974.

32. "Memorandum," Gree to Laurin B. Askew, January 24, 1973, Box 1436, Subject Numeric Files, 1970–3, Records of the Department of State, RG 59, NA.

33. Bunker to State, July 2, 1972, box 1435, Central Foreign Policy Files, 1970–73, Records of the Department of State, RG 59, NA; "Board of Trustees Report, AAFLI, 1972," 67/26, Meany Papers, GMMA; *Texarkana Gazette,* March 30, 1973. Buu complained bitterly to anyone who would listen of Viet Cong terrorism directed against the CVT. He argued that, with Chinese and Russian support, the VC had picked up the pace of its campaign of violence and aimed it directly at the CVT, one of the last democratic forces in the country.

34. "Political Round-Up," June 10, 1969, FCO 15/1001, PRO. Beginning in May 1969, RMK-BRJ began laying off fifteen hundred Vietnamese workers per month.

35. *New York Times,* June 4, 1972; *Free Trade Union News,* November 1972; Dacy, *Foreign Aid, War, and Economic Development,* 17–18; Bunker to State, July 2, 1972, box 1435, Central Foreign Policy Files, 1970–73, Records of the Department of State, RG 59, NA; Ngo Vinh Long, "South Vietnam," 90; Arnold Isaacs, *Without Honor: Defeat in Vietnam and Cambodia* (Baltimore, 1983), 300. By 1974, unemployment in South Vietnam had reached 14 percent and an estimated three to four million people were idle. Meanwhile, real wages dropped by approximately 30 percent. The government's imposition of a "value added" tax in 1973 only added to the economic pressure felt by the average South Vietnamese citizen.

36. Nguyen-Duc-Dat, interview.

37. Vy Pham, interview.

38. Bunker to State, July 2, 1972, box 1435, Central Foreign Policy Files, 1970–73, Records of the Department of State, RG 59, NA. CVT General Secretary Quyen, always something of a militant within the organization, saw unemployment as the "natural consequence of the government's own socio-economic policy."

39. Saigon to State, July 18, 1972, box 1436, Subject Numeric Files, 1970–3, Records of the Department of State, RG 59, NA. Buu issued his no-strike pledge on July 15, 1972.

40. Bunker to State, July 24, 1972, box 1436, Subject Numeric Files, 1970–3, Records of the Department of State, RG 59, NA.

41. Bunker to State, October 30, 1972, box 1436, Subject Numeric Files, 1970–3, Records of the Department of State, RG 59, NA.

42. *Chicago Tribune,* December 29, 1972.

43. Vy Pham, interview.

44. Appling to State Department, November 14, 1973, box 1435, Subject Numeric Files, 1970–3, Records of the Department of State, RG 59, NA. The threat came at the CVT's seventh triennial convention in October 1973.

45. "The Situation of Workers and Peasants in the Present War," *Cong Nong Student's Magazine,* no. 2, private papers of Robert Senser; Nam Pham, interview. The CVT created its student auxiliary to counter the success of communist agents in infiltrating other student groups. According to Nam Pham, a leader of the CVT student group, communists had infiltrated their group as well. The strongest force mov-

ing CVT students, however, was war weariness. By 1972, according to Pham, the students "were very tired of war, tired of Americans and interference with internal affairs, tired of politics, and tired of Thieu. Yet most had an understanding that communists would make things worse. The Tet Offensive made clear, for even those who did not understand communism, that things would not get better under communists. So Thieu still had our overall support, not because of his politics but because he represented resistance to the invading army."

46. Senser, interview.

47. Bunker to Kissinger, December 18, 1972; Bunker to Haig, December 13, 1972, box 2, NSC Convenience Files, U.S. Embassy Saigon, Ford Library.

48. Bunker to State, July 2, 1972, box 1435, Central Foreign Policy Files, 1970–73, Records of the Department of State, RG 59, NA.

49. *Washington Post,* March 10, 1973.

50. Frank Snepp, *A Decent Interval: An Insider's Account of Saigon's Indecent End* (New York, 1977), 14–15, 147; David Corn, *Blond Ghost: Ted Shackley and the CIA's Crusades* (New York, 1994), 210. According to Snepp, the CIA's Saigon station chief helped Buu write letters asking for aid to U.S. labor leaders: "No one in the station's front office seemed bothered by the fact that this was a violation of the CIA charter which prohibits the agency from dabbling in U.S. domestic politics."

51. Saigon to State, n.d., box 1433, Subject Numeric Files, 1970–3, Records of the Department of State, RG 59, NA.

52. Tran Kim Phoung to Meany, March 28, 1973, box 516, Lovestone Papers, Hoover.

53. Memorandum, "AFL-CIO Talk with Thieu," April 7, 1973, box 1433, Subject Numeric Files, 1970–73, Records of the Department of State, RG 59, NA; Goldberg to Meany, September 18, 1973, box 518, Lovestone Papers, Hoover. Also present at the meeting were Lane Kirkland, Hunter Wharton, Ernest Lee, Harry Goldberg, and Jay Lovestone. Meany also used the occasion to lobby for the long-delayed construction of a hiring hall for Saigon dockworkers and to press for "new legislation" to empower private groups to establish producer and consumer cooperatives.

54. *Washington Post,* June 23, 1973; "Annual Meeting of Board of Trustees of AAFLI," March 8, 1973, 10/1, Keenan Papers, Catholic University. On Thieu's Democracy Party, see Ta Van Tai and Jerry Mark Silverman, "Elections and Political Party Constraints following the 1972 Offensive," in *Electoral Politics in South Vietnam,* edited by John C. Donnell and Charles A. Joiner (Lexington, MA, 1974).

55. Saigon to State, 28 June 1973, box 1435, Subject Numeric Files, 1970–3, Records of the Department of State, RG 59, NA; Ta Van Tai and Silverman, "Elections and Political Party Constraints following the 1972 Offensive," 129–30. On December 27, 1972, Thieu issued a decree placing further constraints on party organization, ostensibly to quell the fragmentation and chaos that were so much a feature of South Vietnamese politics. The decree limited political participation to "broadly based and publicly known parties." Although Buu publicly approved of the changes, the new restrictions were so stringent that the CVT's Cong Nong Party proved unable to qualify for elections. In desperation, it joined with other parties to form the Democratic Socialist Alliance (Lien Minh Dan Chu Xa Hoi).

56. Saigon to State, June 28, 1973, box 1435, Subject Numeric Files, 1970–3,

Records of the Department of State, RG 59, NA; *Washington Post,* June 23, 1973. Immediately following the strike, officials arrested twenty-six strikers and later jailed four prominent strike leaders, including the vice president and president of the rail workers, the president of the petroleum workers, and the president of the bank workers union.

57. Joel Seagall, "Memorandum for the Secretary, Subject: Your Meeting with Minister Hien of South Vietnam," November 5, 1973, box 48, Office of Secretary, Peter Brennan, General Records of the Department of Labor, RG 174, NA.

58. Goldberg to Meany, September 18, 1973, box 518, Lovestone Papers, Hoover.

59. Joel Seagall, "Memorandum for the Secretary, Subject: Your Meeting with Minister Hien of South Vietnam," November 5, 1973, box 48, Office of Peter Brennan, General Records of the Department of Labor, RG 174, NA; Benjamin A. Sharman, interview with the author, Rockville, MD, June 11, 1997.

60. "Harloses Schlid," *Der Spiegel,* April 16, 1973; Morgan, *A Covert Life,* 344.

61. Vy Pham, interview.

62. Karnow, *Vietnam,* 661; Bunker to State, August 17, 1972, box 1435, Subject Numeric Files, 1970–3, Records of the Department of State, RG 59, NA. American officials were well aware of the problem of nepotism and corruption in CVT-owned businesses and fretted that it was causing cleavages within the movement.

63. James H. Willbanks, "Neither Peace nor Honor: Vietnamization, U.S. Withdrawal, and the Fall of South Vietnam," Ph.D. diss., University of Kansas, 1998, 432.

64. *Saigon Post,* May 24, 1973.

65. Vo Van Giao to Editor and Chief of *Der Spiegel,* n.d., 39/11, Irving Brown Papers, GMMA.

66. Vien Lao-Dong Tu-Do, "Report of Activities for the Month of August 1974," 64/17, Meany Papers, GMMA.

67. Paul Barton to Lovestone, December 2, 1972, 10/1, Jay Lovestone Papers, GMMA; Patrick Pasture, *Christian Trade Unionism in Europe since 1968* (Brookfield, VT, 1994), 85–96.

68. Appling to State, November 14, 1973, box 1435, Subject Numeric Files, 1970–3, Records of the Department of State, RG 59, NA.

69. Buu to Comrades in Non-aligned Conference, August 20, 1973, box 580, Lovestone Papers, Hoover.

70. Les Unions Departmentales CFDT-CGT, "Une Exigence La Paix au Vietnam," 7H 700, CFDT Archives; Esperet to Buu, October 17, 1969, 7H 700, CFDT Archives. CFDT president Gerard Esperet politely turned down Buu's invitation to attend the CVT's twentieth anniversary celebration for "purely material reasons." See CFDT, "Resolution Sur Le Problem de la Paix," October 2–3, 1965, 7H 697, CFDT Archives. As early as the fall of 1965, the CFDT was urging immediate negotiations in Vietnam and moving to "condemn the intervention of one state in another."

71. Lovestone to Meany, March 24, 1974, box 280, Lovestone Papers, Hoover.

72. AAFLI, "Report of Activities for 1972" and "Minutes of Annual Meeting of Board of Trustees of AAFLI," March 8, 1973, 10/1, Keenan Papers, Catholic.

73. Truong Nhu Tang, *A Vietcong Memoir,* 234–37; *Washington Post,* March 10, 1973. Buu claimed to have in his possession a captured VC document rebuking

cadres for not making inroads with workers, despite their success with intellectuals and students. Also see Pike, *Viet Cong,* 178–79. Vietnam expert Douglas Pike likewise noted: "It is an important commentary that the NLF could generate so little support among the great foreign-owned rubber plantation and the textile and other factories in Saigon." Pike credited the "intelligent and militant leadership" of the CVT, "leadership particularly skilled in battling the NLF in meaningful terms on the worker level."

74. Board of Trustees Report, AAFLI, 1973, 67/27, Meany Papers, GMMA.

75. Bunker to State, September 25, 1972, box 1435, Subject Numeric Files, 1970–3, Records of the Department of State, RG 59, NA.

76. Board of Trustees Report, AAFLI, 1972, 67/26, Meany Papers, GMMA.

77. Bunker to State, January 6, 1972, box 1435, Subject Numeric Files, 1970–3, Records of the Department of State, RG 59, NA.

78. Bunker to State, May 4, 1973, box 1435, Subject Numeric Files, 1970–3, Records of the Department of State, RG 59, NA.

79. Board of Trustees Report, AAFLI, 1972, 67/26, Meany Papers, GMMA.

80. Dam-Sy-Hien to Brennan, May 18, 1973, box 6, Office of Secretary, James D. Hodgson, General Records of the Department of Labor, RG 174, NA.

81. AAFLI Saigon, "Report of Activities for the Month of August 1974," 64/17, Meany Papers, GMMA.

82. *New York Times,* October 30, 1974; Isaacs, *Without Honor,* 322–23. In attacking Thieu, Buu aligned the CVT with Roman Catholics, veterans, and other Saigon interest groups protesting governmental corruption.

83. Olivier Todd, *Cruel Avril: 1975, la Chute de Saigon* (Paris, 1987), 129–32. In conversations with journalists, Buu was asked about Madame Ngo Da Thanh, then jailed by the Saigon government as a suspected Viet Cong agent. Commenting that he had worked with the dissident's father, who was minister of labor in 1954, Buu added: "As in many families, she goes from one extreme to the other."

84. Meany to Ford, January 10, 1975, box 2131, White House Central Files, Name Files, Ford Library.

85. "Meany to Senate," *Free Trade Union News,* March–April 1975.

86. *Saigon Post,* February 23, 1975.

87. *Free Trade Union News,* March–April 1975.

88. Kissinger to Ford, March 25, 1975, box 59, WHCF, CO 165-2, Ford Library.

89. "Memorandum of Conversation," March 25, 1975, box A1, Kissinger and Scowcroft Temporary Parallel Files, Ford Library. On the 1975 appropriations battle over South Vietnam, see T. Christopher Jespersen, "Kissinger, Ford, and Congress: The Very Bitter End in Vietnam," *Pacific Historical Review* 71 (August 2002): 439–73.

90. Nguyen Cao Ky, *Twenty Years and Twenty Days* (New York, 1976), 203; Bui Diem, with David Chanoff, *In the Jaws of History* (Boston, 1987), 6–7.

91. *Saigon Post,* April 6, 1975. Can left the Cong Nong Party in 1972 to join Thieu's Democracy Party, and was later elected to the lower house of the General Assembly. Nevertheless, he reportedly remained on good terms with Buu.

92. Meany to Selected Members of Congress, April 18, 1975, WHCF, CO 165, Vietnam, Ford Library.

93. *New York Times,* April 26, 1975.

94. Graham Martin to Meany, April 11, 1975, 63/14, Meany Papers, GMMA; David Butler, *The Fall of Saigon: Scenes from the Sudden End of a Long War* (New York, 1985), 145.

95. *Saigon Post,* April 12, 1975.

96. *Saigon Post,* April 3, 1975.

97. Martin to Kissinger, April 26, 1975, box 5, NSC Convenience Files, Copies of Materials for the U.S. Embassy Saigon, Ford Library; Meany to Ford, May 1, 1975, box 195, William Seidman Files, Ford Library. The day following the fall of Saigon, Meany commended Martin's work on behalf of the CVT to President Ford.

98. Vy Pham, interview; Su Tri Nguyen, interview; Karnow, *Vietnam,* 668. Henry Kissinger, *Years of Renewal* (New York, 1999), 544. Secretary of State Kissinger personally reassured Meany, late in the afternoon of April 29, that South Vietnamese labor leaders had been "rescued." On the "sealift" of refugees from Saigon, a relatively neglected side of the collapse of the city, see Donald Berney, "Self-Preservation," in *White Christmas in April: The Collapse of South Vietnam, 1975,* edited by J. Edward Lee and Toby Haynsworth (New York, 2000), 169–75.

99. *New York Times,* May 3, 1975; Terzani, *Giai Phong!* 183–84.

100. Hugh Sheehan to Robert L. Moeller, May 28, 1975, 68/20, Meany Papers, GMMA.

101. *Free Trade Union News,* May 1975; Vy Pham, interview; Victor Riesel, "Labor and the Refugees," in *All Quiet on the Eastern Front: The Death of South Vietnam: A Symposium,* edited by Anthony Bouscaren (Old Greenwich, CT, 1977).

102. Unsigned letter, April 23, 1975, 39/7, Brown Papers, GMMA.

103. James Ring Adams, "Battle Royal among the Socialists," *Wall Street Journal,* December 8, 1972. Also see Michael Massing, "From Bolshevism to Reaganism: Trotsky's Orphans," *New Republic,* June 22, 1987; Maurice Isserman, "Michael Harrington and the Vietnam War: The Failure of Anti-Stalinism in the 1960s," *Peace and Change* 21 (October 1996), 400–401; and James Miller, *Democracy Is in the Streets: From Port Huron to the Siege of Chicago* (Boston, 1994), 74–75, 113–14. Social Democrats-USA members included Kahn, Tom Milstein, Rachelle Horowitz, and Penn Kemble.

104. *Saigon Post,* February 23, 1975.

105. Meany to Mark Stone, December 1, 1975, 68/20, Meany Papers, GMMA; Lane Kirkland, interview with author, Silver Spring, MD, July 23, 1997. Meany aide and AFL-CIO secretary treasurer Lane Kirkland was at a loss to explain Meany's *Cavett Show* comments, with which he strongly disagreed.

106. Leon Davis, "Meany's Reversal on Vietnam," *1199 News,* January 1975. In other public comments, Meany showed no such second thoughts. See also *Washington Star,* April 30, 1975. In a newspaper column reflecting on how American involvement in Vietnam changed the United States, Meany assailed the rising tide of neo-isolationism, and demanded: "Where is the public outcry against documented communist atrocities in South Vietnam—against democratic union leaders for example?"

107. *New York Times,* May 7, 1975.

108. Julia Vadala Taft to Ford, July 25, 1975, box 65, White House Central Files, ND 18–2, Ford Library; *Free Trade Union News,* June 1975.

109. *Free Trade Union News,* May 1975.

110. Perlis to Meany, June 27, 1975, 68/20, Meany Papers, GMMA.

111. Andrew Kornylak to John Eisenhower, May 29, 1975; E. Douglas Kenna to Kornylak, May 30, 1975; Lee Perlis to James J. Delaney, August 8, 1975, all in 68/20, Meany Papers, GMMA.

112. Keith Johnson to Meany, August 13, 1975, 68/20, Meany Papers, GMMA.

113. Julia Vadala Taft to Ford, August 15, 1975, box 65, WHCF, ND 18–2, Ford Library; Perlis to Meany, August 15, 1975, 68/20, Meany Papers, GMMA; *Denver Post,* August 15, 1975.

114. *American Federationist,* April 1974. Solzhenitsyn paid tribute to Meany's anticommunism in a 1974 letter to him: "As I saw it and figured it out during my many years in the Soviet Union, you always stood out as one of the most farsighted, reasonable and steadfast public figures in the U.S." See Meany to Patricia Derian, January 11, 1979, 68/20, Meany Papers, GMMA. One of the last causes that Meany took up was that of Vietnamese dissident Nguyen Thanh Vinh, who escaped Vietnam by boat in 1978. Vinh wound up in a refugee camp in Australia, and Meany pressured the State Department to admit him to the United States.

115. *Washington Star,* August 22, 1975. For similar criticisms of Meany, see Philip Shabecoff, "Labor's Credibility Crisis," *Nation,* January 1, 1973; and B. J. Widick, "Exit Lovestone, the Alienator," *Nation,* September 7, 1974.

116. As quoted in the *Free Trade Union News,* October 1974.

117. Helen Dewar, "Old George Meany Just Keeps Rolling While Brothers Sigh," *Washington Post,* February 6, 1979.

118. Herbert Parmet, *The Democrats: The Years after FDR* (New York, 1976), 314.

119. Norman Mailer, *Why Are We in Vietnam? A Novel* (New York, 1967). Works directly addressing the "why" questions include Michael Charlton and Anthony Moncrieff, *Many Reasons Why: The American Involvement in Vietnam* (New York, 1978); and Jeffrey Record, *The Wrong War: Why We Lost in Vietnam* (Annapolis, 1998). For a treatment of the current literature on the question, see Alan Brinkley, "Why We Were in Vietnam," *New York Times Book Review,* April 8, 2001.

Bibliography

1. Manuscript Sources

A. Published Document Collections

Public Papers of the Presidents of the United States.
John F. Kennedy, 1962. Washington, DC, 1963.
Lyndon Baines Johnson, 1966. Washington, DC, 1967.
Richard Nixon, 1969. Washington, DC, 1974.
U.S. Department of State. *Foreign Relations of the United States.* Washington, DC.
Vietnam, 1958–1960, vol. 1.
Vietnam, 1961–1963, vols. 1, 3, and 4.
Vietnam, 1964–1966, vol. 1.

B. Archival Sources

George Meany Memorial Archives (GMMA), Silver Spring, MD
George Meany Papers
AFL Secretary Treasurer Papers
AFL, AFL-CIO Presidential Papers
Jay Lovestone Papers
Irving Brown Papers
Stanley Ruttenberg Papers
Nathaniel Goldfinger Papers
Michael Ross Papers
William Schitzler Papers
International Affairs Department, Country Files
Presidential Papers, Microfilm 81
Government Departments, Microfilm 7
Legislative Department Files
Oral Histories
AFL, AFL-CIO Executive Council Minutes

Library of Congress (LC), Washington, DC
- Arthur Goldberg Papers
- Averell Harriman Papers

Hoover Institute on War, Revolution, and Peace (Hoover), Stanford, CA
- Jay Lovestone Papers
- Robert F. Turner Papers
- Allan E. Goodman Papers

Kheel Center for Management-Labor Documentation and Archives (Kheel), Cornell University, Ithaca, NY
- International Ladies Garment Workers Union
  - David Dubinsky Papers
  - Benjamin Schlesinger Papers
  - Jay Lovestone Papers
- Amalgamated Clothing Workers of America Papers
- National Union of Hospital and Health Care Employees, Local 1199

Gerald R. Ford Presidential Library, Ann Arbor, MI
- White House Central Files
- National Security Files

Lyndon B. Johnson Presidential Library (LBJ), Austin, TX
- White House Central Files
  - Country Files
  - Name Files
- National Security Council Files (NSC)
- Vice Presidential Security Files
- Confidential Files
- Oral Histories

John F. Kennedy Presidential Library (JFK), Boston, MA
- President's Office Files
- Oral Histories

Robert Wagner Labor Archives (Wagner), New York University, New York, NY
- New York Building Trades Council, Secretary's Minute Book
- Communications Workers of America, Presidential Papers
- Vertical Files

National Archives (NA), College Park, MD
- RG 59, General Records of the Department of State, Central Foreign Policy Files
- RG 84, Records of Foreign Service Posts of Department of State, Saigon Embassy, Files of Ambassador
- RG 92, Office of the Quartermaster General, Procurement Policy Branch
- RG 174, General Records of the Department of Labor, Office of Secretary
- RG 469, Records of the U.S. Foreign Assistance Agencies, 1948–61, Office of Labor Affairs, Far East Country Files
- Joint Chiefs of Staff Central Files, Records of John F. Kennedy
- CIA Declassification Database
- Richard Nixon White House Materials
  - Colson Contested Materials
  - White House Staff Member and Office Files
  - White House Central Files

White House Special Files
National Security Files
Catholic University of America Archives (Catholic), Washington, DC
Papers of Joseph Keenan
National Security Archives (NSA), Washington, DC
Edward Lansdale Materials
Walter Reuther Library (Reuther), Wayne State University, Detroit, MI
Papers of the CIO Secretary Treasurer
Papers of Detroit Coalition to End the War Now!
Papers of Jay Krane
Presidential Papers of Walter Reuther
UAW International Affairs Department
Confédération Française Démocratique du Travail Archives (CFDT), Paris, France
Le Centre des Archives d'Outre-Mer (CAOM), Aix-en-Provence, France
Haut-Commissariat de France pour L'Indochine (HCI)
Conseiller aux Affaires Sociales (CS)
Service de Protection du Corps Expéditionnaire (SPCE)
National Archives of the United Kingdom, Public Records Office (PRO), Kew, England
Foreign Office (FO)
Foreign and Commonwealth Office (FCO)

2. Selected Secondary Sources

Abramson, Michael. "Delusions of Development: The Eisenhower Administration and the Foreign Aid Program in Vietnam, 1955–1960." *Journal of American-East Asian Relations* 5 (summer 1996).

Adams, James Ring. "Battle Royal among the Socialists" *Wall Street Journal*, December 8, 1972.

Alexander, Robert. *The Right Opposition: The Lovestonites and the International Communist Opposition of the 1930s*. Westport, CT, 1981.

Alsop, Stewart. "Labor and the Liberals." *Newsweek*, January 22, 1971.

Ambrose, Stephen. *Eisenhower*. Vol. 2: *The President*. New York, 1984.

Anderson, David. *Trapped by Success: The Eisenhower Administration and Vietnam, 1953–1961*. New York, 1991.

Anderson, Jervis. *Bayard Rustin: Troubles I've Seen, a Biography*. New York, 1997.

Appy, Christian. *Working-Class War: American Combat Soldiers and Vietnam*. Chapel Hill, NC, 1993.

Brancroft Griffing. "Racism, Reaction and George Wallace." *American Federationist*, September 1968.

Bain, Chester. *Vietnam: The Roots of Conflict*. Englewood Cliffs, NJ, 1967.

Bell, Daniel. *The End of Ideology: On Exhaustion of Political Ideas in the Fifties*. New York, 1961.

Berger, Graenum. *Not So Silent an Envoy: A Biography of Ambassador Samuel Berger*. New York, 1992.

Berman, Larry. *Planning a Tragedy: The Americanization of the War in Vietnam*. New York, 1982.

Berman, William. *William Fulbright and the Vietnam War*. Kent, OH, 1988.

Bernard, John. *Walter Reuther and the Rise of the Auto Workers*. Boston, 1983.

Berney, Donald. "Self-Preservation." In *White Christmas in April: The Collapse of South Vietnam, 1975,* edited by J. Edward Lee and Toby Haynsworth. New York, 2000.

Bernstein, Irving. *Guns or Butter: The Presidency of Lyndon B. Johnson*. New York, 1996.

Beschloss, Michael. *Reaching for Glory: Lyndon Johnson's Secret White House Tapes, 1964–1965*. New York, 2001.

Bodard, Lucien. *The Quicksand War: Prelude to Vietnam*. Boston, 1967.

Boyle, Kevin. *The UAW and the Heyday of American Liberalism, 1945–1968*. Ithaca, NY, 1995.

Braden, Thomas. "I'm Glad the CIA Is Immoral." *Saturday Evening Post,* May 20, 1967.

Bradley, Mark Philip. *Imagining Vietnam and America: The Making of Postcolonial Vietnam, 1919–1950*. Chapel Hill, NC, 1999.

Brands, H. W. *The Specter of Neutralism: The United States and the Emergence of the Third World, 1947–1960*. New York, 1989.

Brinkley, Alan. *End of Reform: New Deal Liberalism in Recession and War*. New York, 1995.

———. "Why We Were in Vietnam." *New York Times Book Review,* April 8. 2001.

Brigham, Robert. "Why the South Lost the American War in Vietnam." In *Why the North Won the Vietnam War,* edited by Marc Jason Gilbert. New York, 2002.

Brody, David. "The New Deal and World War II." In *The New Deal,* edited by John Braeman et al. Columbus, 1975.

———. *Workers in Industrial America: Essays on the Twentieth-Century Struggle*. New York, 1980.

———. "The Breakdown of Labor's Social Contract." *Dissent* 39 (winter 1992).

Brophy, John. *A Miner's Life*. Madison, 1964.

Brown, Irving. "Democracy Wins a Battle." *American Federationist,* May 1948.

Buhle, Paul. "Lovestonites." In *Encyclopedia of the American Left,* edited by Mari Joe Buhle, Paul Buhle, and Dan Georgakas. New York, 1990.

———. *Taking Care of Business: Samuel Gompers, George Meany, Lane Kirkland, and the Tragedy of American Labor*. New York, 1999.

Bui Diem with David Chanoff. *In the Jaws of History*. Boston, 1987.

Burns, Arthur F. *Reflections of an Economic Policy Maker: Speeches and Congressional Statements, 1969–1978*. Washington, DC, 1978.

Burwood, Stephen. "American Labor and the Industrial Unrest in France, 1947–1952." Ph.D. diss., State University of New York at Binghamton, 1991.

Butler, David. *The Fall of Saigon: Scenes from the Sudden End of a Long War*. New York, 1985.

Buttinger, Joseph. *Vietnam: A Dragon Embattled*. New York, 1967.

———. *Vietnam: A Political History*. New York, 1968.

Cable, James. *The Geneva Conference of 1954 on Indochina*. New York, 1986.

Calleo, David. *The Imperious Economy*. Boston, 1982.

Callison, C. Stuart. *The Land-to-the-Tiller Program and Rural Resource Mobilization in the Mekong Delta of South Vietnam*. Athens, OH, 1974.

Campagna, Anthony S. *The Economic Consequences of the Vietnam War*. New York, 1991.

Carew, Anthony. "Conflict within the ICFTU: Anticommunism and Anticolonialism in the 1950s." *International Review of Social History* 41 (1996).

———. *Labour under the Marshall Plan: The Politics of Productivity and the Marketing of Management Science*. Detroit, 1987.

———. "The American Labor Movement in Fizzland: The Free Trade Union Committee and the CIA." *Labor History* 39 (February 1998).

Caro, Robert. *Years of Lyndon Johnson: Master of the Senate*. New York, 2002.

Chamberlin, William Henry. "A New Deal for French Indo-China?" *Asia* 37 (July 1937).

Charlton, Michael, and Anthony Moncrieff. *Many Reasons Why: The American Involvement in Vietnam*. New York, 1978.

Clifford, Gary. "Leonard Wood, Samuel Gompers, and the Plattsburg Training Camps," *New York History* 52 (1971).

Clos, Max. "La Capitale Paralysée Hier Matin Par Grève." *Le Figaro*, September 22, 1964.

Cochran, Bert. *Labor and Communism: The Conflict That Shaped American Unions*. Princeton, 1977.

Cohen, Alvin. "Leon Keyserling." In *Biographical Directory of the Council of Economic Advisers*, edited by Robert Sobel and Bernard S. Katz. New York, 1988.

Colander, David, and Harry Landreth, eds. *The Coming of Keynesianism to America: Conversations with the Founders of Keynesian Economics*. Brookfield, VT, 1996.

Cole, Gordon. "Vietnam Labor's Unifying Role." *American Federationist*, September 1971.

Collins, Robert M. "Growth Liberalism in the Sixties: Great Societies at Home and Grand Designs Abroad." In *The Sixties: From Memory to History*, edited by David Farber. Chapel Hill, NC, 1994.

———. *More: The Politics of Economic Growth in Postwar America*. New York, 2000.

Conin, Ernest. "Meany's Folly May Help Reds." *Los Angeles Times*, March 2, 1969.

Cooper, Chester. *The Lost Crusade: America in Vietnam*. New York, 1969.

Corn, David. *Blond Ghost: Ted Shackley and the CIA's Crusades*. New York, 1994.

Culhane, Charles. "White House Report." *National Journal*, January 30, 1971.

Currey, Cecil B. *Edward Lansdale: The Unquiet American*. Boston, 1988.

Dacy, Douglas. *Foreign Aid, War, and Economic Development: South Vietnam, 1955–1975*. New York, 1986.

Davis, Leon. "Meany's Reversal on Vietnam." *1199 News*, January 1975.

Davis, Michael. *Prisoners of the American Dream: Politics and Economics in the History of the U.S. Working Class*. London, 1986.

Dawley Alan. *Class and Community: The Industrial Revolution in Lynn*. Boston, 1976.

Dean, John. *Blind Ambition: The White House Years*. New York, 1976.

Department of Health, Education and Welfare. *Work in America: Report of a Special Task Force to the Secretary of Health, Education, and Welfare*. Cambridge, MA, 1973.

Derickson Alan. "Health Security for All? Social Unionism and Universal Health Insurance, 1935–1958." *Journal of American History* 80 (March 1994).

Despuech, Jacques. *Le Trafic des Piastres*. Paris, 1974.

Dewar, Helen. "Old George Meany Just Keeps Rolling While Brothers Sigh." *Washington Post,* February 6, 1979.

DiBendedetti, Charles, and Charles Chatfield. *An American Ordeal: The Antiwar Movement of the Vietnam Era.* Syracuse, 1990.

Dickow, Raymond. "Vietnam: Dissent within Labor." *Butcher Workman,* February 1967.

Diggins, John Patrick. *The Rise and Fall of the American Left.* New York, 1992.

Direr, Françoise. "L'Économie." In *Vietnam, L'histoire, la terre, les hommes,* edited by Alain Ruscio. Paris, 1993.

Divine, Robert, ed. *The Johnson Years.* Vol. 2. Lawrence, KS, 1987.

Dommen, Arthur. *The Indochinese Experience of the French and Americans: Nationalism and Communism in Cambodia, Laos, and Vietnam.* Bloomington, IL, 2001.

Donnell, John C., and Charles A. Joiner, eds. *Electoral Politics in South Vietnam.* Lexington, MA, 1974.

Draper, Theodore. *The Roots of American Communism.* New York, 1957.

———. *American Communism and Soviet Russia.* New York, 1960.

Dubinsky, David, and A. H. Raskin. *A Life with Labor.* New York, 1977.

Dubofsky, Melvyn. "George Meany: The Perfect Bureaucrat." *New Politics* 10 (winter 1973).

———. *The State and Labor in Modern America.* Chapel Hill, NC, 1994.

Dubofsky, Melvyn, and Warren Van Tine. *John L. Lewis: A Biography.* New York, 1978.

Dubofsky, Melvyn, and Warren Van Tine, eds. *Labor Leaders in America.* Urbana, IL, 1987.

Dudman. Richard. "Agent Meany." *New Republic,* May 3, 1969.

Duiker, William. *The Communist Road to Power in Vietnam.* Boulder, 1981.

———. *Vietnam: Nation in Revolution.* Boulder, 1983.

———. *Ho Chi Minh.* New York, 2000.

Dulles, Foster Rhea. "French Problems in Indo-China." *Current History* 26 (May 1927).

Durr, Kenneth. *Behind the Backlash: White Working-Class Politics in Baltimore, 1940–1980.* Chapel Hill, NC, 2003.

Duscha, Jules. "Arms and the Big Money Men: Congressmen, Contractors, and the 'Defense' Pork Barrel." *Harper's,* March 1964.

Edsall, Thomas, and Mary Edsall. *Chain Reaction: The Impact of Race, Rights, and Taxes on American Politics.* New York, 1991.

Eisele, Albert. *Almost to the Presidency.* San Francisco, 1972.

Fall, Bernard. *The Vietminh Regime.* New York, 1956.

———. *The Two Vietnams: A Political and Military Analysis.* New York, 1963.

Fejto, Francois. *The French Communist Party and the Crisis of International Communism.* Boston, 1967.

Filippelli, Ronald. "The History Is Missing Almost: Philip Murray, the Steelworkers, and the Historians." In *Forging a Union of Steel: Philip Murray, SWOC, and the United Steelworkers,* edited by Paul F. Clark, Peter Gottlieb, and Donald Kennedy. Ithaca, NY, 1987.

———. *American Labor and Postwar Italy, 1943–1953.* Stanford, 1989.

Fink, Gary, ed. *AFL-CIO Executive Council Statements, 1956–1975.* Westport, CT, 1977.

FitzGerald, Frances. *Fire in the Lake: The Vietnamese and the Americans in Vietnam*. New York, 1972.

Foner, Eric. *Free Soil, Free Labor, Free Men*. New York, 1970.

———. *Tom Paine and Revolution*. New York, 1976.

Foner, Philip. *U.S. Labor and the Vietnam War*. New York, 1989.

Fones-Wolf, Elizabeth. *Selling Free Enterprise: The Business Assault on Labor and Liberalism, 1945–1960*. Urbana, IL, 1994.

Fraser, Steven. "Dress Rehearsal for the New Deal: Shop-Floor Insurgents, Political Elites, and Industrial Democracy in the ACW." In *Working-Class America,* edited by Daniel Walkowitz and Michael Frish. Urbana, IL, 1983.

———. "Sidney Hillman." In *Labor Leaders in America,* edited by Melvyn Dubofsky and Warren Van Tine. Urbana, IL, 1987.

———. *Labor Will Rule: Sidney Hillman and the Rise of American Labor*. New York, 1991.

Fraser, Steven, and Gary Gerstle, eds. *The Rise and Fall of the New Deal Order, 1930–1980*. Princeton, 1989.

Freeman, Joshua. "Hardhats: Construction Workers, Manliness, and the 1970 Pro-war Demonstrations." *Journal of Social History* 26 (1993).

Friedberg, Aaron. "Why the U.S. Didn't Become a Garrison State." *International Security* 16 (spring 1992).

Gaddis, John Lewis. *Strategies of Containment: A Critical Appraisal of Postwar American National Security Policy*. New York, 1982.

Galambos, Louis. "Paying the Price of the Vietnam War." *Journal of Policy History* 8 (fall 1996).

Galbraith, John Kenneth. *The Affluent Society*. New York, 1958.

———. *The New Industrial State*. New York, 1967.

Galenson, Walter. *The CIO Challenge to the AFL: A History of the American Labor Movement, 1935–1951*. Cambridge, MA, 1960.

Gannon, Francis. *Joseph D. Keenan: Labor's Ambassador in War and Peace*. New York, 1984.

Gannon, James P. "Wobble in Labor's Pro-Vietnam Stance." *Wall Street Journal,* November 9, 1967.

Gardner, Lloyd C. *Pay Any Price: Lyndon Johnson and the War for Vietnam*. Chicago, 1995.

Gerstle, Gary. "The Politics of Patriotism: Americanization and the Formation of the CIO." *Dissent* 33 (1986).

———. *Working-Class America: The Politics of Labor in a Textile City, 1914–1969*. Cambridge, MA, 1989.

———. "Catholic Corporatism, French Canadian Workers, and Industrial Unions in Rhode Island." In *Labor Divided: Race and Ethnicity in United States Labor Struggles, 1835–1960,* edited by Robert Asher and Charles Stephenson. Albany, 1990.

Gilbert, Marc Jason, ed. *Why the North Won the Vietnam War*. New York, 2002.

Giles, Frank. *The Locust Years: The Story of the Fourth French Republic, 1946–1958*. New York, 1994.

Gillon, Steven M. *Politics and Vision: The ADA and American Liberalism, 1947–1985*. New York, 1987.

Gitlin, Todd. *The Sixties: Years of Hope and Days of Rage*. New York, 1987.

Goldberg, Arthur J. *AFL-CIO: Labor United*. New York, 1956.

Gompers, Samuel. *American Labor and the War*. New York, 1984.
———. "Our Shield against Bolshevism." *McClure's*, May 1919.
———. *Seventy Years of Life and Labor: An Autobiography*. New York, 1925.
Gompers, Samuel, and William English Walling. *Out of Their Mouths: A Revelation and Indictment of Sovietism*. New York, 1921.
Goodman, Allan E.. *Politics in War: The Bases of Political Community in South Vietnam*. Cambridge, MA, 1973.
Gordon, Jerry. *Cleveland Labor and the Vietnam War*. Cleveland, 1990.
Goulden, Joseph. *Meany*. New York, 1972.
———. *Jerry Wurf, Labor's Last Angry Man*. New York, 1982.
Green, William. "Free Trade Unions." *American Federationist*, November 1944.
Greene, Julie. *Pure and Simple Politics, the AFL and Political Action, 1887–1917*. New York, 1998.
Greenstone, J. David. *Labor in American Politics*. New York, 1969.
Grenville, Kenneth. *The Saving of South Vietnam*. Sydney, 1972.
Halberstam, David. *The Best and the Brightest*. New York, 1972.
———. *Ho*. New York, 1987.
Haldeman, H. R. *The Haldeman Diaries: Inside the Nixon White House*. New York, 1994.
Hamby, Alonzo. *Beyond the New Deal: Harry S. Truman and American Liberalism*. New York, 1973.
Hamil, Pete. "The Revolt of the White Lower-Middle Class." *New Yorker*, March 14, 1969.
Hammer, Ellen. *A Death in November: America in Vietnam, 1963*. New York, 1987.
Hanks, Lucien M. "American Aid is Damaging Thai Society." In *America and the Asian Revolutions*, edited by Robert Jay Lifton. Chicago, 1970.
Harris, Seymour. "Economics of the Kennedy Years." In *John F. Kennedy and the New Frontier*. New York, 1966.
Hawley, Ellis. *The Great War and the Search for Modern Order*. New York, 1970.
Heale, M. J. *American Anticommunism: Combating the Enemy Within, 1830–1970*. Baltimore, 1990.
Heller, Walter. *New Dimensions of Political Economy*. New York, 1967.
Helsing, Jeffrey. *Johnson's War/Johnson's Great Society: The Guns and Butter Trap*. Westport, CT, 2000.
Herring, George. *America's Longest War*. New York, 1986.
———. "'Peoples Quite Apart': Americans, South Vietnamese, and the War in Vietnam." *Diplomatic History* 14 (winter 1990).
Hill, Herbert. "The Importance of Race in American Labor History." *International Journal of Politics, Culture, and Society* 9 (winter 1995).
Hogan, Michael. "Corporatism: A Positive Appraisal." *Diplomatic History* 10 (fall 1986).
———. *The Marshall Plan: America, Britain, and the Reconstruction of Western Europe, 1947–1952*. New York, 1987.
Hoffman, Paul. "For More and More Jobs." *American Federationist*, May 1945.
Hue-Tam Ho Tai. *Radicalism and the Origins of the Vietnam Revolution*. Cambridge, MA, 1992.
Hunt, Michael. *Ideology and U.S. Foreign Policy*. New Haven, 1987.

Immerman, Richard. "Between the Unattainable and the Unacceptable: Eisenhower and Dienbienphu," in *Reevaluating Eisenhower: American Foreign Policy in the 1950s,* edited by Richard A. Melanson and David Mayers. Urbana, IL, 1987.

Iriye, Akira. "Culture." *Journal of American History* 77 (1990).

Isaacs, Arnold. *Without Honor: Defeat in Vietnam and Cambodia.* Baltimore, 1983.

Isserman, Maurice. *If I Had a Hammer: The Death of the Old Left and the Birth of the New Left.* New York, 1987.

———. "Michael Harrington and the Vietnam War: The Failure of Anti-Stalinism in the 1960s." *Peace and Change* 21 (October 1996).

Jacobs, Meg. "'How about Some Meat': The OPA, Consumption Politics, and the Building from the Bottom Up, 1941–1946." *Journal of American History* 84 (December 1997).

Jamieson, Neil. *Understanding Vietnam.* Berkeley, 1993.

Jeffreys-Jones, Rhodri. *Peace Now! American Society and the Ending of the Vietnam War.* New Haven, 1999.

Jespersen, T. Christopher. "Kissinger, Ford, and Congress: The Very Bitter End in Vietnam." *Pacific Historical Review* 71 (August 2002).

Kahin, George M. *Intervention: How America became Involved in Vietnam.* New York, 1986.

Kahin, George M., and John W. Lewis. *The United States in Vietnam.* New York, 1967.

Kampelman, Max. *The Communist Party versus the CIO: A Study in Power Politics.* New York, 1957.

Kantrowitz, Jack. "L'Influence Américaine sur Force Ouvrière: Myth ou Réalité?" *Revue Française de Science Politique* 28 (1978).

Karnow, Stanley. *Vietnam: A History.* New York, 1983.

Kaufman, Burton. *Trade and Aid: Eisenhower's Foreign Economic Policy, 1953–1961.* Baltimore, 1982.

———. "Foreign Aid and the Balance of Payments Problem in Vietnam: Vietnam and Johnson's Foreign Economic Policy." In *The Johnson Years,* edited by Robert Divine. Lawrence, KS, 1987.

Kaufman, Stuart B. *Samuel Gompers and the Origins of the AFL, 1848–1896.* Westport, CT, 1973.

Kaufman, William. *The McNamara Strategy.* New York, 1964.

Kazin, Michael. *The Populist Persuasion: An American History.* New York, 1995.

Kettl, Donald. "The Economic Education of Lyndon Johnson: Guns, Butter, and Taxes." In *The Johnson Years,* edited by Robert A. Divine. Vol. 2. Lawrence, KS, 1987.

Keynes, John Maynard. *General Theory of Employment, Interest, and Money.* New York, 1936.

Keyserling, Leon. "Housing and Full Employment." *American Federationist,* June 1946.

———. *Progress or Poverty: The U.S. at a Cross-Roads.* Washington, DC, 1964.

———. *The Toll of Rising Interest Rates.* Washington, DC, 1964.

———. *The Scarcity School of Economics.* Washington, DC, 1973.

———. *Liberal and Conservative National Economic Policies and Their Consequences, 1919–1979.* Washington, DC, 1979.

Kimball, Jeffrey. *Nixon's Vietnam War*. Lawrence, KS, 1998.

Kirk, Donald. "Presidential Campaign Politics: The Uncontested 1971 Election." In *Electoral Politics in South Vietnam*, edited by John C. Donnell and Charles A. Joiner. Lexington, MA, 1974.

Kissinger, Henry. *Years of Renewal*. New York, 1999.

Klehr, Harvey, and John E. Haynes. "Communists and the CIO: From the Soviet Archives." *Labor History* 35 (1994).

Kofas, Jon V. "U.S. Foreign Policy and the World Federation of Trade Unions, 1944–1948." *Diplomatic History* 26 (winter 2002): 21–60.

Koistinen, Paul. *The Hammer and the Sword: Labor, the Military, and Industrial Mobilization, 1920–1945*. New York, 1979.

Gabriel, Kolko. *Anatomy of a War: Vietnam, the United States, and the Modern Historical Experience*. New York, 1985.

Kornblum, William. *Blue Collar Community*. Chicago, 1974.

Lacouture, Jean. *Vietnam between Two Truces*. New York, 1966.

LaCroix-Riz, Annie. "Autour d'Irving Brown: L'AFL et la Sicission Syndicale Française, 1944–1947." *Mouvement Sociale* 151 (1990).

Lafont, Pierre-Bernard. "Les sects Religieuses." In *Vietnam L'histoire, la terre, les hommes*, edited by Alain Ruscio. Paris, 1993.

Lancaster, Donald. *The Emancipation of French Indo-China*. New York, 1961.

Lansdale, Edward. *In the Midst of Wars: An American's Mission to Southeast Asia*. New York, 1972.

Larson, Simeon. *Labor and Foreign Policy; Gompers, the AFL, and the First World War, 1914–1918*. Cranbury, NJ, 1975.

Lee, J. Edward, and Toby Haynsworth, eds. *White Christmas in April: The Collapse of South Vietnam, 1975*. New York, 2000.

Lens, Sidney. *The Crisis of American Labor*. New York, 1959.

Levenstein, Harvey A. *Communism, Anti-communism, and the CIO*. Westport, CT, 1981.

Levenstein, Jerome, and Juan de Onis. *The Alliance That Lost Its Way: A Critical Report on the Alliance for Progress*. Chicago, 1970.

Levitan Sar. *Blue-Collar Workers: A Symposium on Middle America*. New York, 1971.

Levy, Peter. *The New Left and Labor in the 1960s*. Urbana, IL, 1994.

Liazos, Theodore C. "Big Labor, George Meany, and the Making of the AFL-CIO, 1894–1955." Ph.D. diss., Yale University, 1998.

Lichtenstein, Nelson. *Labor's War at Home, The CIO in World War II*. New York, 1982.

———. "From Corporatism to Collective Bargaining: Organized Labor and the Eclipse of Social Democracy in the Post-war Era." In *The Rise and Fall of the New Deal Order, 1930–1980*, edited by Gary Gerstle and Steven Fraser. Princeton, 1989.

———. *The Most Dangerous Man in Detroit: Walter Reuther and the Fate of American Labor*. New York, 1995.

———. "American Trade Unions and the 'Labor Question': Past and Present." In *What's Next for Organized Labor? The Report of the Century Foundation Task Force on the Future of Unions*. New York, 1999.

Lichtenstein, Nelson, and John Harris Howel, eds. *Industrial Democracy in America: The Ambiguous Promise*. Cambridge, MA, 1993.

Linder, Mark. *Wars of Attrition: Vietnam, the Business Roundtable, and the Decline of Construction Unions.* Iowa City, 1999.
Lipset, Martin Seymour. "The President, the Polls, and Vietnam." In *America and the Asian Revolutions,* edited by Robert Jay Lifton. Chicago, 1970.
Lipsitz, George. *Rainbow at Midnight: Labor and Culture in the 1940s.* Champaign and Chicago, 1994.
Logevall, Fredrik. *Choosing War: The Lost Chance for Peace and the Escalation of War in Vietnam.* Berkeley, 1999.
Lomperis, Timothy J. *The War Everyone Lost—and Won: America's Intervention in Viet Nam's Twin Struggles.* Washington, DC, 1987.
Lorwin, Val. *The French Labor Movement.* Boston, 1954.
Loss, John. "The Rise of the Labor Movement in South Vietnam." M.A. thesis, University of Texas, 1975.
Lowi, Theodore J. *The End of Liberalism: The Second Republic of the United States.* 2d ed. New York, 1979.
Lukas, J. Anthony. *Common Ground: A Turbulent Decade in the Lives of Three American Families.* New York, 1986.
MacShane, Denis. *International Labour and the Origins of the Cold War.* New York, 1992.
Mailer, Norman. *Why Are We in Vietnam? A Novel.* New York, 1967.
Malmgrem, Harold. "Willing to Help." *New Republic,* November 1, 1969.
Marr, David G. *Vietnamese Tradition on Trial, 1920–1945.* Berkeley, 1981.
———. *Vietnam, 1945: The Quest for Power.* Berkeley, 1995.
Massing, Michael. "From Bolshevism to Reaganism: Trotsky's Orphans." *New Republic,* June 22, 1987.
Matusow, Allen J. *The Unraveling of America: A History of Liberalism in the 1960s.* New York, 1984.
———. *Nixon's Economy: Booms, Busts, Dollars, and Votes.* Lawrence, KS, 1998.
May, Ernest, ed. *American Cold War Strategy: Interpreting NSC-68.* Boston, 1993.
McCracken, Paul. "Economic Policy in the Nixon Years." *Presidential Studies Quarterly* 26 (winter 1996).
McKillen, Elizabeth. "The Corporatist Model, World War I, and the Public Debate over the League of Nations." *Diplomatic History* 15 (spring 1991).
———. *Chicago Labor and the Quest for a Democratic Diplomacy, 1914–1924.* Ithaca, NY, 1995.
McLoad, Mark, and Nguyen Thi Deiu. *Culture and Customs of Vietnam.* Westport, CT, 2001.
McMahon, Robert J. "Eisenhower and the Third World Nationalism: A Critique of the Revisionists." *Political Science Quarterly* 101 (fall 1986).
———. "U.S.-Vietnamese Relations: A Historiographical Survey." In *Pacific Passages: The Study of American-East Asian Relations on the Eve of the Twenty-First Century,* edited by Warren I. Cohen. New York, 1996.
Meany, George. "Labor Day Guest Editorial." *Camden Union Reporter,* August 14, 1946.
———. "Let's Get Back to Collective Bargaining." *American Federationist,* October 1946.
———. "Free Trade Unionism: Its Aims in the Struggle against the Totalitarian Menace." *Free Trade Union News,* August 1951.

———. "Turn for the Better in Vietnam." *American Federationist,* October 1965.

———. "The Economic Disaster." *American Federationist,* August 1971.

Melman, Seymour. *The Permanent War Economy: American Capitalism in Decline.* New York, 1974.

Milkis, Sidney. *The President and the Parties: The Transformation of the American Party System since the New Deal.* New York, 1993.

Miller, James. *Democracy Is in the Streets: From Port Huron to the Siege of Chicago.* Boston, 1994.

Mills, C. Wright. *The New Men of Power: America's Labor Leaders.* New York, 1948.

Mohan Das, S. R. "Ho Chi Minh: Vietnamese Nationalist or Soviet Agent?" *Free Trade Union News,* January 1951.

Moise, Edwin E. "Land Reform and Land Reform Errors in North Vietnam." *Pacific Affairs* 49 (spring 1976).

———. *Land Reform in China and North Vietnam.* Chapel Hill, NC, 1983.

Monet, Paul. *Les Jauniers.* Paris, 1930.

Mongold, Thomas. *Cold Warrior: James Jesus Angleton, the CIA's Master Spy Hunter.* New York, 1991.

Moody, Kim. *An Injury to All: The Decline of American Unionism.* London, 1988.

Morgan, Ted. *A Covert Life: Jay Lovestone—Communist, Anti-communist, and Spymaster.* New York, 1999.

Mortimer, Edward. *The Rise of the French Communist Party, 1920–1947.* Boston, 1984.

Ngo Van. *Vietnam, 1920–1945: Révolution et contre-révolution sous la domination coloniale.* Paris, 1995.

Ngo Vinh Long. "South Vietnam." In *The Vietnam War,* edited by Peter Lowe. New York, 1998.

Nguyen Cao Ky. *Twenty Years and Twenty Days.* New York, 1976.

Nguyen Duy Hinh and Tran Dinh Tho. *The South Vietnamese Society.* Washington, DC, 1980.

Nguyen Ngoc Huy. "The Possible Role of Elections in a Political Settlement." In *Electoral Politics in South Vietnam,* edited by John C. Donnell and Charles Joiner. Lexington, MA, 1974.

Nguyen Ngoc Linh. *The Working Man in Vietnam.* Saigon, 1970.

Nieburg, H. L. *In the Name of Science.* Chicago, 1966.

Nixon, Richard. *RN: The Memoirs of Richard Nixon.* New York, 1978.

Nossiter, Bernard. "The Hidden Affair between Big Business and Big Labor." *Harper's,* July 1959.

———. "Labor and Government Cooperate on Foreign Policy." *Washington Post,* April 28, 1969.

Okun, Arthur. *The Political Economy of Prosperity.* New York, 1970.

Orren, Karen. "Union Politics and Postwar Liberalism in the U.S., 1946–1979." *Studies in American Political Development* 1 (1986).

Parenti, Michael. *The Anti-communist Impulse.* New York, 1969.

Parmet, Herbert S. *The Democrats: The Years after FDR.* New York, 1976.

———. *JFK: The Presidency of John F. Kennedy.* New York, 1983.

Pasture, Patrick. *Christian Trade Unionism in Europe since 1968.* Brookfield, VT, 1994.

Paterson, Thomas G., and Les Adler. "The Merger of Nazi Germany and Soviet Russia in the American Image of Totalitarianism, 1930s–1950s." *American Historical Review* 7 (April 1970).

Patterson, James T. *Congressional Conservatism and the New Deal: The Growth of the Conservative Coalition in Congress, 1933–1939.* Lexington, KY, 1967.

———. *America's Struggle against Poverty, 1900–1985.* Cambridge, MA, 1986.

———. *Grand Expectations: The United States, 1945–1974.* New York, 1996.

Pesce, Michael. "Notes toward a Blue Collar Reform Movement." In *Pieces of a Dream: The Ethnic Worker's Crisis in America,* edited by Michael Wenk et al. New York, 1972.

Peterson, Wallace. *Silent Depression: The Fate of the American Dream.* New York, 1994.

Pham, David Lan. *Two Hamlets in Nam Bo: Memoirs of Life in Vietnam through the Japanese Occupation, the French and American Wars, and Communist Rule, 1940–1986.* London, 2000.

Phelan, Craig. *William Green: Biography of a Labor Leader.* Albany, 1989.

Pierson, John H. G. "A Full Employment Program." *American Federationist,* August 1945.

Pike, Douglas. *Viet Cong: The Organization and Techniques of the National Liberation Front of South Vietnam.* Boston, 1966.

———. *History of Vietnamese Communism, 1925–1976.* Stanford, 1978.

Pike, Douglas, ed. *The Bunker Papers, Reports to the President from Vietnam, 1967–1973.* Berkeley, 1990.

Plotke, David. *Building a Democratic Political Order: Reshaping American Liberalism in the 1930s and 1940s.* New York, 1996.

Polenberg, Richard. *One Nation Divisible: Race, Class, and Ethnicity in America since 1938.* New York, 1980.

Powers, Richard Gid. *Not without Honor: The History of American Anticommunism.* New Haven, 1998.

Powers, Thomas. *The Man Who Kept the Secrets: Richard Helms and the CIA.* New York, 1979.

Prados, John. "Impatience, Illusion, and Asymmetry: Intelligence in Vietnam." In *Why the North Won the Vietnam War,* edited by Marc Jason Gilbert. New York, 2002.

Proceedings of the Seventh Constitutional Convention of the AFL-CIO. Washington, DC, 1968.

Proceedings of the Ninth Constitutional Convention of the AFL-CIO. Bal Harbor, FL, 1971.

Prosterman R. L. "Vietnam's Land Reform Begins to Pay." *Wall Street Journal,* February 5, 1971.

Radosh, Ronald. *American Labor and United States Foreign Policy.* New York, 1969.

Randle, Robert F. *Geneva, 1954.* Princeton, 1969.

Rathburn, Ben. *The Point Man: Irving Brown and the Deadly Post-1945 Struggle for Europe and Africa.* London, 1996.

Record, Jefferey. *The Wrong War: Why We Lost in Vietnam.* Annapolis, 1998.

Renshaw, Patrick. *American Labor and Consensus Capitalism, 1935–1990.* Jackson, MS, 1991.

"Report of the AFL-CIO Economic Policy Committee Submitted to the Executive Council." In *AFL-CIO Executive Council Statements and Reports, 1956–75,* edited by Gary Fink. Westport, CT, 1977.

Reuther, Victor. *The Brothers Reuther and the Story of the UAW: A Memoir.* Boston, 1976.

Reuther, Walter. "Our Fear of Abundance." *New York Times Magazine,* September 16, 1945.

Rice-Maximin, Edward. *Accommodation and Resistance: The French Left, Indochina, and the Cold War.* New York, 1986.

Rieder, Jonathan. *Canarsie: The Jews and Italians of Brooklyn against Liberalism.* Cambridge, MA, 1985.

Riesel, Victor. "Hungry Viet Workers." *New York Journal American,* September 25, 1964.

———. "Labor and the Refugees." in *All Quiet on the Eastern Front: The Death of South Vietnam: A Symposium,* edited by Anthony Bouscaren. Old Greenwich, CT, 1977.

Robinson, Archie. *George Meany and His Times.* New York, 1981.

Romero, Federico. *The United States and the European Trade Union Movement, 1944–1951.* Chapel Hill, NC, 1992.

Ross, George. *Workers and Communists in France: From Popular Front to Eurocommunism.* Berkeley, 1982.

Rosswurm, Steve, ed. *The CIO's Left-Led Unions.* New Brunswick, NJ, 1992.

Ruscio, Alain. *Les Communistes français et la guerre d'Indochine, 1944–1954.* Paris, 1985.

Ruscio, Alain, ed. *Vietnam, L'histoire, la terre, les hommes.* Paris, 1993.

Ruttenberg, Stanley. "For a Free World: Alliance for Progress." *Free Trade Union News,* June 1962.

SarDesai, D. R. *Vietnam: The Struggle for National Identity.* Boulder, 1992.

Savatore, Nick. "Introduction." In Samuel Gompers, *Seventy Years of Life and Labor: An Autobiography.* New York, 1984.

Sauders, Frances Stonor. *The Cultural Cold War: The CIA and the World of Arts and Letters.* New York, 1999.

Schlesinger, Arthur, Jr. *A Thousand Days.* New York, 1965.

Schulzinger, Robert. *A Time for War: The United States and Vietnam, 1941–1975.* New York, 1997.

Scigliano, Robert. *South Vietnam: Nation under Stress.* Boston, 1963.

Scott, James. *The Moral Economy of the Peasant.* New Haven, 1976.

Seaton, Douglas. *Catholics and Radicals.* New York, 1981.

Sexton, Brendan. "Middle-Class Workers and the New Politics." In *Twenty-five Years of Dissent,* edited by Irving Howe. New York, 1979.

Sexton, Brendan, and Patricia Sexton. *Blue Collars and Hard Hats: The Working Class and the Future of American Politics.* New York, 1971.

Shabecoff, Philip. "Labor's Credibility Crisis." *Nation,* January 1, 1973.

Shadegg, Stephen C. *Winning's a Lot More Fun.* New York, 1969.

Shaplen, Robert. *The Lost Revolution: The U.S. in Vietnam, 1946–1966.* New York, 1966.

———. *The Road from War; Vietnam, 1965–1971.* New York, 1971.

Sheehan, Neil. *A Bright Shining Lie.* New York, 1988.

Sherry, Michael. *In the Shadow of War: The United States since the 1930s*. New Haven, 1995.

Short, Anthony. *The Origins of the Vietnam War*. London, 1989.

Shulman, Bruce. *Lyndon Johnson and American Liberalism*. Boston, 1995.

Shurcliff, Alice. "The Trade Union Movement in Vietnam." *Monthly Labor Review* 72 (January 1951).

Sibley, Katherine. "American Foreign Aid." In *The Encyclopedia of American Foreign Policy*, edited by Alexander DeConde, Richard Dean Burns, and Fredrik Logevall. New York, 2002.

Siemiller, P. L. "The Advanced Planning Briefing for the Department of Defense." *AFL-CIO News*, April 16, 1966.

Silk, Leonard. *Nixonomics*. New York, 1972.

Silverman, Victor. *Imagining Internationalism in American and British Labor, 1939–1949*. Urbana, IL, 1999.

Sims, Beth. *Workers of the World Undermined*. Boston, 1992.

Sloan, John W. *Eisenhower and the Management of Prosperity*. Lawrence, KS, 1991.

Small, Melvin. *Johnson, Nixon, and the Doves*. New Brunswick, NJ, 1988.

Smith, Jean Edward. *Lucius D. Clay: An American Life*. New York, 1990.

Smith, R. B. *An International History of the Vietnam War*. New York, 1983.

Snepp, Frank. *A Decent Interval: An Insider's Account of Saigon's Indecent End*. New York, 1977.

Spector, Ronald. *After Tet: The Bloodiest Year in Vietnam*. New York, 1993.

Stanley, Nadel. "Reds versus Pinks: A Civil War in the International Ladies Garment Workers Union." *New York History* 66 (1985).

Stearn, Gerald. *Gompers*. Englewood Cliffs, NJ, 1971.

Stebenne, David. *Arthur Goldberg, New Deal Liberal*. New York, 1996.

Stein, Herbert. *The Fiscal Revolution in America*. Chicago, 1969.

———. *Presidential Economics: The Making of Economic Policy from Roosevelt to Reagan and Beyond*. New York, 1985.

Stevens, Robert Warren. *Vain Hopes, Grim Realities: The Economic Consequences of the Vietnam War*. New York, 1976.

Strober, Gerald, and Deborah Strober, eds. *Let Us Begin Anew: An Oral History of the Kennedy Presidency*. New York, 1993.

Suffridge, James. "The Urgent Needs of Asian Workers." *American Federationist*, July 1961.

Sugrue, Thomas. *The Origins of the Urban Crisis: Race and Inequality in Postwar Detroit*. Princeton, 1996.

Sullivan, David. "Report on Vietnam." *American Federationist*, October 1967.

Ta Van Tai and Jerry Mark Silverman. "Elections and Political Party Constraints following the 1972 Offensive." In *Electoral Politics in South Vietnam*, edited by John C. Donnell and Charles A. Joiner. Lexington, MA, 1974.

Taft, Philip. *Defending Freedom: American Labor and Foreign Affairs*. Los Angeles, 1973.

Taylor, Maxwell. *Swords and Plowshares*. New York, 1972.

Terzani, Tiziano. *Giai Phong! The Fall and Liberation of Saigon*. New York, 1976.

Thompson, Heather. *Whose Detroit? Politics, Labor, and Race in a Modern American City*. Ithaca, NY, 2001.

Thompson, Virginia. *French Indochina*. London, 1937.

Thorne, Florence. *Samuel Gompers, American Statesman.* New York, 1957.

Tien Hung Nguyen and Jerrold Schechter. *The Palace File.* New York, 1986.

Todd, Olivier. *Cruel Avril: 1975, la Chute de Saigon.* Paris, 1987.

Tomlins, Christopher L. "The AFL Unions in the 1930s: Their Performance in Historical Perspective." *Journal of American History* 65 (summer 1979).

———. *The State and the Unions: Labor Relations, Law, and the Organized Labor Movement in America, 1880–1960.* New York, 1986.

Ton Vy. "The Workers' Struggle." In *Vietnamese Studies, no. 8: South Vietnam, 1954–1965.* Hanoi, 1966.

———. "The U.S.-Diem Regime." *Vietnam Studies* 18–19 (1968).

Tonnesson, Stein. *The Vietnamese Revolution of 1945: Roosevelt, Ho Chi Minh, and De Gaulle in a World at War.* London, 1991.

Topmiller, Robert. "The Lotus Unleashed: The Buddhist Struggle Movement in South Vietnam, 1964–66." Ph.D. diss., University of Kentucky, 1998.

Townsend, Ed. "Western-Style Labor Movement." *Christian Science Monitor,* December 8, 1969.

Tran Tu Binh, *The Red Earth: A Vietnamese Memoir of Life on a Colonial Rubber Plantation.* Athens, OH, 1985.

Tran Van Don. *Our Endless War: Inside Vietnam.* San Rafael, CA, 1978.

Trinh Quang Quy. *Phong Trào lao-dông Viêt-Nam.* Saigon, 1970.

Trinh Van Thao. *Vietnam du Confucianisme au Communisme: Un essai itinéraire intellectuel.* Paris, 1990.

Trumka, Richard. "On Becoming a Movement." *Dissent* 39 (winter 1992).

Truong Nhu Tang. *A Vietcong Memoir.* New York, 1985.

Tull, Theresa. "Broadening the Base: South Vietnamese Elections, 1967–1971." In *Electoral Politics in South Vietnam,* edited by John Donnell and Charles Joiner. Lexington, MA, 1974.

Turgeon, Lynn. *Bastard Keynesianism: The Evolution of Policy Making since World War II.* Westport, CT, 1996.

Tyler, Gus. *The Labor Revolution: Trade Unions in a New America.* New York, 1967.

———. *George Meany: The Making of a Freedom Fighter.* New York, 1979.

———. *Look for the Union Label: A History of the International Ladies' Garment Workers' Union.* Armonk, NY, 1995.

Tyson, James T. *Target America: The Influence of Communist Propaganda on U.S. Media.* Chicago, 1981.

Vatter, Harold G. *The U.S. Economy in the 1950s: An Economic History.* New York, 1963.

Walker, John F., and Harold G. Vatter. "The Princess and the Pea; or the Alleged Vietnam War Origins of the Current Inflation." *Journal of Economic Issues* 16 (June 1982).

Wehrle, Edmund F. "For a Healthy America: Labor's Struggle for National Health Insurance, 1943–1949." *Labor's Heritage* 5 (summer 1993).

———. "Welfare and Warfare: Organized Labor Approaches the Military Industrial Complex, 1949–1964." *Armed Forces and Society* 4 (summer 2003).

Weidenbaum, Murray L. *Economic Impact of the Vietnam War.* Washington, DC, 1967.

Weiler, Peter. "The U.S., International Labor, and the Cold War: The Breakup of the World Federation of Trade Unions." *Diplomatic History* 5 (winter 1981).

———. *British Labour and the Cold War*. Stanford, 1988.

Wenk, Michael, S. M. Tomasi, and Geno Baroni, eds. *Pieces of a Dream: The Ethnic Worker's Crisis in America*. New York, 1972.

Widick, B. J. "Exit Lovestone, the Alienator." *Nation*, September 7, 1974.

Willbanks, James H. "Neither Peace nor Honor: Vietnamization, U.S. Withdrawal, and the Fall of South Vietnam." Ph.D. diss., University of Kansas, 1998.

Williams, Philip. *Politics in Post-war France: Parties and the Constitution in the Fourth Republic*. London, 1953.

Woll, Matthew. "Now It Can Be Told." *American Federationist*, June 1945.

———. "The Main Issue before Mankind: Human Rights versus State Power." *American Federationist*, October 1947,

———. "Slavery Old and New." *American Federationist*. December 1948.

———. "Woll Talks Plainly to NAM." *American Federationist*, December 1948.

———. "An Historic Declaration." *Free Trade Union News*, July 1953.

Woods, Randall. *Fulbright: A Biography*. New York, 1995.

Woodside, Alexander. *Community and Revolution in Modern Vietnam*. Boston, 1976.

Young, Marilyn B. *The Vietnam Wars, 1945–1990*. New York, 1991.

Young, Stephen B. "The Mandate and Politics in Vietnam." In *Electoral Politics in South Vietnam*, edited by John C. Donnell and Charles A. Joiner. Lexington, MA, 1974.

———. "Power to the People: Local Development in Vietnam, 1968–1971." In *Electoral Politics in South Vietnam*, edited by John C. Donnell and Charles A. Joiner. Lexington, MA, 1974.

Z. "The War in Vietnam: We Have Not been Told the Whole Truth." *New Republic*, March 12, 1962.

Zausner, Philip. *Unvarnished: The Autobiography of a Union Leader*. New York, 1941.

Zeiler, Thomas. "Development Do It! Globalization for Diplomatic Historians." *Diplomatic History* 25 (2001).

Zieger, Robert H. *Republicans and Labor, 1919–1929*. Lexington, KY, 1969.

———. *American Workers, American Unions, 1920–1985*. New York, 1986.

———. "George Meany: Labor's Organization Man." In *Labor Leaders in America*, edited by Melvyn Dubofsky and Warren Van Tine. Urbana, IL, 1987.

———. *The CIO, 1935–1955*. Chapel Hill, NC, 1995.

Index

AAFLI. *See* Asian American Free Labor Institute
Abel, I. W., 136, 137
ACWA. *See* Amalgamated Clothing Workers of America
ADA. *See* Americans for Democratic Action
Adenauer Foundation, 185
AFL. *See* American Federation of Labor
AFL-CIO. *See* American Federation of Labor–Congress of Industrial Organizations
African Labor College (ALC), 79
AFSCME. *See* American Federation of State, County and Municipal Employees
Agency for International Development (AID), 78–79, 92, 120, 123, 126, 143–45, 152, 154, 168, 181. *See also* Foreign aid
AID. *See* Agency for International Development
AIFLD. *See* American Institute for Free Labor Development
Air America, 127
Air Vietnam, 151
ALA. *See* Alliance for Labor Action
ALC. *See* African Labor College
Alliance for Labor Action (ALA), 139–40, 152, 198
Alliance for Progress, 78–79, 87
ALP. *See* American Labor Party
Altaffer, Thomas, 97–98, 102–5
Amalgamated Clothing Workers of America (ACWA), 11, 87, 112, 117–18, 176, 193. *See also* Hillman, Sidney
Amalgamated Meat Cutters and Butcher Workmen of North America, 158–59
American Federation of Labor (AFL), 10–12, 16–27, 43–46, 48–49, 51, 56–62. *See also* Meany, George
American Federation of Labor–Congress of Industrial Organizations (AFL-CIO), 17; convention (1965), 110–12; electrical workers strike, 129–30; and foreign aid, 78–81, 153–55, 165–66; formation of, 61–62; and George Wallace, 137–38, and Humphrey campaign, 136–38; and ICFTU, 140–42; and John F. Kennedy, 75–81. *See also* Meany, George
American Federation of State, County and Municipal Employees (AFSCME), 48, 157, 188
American Friends of Vietnam, 71
American Institute for Free Labor Development (AIFLD), 79, 109, 113
American Labor Party (ALP), 17

Americans for Democratic Action (ADA), 118–19, 136
AMF-Head, 193
Anglo-Soviet Union Committee, 20
Asian American Free Labor Institute (AAFLI), 98, 174; formation of, 122–23; mission to Vietnam, 142–45, 153, 163, 166, 170, 183, 185–87, 190. *See also* Foreign aid
Audie, Fernand, 143–45

Baehr, Lutz, 108
Baker, Desmond, 165
Baldanzi, George, 97–98, 102
Ball, George, 103
Bao Dai, 37, 39, 40, 47, 65
Bazin, René, 31
Becu, Omer, 19
Beichman, Arnold, 91–92, 103
Berger, Samuel, 43, 144, 148
Biemiller, Andrew, 117
Bierne, Joseph, 61, 118, 136, 154, 177
Binh Xuyen, 68
"blue-collar strategy" 160, 166, 174. *See also* Nixon, Richard
Blum, Léon, 32
Braden, Thomas, 114–15
Brandt, Willy, 141
Brennan, Peter, 162, 178
Bridges, Harry, 112, 123, 174
Brophy, John, 48
Brown, Irving, 1, 26–27, 45, 56, 90, 96, 144, 148, 162; background of, 26–27; and CIA, 43; and CVT, 81–83; and Jay Lovestone, 27; and OSS, 27; and Tet Offensive, 131–33; and Vietnamese colonialism, 46–48
Buddhist Institute for Secular Affairs, 93, 102, 105
Bui Diem, 189
Building and Construction Trades Council of Greater New York, 162, 178
Bui Luong, 98, 108
Bundy, McGeorge, 85
Bundy, William, 132
Bunker, Ellsworth, 130, 147, 167
Burns, Arthur, 55, 164
Business Week, 129
Buttinger, Joseph, 40

cai recruiters, 30, 170
Califano, Joseph, 117
Cambodian incursion, 157, 161–62
Can Lao Party, 67, 70, 98, 148
Cao Dai, 34–35, 149
Carey, James, 61
Cavett, Dick, 192
CEE. *See* Compagnie des Eaux et de l'Électricité
Central Intelligence Agency (CIA), 3, 43, 47, 81, 92, 104, 113–15, 123, 155–56, 171, 182
CFTC. *See* French Confederation of Christian Workers
CGT. *See* Confédération Générale du Travail
Chamberlin, William Henry, 32
chambres mixtes de métiers, 37, 69, 72
Chapman, Gordon, 48
Church, Frank, 166
CIA. *See* Central Intelligence Agency
CIO. *See* Congress of Industrial Organizations
Citizens Committee for Peace and Freedom in Vietnam, 167
Citrine, Walter, 20
civilian military training, 150
Clay, Lucius, 80
Cleveland Council on World Affairs, 159
Cleveland labor and Vietnam War, 159
Cogen, Charles, 124
Colson, Charles, 161–64, 174–75
Comité Méditerranéen, 47
Committee for Political Education (COPE), 148
Committee to Defend America by Aiding the Allies, 19
Communications Workers of America (CWA), 61, 118, 119. *See also* Biérne, Joseph
Compagnie des Eaux et de l'Électricité

(CEE), 126–29. *See also* Vietnamese Confederation of Labor
Condon, John, 96, 105
Confédération Générale du Travail (CGT), 26, 27, 42, 44, 46
Conference for Progressive Political Action, 15
Conference on Economic Progress, 59–60
Cong Nong Party, 148–52, 167, 182–83, 186–87
Congress of Industrial Organizations (CIO), 42–45, 51, 61–62. *See also* American Federation of Labor–Congress of Industrial Organizations
Connally, John, 165
Connally Act, 21
Conway, Jack, 88
COPE. *See* Committee for Political Education
Cruickshank, Nelson, 48
Curran, Joseph, 125
CVT. *See* Vietnamese Confederation of Labor
CVTC. *See* Vietnamese Confederation of Labor
CWA. *See* Communications Workers of America

Dai Viet Nationalist Party, 67
Darrow, Clarence, 13
Davis, Leon, 112, 124, 192
Defense spending, 60–61, 76–77, 177
Delaney, George, 96
Der Spiegel, 184
Détente, 173, 174, 194
Detroit Women for Peace, 112
Deverall, Richard, 48, 71
Dewey, Thomas, 20
Dien Bien Phu, 57, 71
doan the, 31, 34, 37, 38, 40, 66, 90, 104, 197
dockworkers, 32, 68, 119–20, 170
Dole, Robert, 166
Donovan, Michael, 162
Dooley, Thomas, 71
Douglas, Paul, 57
Dubinsky, David, 4; and AFL, 17, 19, 61; and anticommunism, 16; background of, 16; and New Deal, 18
Dubrow, Evelyn, 136
Dudman, Richard, 155–56
Dulles, John Foster, 55

Eggers, Jodie, 73–74
Eisenhower, Dwight, 51, 54–55, 58, 74
Employment Act (1946), 24, 194. *See also* Keyserling, Leon
European Recovery Program. *See* Marshall Plan

Federation of Commercial, Clerical and Technical Employees, 143
Federation of Railroad Workers, 169
Federation of Textile Workers, 151
Ferri-Pisani, Pierre, 47
Force Ouvrière, 36, 42, 47
Foreign aid, 77–81, 153–55, 165–66, 174. *See also* Agency for International Development; International Cooperation Administration; Liberal developmentalism; Mutual Security Agency
Fraser, Douglas, 113
Free Trade Union Committee (FTUC), 20, 26, 43, 45, 47
Free Trade Union News, 48
Free Trade Unionism, 3; and anticommunism, 10, 12, 15–16, 22–23, 195; contradictions of, 10, 24, 28; and Munich analogy, 18, 112, 124; and "Red Fascism," 18; and trade union autonomy, 9–10, 23
French Confederation of Christian Workers (CFTC), 36, 67, 186
Friedman, Milton, 164
Ford, Gerald, 188, 192, 194
Forrestal, Michael, 85, 90
FTUC. *See* Free Trade Union Committee
Fulbright, William, 156–57, 165
full employment economics, 24–25, 59–61, 76–77, 116–17, 164, 195–96

Galbraith, John, 123
Gaud, William S., 154
Geneva Conference on Indochina, 56–58
German Labor Chest, 18
Gibbons, Harold, 130, 139, 176
Ginh Xuy, 68
Gleason, Thomas, 119–20, 170
Goldberg, Harry, 56–57, 77, 84, 106, 143
Gompers, Samuel, 4, 10–12; anti-radicalism of, 10; and bolshevism, 12; and George Meany, 16; and Marxism, 12; pragmatism of, 10; and World War I, 11
Gorman, Patrick, 109, 158, 159, 165
Green, William, 22
Gulf of Tonkin Resolution, 102

Habbib, Philip, 133
Haig, Alexander, 174
Haldeman, H. R., 162, 165
hard hat rallies, 1–2, 161–62
Harrington, Michael, 191
Heath, Donald, 38
Herling, John, 83, 129
Herring, George, 6
Hillman, Sidney, 10, 12–14, 41; background of, 13; and bolshevism, 13; and new unionism, 13–14, 20–21; and WFTU, 26. *See also* ACWA
Hillquit, Morris, 15
Hilsman, Roger, 85
Hotel Employees and Restaurant Employees International Union, 117–18
Ho Thuong Minh, 85
Hughes, Harold, 165
Humphrey, Hubert, 80, 110, 114, 121, 136–38, 157, 175, 196
Huynh Ngoc Nu, 169

ICFTU. *See* International Confederation of Free Trade Unions
IFCTU. *See* International Federation of Christian Trade Unions
ILA. *See* International Longshoremen's Association
ILGWU. *See* International Ladies Garment Workers Union
ILO. *See* International Labor Organization
ILWU. *See* International Longshore and Warehouse Union
International Association of Machinists, 184
International Confederation of Free Trade Unions (ICFTU), 19, 48, 52, 79, 185; in Asia, 71–72; disaffiliation of AFL-CIO, 140–42; formation of, 44–45; in Vietnam, 71, 83–84
International Cooperation Administration, 73. *Also see* Foreign aid
International Federation of Christian Trade Unions (IFCTU), 38, 53–54, 65, 72, 78–79, 84, 91, 185
International Labor Organization (ILO), 38
International Ladies Garment Workers Union (ILGWU), 13, 16–17
International Longshore and Warehouse Union (ILWU), 112, 174
International Longshoremen's Association (ILA), 116, 120, 170, 174
International Monetary Fund, 154
International Union of Electrical and Machine Workers of America (IUE), 106, 108
International Woodworkers of America, 193
IUE. *See* International Union of Electrical and Machine Workers of America

Jackson, Henry, 175, 188
Jakovlev, F. G., 48
Johnson, Keith, 193
Johnson, Lyndon, 3, 110, 136, 154; and ADA, 118–19; and organized labor, 86–88, 115–19, 196; and Tran Quoc Buu, 90; trip to Vietnam, 86–87
Johnson, U. Alexis, 96, 110
Jouan, Gilbert, 36–38, 48, 65, 72. *See*

also Vietnamese Confederation of Labor

Kahn, Thomas, 191
Kansas State AFL-CIO, 193
Kazin, Michael, 198
Keenan, Joseph, 87, 105, 122–23, 133, 162, 177
Kenin, Herman, 158
Kennedy, Edward M., 175, 188
Kennedy, John F., 75–81, 83, 85–88
Kennedy, Robert F., 136–38
Keyserling, Leon, 13, 24, 75–79, 116–17, 124, 136, 163–64; and Conference on Economic Progress, 59–61; and Employment Act of 1946, 24; and defense spending, 25, 60. *See also* full employment economics
Khrushchev, Nikita, 63, 141
Killian, James, 92
King, Jr., Martin Luther, 123–24, 137, 176
Kirsch, Henry, 103–4, 143
Kissinger, Henry, 163, 188, 190, 192
Krulak, Victor, 85

Labor Advisory Committee on Foreign Assistance, 79, 102, 133
Labor for Peace, 176
Labor's League for Human Rights, Freedom and Democracy, 18
Lacouture, Jean, 94–95
LaFond, André, 47
la lutte pour la paix, 46–47
Lambretta drivers, 91, 168
land reform, 150–51, 168. *See also* land-to-the-tiller program
Lansdale, Edward, 66–67, 106, 132, 143, 150
land-to-the-tiller program, 150–51, 168. *See also* land reform
Le Duan, 34
Le Duc Tho, 176
Lee, Ernest, 105
LeMay, Curtis, 137
Lewis, John L., 17, 21, 42
Liberal developmentalism, 72, 77–78. *See also* Foreign aid
Lichtenstein, Nelson, 2
Lien Minh (National Alliance for Social Revolution), 147–48, 167
Lindahl, Emil, 106, 143, 190
Lodge, Henry Cabot, 86, 89
Logevall, Frederick, 88
Lovestone, Jay, 1, 90, 109, 112–13, 133; background of, 16–17; and CIA, 43; and Charles Colson, 161–62; and FTUC, 20; and OSS, 19; resignation of, 191; and the Tet Offensive, 131

Mailer, Norman, 194
Mann, Thomas, 116
Mansfield, Mike, 57, 166
Maritime trade unions, 116
Marshall Plan (European Recovery Program), 29, 42–46
Martin, Graham, 184, 189–90
"massive retaliation," 55, 78
Mazey, Emil, 109, 111, 123, 125, 176
McCarthy, Eugene, 123, 136
McCracken, Paul, 164
McDonald, David, 44, 61
McGory, Mary, 156
McGovern, George, 175–78
McNamara, Robert S., 76, 87
Meany, George, and anticommunism, 15–17, 23, 42, 105, 110, 166, 173; and antiwar protests, 110, 124–25, 163; as business agent, 15; and Catholic organizations, 71; and the Eisenhower administration, 55; election as president of AFL, 51; and electrical workers strike, 129–30; and foreign aid, 80, 165–66; and Fulbright, 156; and Gompers, 16; and Hubert Humphrey, 136–38; and ICTFU, 78–79; and John F. Kennedy, 75; and Lyndon Johnson, 86–87, 101; and New Deal, 17, 18; and new unionism, 14; and New York City Trades Council, 15; personality of, 15; and Philip Zausner, 15–16; and Plumbers local, 463, 14; and Nixon,

Meany, George (*continued*)
Richard, 155, 173–79, 192; speech to TUC, 25–26; and Vietnamese refugees, 192–94; and Walter Reuther, 112–15, 138–40, 158; and War Labor Board, 21. *See also* American Federation of Labor; American Federation of Labor–Congress of Industrial Organizations
Moyers, Bill, 117
Munich analogy, 18, 57, 112, 124. *See also* free trade unionism
Murray, Philip, 14, 21, 37, 44
Muskie, Edmund, 175
Muste, A. J., 15
Mutual Security Agency, 49, 52, 54. *See also* Foreign aid
My Lai massacre, 163

National Association of Manufacturers, 193
National Civic Federation, 11
National Confederation of Labor, 169
National Industrial Recovery Act, 13
National Labor Assembly for Peace, 123–25, 157
National Labor Committee for the Election of McGovern-Shriver, 177
National Religion and Labor Foundation, 63
National Union of Hospital and Health Care Employees (Local 1199), 112, 124, 192
Negotiations Now!, 167
Nehru, Jawaharlal, 63
New Republic, 155
"new unionism," 10, 13–14, 15, 20–21
New York Times, 115, 125, 132, 159
Ngo Dinh Can, 68
Ngo Dinh Diem, 5, 52, 67–73, 81–85
Ngo Dinh Nhu, 67–68
Nguyen Ba Can, 189
Nguyen Cao Ky, 103, 105–8, 128, 167
Nguyen Duc Dat, 143
Nguyen Khanh, 89–90, 92–97, 102
Nguyen Ngoc Loan, 107–8, 127–29, 130–33, 142
Nguyen Ton Hoan, 67, 85
Nguyen Van Thieu, 121, 130, 132, 147–51, 153, 167, 179, 181–84, 187–89
Nixon, Richard, 3, 146, 153–55, 160–66, 174–80, 192, 196. *See also* Colson, Charles

Office of Labor Advisers in the European Recovery Program, 42, 44
Office of Strategic Services (OSS), 19, 27
Oldenbroek, J. H., 19, 65, 73–74. *See also* International Confederation of Free Trade Unions
Operation Booster, 76–77
OSS. *See* Office of Strategic Services
Ostpolitik, 141
Overseas Private Investment Corporation, 154. *See also* Foreign aid

Palladino, Morris, 184, 186. *See also* Asian American Free Labor Institute
Pan American Airlines, 127
Pella, Heinz, 184
People's Front against Communist Aggression, 181
Perrier, Pierre, 38
Petroleum and Chemical Workers Union, 181
Pham Nam, 65
Pham Van Dong, 44
Phan Chau Trinh, 31
Phan Quang Dan, 56, 57, 82
Plantation Workers Union, 91
Polgar, Thomas, 182
Pollack, William, 158
Port and Allied Workers Union of Saigon, 186
Potofsky, Jacob, 11, 87, 110, 157–58. *See also* Amalgamated Clothing Workers of America
"Problem of the Blue Collar Worker, The," 163

Radio Hanoi, 129
Radosh, Ronald, 6

Raiffeisen Cooperatives, 72
Retail, Wholesale, and Department Store Union, 118
Reuther, Victor, 45, 113–15, 119, 123, 141
Reuther, Walter, 14, 51, 88, 135; and AFL-CIO merger, 61–64; and antiwar movement, 111, 113, 138; and CIA, 114–15; and George Meany, 113–15, 138–40; and ICFTU, 78–79; and John F. Kennedy, 75. *See also* United Auto Workers
RMK-BRJ (Raymond International and Morrison-Knudsen, and Brown and Root and J. A. Jones), 109, 180
Rogers, William, 155
Romine, Auda, 159
Roosevelt, Eleanor, 64
Roosevelt, Franklin D., 13, 20
Rosenblum, Frank, 11, 158, 176
Rosow, Jerome, 163
Ross, Michael, 62
Rostow, Walt Whitman, 72, 77, 87, 147
Rowan, Carl, 194
Rubber Plantations, 30–31, 69
Rumsfeld, Donald, 165
Rusk, Dean, 78, 83, 96, 111, 130–31
Ruttenberg, Stanley, 55

San Francisco Bay Area Labor Assembly for Peace, 158
Scholle, Gus, 159
Schrade, Paul, 113, 125, 138
Seamen's International Union, 84
Sexton, Brendan, 88
Shachtman, Max, 191
Sharman, Benjamin, 184
Shultz, George, 165, 177, 179
Sidey, Hugh, 165
Skull, Leon, 118
Snepp, Frank, 182
Social Democrats USA, 191
Solzhenitsyn, Alexander, 194
Stagflation, 178
Stalin, Joseph, 17
Stevenson, Adlai, 97
Stulberg, Louis, 136
Suffridge, James, 86
Sullivan, David, 111, 121
Sûreté Générale, 31, 36, 38

Taft-Hartley Act, 41, 86
Taylor, Maxwell, 93, 97
Teamsters, 139–40
Tenant Farmers' Union, 69–70, 91, 107, 151, 185
Tessier, Gaston, 67
Tet Offensive, 126, 130–32, 135, 142
Thompson, Virginia, 31
Thorez, Maurice, 46
TLD. *See* Tong Lien Doan Lao Dong
Tomlins, Christopher, 5
Ton Duc Thang, 31
Tong Lien Doan Lao Dong (TLD), 36
Trade Union Congress (TUC), 20, 26, 44, 149
Trade Union Division of the National Committee for Sane Nuclear Policy, 118, 123
Tran Huu Quyen, 34, 129, 132, 144, 170, 181
Tran Quoc Buu, 53, 108; arrest of, 96–97; assassination attempt on, 168; and *Cao Dai,* 34–35; and the CIA, 67, 182–83; and civilian military training, 150; and Cong Nong Party, 148–52; and the division of Vietnam, 65–66; and *doan the,* 37; and general strike (1964), 94–96; and Gilbert Jouan, 37; and health, 170; and Henry Kirsch, 104; and ICFTU, 53–54, 141–42; and Irving Brown, 82–83; and land-to-the-tiller program, 150–51; and Ngo Family, 67–71; and Nguyen Cao Ky, 103, 105–8; and Nguyen Khan, 89; and Nguyen Van Thieu, 147–51, 181–84, 187–89; and Paris Peace Accords, 179, 187; personality of, 37; at Poulo Condore prison, 33–34, 129; as presidential candidate, 167; and Tet Offensive, 131–32; and Vietnamization, 145–47; youth of, 33. *See also* Vietnamese Confederation of Labor

Tran Quoc Khanh, 169
Tran Van Don, 147
Trinh Quang Quy, 35, 151
Tripathi, K. Prasas, 64
Tronchet, Lucien, 53, 57, 65
Truman Doctrine, 29, 41
Trumka, Richard, 2
TUC. *See* Trade Union Congress
Turconi, Luigi, 84
Tyler, Gus, 118–19

UAW. *See* United Auto Workers
United Auto Workers (UAW), 117, 138–41, 157, 159, 165, 169
UOV. *See* Workers' Union of Vietnam

Vandistendael, August, 72
Viet Cong, 82, 94, 104, 130–32, 142, 146, 168, 173, 186, 190
Viet Minh, 30, 47, 65
Vietnamese Confederation of Labor (CVTC and CVT), 4; and Buddhism, 93; and CIA, 66–67; and civilian military training, 150; and Cong Nong Party, 148–52; and division of Vietnam, 58, 65–66; early activities, 39–41; and elections, 120–21; and electrical workers strike, 126–30; evacuation (1975), 190–91; formation of, 36–39; and general strike (1964), 94–96; and the ICFTU, 53–54; land-to-the-tiller program, 150–51; and Ngo family, 67–71, 74, 81–86; and Nguyen Cao Ky, 103, 105–8; and Nguyen Van Thieu, 147–51, 167, 181–84, 187–89; paramilitary use of, 83, 92–93, 131, 150; and Tet Offensive, 130–33; and terrorism, 168. *See also* Tran Quoc Buu
Vietnamese Nationalist Party (VNQDD), 32
Vietnamese Revolutionary Farmers' Party, 146
Vietnam Moratorium Day, 139
Vietnam's Workers' and Farmers' Association, 146
Vimytex mill, 93
voluntarism, 10–11
Vo Van Gio, 34, 107, 151, 185
Vo Van Tai, 94, 98, 108, 126–33, 169

Wagner, Robert, 13, 22, 59
Walkinshaw, Robert, 140, 169
War Labor Board, 21
Washington Post, 115, 132, 155
Washington Star, 64
Watergate, 179
Weaver, George, 155–56
West German International Support Institute, 185
WFTU. *See* World Federation of Trade Unions
Wilson, Edwin, 84
Wilson, Woodrow, 12
Wirtz, Willard, 114, 117–18
Woll, Matthew, 19, 22, 63
Woodcock, Leonard, 165
Woodside, Alexander, 30, 31, 35
Workers' Union of Vietnam (UOV), 71, 84
Works Progress Administration, 18
World Bank, 154
World Council of Labor, 185
World Federation of Trade Unions (WFTU), 13, 26, 27, 43; and Vietnamese workers, 44, 140
Wurf, Jerry, 157–58, 188

Zack, Albert, 137
Zausner, Philip, 15–16
Zieger, Robert, 198
Zimmerman, Charles, 45
Zisman, Joseph, 49, 52